Freeway

Allgemeine Ausgabe
Englisch für das Berufskolleg
Baden-Württemberg

von
Catherine Küpper
Wolfgang Rosenkranz (Hrsg.)
Graham Tucker

Ernst Klett Verlag
Stuttgart · Leipzig

So arbeiten Sie mit Freeway

Unitaufbau
Basic course (Units 1–5) und Advanced course (Units 6–10)

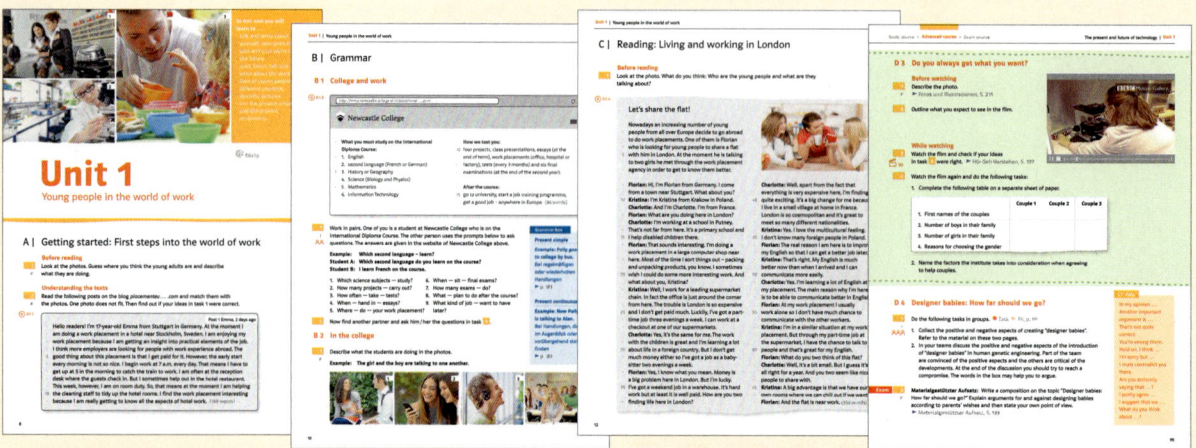

A Getting started
Motivierender Einstieg und Überblick über die Lernziele

B Grammar
Systematisches Wiederholen und Üben der Grammatikthemen

C Reading
Intensive Textarbeit zur Vorbereitung auf die Abschlussprüfung

D Practice
Üben von Hörverstehen/ Hör-Seh-Verstehen

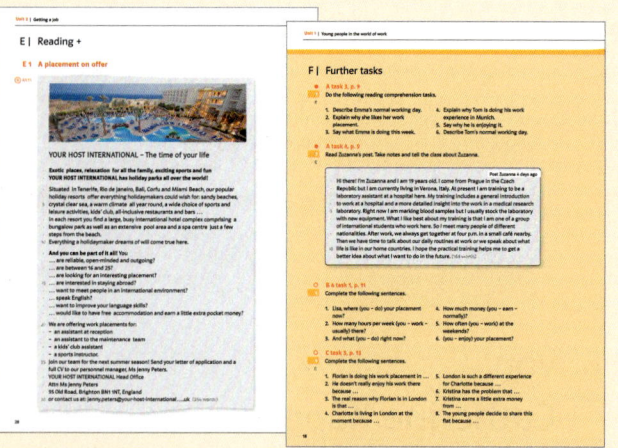 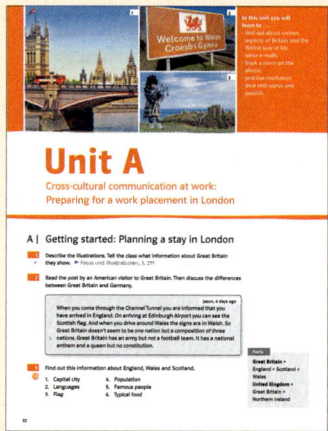 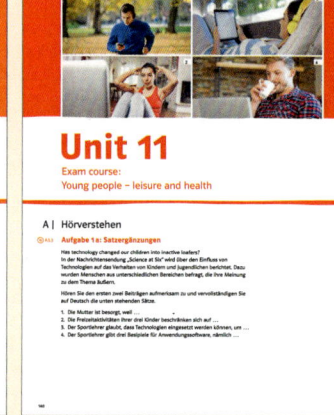

E Reading +
Intensive Textarbeit mit längeren, z.T. authentischen Texten

F Further Tasks
Anspruchsvollere oder leichtere Aufgaben und Hilfestellungen zur Differenzierung

Cross-cultural communication at work
Die Units A bis C bieten interkulturelles Lernen im beruflichen Alltag.

Exam course
Die Units 11–15 bieten fünf komplette Musterprüfungen für Baden-Württemberg.

Differenziert üben = Intensiv üben!
Bei einigen Aufgaben in den Teilen **A** bis **E** finden Sie Verweise auf Hilfestellungen Help ○ oder Zusatzaufgaben Task ○, Task ● im Teil F der Unit (Further Tasks).

B 3 A job for you?

1. Linda Smith has applied for a job in a big supermarket. In an interview she has to talk about her life and career. In pairs, take her role and the role of the interviewer using the role cards on page 170 and prepare the interview. ○ Help ▶ F2, p. 30

○ **B 3 task 1, p. 23**
2. You are Linda Smith. Talk about your life

B | Grammar

B1 College and work

🔊 A1.3

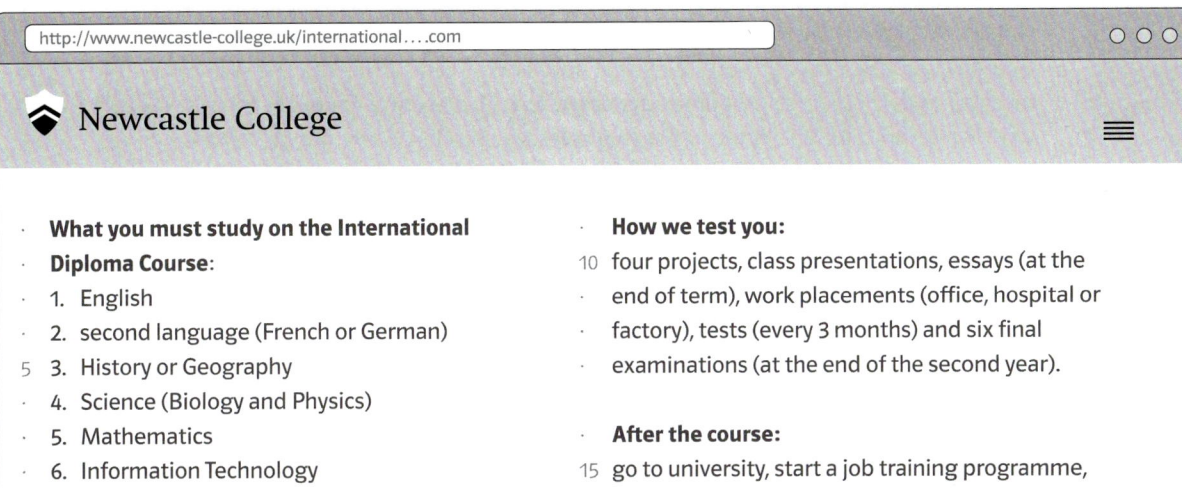

Newcastle College

- **What you must study on the International**
- **Diploma Course:**
- 1. English
- 2. second language (French or German)
- 3. History or Geography
- 4. Science (Biology and Physics)
- 5. Mathematics
- 6. Information Technology

- **How we test you:**
- four projects, class presentations, essays (at the end of term), work placements (office, hospital or factory), tests (every 3 months) and six final examinations (at the end of the second year).

- **After the course:**
- go to university, start a job training programme, get a good job – anywhere in Europe (86 words)

1 Work in pairs. One of you is a student at Newcastle College who is on the International Diploma Course. The other person uses the prompts below to ask questions. The answers are given in the website of Newcastle College above.

Example: Which second language – learn?
Student A: Which second language do you learn on the course?
Student B: I learn French on the course.

1. Which science subjects — study?
2. How many projects — carry out?
3. How often — take — tests?
4. When — hand in — essays?
5. Where — do — your work placement?
6. When — sit — final exams?
7. How many exams — do?
8. What — plan to do after the course?
9. What kind of job — want to have later?

2 Now find another partner and ask him/her the questions in task **1**.

Grammar box

Present simple

Example: Polly goes to college by bus.
Bei regelmäßigen oder wiederholten Handlungen
▶ p. 183

Present continuous

Example: Now Polly is talking to Alan.
Bei Handlungen, die im Augenblick oder vorübergehend stattfinden
▶ p. 184

B2 In the college

1 Describe what the students are doing in the photos.

Example: The girl and the boy are talking to one another.

Basic course > Advanced course > Exam course　　　　　　　　　　　Young people in the world of work | **Unit 1**

A1.2

Post 2: Tom 3 days ago

Hi everyone! I'm Tom from Beaconsfield, a small town in England, and I am 18 years old. Every year my college organizes work placements for their students somewhere in Europe. So as part of my college course I am currently doing three weeks' work experience in a nursery school on the outskirts of Munich, Germany.
5　I am having a very interesting and challenging time here at the moment. It is a wonderful experience to see children learn so quickly and I also like the teamwork. I usually help the children with breakfast and lunch, I read stories to the children or I play with them. We sometimes also plan special activities. Today we are working on an outing to the zoo, for example. My working hours are ok. I work
10　from nine o'clock in the morning until five o'clock in the afternoon. Every Monday and Thursday I play football in a club nearby. This helps me to improve my German language skills and find friends here. (166 words)

3 Which of the following statements about the young people are true and which
R are false? Correct the false statements.
● Task ▶ F1, p. 18 ▶ Leseverstehen, S. 199

1. Emma is currently doing work experience in a restaurant.
2. Emma gets money for her work.
3. Emma goes to work by car.
4. Emma is tidying up the hotel rooms at the moment.
5. Tom is living in Beaconsfield right now.
6. Tom likes working in a team.
7. Tom doesn't like his working hours.
8. Tom hopes to improve his German language skills in his free time.

4 Copy the table below into your exercise book. Write down what the young people usually do and what they are currently doing. ● Task ▶ F2, p. 18

What he / she usually does	What he / she is currently doing
Example: Emma usually lives …	She is currently …

Exam 5 Mediation: Sie haben im Internet Emmas Post gelesen und erzählen Ihrem
M Freund / Ihrer Freundin auf Deutsch, was Sie über Emma wissen.
▶ Mediation, S. 228

6 Say which of the workplaces you like best. Say why.
P

After reading

7 Interview a partner. Find out the information below about him / her and write it
I down. Then present your partner to your class. You can use the expressions in
👥 the *Help* box for the presentation. ▶ Präsentieren, S. 217

name – age – family – home town – interests – likes and dislikes – personality – favourite music – future plans

8 Write your own personal post for a social networking website.
P

○ **Help**
- I would like to introduce…
- He / She is …
- He / She has …
- He / She comes from …
- He / She lives in …
- In his / her free time …
- He / She likes / enjoys / loves / can't stand …
- He / She plans to …

Lernen, Üben, Anwenden

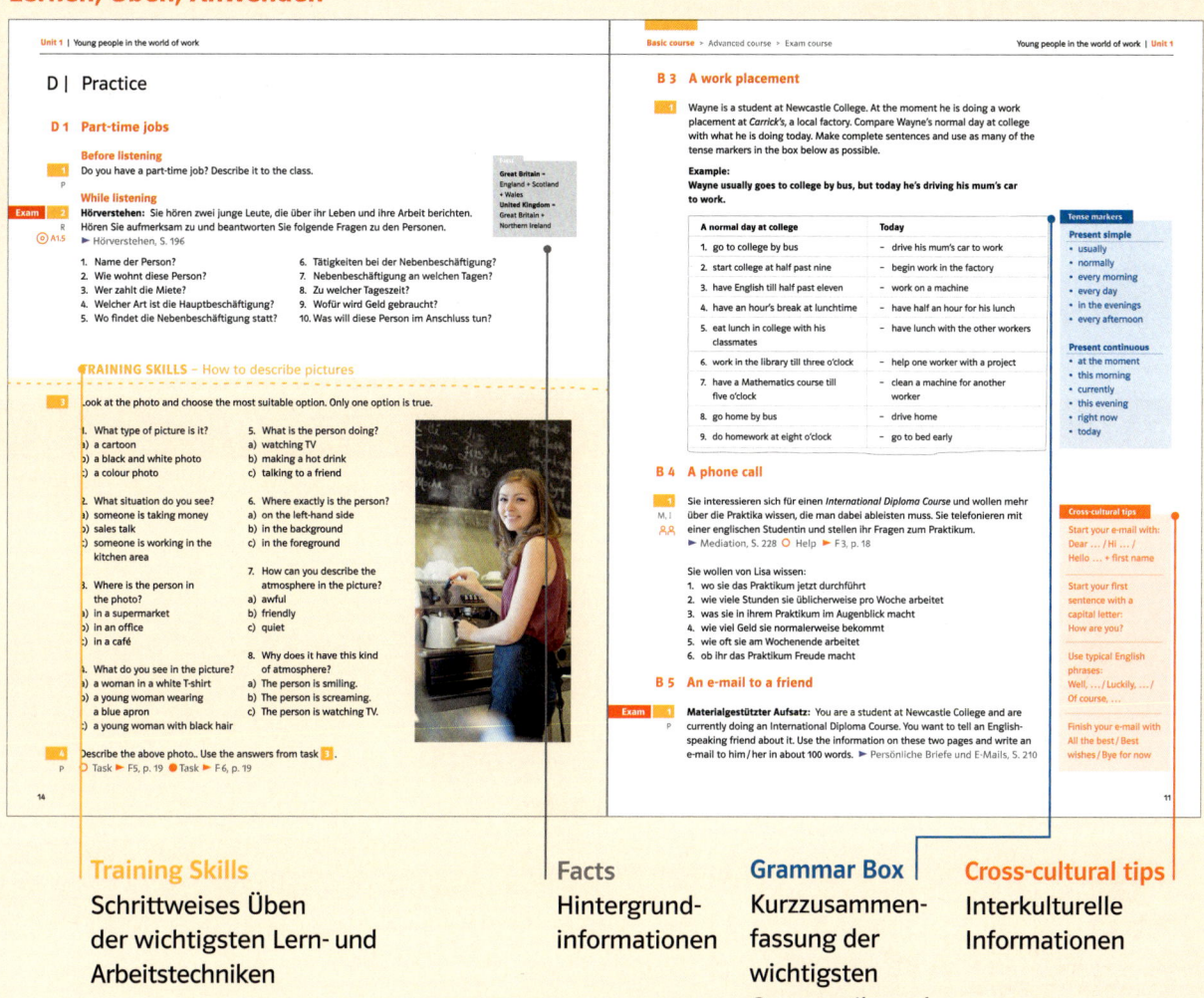

Training Skills
Schrittweises Üben der wichtigsten Lern- und Arbeitstechniken

Facts
Hintergrundinformationen

Grammar Box
Kurzzusammenfassung der wichtigsten Grammatikregeln

Cross-cultural tips
Interkulturelle Informationen

Symbole und Verweise

		Differenziert üben:
Help	○	Verweis auf eine Hilfestellung
Task	○	Verweis auf eine leichte Zusatzaufgabe
Task	●	Verweis auf eine schwierige Zusatzaufgabe

Exam Aufgaben, die auf die Prüfungen zu **Hörverstehen, Mediation** und **Materialgestütztem Aufsatz** vorbereiten

HOT Aufgaben mit Schwerpunkt **Handlungsorientierte Themenbearbeitung**

P, M, I, R Kompetenzen: **Produktion, Mediation, Interaktion, Rezeption**

A1.1 ◉ Audioverweis mit Tracknummer

V1 🎞 Videoverweis mit Tracknummer

▶ Verweis auf *Skills files* im Anhang

▶ Verweis auf *Grammar files* im Anhang

👥 / 👥👥 Partneraufgabe/Gruppenaufgabe

🌐 Internet-Rechercheaufgabe

f8iz7p 🌐 **Zusatzangebot im Internet:** Freeway-Codes führen zu weiteren Materialien im Internet. Geben Sie einfach den Code auf **www.klett.de** ein.

Contents

Basic course

Unit 1	Young people in the world of work						08
Themes	**Texts**	**Grammar**	**Training skills**	**Video lounge**	**Further tasks**		
Work experience abroad • Colleges and jobs • Volunteering	First steps into the world of work • Let's share the flat • Work on a farm – and see the world for free (The Guardian)	Present simple • Present continuous	How to describe pictures	Gap year (BBC)	Aufgaben zur Differenzierung		

Unit 2	Getting a job						20
Themes	**Texts**	**Grammar**	**Training skills**	**Video lounge**	**Further tasks**		
A big company • Applying for a job • Job interviews	A name behind many names • Looking for a work placement as a hotel assistant? • Job advertisement: YOUR HOST INTERNATIONAL – The time of your life	Past simple • Present perfect simple • Present perfect continuous	How to describe statistics	A suitable candidate? (Klett)	Aufgaben zur Differenzierung		

Cross-cultural communication at work:

Unit A	Preparing for a work placement in London		32
Themes		**Video lounge**	
Planning a stay in London • Writing e-mails • Booking a room on the telephone • Preparing to drive in Britain		London (AP Archive)	

Unit 3	The youth market						36
Themes	**Texts**	**Grammar**	**Training skills**	**Video lounge**	**Further tasks**		
Young people's attitudes to branded products • Protecting young consumers • Analyzing ads • Modern media and advertising	Young consumers hold the key to change • Buyers' training at schools • Digital advertising on the move	Past simple • Past perfect simple • Past continuous	How to do a role play	Heinz and Packaging (BBC)	Aufgaben zur Differenzierung		

Unit 4	Media in our lives						48
Themes	**Texts**	**Grammar**	**Training skills**	**Video lounge**	**Further tasks**		
Young people and media consumption • Pros and cons of computers and the Internet • Modern media at college • The changing workplace	Ofcom report identifies emerging 'generation gap' in young people's TV viewing (The Guardian) • Internet chances and dangers • The Internet generation	Will-future • Future with 'going to' • Adjectives • Adverbs	How to write a composition I • How to describe a cartoon	Trends in social media (BBC)	Aufgaben zur Differenzierung		

Unit 5	Social change					60
Themes	**Texts**	**Grammar**	**Training skills**	**Video lounge**	**Further tasks**	
Changing society • Problems of young people • The welfare state • Gender roles	Academic performance: top reason for teen stress • Home sharing in Greenwich • What's behind the rise of stay-at-home dads? *(BBC News Magazine)*	Relative clauses • Modal auxiliaries	How to anticipate, skim and scan	Combining a career with family life *(BBC)*	Aufgaben zur Differenzierung	

Cross-cultural communication at work:

Unit B	Living in London		72
Themes		**Video lounge**	
Travelling in London • Giving directions • Small talk • Differences in British and German life		British weather *(AP Archive)*	

Advanced course

Unit 6	Ecology					76
Themes	**Texts**	**Grammar**	**Training skills**	**Video lounge**	**Further tasks**	
Climate change • Food production • Action for sustainability • Saving nature	Tackling climate change • You are what you eat • Earth has lost half its wildlife in the past 40 years *(The Guardian)*	Reported speech	How to work with a dictionary	Sustainability *(BBC)*	Aufgaben zur Differenzierung	

Unit 7	The present and future of technology					88
Themes	**Texts**	**Grammar**	**Training skills**	**Video lounge**	**Further tasks**	
Sustainable energy production • Medical technology • Genetically-modified food	Scotland – fossil-free by 2030? • Tidal lagoon power • There's no choice: we must grow GM crops now *(The Guardian)*	Passive voice	How to write a composition II	Do you always get what you want? *(BBC)*	Aufgaben zur Differenzierung	

Unit 8	The service industry					100
Themes	**Texts**	**Grammar**	**Training skills**	**Video lounge**	**Further tasks**	
Developments in the service sector • Pros and cons of mass tourism • Fitness and health • Minimum wages in the service sector	Careers in tourism and leisure • It's not only sunshine and fun • Living on $2.13 an hour and tips… *(The Guardian)*	Conditionals • If-clauses	How to answer questions on a text	Physical activity and fitness *(BBC)*	Aufgaben zur Differenzierung	

Contents

Cross-cultural communication at work:

Unit C | Working in London | 112

Themes		Video lounge	
Working at reception • Dealing with guests • Showing people around • Intercultural misunderstandings		A job placement at reception (Klett)	

Unit 9 | Living and working in a globalized world | 116

Themes	Texts	Grammar	Training skills	Video lounge	Further tasks
Migrant workers • Working conditions in the textile industry • Advantages and disadvantages of globalization	What's your story? • £3 per hour! A fair deal? • Not all Asian clothing factories are unethical (The Guardian) • Clothes join rubbish of our throwaway society (The Telegraph)	Infinitive • Gerund	How to do mediation exercises	Emerging markets: India (BBC)	Aufgaben zur Differenzierung

Unit 10 | International organizations and politics | 128

Themes	Texts	Grammar	Training skills	Video lounge	Further tasks
Human rights • Mass surveillance • Development of democracy • Dealing with refugees	Are we all born equal and free? • Mass surveillance is fundamental threat to human rights… (The Guardian) • Der große Bruder macht Pause (Süddeutsche Zeitung) • Migrant boat disaster … (The Independent)	Present participle • Past participle	How to write a material-based composition	Prime Minister's question time (Parliamentlive.tv)	Aufgaben zur Differenzierung

Exam course

Unit 11 | Young people – leisure and health | 140

Hörverstehen	Mediation	Materialgestützter Aufsatz
Young people: new technology and fitness	Teenage girls are skipping meals as weight anxiety soars (The Guardian)	The impact of drugs: Binge drinking as a teenager… (The Daily Mail) • Keine E-Shisha unter 18… (Die Welt)

Unit 12 | Modern media and advertising | 146

Hörverstehen	Mediation	Materialgestützter Aufsatz
Use of social media and its dangers	Cyberbullying … (The Independent)	Ban on adverts targeting children: Wie gefährlich Werbung für Kinder ist (familie.de) • Marketing and advertising to children (The Guardian)

Unit 13 | Young people and society | 152

Hörverstehen	Mediation	Materialgestützter Aufsatz
The situation of young people in Britain	Young people with disabilities campaign for the right to learn *(The Guardian)*	Racial equality in the US: Ferguson, 11 days on: "We're sitting on a powder keg" *(The Guardian)* • Abschied vom Traum einer postrassistischen Gesellschaft *(Die Zeit)*

Unit 14 | Technology, energy and environment | 158

Hörverstehen	Mediation	Materialgestützter Aufsatz
Campaigning for environmental protection	Plan launched to prevent critical climate change … *(The Independent)*	Technological developments: Technology has created more jobs than it has destroyed… *(The Guardian)* • Immer größere Risiken für Mensch und Umwelt *(Der Spiegel)*

Unit 15 | Globalization and migration | 164

Hörverstehen	Mediation	Materialgestützter Aufsatz
Experiences of migrants	Improving conditions for women has a domino effect *(The Guardian)*	Fair trade: Scottish co-op launches Fairtrade football campaign *(The Guardian)* • Fairtrade: Wenn Kaffee bitter schmeckt *(Die Zeit)*

Anhang

Role cards	170
Grammar files	175
Skills files	193
Exam skills Hörverstehen • Einen Materialgestützten Aufsatz schreiben • Eine Mediation schreiben	
Basic vocabulary	246
Unit vocabulary	256
Alphabetical vocabulary	315
Operatoren	332
Phrases for speaking / Phrases for writing	333
Connectives / Phrases to describe statistics	334
Bild- und Textquellennachweis	335
Contents of Grammar files	I
Contents of Skills files	II
Irregular verbs	III

In this unit you will learn to . . .
- talk and write about yourself, your (part-time) jobs and your plans for the future.
- read, listen, talk and write about the work and lives of young people in different countries.
- describe pictures.
- use the present simple and the present continuous.

 f8iz7p

Unit 1
Young people in the world of work

A | Getting started: First steps into the world of work

Before reading

1 Look at the photos. Guess where you think the young adults are and describe what they are doing.
P

Understanding the texts

2 Read the following posts on the blog *placementeu... .com* and match them with
R the photos. One photo does not fit. Then find out if your ideas in task 1 were correct.

◎ A1.1

Post 1 Emma, 2 days ago

Hello readers! I'm 17-year-old Emma from Stuttgart in Germany. At the moment I am doing a work placement in a hotel near Stockholm, Sweden. I am enjoying my work placement because I am getting an insight into practical elements of the job. I think more employers are looking for people with work experience abroad. The
5 good thing about this placement is that I get paid for it. However, the early start every morning is not so nice. I begin work at 7 a.m. every day. That means I have to get up at 5 in the morning to catch the train to work. I am often at the reception desk where the guests check in. But I sometimes help out in the hotel restaurant. This week, however, I am on room duty. So, that means at the moment I am helping
10 the cleaning staff to tidy up the hotel rooms. I find the work placement interesting because I am really getting to know all the aspects of hotel work. (169 words)

Basic course > Advanced course > Exam course   Young people in the world of work | Unit 1

B3 A work placement

1 Wayne is a student at Newcastle College. At the moment he is doing a work placement at *Carrick's*, a local factory. Compare Wayne's normal day at college with what he is doing today. Make complete sentences and use as many of the tense markers in the box below as possible.

Example:
Wayne usually goes to college by bus, but today he's driving his mum's car to work.

A normal day at college	Today
1. go to college by bus	– drive his mum's car to work
2. start college at half past nine	– begin work in the factory
3. have English till half past eleven	– work on a machine
4. have an hour's break at lunchtime	– have half an hour for his lunch
5. eat lunch in college with his classmates	– have lunch with the other workers
6. work in the library till three o'clock	– help one worker with a project
7. have a Mathematics course till five o'clock	– clean a machine for another worker
8. go home by bus	– drive home
9. do homework at eight o'clock	– go to bed early

Tense markers

Present simple
- usually
- normally
- every morning
- every day
- in the evenings
- every afternoon

Present continuous
- at the moment
- this morning
- currently
- this evening
- right now
- today

B4 A phone call

1
M, I
Sie interessieren sich für einen *International Diploma Course* und wollen mehr über die Praktika wissen, die man dabei ableisten muss. Sie telefonieren mit einer englischen Studentin und stellen ihr Fragen zum Praktikum.
▶ Mediation, S. 228 ◯ Help ▶ F3, p. 18

Sie wollen von Lisa wissen:
1. wo sie das Praktikum jetzt durchführt
2. wie viele Stunden sie üblicherweise pro Woche arbeitet
3. was sie in ihrem Praktikum im Augenblick macht
4. wie viel Geld sie normalerweise bekommt
5. wie oft sie am Wochenende arbeitet
6. ob ihr das Praktikum Freude macht

Cross-cultural tips

Start your e-mail with:
Dear … / Hi … /
Hello … + first name

Start your first sentence with a capital letter:
How are you?

Use typical English phrases:
Well, … / Luckily, … /
Of course, …

Finish your e-mail with
All the best / Best wishes / Bye for now

B5 An e-mail to a friend

xam **1**
P
Materialgestützter Aufsatz: You are a student at Newcastle College and are currently doing an International Diploma Course. You want to tell an English-speaking friend about it. Use the information on these two pages and write an e-mail to him / her in about 100 words. ▶ Persönliche Briefe und E-Mails, S. 210

C | Reading: Living and working in London

Before reading

1 Look at the photo. What do you think: Who are the young people and what are they talking about?

A1.4

Let's share the flat!

Nowadays an increasing number of young people from all over Europe decide to go abroad to do work placements. One of them is Florian who is looking for young people to share a flat
5 with him in London. At the moment he is talking to two girls he met through the work placement agency in order to get to know them better.

Florian: Hi, I'm Florian from Germany. I come from a town near Stuttgart. What about you?
10 **Kristina:** I'm Kristina from Krakow in Poland.
Charlotte: And I'm Charlotte. I'm from France.
Florian: What are you doing here in London?
Charlotte: I'm working at a school in Putney. That's not far from here. It's a primary school and
15 I help disabled children there.
Florian: That sounds interesting. I'm doing a work placement in a large computer shop near here. Most of the time I sort things out – packing and unpacking products, you know. I sometimes
20 wish I could do some more interesting work. And what about you, Kristina?
Kristina: Well, I work for a leading supermarket chain. In fact the office is just around the corner from here. The trouble is London is so expensive
25 and I don't get paid much. Luckily, I've got a part-time job three evenings a week. I can work at a checkout at one of our supermarkets.
Charlotte: Yes, it's the same for me. The work with the children is great and I'm learning a lot
30 about life in a foreign country. But I don't get much money either so I've got a job as a baby-sitter two evenings a week.
Florian: Yes, I know what you mean. Money is a big problem here in London. But I'm lucky.
35 I've got a weekend job in a warehouse. It's hard work but at least it is well paid. How are you two finding life here in London?

Charlotte: Well, apart from the fact that everything is very expensive here, I'm finding it
40 quite exciting. It's a big change for me because I live in a small village at home in France. London is so cosmopolitan and it's great to meet so many different nationalities.
Kristina: Yes. I love the multicultural feeling.
45 I don't know many foreign people in Poland.
Florian: The real reason I am here is to improve my English so that I can get a better job later.
Kristina: That's right. My English is much better now than when I arrived and I can
50 communicate more easily.
Charlotte: Yes. I'm learning a lot of English at my placement. The main reason why I'm here is to be able to communicate better in English.
Florian: At my work placement I usually
55 work alone so I don't have much chance to communicate with the other workers.
Kristina: I'm in a similar situation at my work placement. But through my part-time job at the supermarket, I have the chance to talk to
60 people and that's great for my English.
Florian: What do you two think of this flat?
Charlotte: Well, it's a bit small. But I guess it's all right for a year. And you two seem like nice people to share with.
65 **Kristina:** A big advantage is that we have our own rooms where we can chill out if we want.
Florian: And the flat is near work. (558 words)

Basic course > Advanced course > Exam course   Young people in the world of work | **Unit 1**

Understanding the text

2
R
Find the most suitable options according to the text. Only one option is true.

1. All three of the young people come from …
   a) Eastern Europe.
   b) small towns in Europe.
   c) large towns in Europe.
   d) European countries.

2. They need to earn extra money so they all …
   a) have more than two jobs.
   b) have part-time jobs.
   c) work at the weekends.
   d) work in shops.

3. They all like living in Britain because they …
   a) can go to a good college there.
   b) are with people from their own countries.
   c) are able to meet people from all over the world.
   d) like English food.

3
R
Answer the following questions in complete sentences. ○ Help ▶ F4, p. 18
▶ Leseverstehen, S. 199

1. Where is Florian doing his work placement?
2. Why doesn't he really enjoy his work there?
3. What is Florian's real reason for his stay in London?
4. What is Charlotte's main motivation for coming to London?
5. Why does Charlotte find London so different to her home?
6. What problem does Kristina have?
7. How does she solve this problem?
8. Why, do you think, do the young people decide to share this flat?

Exam **4**
M
Mediation: Florian schreibt eine E-Mail nach Deutschland, in der er einem Freund von seinen neuen Mitbewohnerinnen in der Wohngemeinschaft berichtet. Schreiben Sie diese E-Mail auf Deutsch für ihn. ▶ Mediation, S. 228

After reading

HOT **5**
I
👥
Rollenspiel: The agency which found the placements for the three young people wants to find out more about their experiences in London. An employee phones up one of the students. ▶ Telefongespräche, S. 225

Work in pairs. Prepare the phone call and then act it out.
Student A is the employee at the work placement agency. Use the role card on page 170 to find out about the young European.
Student B is Florian, Charlotte or Kristina. Answer the employee's questions.
Use the information from the text and add your own ideas.

6
P
The employee at the agency asks the three young people to write an e-mail to him/her about their experiences as young Europeans in London. Choose one of the young people in the dialogue and write their e-mail.
▶ Formelle Briefe und E-Mails, S. 205

D | Practice

D1 Part-time jobs

Before listening

1 Do you have a part-time job? Describe it to the class.
P

While listening

Exam 2 **Hörverstehen:** Sie hören zwei junge Leute, die über ihr Leben und ihre Arbeit berichten.
R Hören Sie aufmerksam zu und beantworten Sie folgende Fragen zu den Personen.
⊙ A1.5 ▶ Hörverstehen, S. 196

1. Name der Person?
2. Wie wohnt diese Person?
3. Wer zahlt die Miete?
4. Welcher Art ist die Hauptbeschäftigung?
5. Wo findet die Nebenbeschäftigung statt?
6. Tätigkeiten bei der Nebenbeschäftigung?
7. Nebenbeschäftigung an welchen Tagen?
8. Zu welcher Tageszeit?
9. Wofür wird Geld gebraucht?
10. Was will diese Person im Anschluss tun?

TRAINING SKILLS – How to describe pictures

3 Look at the photo and choose the most suitable option. Only one option is true.

1. What type of picture is it?
   a) a cartoon
   b) a black and white photo
   c) a colour photo

2. What situation do you see?
   a) someone is taking money
   b) sales talk
   c) someone is working in the kitchen area

3. Where is the person in the photo?
   a) in a supermarket
   b) in an office
   c) in a café

4. What do you see in the picture?
   a) a woman in a white T-shirt
   b) a young woman wearing a blue apron
   c) a young woman with black hair

5. What is the person doing?
   a) watching TV
   b) making a hot drink
   c) talking to a friend

6. Where exactly is the person?
   a) on the left-hand side
   b) in the background
   c) in the foreground

7. How can you describe the atmosphere in the picture?
   a) awful
   b) friendly
   c) quiet

8. Why does it have this kind of atmosphere?
   a) The person is smiling.
   b) The person is screaming.
   c) The person is watching TV.

4 Describe the above photo.. Use the answers from task **3**.
P ○ Task ▶ F 5, p. 19 ● Task ▶ F 6, p. 19

D2 Qualified jobs

1 Look at the photos. Match them with the jobs below. Five jobs do not match.

> fashion designer – chef – web designer – salesperson – social worker – motor mechanic – office worker – nursery school teacher – IT technician – architect – street worker

2 Explain the jobs in the box using the phrases below.

Example: A fashion designer is a person who creates new clothes.

> **create** – repair – meals in a restaurant – design – firms in creating their own home page – read – buildings – people in need – stories to little children – help – sell – **new clothes** – type – cook – programs – goods in a shop – cars – install – give – advice to teenagers in trouble – support – e-mails to customers

3 Choose one of the jobs in task **1** that interests you most, find out about it and present it to your class in detail. If you want to, you can choose a job that is not in the list. Talk about the workplace, the tasks and wages, and things you like or dislike about this job.

4 Write a short text about the job you would like to do.

E | Reading +

E1 Work and travel

Before reading

1 Look at the photo and headline. Say what you think the article is about.

Work on a farm – and see the world for free

[…] **How does it work?**
Lots of farms, especially those involved with alternative and eco-friendly projects, invite people to volunteer in exchange for free food and accommodation. If you're willing to get your hands dirty, it's a fantastic way to learn about rural life around the world and enjoy a long-term visit on the cheap. You can look for farms that are open to volunteers through sites such as wwoof.net (World Wide Opportunities on Organic Farms) or Growfood and contact the owners directly to arrange your visit.

How long can I stay?
Most farms require you to stay for at least one or two weeks, but the length of your stay really has to be negotiated with your hosts as it can vary immensely. Some hosts are happy to show you around for a day or two, while others will let you really dig in and stay for several months. One farm listed on Growfood, Wayback Farm in Maine, invites apprentices to spend an entire season learning about all-natural, biodynamic farming practices.

What will I do?
You could be doing anything from picking grapes to building a smokehouse, learning about organic crops or setting up an irrigation system. Of course there are plenty of opportunities out there to milk cows or plough a field, should you wish to partake in some more traditional farm labour. Working days can range from a full seven to eight hours of physical labour to a couple of hours helping with the daily chores. Look carefully through the information listed for each post and make sure to check with the owners beforehand how much time each day you will be expected to contribute.

When can I do it?
All year round.

Is it safe?
Safety checks on hosts can depend on the organisation and the country you are choosing to visit. Some regional WWOOF groups visit hosts before they are accepted and some do further checks and references, but this isn't always the case. Some WWOOF groups also have a feedback or reference system where guests can rate the hosts. On the Growfood site, you can find feedback from guests beneath each farm. However, you should still take the same precautions you would normally take if staying with strangers – if you are feeling unsure, you might prefer to go as a couple or with a friend.

Where do I sign up?
[…] There are more than 50 WWOOF groups around the world, so to get involved you need to first choose your destination and join the regional group, which then gives you access to a database of farms that you can contact directly to arrange a visit. Subscription fees for WWOOF groups depend on the country and can range from nothing to £50. […] (466 words)

Quelle: By Will Coldwell, the guardian.com, November 26, 2013.

Basic course > Advanced course > Exam course   Young people in the world of work | **Unit 1**

Understanding the text

2 Answer the questions within the article in one complete sentence each.
R ○ Task ► F7, p. 19 ► Leseverstehen, S. 199

Exam **3** **Mediation:** Für einen Freund, der sein Englisch im Ausland verbessern möchte,
M fassen Sie die wichtigsten Informationen aus dem Artikel auf Deutsch zusammen.
Formulieren Sie ganze deutsche Sätze. ► Mediation, S. 228

After reading

4 You are planning to do "Work and Travel" in your next summer holidays.
Check the Internet and find out about jobs abroad that would interest you.
Present your findings to the class. ► Präsentieren, S. 217

Internet key words: WWOOF – Work and travel

Exam **5** **Materialgestützter Aufsatz:** Write an e-mail to your friend Arvid / Elsa in Sweden.
P Tell him / her about an interesting offer for a "Work and Travel" holiday and try
to convince him / her to join you. Use the information from the article, "Work on
a farm", and from task **4** . ► Materialgestützter Aufsatz, S. 199

E2 From high school to college

Before watching

1 Describe the photo and guess what kind of game
P they are playing.
V1

While watching

2 Watch the beginning of the film (the first forty
seconds) and describe the game Jake is playing.

3 Watch the whole film and complete the following
sentences. ► Hör-Seh-Verstehen, S. 197

1. Jake is not only a team member but he is also …
2. Jake wanted to go to a good …
3. There he applied for an athletic …
4. Jake received a lot of letters of …
5. The numbers of Jake's SAT score were …
6. But Jake's SAT had been scored …
7. The corrected score was …
8. When he heard that Jake was …
9. When Jake received his corrected score most schools had finished granting …
10. Bruce Poch, the admissions director at Pomona College, thinks the situation
    for some students is …
11. In the end Jake was lucky to receive a scholarship at the …

After watching

4 What alternatives would be interesting for you after your examinations?
Give reasons for your choice.

Unit 1 | Young people in the world of work

F | Further tasks

A task 3, p. 9

1 Do the following reading comprehension tasks.

1. Describe Emma's normal working day.
2. Explain why she likes her work placement.
3. Say what Emma is doing this week.
4. Explain why Tom is doing his work experience in Munich.
5. Say why he is enjoying it.
6. Describe Tom's normal working day.

A task 4, p. 9

2 Read Zuzanna's post. Take notes and tell the class about Zuzanna.

> Post Zuzanna 4 days ago
>
> Hi there! I'm Zuzanna and I am 19 years old. I come from Prague in the Czech Republic but I am currently living in Verona, Italy. At present I am training to be a laboratory assistant at a hospital here. My training includes a general introduction to work at a hospital and a more detailed insight into the work in a medical research
> 5 laboratory. Right now I am marking blood samples but I usually stock the laboratory with new equipment. What I like best about my training is that I am one of a group of international students who work here. So I meet many people of different nationalities. After work, we always get together at four p.m. in a small café nearby. Then we have time to talk about our daily routines at work or we speak about what
> 10 life is like in our home countries. I hope the practical training helps me to get a better idea about what I want to do in the future. (168 words)

B 4 task 1, p. 11

3 Complete the following sentences.

1. Lisa, where (you – do) your placement now?
2. How many hours per week (you – work – usually) there?
3. And what (you – do) right now?
4. How much money (you – earn – normally)?
5. How often (you – work) at the weekends?
6. (you – enjoy) your placement?

C task 3, p. 13

4 Complete the following sentences.

1. Florian is doing his work placement in …
2. He doesn't really enjoy his work there because …
3. The real reason why Florian is in London is that …
4. Charlotte is living in London at the moment because …
5. London is such a different experience for Charlotte because …
6. Kristina has the problem that …
7. Kristina earns a little extra money from …
8. The young people decide to share this flat because …

D 1 task 4, p. 14

5 P

Describe photo 1. Fill in the gaps.

This picture is a (1) … photo. It shows a checkout at a (2) …. A young (3) … is standing on the (4) …. Her shopping is in plastic (5) … in front of her. A shop (6) … is sitting at the checkout in the (7) … of the photo. He is wearing a (8) … shirt and he is (9) … at the customer. It looks as if she wants to (10) …. Maybe she is giving him her credit (11) …. The atmosphere seems to be very (12) ….

Help		
in the top left-hand corner	in the background	in the top right-hand corner
on the left	in the centre	on the right
in the bottom left-hand corner	in the foreground	in the bottom right-hand corner

D 1 task 4, p. 14

6 P

Describe photo 2. You can use the words and phrases in the box.

colour photo – sofa – on the left – next to him – drawing – atmosphere

E 1 task 2, p. 17

7 R

Which of the following statements about the young people are true and which are false according to the text? Correct the false statements.

1. You can work on farms all over the world and get paid for it.
2. A lot of these farms do environmentally friendly farming.
3. There are some Internet sites which offer contact to farmers.
4. The volunteers can choose how long they want to stay on a farm.
5. The farms offer very different jobs.
6. The working hours vary from a few hours to a full working day.
7. All farmers are checked by the organizations before they can become hosts.
8. It may be safer not to go to a farm alone.
9. You do not have to become a member of one of the organizations if you want to use their services.

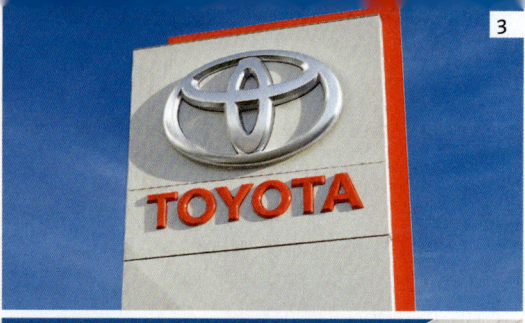

In this unit you will learn to ...
- analyze company descriptions and job advertisements.
- write applications and do job interviews.
- describe statistics.
- use the past and present perfect simple.

 k2q2fc

Unit 2
Getting a job

A | Getting started: Big companies

Before reading

1 The logos in the pictures stand for big international companies. Tell your classmates what you know about them and their products. ○ Help ▶ F1, p. 30

2 Guess what the headline of the text on page 21 could mean.

Understanding the text

3 Read the first two paragraphs of the text and find out if your ideas in task **2** were correct.
R

4 Make a list in your exercise book using the following key words. Then complete
R your list with the information in the text. You may add other products you know or have looked up on the Internet or have at home.

> company name – origin – business fields – brands – sales – customers in – manufacturing plants in – further information in text

5 Use your list in task **4** to describe the company without looking at the text.
P

Basic course > Advanced course > Exam course   Getting a job | Unit 2

◉ A1.6

A name behind many names

Who does not know the brand names Pampers, Ariel and Gillette?

They are just a few examples of the wide range of consumer goods on offer all over the
5 world. But what we usually do not know is that all these brands belong to one multinational company: *P&G* (short for *Procter & Gamble*).

In 2012 *P&G* celebrated their 175th anniversary and were proud to look back at their commercial
10 history. In 1837 candle maker William Procter and soap maker James Gamble – immigrants from England and Ireland – founded a new company in Cincinnati, USA: *Procter & Gamble*. When the founders launched their first
15 branded product, "Ivory Soap", nobody expected that this was the start of an immensely successful multinational company which was to become well-known all over the world.

In order to meet growing demand the
20 company built new factories all over the USA and soon became an international corporation. With their headquarters still in Cincinnati, *P&G* are now marketing their products in more than 180 countries. *P&G* products are available in
25 North and Latin America, Europe, the Middle East, Africa, Asia, Australia and New Zealand. Meanwhile, *P&G* have acquired several other companies and have become one of the largest consumer goods companies in the world.
30 In 2014/15 net sales were about 76.3 billion

dollars. Manufacturing units can be found not only in the USA but also in Europe, Asia, Africa and Australia. In Germany alone about 13,000 people have found employment with
35 *P&G*.

P&G have focused mainly on their brands in two fields: beauty/grooming and household care. Examples of these are "Head and Shoulders" shampoos and "OLD SPICE"
40 fragrances on the one hand, and "Dash" washing powder, "Swiffer" cleaning tools and "Charmin" toilet paper on the other. Most of these well-known brands have become so-called 'billion-dollar-brands'. (335 words)

Exam 6 Mediation: Fassen Sie für eine kurze Unternehmensvorstellung
M   wesentliche Informationen zu *Procter & Gamble* auf Deutsch zusammen.
▶ Mediation, S. 228

After reading

7 Find relevant information about another international company in the
P   consumer goods sector and create a similar list to the one in task **4** .
⊕   Present your results in class. ▶ Präsentieren, S. 217

HOT 8 Projekt: Informieren Sie sich über ein lokales oder regionales Unter-
M   nehmen, das noch keinen englischsprachigen Internetauftritt hat. Sie
⊕   machen ein Praktikum für dieses Unternehmen und werden gebeten, eine
⧍⧍⧍ englischsprachige Homepage zu gestalten. Stellen Sie anschließend Ihren
    Vorschlag für die Homepage der Geschäftsleitung vor. ▶ Mediation, S. 228

Facts

It is said that the term 'soap opera' comes from the early days of radio and TV serials. These were sponsored by soap makers, such as *P&G*, who also ran their commercials during the programmes.

B | Grammar

B1 The rise of Britain's biggest supermarket

1 Complete the information about *Tesco* using the past tense.

In 1919 Jack Cohen started to sell food at a market in the East End of London. He made a profit of £1 on his first day! The name *Tesco* (1. come) to life five years later when Mr Cohen (2. buy) tea from Mr T. E. Stockwell and Mr Cohen (3. use) the first letters of their names. In 1929 he (4. open) the first store in North London. More and more stores (5. follow). The company (6. continue) to grow in the 1930s when Mr Cohen (7. build) large office buildings and a warehouse. In the 1950s *Tesco* (8. expand) quickly by buying other stores, and selling more and more products. *Tesco* Leicester (9. go) into the *Guinness Book of Records* in 1961 as the largest store in Europe. Seven years later *Tesco* (10. develop) its first 'superstore'. At that time supermarkets (11. change) the way in which people (12. shop). In 1974 *Tesco* (13. begin) to sell petrol and (14. become) the UK's largest independent petrol dealer. In 1995 the company (15. manage) to become the largest food retailer in the UK. A year later *Tesco* (16. introduce) its first 24-hour store. In 2000 Tesco.com (17. enter) the online shopping market.

2 Complete the following information about *Tesco*. Use negative forms.

Example: On his first day Mr Cohen made a <u>small</u> profit. He did not make a <u>big</u> profit.

1. Mr Cohen bought tea from Mr Stockwell. He did not …
2. He used the first letters of their names. He …
3. In 1929 Mr Cohen opened his first store in North London.
4. *Tesco* built large office buildings in the 1930s.
5. In the 1950s the company expanded quickly.
6. In 1961 *Tesco* Leicester became the largest store in Europe.

B2 Big supermarkets, small supermarkets

1 Describe what has happened to *Tesco* and *Royce & Sons* in the last few years.

Example: *Tesco* has been in North London for many years. *Royce & Sons* have been in North London since 2012.

	Tesco	Royce & Sons
1. be in North London	for many years	since 2012
2. open	a lot of supermarkets up to now	only two little shops so far
3. make a profit	always	only once
4. start business in the USA	just	not yet
5. break a record	already	never

Grammar box

Past simple
Example: Sue lived in Glasgow from 2008 – 2014.
Bei Handlungen zu einem bestimmten Zeitpunkt oder in einem abgeschlossenen Zeitraum in der Vergangenheit
► p. 185

Present perfect simple
Example: Sue has lived in Leeds since 2010.
Mit einem Zeitraum, der noch andauert, und mit bestimmten Zeitbestimmungen und Adverbien
► p. 186

Basic course > Advanced course > Exam course   Getting a job | Unit 2

B3   A job for you?

1   Linda Smith has applied for a job in a big supermarket. In an interview she has to talk about her life and career. In pairs, take her role and the role of the interviewer using the role cards on page 170 and prepare the interview. ○ Help ▶ F 2, p. 30

2   Work in pairs and prepare a talk about yourselves. Ask and answer questions about the following:

> date of birth – school – college – exams – address – trips abroad – fluency in English – work experience – hobbies

B4   How long or how many?

1   Work in pairs. Use the verbs in brackets to ask and answer questions.

1. Daniel Jones got a job with a big supermarket chain a year ago. His job has been to work on two projects so far. (work)

   Example:
   Questions: How long has Daniel been working for the supermarket?
                  – How many projects has he worked on?
   Answers: He has been working for the supermarket for a year.
                  – He has worked on two projects.

2. Daniel's secretary Jane began to type letters an hour ago. Six letters are complete now. (type)
3. At the moment Larry, one of the shop assistants, is serving his 45th customer. He started work three hours ago. (serve)
4. Trudy's job is to look after the customers' children. Today she started at eight o'clock in the morning. She has just said hello to the 20th child. (look after)
5. The baker in the supermarket began work eight hours ago. Now there are five hundred fresh loaves of bread. (make)
6. Lucy is just finishing the third and last page of her homework. She sat down at her desk two hours ago. (do)

B5   The story of ???

Exam 1   **Materialgestützter Aufsatz:** Find information about the development of an interesting company or organization on the Internet. Take notes. Use your notes to write about the company in about 100 words.
▶ Materialgestützter Aufsatz, S. 199

> **Internet key words**
> company – development – history – organization
> (Or just use the name of the company that you are interested in.)

2   Read the text to the class but do not mention the name of the company or organization. The rest of the class have to find out the name.

○ **Help**

How to pronounce years in English:
1995 nineteen ninety-five or nineteen hundred (and) ninety-five
2005 twenty oh five or two thousand (and) five
2011 twenty eleven or two thousand (and) eleven

Grammar box

Present perfect simple
Example: John has repaired the car.
Bei Handlungen in der Vergangenheit ohne Zeitangabe, das Ergebnis ist wichtig
▶ p. 186

Present perfect continuous
Example: Alex has been repairing his car for two hours.
Bei Handlungen, die in der Vergangenheit begonnen haben und noch andauern
▶ p. 187

C | Reading: Applications

A

Looking for a WORK PLACEMENT as a hotel assistant?

You like working with people from different countries? You speak different languages? Then we look forward to getting your application.
As a hotel assistant you will work in different parts of the hotel such as the restaurant, the bar, the reception as well as the housekeeping department.

5 Essential requirements:
– You need to speak English and German fluently.
– You must be able to work in a team.
– You must have basic computer skills.

We offer work placements for one year. If you are interested, please send
10 your letter of application and CV to: Grange City Hotel, Mr Joseph Wildbloom, 8–14 Cooper's Row, London EC3N 2BQ. (116 words)

B

Arnoldstr. 41a
74081 Heilbronn
Germany   20 September 20…

Grange City Hotel
5 Mr Joseph Wildbloom
8–14 Cooper's Row
London EC3N 2BQ
Great Britain

Dear Mr Wildbloom
10 **Your advertisement for a hotel assistant**
With reference to the advert on your homepage, I would like to apply for a work placement as a hotel assistant. I am German and 18 years old.
I am an open-minded person and I am interested in working in new areas.
I have already got some experience in hotel work: I had a part-time job at
15 the Madison Hotel last year. I worked in reception and in housekeeping.
My present aim is to get to know about hotel work as my long-term aim is to become a hotel manager. In order to achieve this aim I want to study at the Australian International Hotel School (AIHS) in Canberra.
Your hotel is my first choice because of its size and its high class facilities.
20 I believe the work placement would be interesting and rewarding.
I enclose my CV and copies of certificates.
I look forward to hearing from you.
Yours sincerely

Julia Meyer
25 Julia Meyer
Encs. (202 words)

Basic course > Advanced course > Exam course   Getting a job | Unit 2

C

🔊 A1.9

Julia Meyer
Arnoldstraße 41a   Mobile: +49 (0)171 23456789 …
74081 Heilbronn   julia.meyer@mynewjob.….de

Personal Statement
5 I am a student at a college of further education who is looking for a work
placement in a hotel with a good reputation. I enjoy working with people
and I am interested in getting experience of hotel work. I am also looking
for a challenge where I can use and improve my skills.

Education
10 2014–2016 Berufliche Schule West (college of further education)
            Fachhochschulreife (exam enabling a student to enrol at
            a polytechnic university) in 2016 – Business studies A,
            Mathematics B, Social studies A
    2008–2014 Mörike-Realschule (intermediate secondary school)
15   *Realschulabschluss* (secondary school certificate comparable
            to GCSEs) in 2014

Work experience
Part-time job at Madison Hotel GmbH, Stuttgart
Reception desk and housekeeping

20 **Interests**
Sports: I am an active volleyball and tennis player, and I also enjoy
             watching football.
Leadership: I train a 9-12 year old volleyball team at a sports club.

Skills
25 Languages: I speak English and German fluently. I have a good working
             knowledge of French and Spanish.
Computing: I have good computer skills in Word, Excel, Access, and
             PowerPoint.
Driving: full driving licence (190 words)

Understanding the text

1 Match the terms *job advertisement*, *curriculum vitae* and *letter of application* to the texts A,
R   B and C.

2 Complete the sentences with regard to the three texts. Find at least three aspects.
R   ● Task ▶ F 3, p. 30 ▶ Leseverstehen, S. 199

1. The hotel is looking for somebody who …   3. Julia is …
2. Julia would like to …   4. Julia has some experience …

After reading

3 Would you invite Julia for an interview? Why or why not?

4 Describe your present and future qualifications, and say what kind of job or work
P   placement you would like to apply for.

D | Practice

D1 Finding the right candidate

Before listening

1 Look at the photos and match the interview candidates with suitable jobs in the list below.

> chef – salesperson – motor mechanic – nursery school teacher – nurse –
> computer technician – bank clerk – electrician

2 Give reasons why their clothes suit these jobs.

3 Name other jobs that in your opinion are suitable for these candidates.

While listening

Exam **4** **Hörverstehen:** Sie hören zwei Bewerbungsgespräche. Hören Sie aufmerksam zu
R und vervollständigen Sie auf Deutsch das folgende Raster in Ihrem Heft.
A1.10
● Task ▶ F4, p. 30 ▶ Hörverstehen, S. 196

1. Name der Personalchefin
2. Angebotene Stelle
3. Art des Unternehmens
4. Sitz des Unternehmens
5. Name der Bewerberin / des Bewerbers
6. Grund für die Bewerbung
7. Dauer / Ende des Praktikums
8. Familie
9. Qualifikationen
10. Berufliche Erfahrung
11. Zukunftspläne
12. Fragen an die Personalchefin

Example:

	Interview 1	Interview 2
1. Name der Personalchefin	…	…
2. Angebotene Stelle	…	…

After listening

5 Work in pairs. Discuss and decide which applicant you would give the work
I, P placement to. Then present your results in class. Give reasons.

Basic course > Advanced course > Exam course | Getting a job | Unit 2

D2 Word web: Applying for a job ▶ Wortnetze, S. 236

> **Help**
> skills / qualifications
> interests
> education
> application
> character / personality

1 Copy the word web into your exercise book and write down words from Unit 2 and other words that you know. If necessary use a dictionary. ▶ Umgang mit dem Wörterbuch, S. 234

work experience

2 Work in pairs. Compare your word webs and add more words to them.
● Task ▶ F5, p. 31

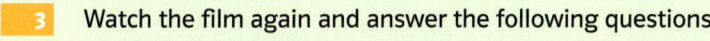

D3 A suitable candidate?

Before watching

1 Describe the photo. What kind of situation do you think this is?
▶ Fotos und Illustrationen, S. 211

While watching

2 Watch the complete film and find out:
▶ Hör-Seh-Verstehen, S. 197

1. the place and country where the interview takes place;
2. the names of the two people;
3. the type and name of the company.

3 Watch the film again and answer the following questions.
○ Task ▶ F6, p. 31

1. What mistake does the applicant make at the beginning of the interview?
2. Why does the applicant want to work there?
3. What skills must a good employee have?
4. How does the applicant see her future?
5. Which areas will she work in as part of the placement?
6. How long do work placements usually last at that company?

After watching

4 Think about the following question and then share your ideas with a partner.

Do you think the applicant will get the job placement? Why / why not?

E | Reading +

E1 A placement on offer

A1.11

YOUR HOST INTERNATIONAL – The time of your life

**Exotic places, relaxation for all the family, exciting sports and fun
YOUR HOST INTERNATIONAL has holiday parks all over the world!**

Situated in Tenerife, Rio de Janeiro, Bali, Corfu and Miami Beach, our popular
holiday resorts offer everything holidaymakers could wish for: sandy beaches,
5 crystal clear sea, a warm climate all year round, a wide choice of sports and
leisure activities, kids' club, all-inclusive restaurants and bars …
In each resort you find a large, busy international hotel complex comprising a
bungalow park as well as an extensive pool area and a spa centre just a few
steps from the beach.
10 Everything a holidaymaker dreams of will come true here.

And you can be part of it all! You
… are reliable, open-minded and outgoing?
… are between 16 and 25?
… are looking for an interesting placement?
15 … are interested in staying abroad?
… want to meet people in an international environment?
… speak English?
… want to improve your language skills?
… would like to have free accommodation and earn a little extra pocket money?

20 We are offering work placements for:
– an assistant at reception
– an assistant to the maintenance team
– a kids' club assistant
– a sports instructor.
25 Join our team for the next summer season! Send your letter of application and a
full CV to our personnel manager, Ms Jenny Peters.
YOUR HOST INTERNATIONAL Head Office
Attn Ms Jenny Peters
35 Old Road, Brighton BN1 1NT, England
30 or contact us at: jenny.peters@your-host-international….uk (256 words)

Basic course > Advanced course > Exam course   Getting a job | **Unit 2**

Understanding the text

1 You have found the advertisement on p. 28 on the Internet. ▶ Leseverstehen, S. 199
R
1. Why could this offer be interesting?
2. Which of the requirements can you meet?
3. What tasks do you think you have to do in the different jobs?
4. Which job and which place or city would you choose for your placement? Say why.

2 Apply for one of the placements in the advertisement. Use the word web on page 27
P to make notes for your application. Then write your letter of application and CV.
▶ Formelle Briefe und E-Mails, S. 205

3 You have been invited for an interview. Work with students who have chosen to
I apply for the same work placement as you. Half of your group play the applicants
(see role card A "applicant" on p. 170) and the other half play the employers
(see role card B "employer" on p. 170). Prepare the interview and act it out.
○ Help ▶ F7, p. 31

4 Decide in class which applicants you would give the work placement to.

TRAINING SKILLS – How to describe statistics

E2 Employment at YOUR HOST INTERNATIONAL

1 Complete the description of chart 1 using the words below. ▶ Diagramme, S. 215
P

> sharply – slowly – rose – fell – remained

Chart 1 shows the changes in the number of employees at YOUR HOST INTERNATIONAL from 1975 until 2015. In the beginning the number of employees was very small. It grew (1)… but steadily until 1985. In the following years the number (2)… at about the same level. However, from 1995 to 2005 the number of employees (3)… (4)… to about 10,000. From 2005 to 2015 the number (5)… slowly for the first time.

2 Describe the development of the number of work placements at YOUR HOST
P INTERNATIONAL in the same way. ● Task ▶ F8, p. 31

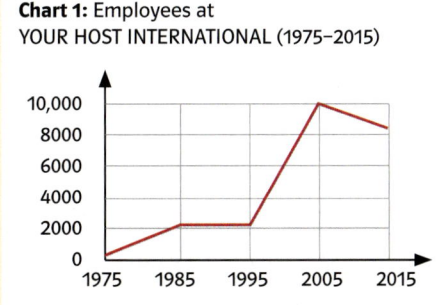

Chart 1: Employees at YOUR HOST INTERNATIONAL (1975–2015)

Chart 2: Work placements at YOUR HOST INTERNATIONAL (1975–2015)

Unit 2 | Getting a job

F | Further tasks

○ **A task 1, p. 20**

1
P

Use the following prompts.

1. company from … (the USA / Germany / …)
2. type of business (producer / store / …)
3. type of products (food / non-food / furniture / …)
4. factories / shops / outlets in … / near your place / in your town
5. your experience with this company / these products

○ **B 3 task 1, p. 23**

2
I

You are Linda Smith. Talk about your life and career using your role card on page 170 and the following phrases.

○ Help

1. I was born in Exeter in …
2. I (live) in Exeter from … to …
3. I (live) in London since …
4. I (go) to college from … to …
5. Then I (work) in …
6. I (be) a shop assistant at Morrisey's since …
7. I (start) learning German …
8. I (… – be) interested in working with people.
9. I (hear) about the job advertisement …

● **C task 2, p. 25**

3
R

Do the following tasks on the three texts in complete sentences.

1. Give details of the company and the job on offer.
2. Describe the qualifications that the applicant should have.
3. Explain Julia's strengths.
4. Give reasons why this placement could be suitable and useful for Julia.

● **D 1 task 4, p. 26**

4
R

Do the following tasks in complete sentences.

First interview:
1. Explain the applicant's plans for the next twelve months.
2. Give reasons why she wants to do a placement at that workplace and in that town.
3. Explain her parents' attitude.
4. Describe the applicant's experience and qualifications.

Second interview:
5. Say why – according to the interviewer – the placement could be a challenge for young people.
6. Explain Christian's reasons for doing a placement there.
7. Describe the applicant's family background.
8. Summarize the interviewer's answer to Christian's question.

Basic course > Advanced course > Exam course   Getting a job | **Unit 2**

● D 2 task 2, p. 27
5 Use your word web and prepare a talk about the things that you have to consider before you write an application.

○ D 3 task 3, p. 27
6 Watch the film again and decide if the following statements are correct.

1. Mr McFarlane asks the first question.
2. Miss Conway wants to try out different jobs before she decides on her future job.
3. Miss Conway is good at working with people and organizing things.
4. She wants to learn German because she did not learn it at school.
5. One of the possibilities for Miss Conway is to work in hotel management in the future.
6. Placements usually last half a year.

○ E 1 task 3, p. 29
7 Consider the following tips when doing your job interview.

- Greet your interviewer with a firm handshake.
- Make regular eye-contact.
- Pay attention to your body language.
- Listen carefully to each question.
- Show interest.
- Make it clear that you would welcome the opportunity to work there.
- Say thank you at the end of the interview.

● E 2 task 2, p. 29
8 Describe the development of unemployment in the UK. ► Diagramme, S. 215

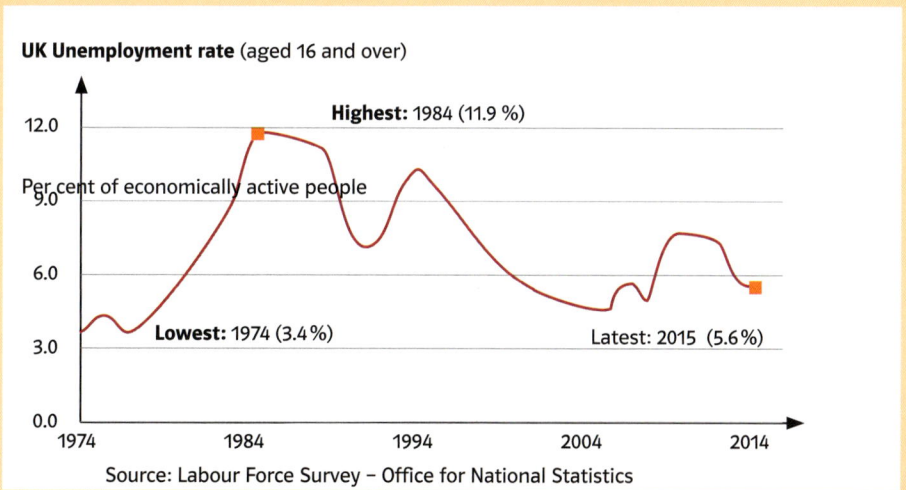

31

In this unit you will learn to ...
- find out about various aspects of Britain and the British way of life.
- write e-mails.
- book a room on the phone.
- practise mediation.
- deal with euros and pounds.

Unit A

 k36gg3

Cross-cultural communication at work:
Preparing for a work placement in London

A | Getting started: Planning a stay in London

1 Describe the illustrations. Tell the class what information about Great Britain they show. ▶ Fotos und Illustrationen, S. 211

2 Read the post by an American visitor to Great Britain. Then discuss the differences between Great Britain and Germany.

> Jason, 6 days ago
>
> When you come through the Channel Tunnel you are informed that you have arrived in England. On arriving at Edinburgh Airport you can see the Scottish flag. And when you drive around Wales the signs are in Welsh. So Great Britain doesn't seem to be one nation but a composition of three
> 5 nations. Great Britain has an army but not a football team. It has a national anthem and a queen but no constitution.

3 Find out this information about England, Wales and Scotland.

1. Capital city
2. Languages
3. Flag
4. Population
5. Famous people
6. Typical food

Facts

Great Britain = England + Scotland + Wales
United Kingdom = Great Britain + Northern Ireland

Basic course > Advanced course > Exam course   Preparing for a work placement in London | Unit A

B | Making preparations

Bastian Topp, a student from Stuttgart, is going to London on a work placement. He intends to work in a hotel there. Bastian contacted a hotel in London and he has received the following e-mail.

A1.12

From:	kate.huggins@hotel-victoria.co….uk	Date: 20.06.20..
To:	bastian.topp@web….de	
Subject:	Your work placement	

Dear Bastian

Having received an enquiry about a work placement from you last week, we are pleased to offer you a position for the period from 3 to 28 August. As you can understand we would appreciate it if you sent us your acceptance as soon
5   as possible.
Most of the work would be on reception, but you would also be required to work in the leisure section of our hotel.
We have no suitable possibilities to accommodate staff in the hotel so we have arranged B&B accommodation near our hotel at the Westward Boarding
10 House. Please contact Ms Lisa Davies to confirm the booking. As far as I know she charges students 30 pounds a night. Her telephone number is: 0044 (0) 20 7871 4627….
As regards pay: it is the hotel's policy to pay students on work placement a small wage (5 pounds an hour). We would also offer you free lunches and
15 evening meals.
Your college teacher gave you a very good reference but it would help us if you could send us more details about yourself. Then I'm sure we can make your stay with us as pleasant as possible.
We look forward to hearing from you soon.

20 Kind regards
Kate Huggins
General Manager,
Hotel Victoria, Barnet, London EN5 5RP, England   (223 words)

Understanding the text

1 Read the e-mail and do the following tasks. ► Leseverstehen, S. 199

1. When can Bastian do a placement at the hotel?
2. Where will he work in the hotel?
3. Where can he get accommodation?
4. How much money will Bastian get per hour in euros? Check the latest exchange rate in the newspaper or on the Internet.

 Internet key words: exchange rate – euro – pound

Unit A | Preparing for a work placement in London

After reading

2 Bastian writes back to Ms Huggins immediately. Write an e-mail for him accepting the placement. Firstly thank her for offering you the placement and tell her that you will come to the hotel in August. Secondly write a few sentences about yourself, your hobbies and why you want to work abroad. Thirdly thank Ms Huggins again and say you are looking forward to coming to the hotel. Finish the e-mail politely. ▶ Formelle Briefe und E-Mails, S. 205

> **Cross-cultural tips**
>
> **English e-mail conventions and etiquette**
> - subject line below e-mail address
> - first name often used: Bastian
> - no comma after salutation: Dear Ms Huggins
> - capital letter to start e-mail: Having…
> - never start with I or We. Use: Having received…
> - be very polite, use: thank you very much, please, excuse me …
> - suitable closing phrase: Kind regards
> - add your address and mobile and / or landline numbers (+49)

C | Booking a room on the telephone

Greg Carter, an American student from Ohio, is going to do a summer job in a restaurant in London. He needs somewhere to stay. He has found the Westward Boarding House on the Internet. He phones the landlady, Ms Davies.

Before listening

1 What do you think Greg is going to ask Ms Davies?

While listening

Exam 2 **Hörverstehen:** Listen and check if your ideas in task **1** were correct.
▶ Hörverstehen, S. 196

3 Hören Sie sich das Telefongespräch ein zweites Mal an und ergänzen Sie die folgenden Aussagen auf Deutsch.

1. Greg informiert Frau Davies, dass er ein Zimmer vom …
2. Das Zimmer, das Greg bucht, kostet …
3. Das Zimmer hat …
4. Greg erklärt, dass er plant, am Samstag …
5. Die Handynummer von Frau Davies lautet …
6. Nur 2 britische Pfund verlangt Frau Davies für…

After listening

HOT 4 **Role play:** Bastian has decided to stay at the Westward Boarding House during his placement, too, so he calls the landlady Ms Davies to confirm the booking. Partner A: You are Bastian. Partner B: You are Ms Davies. Act out the call using the role cards on page 171. ▶ Telefonieren, S. 225

Basic course > Advanced course > Exam course · Preparing for a work placement in London | **Unit A**

D | London: a city full of history and innovation

Before watching

1 In pairs make a list of the sights of London that you know. Then present your results in class.

While watching

2 Watch the video in which three actors and the director of the film "Night at the museum 3" (shot at the British Museum in London) talk about their impressions of London. Find out which sights Ben Stiller (speaker 1), Shawn Levy (speaker 2), Dan Stevens (speaker 3) and Ben Kingsley (speaker 4) mention. ▶ Hör-Seh-Verstehen, S. 197

3 Watch the video again. Find out which speakers (1–4) talk about:

1. history
2. why he gets lost in London
3. architecture
4. art galleries
5. the British Empire

E | Why do the British drive on the left?

1 Mediation: Bekannte von Ihnen wollen in Großbritannien Urlaub mit dem eigenen Auto machen. Erklären Sie ihnen anhand der Aussagen und Tipps auf Deutsch, warum die Briten links fahren und worauf sie sonst noch im Straßenverkehr achten sollten.
▶ Mediaton, S. 228

A "Most people are right-handed. The two main functions when driving are changing gears and steering. You should always have good control of your steering wheel when you change gears."

B "It goes back to Roman times. Riders travelled on the left to keep their sword arm free. Our continental European cousins also used to ride on the left until Napoleon changed it because he didn't like anything British.

C "The reason why the British drive on the left is that the French drive on the right. The British and French don't always get on well."

Cross-cultural tips

Driving in Britain
- **Junctions:** Be careful when you have to turn left or right.
- **Roundabouts:** Give way to traffic and always drive clockwise.
- **Parking:** Double yellow lines mean 'no stopping'. Single yellow lines mean 'no parking'.
- **Lights:** Make changes to your headlights so they do not blind oncoming drivers.
- **Speed limits:** 70 mph on motorways, 60 mph on single carriageways, 30 mph in built-up areas
- **Driving and alcohol:** 80 mg of alcohol per 100 ml of blood in England and Wales, 50 mg per 100 ml of blood in Scotland

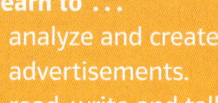

In this unit you will learn to . . .
- analyze and create advertisements.
- read, write and talk about developments in advertising.
- discuss the role of a responsible consumer.
- do a role play.
- use the past perfect simple and the past continuous.

 4t8i6w

Unit 3
The youth market

A | Getting started: Young people as consumers

Before reading

1 Describe the photos and decide which of the activities you like best.

2 Talk about other activities that you enjoy. What kind of equipment do you need? How much does the equipment cost?

3 Make a list of the three consumer goods and services that are most important to you. You can use the items below and / or your own ideas.

> TV – smartphone – cosmetics – bicycle – books – car – trainers – Internet – notebook – cinema – gym – social media – smart clothes

4 Work in pairs. Tell your partner what your three most important things are, and why. Then agree on a common order of the five most important things for both of you. Explain your results to the class. ○ Help ▶ F1, p. 46

5 Prepare a short talk or text about the following questions: "Do I really need the things on my list? How can I live without them?"

Basic course > Advanced course > Exam course   The youth market | **Unit 3**

 A1.14

YOUNG CONSUMERS HOLD THE KEY TO CHANGE

They have the power even if they do not know it. Young adults have the chance to change the world for the better and, later on in life, many of them will have the money and the power to make important decisions for all of us.

Young adults, most of them living in Asia, make up a quarter of the world's population. A large number of them are aware of the global issues which face us today and believe it is their duty to contribute to a better future for our planet. Many of them have strong principles: they often want the products that they buy to be healthy and environmentally friendly, and they want to associate the product with the idea of fair production methods. As a result of this, some large brands which have traditionally used "unfair" and "environmentally unfriendly" methods are experiencing falls in their sales figures.

But why do many young people not act according to their beliefs? Critics say that a lot of alternative or 'green' products are not attractive and do not perform well enough on the market. Moreover, very often people who want to go green are discouraged from doing so by the higher costs they have to pay for 'green' products. They feel that they have to pay more yet they get less in return.

Another reason may be that there are so many different eco-labels and fairtrade labels which confuse consumers. Potential buyers often do not know what the individual label means and what it really stands for. Sometimes so-called green consumer products make false claims so that consumers feel that the companies are cheating them.

So what can be done? Up to now marketing experts have been very creative in selling leading brands. For example they have given fashion labels an image that attracts young consumers. Sometimes the experts even help to 'greenwash' or 'fairwash' the products so that buyers believe that they are supporting humane and environmentally friendly production methods.

But through the Internet and social media, young consumers are now better informed than their parents. Knowing this, many leading companies and their marketing experts are adapting their products accordingly. The more they realize that the young buyers' values and attitudes have changed the more stress they will lay on appropriate products and services. So if companies want to be successful in the youth market in the future, they must stop talking about their environmental and social responsibility and start acting. Otherwise they will lose even more ground among young consumers. And if companies act more responsibly, they will not only help our planet and the people living on it but also make their companies more profitable in the long run. (459 words)

Understanding the text

6 Do the tasks on the text using your own words. ◯ Help ▶ F 2, p. 46
R   ▶ Leseverstehen, S. 199

1. Describe the principles that many young people have today.
2. Say why many young people do not act according to their beliefs.
3. Explain positive developments that could be possible in the future.

 7 **Mediation:** Für einen Vortrag zum Thema "Junge Leute und ihr Kaufverhalten"
M   haben Sie den obigen Text gelesen. Stellen Sie die wesentlichen Aussagen dazu auf Deutsch dar. ● Task ▶ F 3, p. 46 ▶ Mediation, S. 228

B | Grammar

B1 Manchester Shopping Centre

Grammar box

Past simple
Example: Sue lived in Glasgow from 2008 to 2014.
Bei Handlungen zu einem bestimmten Zeitpunkt oder in einem abgeschlossenen Zeitraum in der Vergangenheit
▶ p. 185

Past perfect simple
Example: After Sam had bought a CD he went home.
Für Handlungen oder Zustände, die vor einem Zeitpunkt in der Vergangenheit abgeschlossen waren
▶ p. 186

Past continuous
Example: While Sam was waiting at the bus stop it started to rain.
Bei Handlungen, die in der Vergangenheit schon im Gange waren, als eine neue Handlung eintrat
▶ p. 185

1 Last Sunday Andy went shopping at the shopping centre with his girlfriend Mary. Look at the list and the above plan to find out where they did each thing.

Example: Andy found trainers at Footwear.

Things to do
1. **find trainers (Andy)**
2. try on some new jeans (Mary)
3. buy a birthday present for his mum (Andy)
4. exchange a red T-shirt for a smaller size (Mary)
5. test the new Manchester United football (Andy)
6. put on the new season's make-up (Mary)
7. listen to a new pop CD (Mary and Andy)
8. get a haircut (Mary)

Basic course > Advanced course > Exam course   The youth market | **Unit 3**

2 Andy and Mary wanted to do their shopping quickly. Find the shortest way through the shopping centre and put the list in task **1** in the correct order. They started at the entrance and turned left.

3 Describe Andy and Mary's shopping trip in the following way:

Example: After Andy and Mary had arrived at the shopping centre Mary exchanged a red T-shirt for a smaller size. After Mary had exchanged the T-shirt …

B2 What did you do after …?

1 Read the dialogue below in pairs. Replace the underlined parts and act out the new dialogue.

Student A: What did you do <u>last weekend</u> (yesterday / last week)?
Student B: I <u>went shopping</u>.
Student A: What did you do after you <u>had been shopping</u>?
Student B: After I <u>had been shopping</u> I <u>drank a coffee in a café</u>.

B3 A bad day for shopping

1 While Andy and Mary were going home they met Mark. He had been shopping, too. But some things had gone wrong. Say what happened to him.

1. get dressed / telephone – ring

Example: While Mark was getting dressed the telephone rang.

2. run to – bus stop / bus – leave
3. walk to – shopping centre / start – to rain
4. listen to – an important announcement / meet – his ex-girlfriend
5. look at – book / mobile phone – ring
6. drink – cup of coffee / drop - cup
7. try on – new pair of jeans / fire-alarm – go off
8. sit on – bus / bus – break down

B4 Back from the shopping trip

1 Put the verbs in brackets into the correct form of the past tense.

After Andy and Mary (1. arrive) … at Andy's house they (2. unpack) … all the things they (3. buy) …. After they (4. put) … the things away, they (5. turn on) … the TV. While they (6. watch) … a commercial about trainers, Andy (7. notice) … that he (8. buy) … the wrong shoes. After they (9. discuss) … going back to the shop to change the trainers, they (10. decide) … to get them on their next trip.

B5 Your last shopping trip

1 You have a friend in the US. Write him / her an e-mail. Describe your last shopping
P trip in about 100 words. Use each of the words 'after' and 'while' at least twice.
▶ Persönliche Briefe und E-Mails, S. 210

C | Reading

C1 Protecting young consumers

Before reading

1 Have you ever bought anything on the Internet? Talk about your experiences.

2 What do you think the headline below means?

🔊 A1.15

Buyers' training at schools

Buyers' training? – Buying things has always been relatively simple. If you had the money, you could buy a product. If not, loans could solve your problem but there were several
5 steps to take until you got a bank loan.

A Today buying is often just one click away:
- You need the latest smartphone? Just enter your personal details and click "Buy".
- You want the latest designer jeans? You can
10   have them tomorrow. Buy now, pay later.
- You love football? Bet on your favourite team and win.
- You need a credit card to make your wishes come true? You are 18? Here it is.

15 **B** It is the "spend now and deal with the consequences later" mentality which often runs young people into debt. In Germany more than a million adults under 30 are deep in debt with average debts of about €8,500. In the
20 USA millions of young people have an average of about $1,500 credit card debt before they start college. With plastic money and online shopping at hand, young people tend to buy things today that they cannot afford and end up with debts that they cannot pay back. 25

C That is why last September British schools introduced a special financial education programme. "It's a first step in the right direction," says money expert Percy Ford. "Less than half of young people say that they 30 have an understanding of financial matters. Many avoid contact with financial institutions because they don't even know how to open an account." Pete Stuart, student at Newcastle University remarks: "After two years of business 35 and maths courses I still do not know how to manage my own personal finances." And Percy Ford adds: "Among the millions of people between 20 and 30, four out of five do not save for major purchases. Companies spend billions 40 of pounds on advertising and sales training for their staff and many young people do not really think before they buy something. If the product is modern, attractive and fits their lifestyle, they buy it and then they struggle to cope with 45 the financial consequences."

D Teachers welcome the new education programme which has been included in Maths and other subjects. As one teacher puts it: "I'm sure the next generation of school-leavers will 50 plan their purchases more carefully and will only buy what they can afford. Of course, sometimes it's advisable to take out a loan, for example if you want to buy a house. But people should think first. Maybe we'll even see an effect on 55 parents when their children come home and tell them about the new programme."

Basic course > Advanced course > Exam course   The youth market | Unit 3

> **E** So maybe the next time people go shopping and see "special offers" or a big "sale" sign, they will not just buy because they think it is the cheapest offer they can get. "If you know what you want, you can find a good bargain all year round," says Percy Ford. "Young people are especially at risk when they are online. They are often just one click away from buying things like new apps or the latest hit from the charts. They should always ask themselves some questions first: Have I compared prices? Do I have the money? Do I really need it? If only one answer is "no", don't buy it." (545 words)

Understanding the text

3 Match the following sentences with a suitable paragraph (A – E) in the text.
R   Two of the headings do not match. ▶ Leseverstehen, S. 199

1. The programme can help young people and their parents.
2. Buying has become easy.
3. Think twice before you buy things.
4. Parents must teach their children how to manage money.
5. Many young people cannot manage their money.
6. Millions of young adults in western countries are in debt.
7. Online shopping must be made safer.

4 Do the following tasks on the text in complete sentences. ○ Task ▶ F 4, p. 47
R
1. Give reasons why shopping without actually having enough money has become easier.
2. Describe the somewhat difficult relationship which many young people have with money.
3. Point out the positive effects of the financial education programme.

5 **Mediation:** Sie sind überzeugt, dass es sinnvoll ist, ein ähnliches Programm wie
M   in Großbritannien an Ihrer Schule einzuführen. Schreiben Sie einen Artikel auf Deutsch für Ihre Schulzeitung, in dem Sie die wesentlichen Aussagen des Textes verwenden. ▶ Mediation, S. 228

TRAINING SKILLS – How to do a role play

C2   A sales talk

1 **Rollenspiel:** Work in pairs. Choose a product. Possible products for sale: a smartphone plus contract, the latest designer jeans, cool trainers, a tablet, a cool watch.

2 Choose a role. Student A is a salesperson in a German department store. See role card A "salesperson" on p. 171. Student B is an English-speaking customer. See role card B "customer" on p. 171.

Tips for your role play
1. Read your role card carefully.
2. Think about the situation.
3. Make notes about your ideas.
4. Look up words that you need for your role play.
5. If possible, practise your role with a partner.
6. Ask for feedback from others.
7. Try to be flexible when playing your role.
8. Listen carefully to the other person and react according to your role.
9. Be friendly and polite.

D | Practice

D1 Planning an advertising campaign

Before listening

1 Complete the text with suitable words from the box on the right.

An advertising (1.) … is a business that (2.) … and handles advertising and other forms of promotion. Its (3.) … include companies, non-profit (4.) … and governments. Agencies are hired to produce TV or radio (5.) … as well as online (6.) … or they plan direct sales (7.) … programmes. The (8.) … of large agencies also include market (9.) … or interactive marketing in (10.) … media.

> clients – agency – commercials – social – plans – organizations – research – advertising – services – promotion

While listening

Exam 2 **Hörverstehen:** Hören Sie dem Gespräch in der Werbeagentur zu und ordnen Sie den Fotos die Namen und Berufe der Personen zu. ► Hörverstehen, S. 196

3 Hören Sie dem Gespräch noch einmal genau zu und notieren Sie die fehlenden Informationen zu den folgenden Stichpunkten. ● Task ► F 5, p. 47

1. Name der Werbeagentur
2. Informationen über die Werbeagentur
3. Firma des Kunden
4. Informationen über das Kundenunternehmen
5. Name und Aussehen des Produkts
6. Möglicher Preis des Produkts
7. Zielgruppen
8. Vorteile des Produkts
9. Idee für die Einführung des Produkts
10. Weiteres Vorgehen

After listening

4 How would you advertise a mobile phone for children? Develop ideas in groups, make notes and present them in class.

Basic course > Advanced course > Exam course   The youth market | Unit 3

Facts

The AIDA formula is a theory in marketing: It describes how to sell products to target groups and gets people to buy products.
Attention: attract the target group
Interest: make the target group look more closely
Desire: convince the target group that they want the product or service
Action: make the target group act.

D2 An advertisement for a non-profit organization

1 Do the following tasks based on the advertisement.

1. Describe the advertisement.
2. Match the parts of the AIDA formula in the *Facts* box with the numbers in the above advert.
3. What is the advert for?
4. Who do you think the target group is?
5. What effect does the advert have on you?
6. Do you think the advert is successful? Why? Why not?

2 Find an advert on the Internet and analyze it. Present it in class. ● Task ▶ F 6, p. 47

D3 Does the brand influence your taste?

Before watching

1
I
👥
Talk to a partner about your favourite drink. Tell him/her why you like the taste best. Would you recognize the taste in a neutral bottle?

While watching

2
R
🎬 V4
Watch the film "Heinz & Packaging". Complete the sentences in German. ▶ Hör-Seh-Verstehen, S. 197

1. Zu Beginn ist der Moderator (blau gekleidet) überzeugt, dass wir eine bestimmte Marke wählen, weil wir …
2. Sein Gesprächspartner im dunklen T-Shirt behauptet: Wenn wir glauben, dass eine bestimmte Marke besser schmeckt, dann …
3. Der Moderator füllt zwei gleiche Behälter mit dem gleichen Inhalt, aber …
4. Beim Geschmackstest sagen 10 von 11 Personen, dass der gleiche Inhalt …
5. Am Ende ist die Erkenntnis des Moderators, dass die Marke …

Unit 3 | The youth market

E | Reading+: New trends in advertising

Before reading

1 Work in pairs. Discuss what the headline "Digital advertising on the move" could mean.

Understanding the text

2 Read the first part of the text and check if your ideas in task **1** were correct.
▶ Leseverstehen, S. 199

3 Decide if the following statements are true or false with regard to the text. Correct the false statements. ● Task ▶ F7, p. 47

1. Digital advertising will become the most important way of advertising within the next few years.
2. Users have to forward an e-mail to be provided with adverts.
3. RSS feeds sometimes cost money.
4. Apart from being common in the office, doing a number of activities simultaneously also happens in private homes.
5. Half of TV viewers look for interesting adverts on the Internet.

Exam 4 **Mediation:** Für einen Bericht über die Rolle der Neuen Medien in der Werbung werten Sie diesen Text aus. Fassen Sie dazu die wesentlichen Aussagen auf Deutsch zusammen. ▶ Mediation, S. 228

After reading

HOT 5 **Rollenspiel:** Discuss the topic: "Advertising should be banned in all forms of media that target young people in particular."

1. Work in groups.
   Group A: Take the position of a student. See role card A "student", p. 171.
   Group B: Take the position of a company representative. See role card B "company representative", p. 172.
   Group C: Take the position of a parent. See role card C "parent", p. 172.

2. One person from each group takes part in the discussion. Introduce yourself and state your position.

3. Then discuss the pros and cons of the ban. ▶ Diskussion, S. 219

4. The students in the audience take notes and vote for or against the ban after the discussion. ▶ Notizen, S. 243

Exam 6 **Materialgestützter Aufsatz:** Write a composition about the topic, "Advertising should be banned in all forms of media that target young people in particular." Use information from this unit 3 and your own ideas.
▶ Materialgestützter Aufsatz, S. 199

DIGITAL ADVERTISING ON THE MOVE

A According to experts more than 50% of all advertising will be digital within a few years. As we can already see today more and more people are spending their money online. They are not only buying CDs or downloading music but ordering Christmas presents such as books, household appliances or electronic gadgets for their relatives and friends. Advertisers know all too well that the number of Internet connections – most of them broadband connections – has increased sharply. "But the major focus will lie in the mobile market," as Mark Owen from the market research bureau "Global Research" puts it. "Mobile Internet connections have doubled in the last five years and I expect that this trend will continue. Just look at all those smartphones, net books and web pads."

B There are two basic forms of digital advertising – push and pull. Pull digital advertising means that the user has to search for specific information and he / she can choose (or pull) the content, often via web search. Users click on a specific link in order to view the information required. Push advertising means that both the creator of the information and the user are involved. E-mails, SMS or RSS feeds are examples of push advertising. The sender has to push (send) the message to the user or users so that the message can be received. Often users subscribe to certain providers in order to get information regularly. RSS is a popular form of sharing content, e.g. newspaper headlines, without the need to constantly visit a web site to see if there is anything new. These services are often free, however, they are linked with advertising. This form of marketing can be used by firms to inform potential customers about their new products, special offers or marketing campaigns. If people are not interested in receiving news, they can cancel their subscription.

C Of course, effective marketing does not only rely on one advertising channel and advertisers usually plan campaigns on different channels. Moreover, our consumption of the media available to us is changing rapidly, and multi-tasking is no longer only related to work but has also found its way into our living rooms. A recent survey found out that large numbers of TV viewers still switch channels as they did ten or twenty years ago, but more and more viewers are now turning to the Internet during TV advertising breaks. 40% of TV viewers admit to multi-tasking daily. This could mean that they surf the Internet while they are watching TV, or they work or play on the PC while the TV is on in the background. Although an increasing number of advertisers are switching from TV to online advertising, the report points out that the integration of TV and digital advertising leads to a significant increase in response rates from viewers / users. The same survey also found out that more than half of TV viewers go online to look for a TV commercial which has interested them. In this way the report helps advertisers to find ways to link their messages across the two channels when they are planning their campaigns.

D And this is only the beginning. It will be interesting to see how advertising continues to develop in the future. As we have learnt from past examples, those advertisers who have had a good nose for new developments – particularly in online and mobile communication – have been very successful and able to make an easy dollar. (570 words)

F | Further tasks

A task 4, p. 36

1 The phrases can help you to discuss the order on the list with your partner.

> **Help**
>
> I think that …
> I believe that …
> I feel that …
> In my opinion…
>
> … is most important because …
> … is most useful because …
> … is a lot of fun because …
>
> … comes second because …
> … is not so important because …
> … is not important at all because …
>
> What do you think about …?
> Do you also think that …?
> Do you agree with me?
> What would you say?
>
> I (don't) agree with you.
> I'm sorry but …
> Well, on the other hand you could say that …
> Don't you really think that …?

A task 6, p. 37

2 Decide if the statements are true or false. Correct the false statements.

1. In the future young people will have the influence to support positive developments.
2. A quarter of young people live in Asia.
3. A lot of young people care about their health and the environment.
4. Big companies which have an image of treating workers and the environment badly are losing customers.
5. Many young people follow their ideals and buy environmentally friendly products.
6. The great number of "green" labels helps young consumers to decide.
7. Marketing experts often help to sell a positive image although their companies do not really behave like that.
8. As young people are well-informed, companies will have to act in a humane, environmentally friendly way instead of only talking about it.

A task 7, p. 37

3 Describe the advert and explain how it illustrates the ideas of the text.

C 1 task 4, p. 41

4 Complete the summary of the text with phrases from the text. (— = one word)

1. Today buying new things is easy. When you are online they are only — — —.
2. Many young people in Germany and the USA have run deeply — —.
3. In Britain schools have started a — — — —.
4. A money expert says that many young people do not save money, but they buy expensive things and then have to deal with — —.
5. British teachers feel the buyers' training is a good thing and that in the future young people will think about new purchases and plan them — —.
6. At the end of the text the money expert advises young people not to buy an expensive product spontaneously but always to ask — —.
7. If the answer to one of the questions is negative, they should not — —.

D 1 task 3, p. 42

5 Do the following tasks in complete sentences.

1. Describe Mr Ding's company and its activities on the British market.
2. Give reasons why the company has chosen this advertising agency.
3. Explain why there is not only one target group for the new product.
4. Say how Mr Ding's company wants to reach future customers and give reasons why they have chosen this way.
5. Describe the next steps in the development of the campaign.

D 2 task 2, p. 43

6 You work for an advertising agency and you are developing an advert for a company. Think of a product or service you could advertise with one of the photos below. Complete the illustration with a suitable slogan and further information. Remember the AIDA formula on p. 43.

E task 3, p. 44

7 Do these tasks on the text "Digital advertising on the move" on p. 45. Use your own words..

1. Describe the main trend in digital advertising.
2. Explain the difference between push and pull advertising in one or two sentences.
3. Explain the role of "multi-tasking" in media consumption.
4. Say why it is important for companies to spot new trends first.

Unit 4
Media in our lives

A | Getting started

A1 Where do we get news?

1 Describe the media you see above. Then name other media you know.

2 Where do you get the news? Make a list of the different media and do a survey of their usage in your group or in class. Analyze your results and talk about them.

3 Describe and analyze the chart below. Then compare the results for 2012 with
P   your class survey. ○ Help ► F 1, p. 58

Where Americans Get News: Percentage of Respondents Who Got News "Yesterday" From Each Platform

Year	TV	Radio	Newspaper	Online	Any Digital News (Smartphone, tablet etc.)
2000	56	43	47		
2004	60	40	42	24	
2008	57	35	34	29	
2012	55	33	29	39	50

Quelle: Pew Research Center. "In Changing News Landscape, Even Television is Vulnerable." September 27, 2012; www.journalism.org.

A2 Watching TV

Before reading

1 What do you think the term 'generation gap' in the headline of the text could refer to?

Ofcom[1] report identifies emerging 'generation gap' in young people's TV viewing

Media regulator highlights shift in viewing habits as people aged 16–24 move away from traditional platforms and online consumption grows

Younger people are switching off TV and radio in their droves in favour of online pursuits such as Facebook, leading to a growing "generation gap" in TV and radio.

A report by media regulator Ofcom published on Monday said 16- to 24-year-olds spent an average of 148 minutes a day watching TV in 2013, down from 169 minutes in 2010 and compared to an average of 232 minutes for all viewers. The decline in radio listening has also been precipitous, with 16- to 24-year-olds listening to 15.5 hours a week compared with 21.4 hours a decade earlier (and 21.5 hours across all ages).

Ofcom said it was traditional for younger people to consume less TV and radio, but warned that the latest changes may be part of a structural shift, driven by the digital era, in which TV and radio – in their traditional sense, at least – go permanently out of fashion. The regulator said there had been a "radical change" in the media and communications industry over the past five years, with the rise of on-demand services, from the BBC's iPlayer to commercial service Netflix, and the switch to digital TV. [...]

'Tech natives'

Ofcom said the "generation gap between younger and older audiences appears to be getting wider, with significant differences in opinion, attitude and habits towards [...] television more generally".

It added: "While younger audiences have always watched less television than older audiences, our audience research suggests that the connected generation are watching increasingly less television, and that they may be taking these habits with them as they age."

It identified "tech natives", aged 16 to 30, of whom "less than half now think that the TV is their most important source for relaxing or entertainment". [...] (316 words)

1 Ofcom = Office of Communications

Quelle: John Plunkett, December 15, 2014, www.theguardian.com.

Understanding the text

2 Read the text quickly to find out if your ideas in task 1 were true. ▶ Leseverstehen, S. 199

3 Explain the meaning of the following numbers in the text. ● Task ▶ F 2, p. 58

1. 16 to 24
2. from 169 to 148
3. 232
4. from 21.4 to 15.5
5. 21.5
6. 16 to 30

4 **Mediation:** Für einen Beitrag für Ihre Online-Schulzeitung fassen Sie die wesentlichen Gedanken des Textes über die sich verändernde Mediennutzung von jungen Leuten zusammen. ▶ Mediation, S. 228

B | Grammar

B1 The media in the future

1 Ask your classmates the following questions about the use of media in the future. The words in the *Help* box can help them to answer the questions.

1. people / use / online news services more often

Example: Student A: What do you expect? Will people use online news services more often in the future?
Student B: I suppose people will use online news services more often in the future.

2. people / write / more posts for blogs
3. young people / watch / less TV
4. we / buy / more newspapers
5. students / use / laptops in class
6. use of mobile devices / increase
7. the media / influence people / more

2 Answer the questions using the short form and give reasons.

Example: Student A: What do you expect? Will people use online news services more often in the future?
Student B: Yes, they will because they want to be up-to-date with what is happening in the world.

Help
probably • I expect • I suppose

Grammar box
Will-future
Example: I think the mobile phone will help us in many ways.
Bei unsicheren Vorhersagen
Example: Just a minute, I'll help you!
Bei Entscheidungen, die im Moment des Sprechens getroffen werden
► p. 188

Future with 'going to'
Example: I am going to stay in New York for a week.
Bei Absichten und geplanten Vorhaben
► p. 182

B2 Doing homework on a laptop

1 Make sentences using 'going to' as shown in the example.

1. Jason has opened his laptop and has turned it on.

Example: Jason is going to do some work on his laptop.

2. Jason cannot remember what homework he has to do. He opens an app to chat with a classmate.
3. The homework is to find some information on the Internet. Jason starts his browser.
4. Jason has opened his e-mail program and clicks on the "Create mail" icon.
5. Jason has finished his homework and wants to relax. He clicks on his favourite game on the desktop.
6. It is seven o'clock in the evening. Jason's parents have prepared dinner.
7. After dinner Jason goes back to his room because he wants to watch his favourite series on his laptop.
8. Jason is tired. He switches off the laptop.

B3 The development of a telecommunications company

1 Put the verbs in brackets into the correct future form.

Jim Dawson is managing director of a telecommunications company. He is talking to his staff about the future development of the company.
"Ladies and gentlemen, I would like to talk to you about the future of our company. Management has decided to go ahead with plans for the new office building. We are **going to open** it next March. We hope that it **will secure** the future success of our company. We expect that cloud computing (1. increase) … in the next few years and that we (2. have) … thousands of new customers. Management has plans to invest more in Internet technology, especially in the mobile web. That is why we (3. buy) … new servers and we (4. update) … our network. Since mobile phones and tablets have become more important and the number of users of the mobile web has also increased, the mobile web (5. grow) … in the future. This (6. probably help) … us to be more profitable."

B4 Comparing different kinds of media

1 Complete the text with the suitable form of the words in brackets.

It is **easy** to find information on the Internet. You press a button and a new page opens **quickly**. Usually the Internet works (1. good) … and you can download files (2. accurate) …, but sometimes it breaks down. Newspapers show (3. interesting) … news and are (4. informative) …. What are the (5. real) … advantages of reading a newspaper or magazine compared to using the (6. fast) … Internet? First of all, you can read a newspaper wherever you go. You do not need electricity or a wireless connection. If your newspaper is stolen, you can replace it (7. easy) …, as it is (8. cheap) …. Another advantage is that a newspaper is (9. good) … for the environment because it is (10. recyclable) … and is not made of (11. harmful) … toxic material. If a newspaper prints something which is not (12. correct) …, you can read the correction the next day. Of course, the latest news appears on the Internet more (13. quick) …, but you cannot (14. easy) … find out if it is (15. real) … true.

B5 Managing situations – A new laptop

1 Sie chatten mit einem englischen Freund und berichten ihm von Ihrem Plan, sich
M einen neuen Computer zu kaufen. Übertragen Sie die folgenden Sätze sinngemäß ins Englische. ○ Help ▶ F3, p. 58 ▶ Mediation, S. 228

1. Sie haben gespart und werden sich einen Laptop kaufen.
2. Sie werden wahrscheinlich eine Laptop-Tablet-Kombination *(laptop tablet hybrid)* kaufen.
3. Sie nehmen an, dass Sie überall damit arbeiten können.
4. Sie hoffen, dass Sie viel Spaß damit haben werden.
5. Ihr Lehrer hat Ihnen die Aufgabe gegeben, im Internet Informationen zu suchen. Sie werden das heute Abend tun.
6. Wenn Sie danach noch Zeit haben, werden Sie noch einmal mit Ihrem Freund chatten.

C | Reading: You can't escape it!

Before reading

1 Look at the pictures below. What do you think they could tell us about the Internet and its use?

Understanding the texts

2 Skim through the texts on page 53 and match them with one of the photos.

3 Read the three texts carefully and match them with a suitable headline. Three headlines do not match. ● Task ▶ F 4, p. 58; ○ Task ▶ F 5, p. 59
▶ Leseverstehen, S. 199

1. Net piracy may send parents to prison
2. Beware of the wolf
3. The development of the Worldwide Web
4. Internet fraud on the rise
5. The Internet saves the world
6. The Internet's role in education

Exam 4
M **Mediation:** In Ihrem Politikunterricht sprechen Sie über die Chancen und Gefahren des Internets. Sie erhalten die Aufgabe, ein kurzes Referat über die Risiken des Internets auf Deutsch zu halten. Bereiten Sie dieses Referat mit Hilfe der hier abgedruckten Zeitungsartikel vor.
▶ Mediation, S. 228

TRAINING SKILLS – How to write a composition I

5
R Find advantages and dangers of using the computer and the Internet in the texts on page 53. Write them down in two lists.

6 Work in pairs. Complete the lists of advantages and dangers with ideas of your own.

7
P Comment on this statement: "Children should not have their own computer or Internet access because it is too dangerous." Write at least three arguments for and three against this statement in complete sentences.

Basic course > Advanced course > Exam course   Media in our lives | Unit 4

A1.18

Text A

"I can't believe that there was no Internet when my parents were my age," says 17-year-old John Burns from Newcastle. "They didn't even have mobile phones!"
5   What adults call "new" media nowadays is generally quite normal for the younger generation. Young people use the Internet constantly to buy and sell things, place bets on their favourite football teams or
10 download music. In the last few years the mobile Internet has become more and more important. Both young people and even older people have discovered how easy it is to get in contact with other people
15 on the Internet or to just post their ideas and tips.
    But this all only started about 30 years ago when computer expert Tim Berners-Lee invented the new programming language
20 HTML and put his new software onto the Internet for free. Soon businesses and private people realized how useful the Web could be – and that was the start of a worldwide success story. (158 words)

A1.19

Text B

According to police reports internet crime is still rising sharply in Britain and criminal fantasy seems to be unlimited. In London for example, online fraudsters are targeting
5   students and holidaymakers by offering cheap rooms and flats. People who are interested have to pay deposits in cash before they even see their new homes. Often these homes do not really exist.
10 "Phishing attacks" are also on the rise. Fraudsters try to get people's credit card or account details by sending them e-mails that seem to come from their bank or the government. Many other internet crimes
15 are connected with the buying and selling of goods. The buyer sends the payment, but the goods never arrive. In other cases where the seller may agree to payment after delivery, he or she never receives
20 the money or the buyer may use a stolen credit card to pay. The police warn all internet users to be very careful about using their personal data and only to use the service of internet auction sites which
25 guarantee safe payment up to a certain amount. (178 words)

A1.20

Text C

When newspaper reporter Susan Brady met Detective Sergeant Jones, she was not aware of what would happen in the next few minutes. She was investigating 'child
5   grooming'. In such cases, men or organized gangs approach children in chatrooms in order to get in touch with them. Very often these criminals use false identities.
    Sergeant Jones had already registered
10 Susan with her new username "alice13" and clicked the button to tell other users that she was online. Within a few minutes several people wanted to have a chat with "Alice". As the reporter started chats with
15 some of her anonymous partners, she soon felt that the conversation was going in an unpleasant direction because she was asked very personal details. That is when she stopped the chats.
    Sergeant Jones explained: "The Internet
20 has provided new opportunities for paedophiles. Many of them are waiting online to get in contact with potential victims. But now the police are allowed to become active. We need not wait until a
25 crime is committed, instead we can enter the various meeting places on the Internet and do undercover investigations. In this way we have been quite successful. But there is still a lot to do and you wouldn't
30 believe how many paedophiles there are online right now." (211 words)

53

D | Practice

D1 What's on the radio?

Before listening

1. Look at the three photos. Describe the situations.

While listening

2. **Hörverstehen:** Hören Sie sich die Ausschnitte aus Radiosendungen an. Notieren Sie, in welchem Ausschnitt über welche Medien gesprochen wird.
▶ Hörverstehen, S. 196

3. Hören Sie die Ausschnitte ein zweites Mal. Finden Sie heraus, welche der folgenden Aussagen in den jeweiligen Sendungen gemacht werden. Mehr als eine Antwort kann zutreffen.

Ausschnitt A
1. Die Hälfte der Bewerber informiert sich über den Arbeitgeber online.
2. Arbeitgeber akzeptieren in der Regel keine Bewerber, die Drogen oder maßlos Alkohol konsumieren.
3. Arbeitnehmer bekommen das Facebook-Passwort des Unternehmens.
4. In einigen Fällen finden Arbeitgeber heraus, dass die Bewerber über ihre Qualifikationen gelogen haben.

Ausschnitt B
1. Die interviewte Dame hat zwei Kinder in einem schwierigen Alter.
2. Eine Tochter kann sich gar nicht von ihrem Smartphone trennen.
3. Selbst beim gemeinsamen Mittagessen am Sonntag legen die Töchter die Smartphones nicht zur Seite.
4. Kinder sollten kein eigenes Smartphone haben.

Ausschnitt C
1. Junge Leute verbringen ungefähr 50 Stunden in der Woche vor verschiedenen Bildschirmen.
2. Allein 10 Stunden spielen junge Leute Spiele am Computer oder an Spielkonsolen.
3. Es hat schon Teenager gegeben, die nach langem Spielen ins Krankenhaus gebracht werden mussten.
4. Es wird davon ausgegangen, dass junge Leute, die sehr viel spielen, in der Schule schlechtere Leistungen bringen.

TRAINING SKILLS – How to describe a cartoon

D2 Media, media!

1 **Describe and analyze cartoon 1 . Start with the following phrases.**
P

Description: The illustration shows …
The caption (speech bubble) reads …
Analysis: The cartoonist wants to point out that …
Your opinion: I think this cartoon is …
The words in the *Help*-box on the right can help you to go on.

2 **Describe cartoon 2 in a similar way.** ○ Help ▶ F 6, p. 59
P

> **○ Help**
>
> office • office block • in the background • desk • personnel manager • comfortable office chair • on the right • applicant • on the left

D3 Smartphones at school?

When young people come to college none of them leaves their smartphones at home. During breaks you can see them with their heads down instead of talking to each other. Even more problems arise when smartphones are used without permission during lessons. Head teachers and their staff are trying to find solutions to this problem. Students see the use of mobile phones differently, of course.

HOT **1** **Rollenspiel:** You are at Newcastle College and next week a discussion is going to take place about the use of smartphones and other modern media at college and in the classroom. Prepare a role using the role cards. Use your own ideas, too.

Student A is a student at the college. You are going to speak for the students.
Student B is a head teacher. Student C is a parent. Student D is a police officer.
You can find your role cards on p. 172.

Introduce yourselves and present your statements / arguments. Discuss the pros and cons of smartphones in students' hands. Try to reach an agreement on a mobile device policy for the college at the end of the discussion.

E | Reading +

E1 Trends in social media

Before watching

1 Look at the diagram.
What do you think it shows?

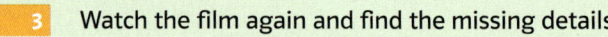

While watching

2 Watch the film and find out if your guess
R in task **1** was true. ▶ Hör-Seh-Verstehen, S. 197

3 Watch the film again and find the missing details.

1. Number of telephones in 1880
2. Number of telephones now
3. Times of peaks
4. Main use of Twitter by
5. Reason for this according to Nicola Millard
6. Use of Facebook by
7. Reason for the use of Facebook
8. The new trend

E2 The Internet on the move

Understanding the text

1 Skim the text on p. 57 and say in one or two sentences what it is about.
R

2 Read the text in detail and match the key points 1–5 with the headings in the text.
R ▶ Leseverstehen, S. 199

1. the first generation that has grown up with computers / the Internet
2. giving up an old job for an interesting new one
3. many young people work after school – online social networks
4. open-minded young generation – study and work abroad
5. time management and multi-tasking skills

3 Answer the questions in your own words. ○ Task ▶ F7, p. 59
R

1. Why does "Jimmy" give up his old job so quickly?
2. Why is Generation Y skilled in the use of new technology?
3. What may be an advantage / a disadvantage of multi-tasking?
4. How do young people often meet other people?
5. In which way have young people become global citizens?

Exam 4 **Mediation:** Erläutern Sie Ihren Freunden auf Deutsch, was Sie in diesem Artikel
M über die Generation Y gelernt haben. ▶ Mediation, S. 228

THE INTERNET GENERATION *by Andrew Moss*

Switching jobs quickly

Let's call him Jimmy. He's buying designer jeans in a new superstore in San Francisco when he meets his old school friend, Derek, who is desperately looking for a computer professional. Jimmy has just finished work on some PC applications in his present job and has only got some dull work to do in the next few weeks. Derek hires him spontaneously. Still in the superstore Jimmy sends an e-mail to his employer: "Sorry. Won't come back. Please send me the rest of my pay by check."

Growing up with new technology

Born in the 1980s or 1990s Jimmy is one of the so-called "Internet generation" or "Generation Y" which is the first generation that has grown up surrounded by new technology. Armed with smartphones and laptops they are online twenty-four hours a day, seven days a week. They rely on new technology to do their jobs better. They prefer to communicate by e-mail or text messaging rather than face-to-face. Online communication with its automatic spell checks and instant messaging (where it takes too long to write "You made me laugh out loud") means that this generation doesn't need to know how to spell, or even speak English properly. Young people LOL and confess ILY.

On the move to better jobs

Nevertheless, members of Generation Y are self-confident, creative and optimistic, independent and goal-oriented. Having grown up in play groups and doing team sports they appreciate team work. They belong to a generation whose free time was carefully planned by their parents when they were kids. That is why they are used to time management and multi-tasking. The flipside of the coin is that multi-tasking talents are unable to concentrate on a single task for a long period of time. A recent survey found that nearly 50% of graduates are planning to stay with their first employer for less than two years.

Online networks replace road networks

Young people today are willing to work and earn money. About 50 % of the students in the 12th grade work more than twenty hours a week, most of them in the retail trade and in the service industry. On the other hand young employees are not only interested in money but also in flexible working hours and a better work / life balance. It is interesting to know that the percentage of car buyers in Germany under thirty has decreased from 17% to 7% within twenty years. Some experts believe that young people today do not need cars any more because they see the world through their computers. Internet connections have replaced road networks and so young people can stay at home and experience the world online in social networks.

Going global

Having grown up with people of other nationalities and cultures and being connected to all continents through the Internet, members of Generation Y are open-minded, they think globally and see everything as being connected. They can truly be called global citizens. They are ready to do placements or study abroad, their jobs may demand that they also work abroad in a more and more global world and they are ready to fit in – as long as it meets their requirements. (540 words)

Unit 4 | Media in our lives

F | Further tasks

A 1 task 3, p. 48

1. Use the phrases from the box to describe the table on p. 48.

> **Help**
>
> **Introduction:** The chart / diagram ... published in / on ... shows where ...
> **Time:** in the year ... • in ... • from ... to ... • between ... and ... • in the last few years
> **Numbers:** percentage of ... • ... per cent
> **Positive development:** increased • grew • rose
> **Negative development:** decreased • fell • declined • sank
> **No change:** remained constant • did not change
> **Rate of change:** slowly • slightly • gradually • sharply • drastically
> **Conclusion:** all in all we can say that ... • to sum up you can say that ...

A 2 task 3, p. 49

2. Do the following tasks on the text on p. 49 in complete sentences.

1. Describe the trend in TV and radio consumption among young people.
2. Compare young people's viewing habits to those of the average viewer.
3. Give reasons why young people are turning away from traditional communication platforms.
4. Describe Ofcom's expectations with regard to young people's television consumption when they grow older.

B 5 task 1, p. 51

3. You are chatting with an English-speaking friend about a new computer you are planning to buy. Fill in the correct future tense.

1. I have saved some money and I (buy) ... a new laptop.
2. I ... probably (buy) ... a laptop tablet hybrid.
3. I suppose that in this way I (be able) ... to work on it anywhere.
4. I hope I (have) ... a lot of fun with it.
5. My teacher has given me the task of looking for some information on the Internet. I (do) ... that this evening.
6. If I have time afterwards, I (chat) ... with you again.

C task 3, p. 52

4. Do the following tasks on the three texts on p. 53 in complete sentences.

1. Describe the reasons for the success of the Internet.
2. Explain the problems that people can have when they buy or sell on the Internet.
3. Explain how paedophiles use the Internet to contact children.

C task 3, p. 52

5 Decide if the following statements are true or false according to the texts on p. 53. Correct the false statements.

1. The Internet is younger than John Burns' parents.
2. The reason for its success was that it was relatively cheap.
3. Sometimes when holidaymakers want to move into their holiday home, they find that it is already occupied.
4. Internet crime is rising in different areas.
5. The newspaper reporter's name was Alice.
6. The reporter started the chats in order to find a new partner.

D 2 task 2, p. 55

6 You can use the words and phrases from the *Help*-box below to describe and analyze cartoon 2 on p. 55.

> **Help**
>
> **Description:** dining room • family of six • grandfather • father • three children • at the table • in the middle • holding smartphones • going to have a meal • mother • standing • on the right • looking at her smartphone • speech bubble reads
> **Analysis:** cartoonist • point out • talk to each other face-to-face • use social networks instead
> **Your opinion:** I think • funny • mother usually asks • like the meal • family members answer on the phone • show a trend • people / friends / family members together • but work / play / chat on mobile devices

E 2 task 3, p. 56

7 Complete the sentences using words or phrases from the text.

1. When Derek meets his old school friend Jimmy, Derek tells Jimmy that he is trying to find —.
2. As Jimmy has no interesting work to do he is interested in the job and Derek —.
3. Jimmy is a member of the —.
4. Mobile devices allow these people always to be —.
5. Their strengths are good — and the ability to do —.
6. But on the other hand young employees do not stay long in their jobs and soon —.
7. Money is not the only thing that young people are interested in. They care about their —.
8. Young people do not need cars or road networks. They rely on —.
9. Members of the Internet generation are open-minded and connected to people all over the world. That is why they —.
10. New challenges require —.

In this unit you will learn to . . .
- talk about social changes in our society.
- anticipate, skim and scan a text.
- talk, read and write about the benefits and problems of our modern welfare state.
- use relative clauses and modal auxiliaries.

 37cm79

Unit 5
Social change

A | Getting started: Challenges of a changing society

Before you read

1 Have you ever seen a board like the one on the right? Have you ever posted any texts or photos? Tell the class about it.

2 Choose a photo that expresses the "challenges of a changing society today" best. Tell a partner why you have chosen it.

Understanding the texts

3 Find headings for each of the messages on p. 61. The phrases in the box can help you. ▶ Leseverstehen, S. 199

4 Complete the sentences in your own words with regard to the messages on p. 61.

1. Many young Europeans today are rejected by …
2. Communication devices occasionally lead to …
3. Hospitals in the UK are having difficulties because …
4. The number of single working mothers in the UK …
5. The EU needs to prepare for population shifts, because …
6. Female employees earn …
7. Frederick Bailey thinks that he must …

> **Help**
> mothers as breadwinners •
> help for the sick •
> gender equality •
> demographic change •
> social isolation •
> homelessness • youth unemployment

60

Basic course > Advanced course > Exam course   Social change | Unit 5

http://www.haveasay....com

A2.2

1 How do we get young people into jobs? Many young Europeans are really worried about their future. They have worked hard to pass their exams. They have written lots of applications and CVs but they have only received rejections.   /Angus Baker

2 Put down your phones, guys! Sometimes communication devices keep us apart.   /Miriam Owen

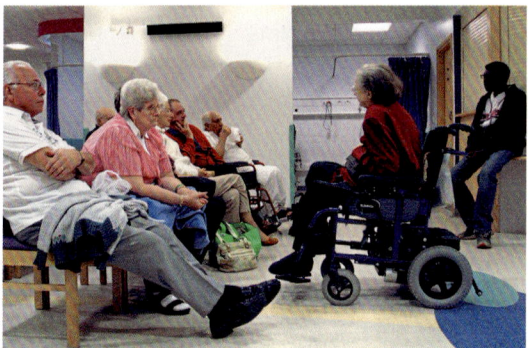

3 Message to the government: Please invest more money in our national health system.   /Jim Roberts

4 The number of single working mothers has reached a record level in the UK. But they still do not get enough support from the government.
/Stacey Cooper

5 The EU is facing extreme changes. The population is ageing, birth rates are low, family structures are changing, migration is increasing and the number of workers is falling.   /Thomas Green

6 Did you know that female employees in Europe still earn 16 % less than male counterparts? In other words: female employees work 59 days a year for free. /
Kira Parker

7 I always wondered why somebody didn't do something. Then I realized that I am somebody.
/Frederick Bailey   (171 words)

After reading

5 Work in pairs. What other social problems which were not mentioned in the texts can you think of? Make a list.

6 Choose one problem and create a page with a picture and message. Present your message in class by pinning it to the board.

B | Grammar

B1 Guessing game

1 Explain the following words using 'who' or 'which'. ○ Task ▶ F1, p. 70

Example: Europeans are citizens who live in Europe.

1. **Europeans**	buildings	move – information from one place to another
2. communication device	piece of information	work – for somebody else in return for payment
3. employee	**citizens**	be in charge of – child
4. demographic change	group of people	accommodate – ill people
5. family	woman	**live – in Europe**
6. message	piece of hardware	describe – age structure – population
7. hospitals	person	send – someone
8. mother	concept	be related – to each other

B2 Challenges: food for thought

1 Complete the following text. Fill in 'who' or 'which' to make non-defining relative clauses.

Birmingham, (1) … is one of ten cities in Britain with a high unemployment rate, now gets support from a inventive woman. Carla Williams, (2) … was raised there, wants to help poor people. Her idea, (3) … is simple but effective, is to cook meals for people in need from surplus produce from large supermarket chains. Williams, (4) … has never needed to work, did not know what to do when her children left home. "My husband, (5) … is a successful engineer, is not at home very often. So when our three children moved out I needed something to do", she says. Williams, (6) … has never done any professional training, thought about her options. "First I started to redecorate our house, (7) … is quite big. But this was not fulfilling. I wanted to make a difference and help poor people, (8) … often cannot afford healthy food." When she talked to her friends, (9) … were also bored, they decided to use their cooking skills in order to help the poor. They found that many large supermarkets throw away leftover, (10) … they cannot sell. Now Williams and her friends collect the food in the evenings and cook healthy meals for poor people during the day.

Grammar box

Defining relative clauses
Example: The man who / that is getting on the bus is on his way home.
Bei Personen werden die Relativpronomen *who* oder *that* verwendet.
Example: The bus which / that is at the bus stop is going to Bristol.
Bei Sachen werden *which* oder *that* verwendet.
Example: The man (–) I saw was a good football player.
Ist das Relativpronomen Objekt des Satzes, kann es weggelassen werden.
▶ p. 182

Non-defining relative clauses
Example: His wife, who is 26, works in an office.
Nicht notwendige Relativsätze werden in Kommas eingeschlossen.
Example: The bus, which was a doubledecker, was waiting.
That wird hier nicht verwendet.
Example: Henry, who I know well, is going to Bali next week.
Ist das Relativpronomen Objekt des Relativsatzes, darf es nicht weggelassen werden.
▶ p. 183

Basic course > Advanced course > Exam course   Social change | Unit 5

B3   Somebody special

1 Complete the text about British comedian, Shazia Mirza, using the information about her life. Decide if a relative clause is necessary or not, and if you can leave out the relative pronoun.

Shazia Mirza (1) …, **who was born in England in 1975**, is a popular woman (2) …. Shazia is the first British Muslim comedian (3) …. When she started doing comedy her parents (4) … did not know about the new profession (5) …. They thought Shazia (6) … was a teacher at a comprehensive school (7) …. Shazia was so successful with her shows (8) … that she gave up her job as a teacher.

Some information about Shazia Mirza's life
a) She had studied science at university.
b) She has her own comedy show.
c) The comprehensive school is in Tower Hamlets, London.
d) She was born in England in 1975.
e) Her parents are very religious Muslims.
f) Shazia had taken up a new profession.
g) Her shows were even broadcast on television.
h) Nearly everybody in Britain knows her.

B4   Changing roles

1 Make sentences about women's roles today with the verbs in brackets.

1. take part in government (can)

Example: Today women can take part in government.

2. go to school (must)
3. study at university (can)
4. wear what they like (can)
5. ask their husbands when they want to go out with friends (needn't)
6. marry the man their parents choose (needn't)
7. read (can)
8. give up their new roles (needn't)

2 Talk about women's roles in the past. Make sentences as in the example.

1. vote (not be allowed to)

Example: 200 years ago women were not allowed to vote.

2. work at home and in the fields (have to)
3. attend university (not be allowed to)
4. stay at home (have to)
5. marry the man their parents chose (have to)
6. wear trousers (not be allowed to)
7. read in most cases (not be able to)
8. take on new roles (not be allowed to)

3
P   Compare men's roles 200 years ago, today and in the future. Use modal auxiliaries and their substitutes.

Example: 200 years ago boys had to go to work when they were 14. Today they must go to school until they are 16. I suppose that in 200 years' time they will have to go to school until they are 18.

> **Grammar box**
>
> **Modal auxiliaries**
> **Example: Cars must / have to stop at red lights.**
> Für modale Hilfsverben können auch entsprechende Ersatzformen verwendet werden.
> **Examples: He was not allowed to park his car there.**
> **You will have to leave at 8 o'clock.**
> Die Ersatzformen werden insbesondere für die Vergangenheit und die Zukunft eingesetzt.
> ▶ p. 182

Unit 5 | Social change

C | Reading – Carefree youth of today?

TRAINING SKILLS – How to anticipate, skim and scan

Before reading

1 Where does the text on p. 65 come from?

2 Describe and analyze the photos that go with the text and guess what it is about. ▶ Fotos und Illustrationen, S. 211

3 Skim through the text, that means you look at the heading and subheadings quickly. Say in a few sentences what it is about.

> **Help**
> 1. The text comes from …
> 2. The photos show … The girl in the first photo … – The photos could indicate …
> 3. The heading and subheadings could mean …

Understanding the text

4
R
Read the text and match the key points with the headings A–E.
● Task ▶ F 2, p. 70 ▶ Leseverstehen, S. 199

1. Increasing pressure – nearly twice as many over-worked students

    Example: These key points match the heading High demands

2. Few job opportunities – hard to make decisions for future
3. Stress reduction impossible – college, work, relationships
4. Managing stress – voluntary activities
5. More competition for university places – youth unemployment

5 Do the tasks in your own words. Your results from task 4 can help you.

1. Describe what the international study shows.
2. Give reasons why college students try to get top grades.
3. Explain how a gap year can help stressed teenagers.
4. Point out other benefits of a gap year mentioned in the text.

Exam **6**
M
Mediation: Sie sollen für die Online-Schülerzeitung Ihrer Schule einen Artikel zum Thema "Schulstress" verfassen. Bei Ihrer Vorbereitung haben Sie den Artikel auf der nächsten Seite entdeckt. Fassen Sie die darin beschriebenen Stressfaktoren zusammen. Formulieren Sie ganze deutsche Sätze. ▶ Mediation, S. 228

After reading

7
P
Create a poster about a gap year programme that would interest you. Present it to your class. ▶ Plakate, S. 244

Internet key words: gap year jobs – gap year programmes – gap year abroad – voluntary work – work experience

8
P
You want to apply for the programme you have just presented. Write a letter of application to an organization which offers such a programme. Give reasons for your application. ▶ Formelle Briefe und E-Mails, S. 205

ACADEMIC PERFORMANCE: top reason for teen stress

A High demands

A recent international study found that teenagers in Europe feel growing pressure to perform well at college. This fact negatively affects nearly every aspect of their lives. Psychologists point out that teenagers today are facing increasing academic and social pressure as college degrees have become more important in our service-oriented world. College students are working harder than ever and the number of stressed-out students has almost doubled since the 1990s.

B Tough job market

University admissions are far more competitive so students are pushing themselves to get top grades. The job market does not offer the best prospects. Employment opportunities for young adults have dropped in recent years. One in four young Europeans is out of work. The good news is the economy is picking up in most European countries and so unemployment levels will fall soon, the study predicts.

C Stress: a factor in teens' daily lives

Most teenagers today have no time to reduce stress, because they are juggling a college education and part-time jobs. At the same time they are trying to catch up with their friends. We spoke with teenagers about the stress factors in their lives.

D Melissa, 17: "I'm hoping to make the right choices!"

"I'd like to become a banker," says 17-year-old Melissa from Santa Luzia, a small town in Portugal. "However, I often hear how poor job prospects are in this sector. And so I ask myself: Should I become a physical therapist? But I think this is not something I'd like to do for the rest of my life. The problem is that I only have months left at school and then I need to decide what to do next year. I feel that right now I am not prepared to make such an important decision which will determine my life in the future. I don't know what to do and that makes me unhappy."

E Gap year – the opportunity for a planned timeout

"We need to protect teenagers much more and help them to cope with pressure and stress," says Madeleine Ward from *TeensNeedHelp*, an organization which supports young adults suffering from academic and social stress. Among other programmes, the organization offers young Europeans, aged 18 to 25, the chance to take time out from college. They

want to help young people to find their true identities and to have time to think about what they really want to do in the future. At the same time young people can express their social commitment through unpaid, full-time voluntary activities in foreign countries. In this way the volunteers get a meaningful job in an environment where they can also improve their language skills. In most cases a gap year not only helps teenagers to make decisions and improve their personal skills, it also upgrades their CVs. (472 words)

Quelle: Ethan Collins, The Parent Mag

D | Practice

D1 Problems of the modern welfare state

While listening

Exam 1
R

Hörverstehen: Sie hören ein Radio-Interview mit einem Wirtschaftsprofessor. Hören Sie aufmerksam zu und vervollständigen Sie auf Deutsch die untenstehenden Sätze mit Informationen aus dem Interview. ▶ Hörverstehen, S. 196

1. Gast der Radio-Sendung ist ein Professor für Wirtschaft in …
2. Der moderne Sozialstaat soll einerseits existenzgefährdenden Risiken vorbeugen und andererseits …
3. Dazu verfügt der moderne Sozialstaat über ein System der …
4. Als Beispiele für existenzgefährdende Risiken nennt Prof. Hamilton …
5. Seiner Ansicht nach muss der moderne Wohlfahrtsstaat abgebaut werden, weil …
6. Prof. Hamilton nennt vier Gründe, die zum Verfall des Wohlfahrtsstaates führen. Erstens, das Sozialversicherungssystem …
7. Zweitens wird ein neuer Generationenvertrag benötigt, weil …
8. Drittens hat der medizinische Fortschritt dazu geführt, dass wir einerseits verbesserte Gesundheitsdienste haben und andererseits …
9. Viertens verursacht der Wohlfahrtsstaat selbst Probleme, indem er verhindert, dass Menschen arbeiten, weil …
10. Nach Ansicht von Prof. Hamilton gibt es für die Probleme des Wohlfahrtsstaats keine …

D2 Demographic changes: Multigenerational living

A2.5

HOME SHARING IN GREENWICH

- **Who we are**
- We are a community of four generations all living together under
- one roof. Our community consists of singles, single parents, married
- and unmarried couples and families with children. Residents range
- 5 in ages from 2 to 89 living together in 20 accommodation units. Our
- project is organized by a charity called SharedLivesOrg which provides
- accommodation units for young and old people in Greenwich.

Basic course > Advanced course > Exam course   Social change | **Unit 5**

What we offer
You will live in a community with
10 people who want to help you with your
everyday life, for example when you
need help doing the shopping or when
you need someone to look after your
children.
15 Apart from a large common living room
and kitchen, we have huge outdoor
facilities with beautiful gardens with flowers, vegetables and trees. We
also have two barbecue areas, car parks and a play area for the children.

What we expect
20 Respect the diversity in our community.
Moreover we expect you to help other
residents, especially when it comes to
illness and dependency on long-term
care.

25 **Interested? You want to join us?**
If you are interested in our home
sharing project, then send a letter of application and a full CV to our
organization.

SharedLivesOrg ++ Home Sharing in Greenwich ++ 210 Mauritius Road ++ Greenwich SE10 ++ England ++ www.sharedlivesorg.co....uk (214 words)

Understanding the text

1 Read the text and answer the questions in your own words.
R   ○ Task ▶ F3, p. 70 ▶ Leseverstehen, S. 199

1. Who are the residents of the home sharing community?
2. What is the benefit of the home sharing project?
3. What facilities are there?
4. What does the project expect from its residents?

After reading

2 You are interested in the home sharing project. Write an application saying why
P   you want to live in the community.

HOT **3** **Rollenspiel:** Work in pairs.
I   **Student A:** You are a college student and are looking for an affordable room. You
have applied to the home sharing project in Greenwich. Read the information on
your role card on p. 172. Introduce yourself and play your role.
Student B: You are a resident of the home sharing community and have lived
there for three years. Read the information on your role card on p. 173. Introduce
yourself and play your role.

E | Reading +

E1 Combining a career with family life

Before watching

1 Describe the photo. What situation do you think the woman is in?
▶ Fotos und Illustrationen, S. 211

While watching

2 Watch the film and answer the following questions. ▶ Hör-Seh-Verstehen, S. 197

1. Why do most mothers have to work today?
2. In what two situations can a mother stay at home full-time?
3. What situations are especially difficult for working mothers?
4. Why does the banker say it is better to be a cocaine addict than a mother?
5. What does Allison Pearson want?
6. How could the mumtrepreneur movement help working mums?

E2 Stay-at-home dads

Before reading

1 Look at the headline and photo on p. 69. Guess what the text is about.

Understanding the text

2 Skim through the article without reading it in detail. Say in one or two sentences what the text is about. Compare your results with your ideas in task **1**.
▶ Antizipieren, Skimming, Scanning, S. 231

3 Find suitable headings for the paragraphs A–H. ○ Help ▶ F 4, p. 71

4 Answer the following questions in your own words. ○ Help ▶ F 5, p. 71

1. How has the number of stay-at-home dads changed?
2. What reasons are given for the rise in stay-at-home dads?
3. How have roles changed within families today?
4. What job prospects do young women have before getting married?
5. What effects did the recession have on the job market?

Exam **5** **Mediation:** Sie stellen die Ergebnisse der Studie des Pew Research Center Ihrer Klasse anhand von Stichpunkten mündlich vor. Entnehmen Sie dazu die wesentlichen Informationen aus dem Text.
● Task ▶ F 6, p. 71 ▶ Mediation, S. 228

What's behind the rise of stay-at-home dads?

A A new study by the *Pew Research Center* shows that the number of dads who choose to stay home and care for their children and families has quadrupled over the past 25 years. Can social and economic factors explain the change?

B Make no mistake – fathers who are the primary caregiver for their children are far from the norm. In fact, they are only 16% of all stay-at-home parents. But that number is up from 10% since 1989, when Pew started analysing data. The steady growth since then suggests that these numbers represent a growing trend [...].

C "It's up from 1.1 million to 2 million," says Gretchen Livingston, one of the study authors. More significantly, the number of men who say they stay at home specifically to take care of their home and children is at an all-time high, more than four times the rate of fathers who gave that same answer in 1989. [...]

D "Stay-at-home dads have a unique situation – we don't have role models so we are kind of doing this on our own and trying to figure out how to navigate the relationships that are different than we expected them to be when we first got married," says Al Watts, the president of the National At-Home Dad Network.

E As women have taken on more high-paying careers, the assumption that they'll stay home with the children has become less automatic.

"My wife and I were earning about the same income at the time just after our daughter was born. We felt that if someone was going to raise our children it would have been one of us," says Watts. "My wife was promoted shortly after she got back from maternity leave and that bump in pay would allow us to live on one income."

When Matt Burr's son was born, there was never any question as to whether his wife would take time off from her job as a doctor. "It was a no-brainer in that situation. She was definitely going to have to work," he says. The question,

then, "was whether I kept doing my job." When they crunched the numbers, including the cost of childcare, it made sense for him to stay home.

F "The rise in stay-at-home dads coincides with a change in social and economic trends regarding women in the workforce," says Farnoosh Torabi, author of *When She Makes More.* "We know that before they even get married, women are out-earning and out-learning men," she says, noting that younger women are now getting more degrees and better paying jobs, on average, than men.

G In lean economic times staying at home is often a fiscal necessity or the only option for some fathers. Twenty-one percent of fathers cite caring for their family as the main reason they're staying at home, while 23% say they cannot find a job. Forty-seven percent of the men in the Pew survey are living at or below the poverty line, says Reynolds.

H The types of jobs that have made a stronger comeback tend to be service-sector, "pink collar" jobs, like healthcare services, retail, and education, that are dominated by women, says Torabi, while well-paying blue collar jobs like manufacturing and construction suffered in the recession.

At the same time, says Watts, men who grew up in households with strict gender divisions want to be more hands-on with their own kids, and are more open to staying at home to do so. [...] (575 words)

Quelle: Kate Dailey, *BBC News Magazine*, June 2014, www.bbc.com.

Unit 5 | Social change

F | Further tasks

○ B 1 task 1, p. 62

1 Fill in 'who' or 'which' in the descriptions of people and things. Then tell the class but don't mention their names. The rest of the class have to find out who / what they are.

Example:
It is a shop … sells food.
You: It is a shop which sells food. (supermarket)
Class: It's a supermarket.
You: That's true.

1. It's a person … sells goods in a shop. (shop assistant, salesperson)
2. It's a vehicle … transports goods. (truck, lorry)
3. It's an appliance … you use to clean rooms. (vacuum-cleaner, hoover)
4. It's a person … makes bread and rolls. (baker)
5. It's an app … helps you to chat with other people who are not present. (WhatsApp, Skype, etc.)
6. It's a person … helps sick people in a hospital. (doctor, nurse)
7. It's an institution … teaches young adults who want to learn a job. (college)
8. It's a person … repairs cars. (car mechanic)
9. It's a device … helps you to talk to people who are far away. (telephone, computer)
10. It's a person … has millions of pounds. (millionaire)
11. It's a vehicle … transports many people. (bus, coach)
12. It's a person … welcomes guests in a hotel. (receptionist)
13. It's a device … you can take photos or make films with. (camera, mobile phone, tablet)
14. It's a person … scores goals with his feet or head. (football player)

● C task 4, p. 64

2 After matching the key points 1–5 with the headings A–E give a summary of the
P text "Academic performance: top reason for teen stress" using these key points.

○ D 2 task 1, p. 67

3 Read the text "Home sharing in Greenwich" and find out if the following
R statements are true or false. Correct the false statements.

1. In this community four people live under one roof.
2. Very young and very old people live in this community.
3. Within the community people have to help each other.
4. There are places within and outside the building which can be used by all residents of the home.
5. In order to make life easier residents should come from the same background and share the same ideals.
6. You can join the project if you send a written application.

Basic course > Advanced course > Exam course   Social change | Unit 5

E 2 task 3, p. 68

4
R
Read the text "What's behind the rise of stay-at-home dads?" in detail and match the headings below with the paragraphs (A–H) in the text.

1. Women still the main caregivers
2. Reasons for staying at home
3. Shifting roles in families
4. Survey findings: increasing number of male caregivers
5. Better career prospects for women without families
6. Women's wages rising
7. Negative impact of recession mainly on manual labour
8. Reasons why fathers stay at home: take care of children and manage household

E 2 task 4, p. 68

5
R
Answer the questions on the text, "What's behind the rise of stay-at-home dads?" The beginnings of the answers will help you.

Help

1. How has the number of stay-at-home dads changed?	The survey shows that there is an increasing… The number is four times… But the survey also shows that… Only 16 percent…
2. What reasons are given for the rise in stay-at-home dads?	The text mentions several… First of all, men's attitudes towards their families… Many fathers stay at home because… Another reason is that high unemployment rates…
3. How have roles changed within families today?	Fathers find themselves in a new situation where… They first need to learn how to deal with… The text states that fathers lack…
4. What job prospects do young women have before getting married?	Career prospects for young women are better today because… Due to these higher qualifications young women get… But the text limits women's better career prospects to…
5. What effects did the recession have on the job market?	The recession led to changes… It mainly had negative effects on… Blue-collar jobs are dominated by… But there were no negative effects on…

E 2 task 5, p. 68

6
P
Write a composition about the topic below. Use information from the film, the article and the photos. "It is better for a family if the father works outside the home and the mother stays at home and takes care of the children."

▶ Materialgestützter Aufsatz, S. 199

In this unit you will learn to . . .
· find out about various aspects of life in Britain.
· give and take directions.
· hold conversations with strangers.
· make small talk.

 b8zr55

Unit B

Cross-cultural communication at work:
Living in London

A | Arriving in London

Before reading

Bastian Topp from Stuttgart is going to do a work placement in London. He has just arrived and is now standing outside High Barnet Underground Station in North London.

1 Describe the photos above. How do you think Bastian has travelled there?
P

2 Bastian wants to get to the Westward Boarding House where he has booked
P a room. He is not sure where the boarding house is so he asks a passer-by.
A2.6 Read the dialogue and answer the following questions.

1. How long does Bastian have to walk to get to the boarding house?
2. Where does he have to take the first turning?

Bastian: Excuse me, could you tell me how to get to Normandy Avenue, please?
Passer-by: Sure. That's about a ten-minute walk from here. Just go down this road until you come to the traffic lights. Turn right there and just walk up Barnet Hill. I think Normandy Avenue is the second road on your left.
Bastian: That sounds easy. Thanks a lot.
Passer-by: That's fine. Take care.

Basic course > Advanced course > Exam course   Living in London | Unit B

3 Look at the map. Was the passer-by right when she told Bastian to take the
R   second turning on the left?

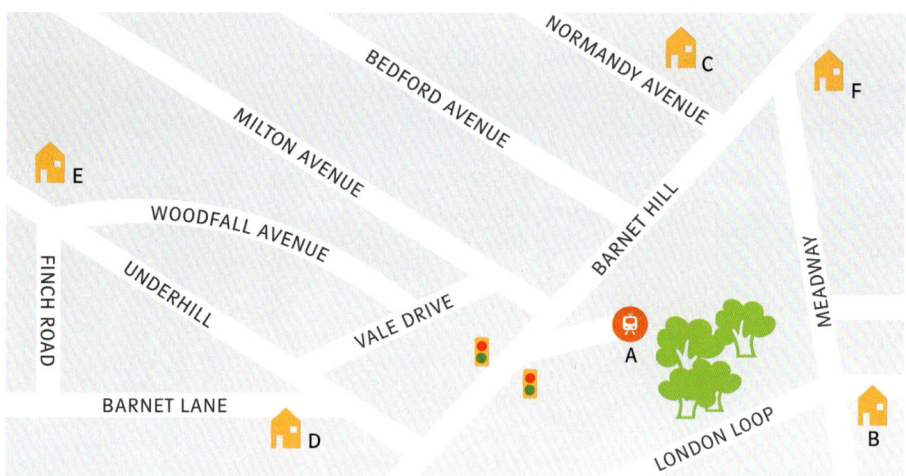

A High Barnet Underground Station
B Hotel Victoria
C Westward Boarding House
D The King's Arms Pub
E The Coop Supermarket
F Peter's Place Fish and Chips Shop

○ **Help**

- Turn right / left at …
- Go straight on
- Go down… / up…
- … until you come to …
- Carry on down / up…
- on your right / left
- You will see …

4 Look at the map of North London. Find out how to get to these places from the
I   underground station. Student A is Bastian who asks the way and student B is a
     passer-by who gives directions.

1. a supermarket
2. a fish and chips shop
3. a pub
4. Hotel Victoria

B | Meeting the landlady

Understanding the text

1 Read the dialogue between Bastian and the landlady. Find out why Bastian
R   apologizes to her.
 A2.7

Bastian: Hello I'm Bastian Topp from Germany.
Landlady: Oh great. Come in dear. I'm Lisa Davies by the way.
Bastian: Pleased to meet you Ms Davies.
Landlady: Nice to meet you, too, and please call me Lisa.
Bastian: Oh I'm sorry.
Landlady: That's all right, dear. Well, did you have a good journey down here? It's a long way, isn't it?
Bastian: Everything went well, thank you. I got all the connections on time. But I'm a bit tired now, you know.
Landlady: I'm sure you are, love. Let me show you your room. It's on the third floor. Just follow me.

After reading

 **2** **Rollenspiel:** In pairs continue the dialogue at the guest house using the role
I   cards on p. 173.

Intercultural tips

The use of *dear*, *love*, *darling* etc. in conversations: Younger people – not only friends but also strangers – are often addressed in this way, especially by older women.

73

Unit B | Living in London

C | Getting used to the British way of life

> **Help**
> queue • school uniform • 3 pin plug • fried eggs • bacon • beans • sausage

1 **P** In the first days in London Bastian experiences some typically British things. Describe the photos and explain the differences to your home country. The words in the *Help* box on the right may help you.

D | Meeting people

While listening

Exam 1 **R** **A2.8** **Hörverstehen:** After a good night's sleep at the Westward Boarding House, Bastian goes down to the dining room for breakfast. He overhears the following conversation between two other young people there. Listen to the dialogue and say what they are talking about. ▶ Hörverstehen, S. 196

2 **A2.8** Hören Sie den Dialog zwischen Anna und Greg noch einmal an und finden Sie heraus:

1. welche Nationalität Anna hat.
2. aus welcher Stadt Greg kommt.
3. was er in London macht.
4. warum Anna eine Sprachschule besucht.
5. was sie beide zum Frühstück bestellen.

Basic course > Advanced course > Exam course   Living in London | **Unit B**

After listening

3 **Rollenspiel:** Student A serves the guests. Student B orders breakfast. Use the role cards on p. 173 and the *Help* box below.

> **○ Help**
>
> cereals: porridge, muesli, cornflakes
> eggs: boiled, fried, scrambled
> meat: sausage, bacon
>
> vegetables: beans, mushrooms, tomatoes
> drinks: tea with milk, coffee, fruit juice

4 **Rollenspiel:** Continue the following dialogue, using the role cards on pp. 173–174.

Bastian gets to know Greg at the Westward Boarding House.
Bastian: Hi there. I saw you at breakfast. I'm Bastian. I'm staying here, too.
Greg: Hi. I'm Greg. Nice to meet you. What are you doing in London?

> **Cross-cultural tips**
>
> **Rules for talking to strangers**
> - Be friendly and polite – use "please" and "thank you".
> - Use complete sentences.
> - Use small talk (weather, journey, where you come from, what you do).
> - Avoid talking about politics, or asking personal questions.

E | British weather

Before watching

1 One of the favourite topics of conversation in Britain is the weather. Consider why. Talk about your ideas.

While watching

2 Copy the table below into your exercise book and fill in the missing information. ▶ Hör-Seh-Verstehen, S. 197

1. Weather forecaster	
2. Weather in Scotland this afternoon	
3. Air pressure	
4. City with the most rain	
5. Driest and sunniest parts	
6. Temperature	
7. Wind	

3 Why does the forecaster say in the end "Thank God, it isn't a bank holiday"?

After watching

4 Look up the weather forecast for London in the next few days and describe the weather that is expected.

In this unit you will learn to ...
- find out about and analyze environmental developments.
- talk and write about environmental problems and possible solutions.
- use reported speech.
- use an English-English dictionary.

 74eg5y

Unit 6
Ecology

A | Getting started: We are all part of it!

Before reading

1 Describe the photo that in your opinion shows the biggest environmental problem. ▶ Fotos und Illustrationen, S. 211

2 Match the headings on the right with the photos. Four headings do not fit.

3 Which of the problems mentioned in the box on the right must be solved first in your opinion? Give reasons for your choice.

Headings
waste – global warming – water pollution – genetically modified (GM) food – air pollution – extinction of animals – rising sea levels – dangerous technology

Tackling climate change

A Rising levels of carbon dioxide (CO_2) and other gases in the atmosphere create a greenhouse effect, trapping the sun's energy and causing the earth and the oceans in particular, to get warmer. In fact, CO_2 levels have increased by a third since the Industrial Revolution began. This increase in CO_2 is mainly caused by the burning of fossil fuels such as coal, oil and gas and by the destruction of forests. In addition a lot of the forests which effectively absorb CO_2 are being systematically destroyed.

Basic course > **Advanced course** > Exam course   Ecology | **Unit 6**

B If global emissions are not reduced, average summer temperatures in
10 Western Europe will almost certainly rise by over 2 degrees Centigrade
by 2040 and up to 4 degrees Centigrade by the 2080s. Rises in global
temperatures will have both direct and indirect effects on us all. The
extreme weather conditions which we have experienced in recent times
seem to be a direct effect of such climate change. Indirectly, Europe's
15 food supply could also be affected as crops in Europe and elsewhere
could fail or be damaged by extreme weather conditions such as severe
changes in temperature, heavy or no rainfall and storms.

C If we take action now, we will help future generations. Hopefully,
they will not have to pay the costs of such dramatic climate change.
20 One company in the UK which is contributing in a positive way to tackle
this problem is *Bentley Motors* in North West England. Its factory, which
employs 4,000 people in Crewe, has one of the UK's largest rooftop solar
panel arrays with some 20,000 solar panels. These panels generate
enough electricity to provide power for the factory during the working
25 day. At weekends and at times of low demand the energy produced is
fed back into the National Grid in order to supply 1,200 local households
with electricity. In this way the Bentley factory is demonstrating how
businesses not only profit from using sustainable energy sources but
also reduce their carbon footprint at the same time. (328 words)

Understanding the text

4 Match the paragraphs (A–C) in the text with the following headings (1–3) and with
R   the key points (a–f). ● Task ▶ F1, p. 86 ▶ Leseverstehen, S. 199

Headings	Key points
1. Reducing CO_2	a) food supply in danger
2. Causes of high levels of greenhouse gases	b) burning of fossil fuels
	c) use of alternative energy sources, e.g. solar power
	d) destruction of forests
3. Effects of rising temperatures	e) positive development, e.g. *Bentley Motors*
	f) extreme weather conditions

5 Summarize the writer's main ideas using the headings and the key points above.
P

xam 6 **Mediation**: Nachdem Sie ein Praktikum bei *Bentley Motors* in Nordwestengland
M   absolviert haben, werden Sie gebeten, bei einer Sitzung des Städtepartnerschafts-
vereins einen Vortrag über die Entwicklung im Bereich Energienutzung in Nordwestengland zu halten. Sammeln Sie dazu Stichpunkte zum Text auf Deutsch und
halten Sie Ihren Vortrag mit Hilfe dieser Stichpunkte auf Deutsch. ▶ Mediation, S. 228

After reading

7 Work in groups. Find other examples of companies or organizations behaving in an
R/P environmentally friendly way. Create a poster and present your results to the class.
 ▶ Plakate, S. 244

B | Grammar

B1 Water for life

1 Dr Emma Roberts, a voluntary worker with *Water for Life*, gave an interview on *Radio Bristol* last month. This is part of the interview. Report what she said using the reporting verbs in the *Help* box.

1. "Every 17 seconds a child in the developing world dies from water-related diseases."

   Example: In the interview Dr Roberts said that every 17 seconds a child in the developing world died from water-related diseases.

2. "Every day people in poor countries face this problem."
3. "They can drink dirty water that can kill them or die of thirst."
4. "It is a gamble that often carries a high price."
5. "It is heartbreaking to see children who are dying."
6. "For £ 2 a month everyone here in Bristol can help."
7. "Whole communities can benefit from this help."
8. "It doesn't really matter how much a person gives."

2 This is what some people said after reading the *Water for Life* advert. Report what they told you. ● Task ▶ F 2, p. 86

1. Ron: "I saw this advert on the Internet, too."

   Example: Ron said / told me that he had seen that advert on the Internet, too.

2. Julie: "My friend showed me the advert."
3. Sam: "I decided to give £2."
4. Tom and Mark: "We donated money online."
5. Nick: "I filled in the form immediately."
6. Jack: "I didn't know much about this problem."
7. Lisa and Sarah: "We have made the decision to give £5 a month."
8. Jenny: "I haven't checked out this website yet."

> **Help**
>
> She …
> - said that …
> - went on to say that …
> - told us that …
> - informed us that …
> - stated that …
> - added that …
> - concluded that …

> **Grammar box**
>
> **Reported speech**
> Example: She said, "I want to help children in Africa."
> wird zu: She said that she wanted to help children in Africa.
> In der indirekten Rede ändern sich die Zeitformen wie folgt:
> *present → past*
> *past → past perfect*
> *present perfect → past perfect*
> *will → would*
> Auch Pronomina, Orts- und Zeitbestimmungen werden angepasst.

Basic course > **Advanced course** > Exam course   Ecology | **Unit 6**

B2 A world without seafood

1 After some people had seen this photo on the Internet, they started to talk about this topic. Report what they said.

1. Sally: "Restaurants will soon have no fish on the menu."

   Example: Sally said that restaurants would soon have no fish on the menu.

2. Christian: "As I understand it, I will have to pay more for my fish and chips in the future."
3. Helen: "I like tuna, but as I see it I won't be able to get it so easily in the supermarket."
4. Alex and Jill: "We won't be able to buy seafood so cheaply."
5. Owen: "In my opinion, I won't have any fish protein to eat."
6. Sharon: "As I see it, governments will have to act quickly."
7. Bill and Ben: "After reading the article that went with the photo we are sure the catastrophe will happen in our lifetime."
8. Donna: "I won't eat so much fish after reading this article."

B3 World Nature Fund

1 Sally Neville belongs to the *World Nature Fund*. Work in pairs. One student reports the questions people have asked Sally, the other student reports what she said.

1. "What do you do in the organization?" (organize activities)

   Example:
   Student A: People often asked Sally what she did in the organization.
   Student B: Sally said that she organized activities.

2. "Where is the nearest branch of the organization?" (have branches in all major cities)
3. "How much do you have to pay to join the organization?" (donate £10 a year)
4. "Where can I get a membership form?" (download online)
5. "Have you sent leaflets about the organization to our college?" (send some brochures some months ago)
6. "When will you come to our college to give us more information?" (come soon)
7. "How long has the organization existed?" (begin in 1961)
8. "When did you join?" (become a member in 2010)
9. "Why did you become a member of WNF?" (read an interesting article about WNF's activities)

B4 Not a drop of water to drink

1 **Rollenspiel:** Work in groups of four. Introduce yourself and discuss the problems relating to water using the role cards on p. 174. Make notes during the discussion.

2 Use your notes to write a report about what your group said.

Example: Patrick thought that people had to …

79

C | Reading: Where does our food come from?

Before reading

  Look at the headline of the text below and guess what it could be about. Then skim through the text without reading it in detail and say if your guess was correct.
► Antizipieren, Skimming, Scanning, S. 231

You are what you eat

You believe you are a good person, don't you? Of course you do! In fact, when it comes to shopping for food the average person cares more and more about where and how their food has been produced. We want the chicken that we eat to have had a nice life and we don't want to eat a meal when its production has harmed the
5 environment.
   Unfortunately, shopping for food with a clear conscience has become increasingly difficult. And we, as consumers, are partly responsible for this development. As we want relatively cheap food we tend to shop in big supermarkets. Due to extreme price competition from these supermarkets a lot of
10 local butchers, bakers and greengrocers have had to close their doors.
   Today, a lot of the food that is on offer in the supermarkets is mass-produced by the food industry. Food products are highly processed which means that they often contain a lot of fats, salt and sugar and they are standardized because consumers always expect identical products. We have got used to eating fruit and vegetables
15 which have little or no taste but look perfect all year round. As a result of this over-processed and unnatural food our health may be suffering. Moreover, many products are packaged in environmentally unfriendly plastic and have gained a massive carbon footprint by the time they reach consumers.
   As a reaction to the growing number of consumers who are demanding
20 environmentally friendly, healthy food, organic supermarket chains are becoming increasingly popular. The latest ones to open their doors are in London and Berlin. They offer customers natural organic food and have made a promise that most of the food on offer has been produced in the area or country where the supermarket is situated. A further trend is that organic supermarkets also try to offer unpackaged
25 food wherever that is possible.
   Most of the food we buy in normal supermarkets has travelled many miles – often by plane – before it arrives on the shelves. Buying locally means that we as consumers help to avoid millions of 'food miles'.
   And why buy organic food? Farmers who produce organically avoid chemical
30 fertilizers and pesticides which are often used in conventional farming: these contribute to the pollution of the groundwater. Another positive aspect is that you can be sure that the food you buy from organic supermarkets has not been genetically modified. Standards and regulations which food must meet before farmers can label it as "organic" are very strict. These same standards do not allow
35 the routine use of antibiotics. In conventional farming there is often a high use of antibiotics on farm animals and this can lead to health risks for the consumer.
   When we buy locally produced organic food we are not only buying healthy, naturally produced food, we are also making a contribution to the protection of our

Basic course > **Advanced course** > Exam course   Ecology | Unit 6

> environment. And don't forget: many people do not only buy organic food
> 40 because they want to face the challenge of reducing their carbon footprint
> but they also say it tastes better. (514 words)

TRAINING SKILLS – How to work with a dictionary

2 The following words are taken from the text. Identify them as nouns, verbs or adjectives in the context of the text.

1. average (l. 2)
2. harm (l. 4)
3. promise (l. 22)
4. contribute (l. 31)
5. label (l. 34)
6. challenge (l. 40)

3 Find the meaning of the above words using the following parts of an English-English dictionary. Words often have more than one meaning so make sure you find the meaning of the word in the text.

> **average (n.)** – **1.** An **average** is what you get by adding two or more numbers and dividing the result by the amount of numbers you added. **2.** An amount or quality that is **average** is the standard or usual amount/quality of a group of things or people.
> **average (adj.)** – **1.** You use **average** to say that a person or thing is typical or normal. **2.** Something that is **average** is ordinary: it is not so good, nor is it so bad.
> **challenge (n.)** – A **challenge** is **1.** something new and difficult and you must make a big effort to do it. **2.** an invitation from a person to compete or argue with them.
> **challenge (v.)** – If you **challenge** a person **1.** you ask them to compete or argue with you. **2.** You want to know whether what they say is true or whether what they do is correct.
> **contribute (v.)** – **1.** If you **contribute** to a thing **1.1.** you try to make it successful. **1.2.** you pay money or you give assistance to something, usually for charitable purposes. **2.** If something **contributes** to a situation, it is one of the reasons for it. **3.** If you **contribute** to a newspaper or magazine, you write articles for them.
> **harm (v.)** – **1.** To **harm** someone means to hurt them and cause them physical pain. **2.** To **harm** something means to damage it or make it less useful.
> **label (n.)** – A **label** is a piece of paper or another material that is placed on an object. It gives information about the object, for example it tells what it is, who owns it, or how you can use it.
> **label (v.)** – **1.** If you **label** something, you put a label on it to mark it. **2.** If you **label** people as something, you describe or think of them in a certain way, even though they do not agree with your opinion.
> **promise (n.)** – **1.** A **promise** is a declaration which you make to a person saying that you will definitely do something or give them something. **2.** If someone or something shows **promise**, it looks as if they will be successful in future.
> **promise (v.)** – **1.** If you **promise** that you will do a thing, you tell a person that you will certainly do it. **2.** If you **promise** someone a thing, you tell them that you will certainly give it to them. **3.** If a situation or event **promises** to have a special quality, you expect it to have that quality.

4 Replace the words in task **2** with words or phrases from the above dictionary.

5 Answer the questions on the text in your own words. ● Task ▶ F 3, p. 86
R
1. Explain why shopping has become more difficult for the environmentally conscious consumer.
2. Describe the disadvantages of much of the food on offer in the big supermarkets.
3. Summarize the advantages of organic food.

Exam 6 **Mediation:** Als umweltbewusster Verbraucher wollen Sie Ihre Freunde über diesen
M Artikel informieren. Stellen Sie dazu die wichtigsten Aussagen des vorliegenden Textes auf Deutsch zusammen. Formulieren Sie ganze Sätze. ▶ Mediation, S. 228

D | Practice

D1 Consuming the world

Before listening

1 Describe and analyze the picture. ▶ Karikaturen, S. 214
P

2 Read the headlines and guess what the listening text is about.

> **Ecology and economy go hand in hand.** 1

> We are all overconsumers. 2

> 'Buy Nothing Day' is only the beginning. 3

> Can you teach an old society new tricks? 4

While listening

3 Hören Sie dem Radiokommentar zu und vergleichen Sie, ob Ihre Ideen zu
R Übung 2 zutreffend waren.
A2.11

Exam 4 **Hörverstehen:** Hören Sie dem Kommentator noch einmal zu und ergänzen Sie
A2.11 die folgenden Aussagen. ▶ Hörverstehen, S. 196

1. Nach seiner Ansicht müssen Ökonomie und Ökologie …
2. Die Menschen verbrauchen heute mehr von der Natur als …
3. 20 % der Menschen verbrauchen …
4. Ein einzelner Haushalt im Vereinigten Königreich hat …
5. Verglichen mit Eisenbahnfahrten kann ein Flug …
6. Der Transport auf der Straße …
7. Beim "Boomerang Trade" werden ähnliche Güter …
8. Der Klimawandel betrifft zuerst … und dann …
9. Ein wesentlicher Konfliktherd wird der Zugang zu …
10. Wir Verbraucher sollten … ändern.
11. Es gibt sehr viel Werbung, die uns zum Konsum anstiften will, aber nur sehr wenig Werbung dafür, dass …
12. Am Ende fordert uns der Kommentator auf, …

After listening

5 Explain the link between the slogan on the right and the commentary
"Consuming the world".

6 Think about electrical appliances in your home and do the tasks.
I
1. Make a list of three items which you believe are necessary and three which are not.
2. Work in pairs. Compare your list with a classmate's list.
3. Make a common list with your partner. Present it to the class. Give reasons for your choice.

Basic course > **Advanced course** > Exam course   Ecology | Unit 6

D2 Eco-colleges – a hopeless dream?

The carbon footprint of English schools and colleges shows that they cause about 10 million tonnes of CO_2. So, the idea of eco-schools and colleges is no longer science fiction but has become a realistic and necessary option.

1
P
Read what the people say and decide what colleges could do to reduce environmental problems. The *Help* box on the right may help you.

1. "The food in our college canteen is not very healthy and I'm sure a lot of it is thrown away at the end of the day." Kirsty – student at Newcastle College
2. "The heating at the college doesn't seem to work efficiently. It's always much too warm in the classrooms." Barney – student at Norwich College
3. "We throw away an enormous amount of waste here at college – paper, bottles, printer cartridges. The list is endless." Paula – teacher at Swindon College

> **Help**
> eco projects •
> curriculum changes •
> food • recycling •
> energy-saving
> strategies

2
P

Work in groups. Collect ideas about how <u>your</u> college could be more eco-friendly. Then prepare a presentation of your ideas.

D3 Sustainability

While watching

1
V8
Watch the film and decide if the statements are true or false. ▶ Hör-Seh-Verstehen, S. 197

1. When IKEA started in the UK, they …
   a) brought many colours to British homes.
   b) had strong competitors.
   c) demanded high prices.
   d) were very successful.

2. At that time IKEA…
   a) changed the way of buying furniture.
   b) contributed to the throwaway attitude.
   c) designed products to be fashionable.
   d) produced goods to last for a lifetime.

3. Steve Howard, Head of Sustainability wants to make it clear that…
   a) adverts can influence consumers' attitudes completely.
   b) IKEA does not make consumers throw away goods any more.
   c) he has training videos for the marketing team.
   d) he is going to talk to the marketing team about sustainability.

 2
M
Mediation: Sie sind Mitglied einer Umweltorganisation. Bei einem Treffen wollen Sie über den Film berichten. Fassen Sie die wesentlichen Punkte – mit Hilfe Ihrer Lösung zu task **1** – auf Deutsch zusammen. Verwenden Sie ganze Sätze. ▶ Mediation, S. 228

E | Reading +: Saving nature

Before reading

1 Describe *WWF's* logo and say what you know about the *WWF*.

2 Describe and analyze the two diagrams. ▶ Diagramme, S. 215

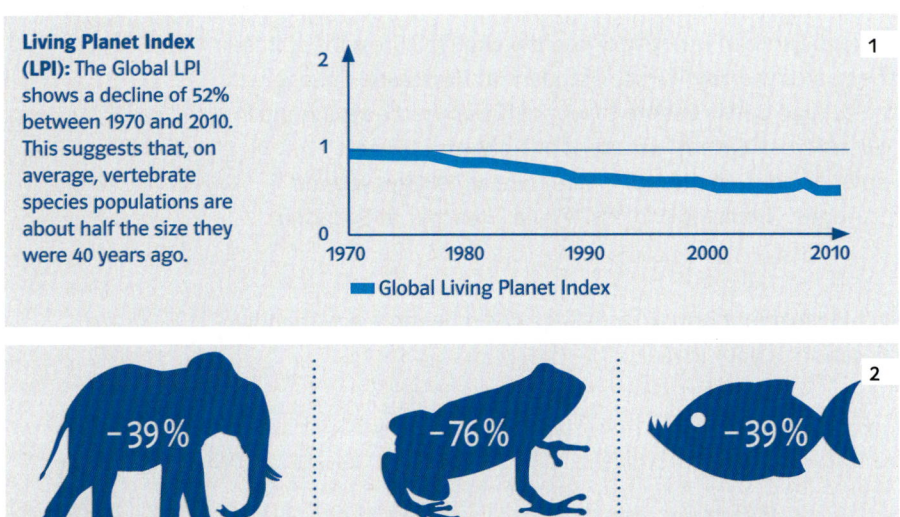

Quelle: Nach www.panda.org.

Understanding the text

3 Read the text on p. 85 and point out what the above diagrams have to do with it.
▶ Leseverstehen, S. 199

4 Answer the questions in your own words as much as possible. ○ Help ▶ F 4, p. 87

1. Why has the number of wild animals decreased by a half?
2. According to *WWF*, how can the problem be solved?
3. What does our ecological footprint show us?
4. Why have freshwater ecosystems become a major problem?
5. How do EU countries contribute to environmental damage?

Exam 5 **Mediation:** Als Mitglied einer Umweltjugendgruppe wollen Sie einen kurzen Vortrag halten über die negativen Veränderungen in der Umwelt und die Gründe dafür. Entnehmen Sie dazu die wichtigsten Informationen aus dem Text und fassen Sie sie auf Deutsch zusammen. ▶ Mediation, S. 228; ● Task ▶ F5, p. 87

Exam 6 **Materialgestützter Aufsatz:** Write a composition about the increasing problems of wildlife on our planet and possible solutions. Refer to the diagrams and the text.
▶ Materialgestützter Aufsatz, S. 199

Earth has lost half its wildlife in the past 40 years

The number of wild animals on Earth has halved in the past 40 years, according to a new analysis. Creatures across land, rivers and the seas are being decimated as humans kill them for food in unsustainable numbers, while polluting or destroying their habitats, the research by scientists at WWF and the *Zoological Society of London* found.

"If half the animals died in London zoo next week it would be front page news," said Professor Ken Norris, ZSL's director of science. "But that is happening in the great outdoors. This damage is not inevitable but a consequence of the way we choose to live." He said nature, which provides food and clean water and air, was essential for human wellbeing.

"We have lost one half of the animal population and knowing this is driven by human consumption, this is clearly a call to arms and we must act now," said Mike Barratt, director of science and policy at *WWF*. He said more of the Earth must be protected from development and deforestation, while food and energy had to be produced sustainably.

The steep decline of animal, fish and bird numbers was calculated by analysing 10,000 different populations, covering 3,000 species in total. "This data was then, for the first time, used to create a representative "Living Planet Index" (LPI), reflecting the state of all 45,000 known vertebrates [...]," said Professor Jonathan Baillie, ZSL's director of conservation. "If we get [our response] right, we will have a safe and sustainable way of life for the future," he said.

If not, he added, the overuse of resources would ultimately lead to conflicts. He said the LPI was an extremely robust indicator and had been adopted by UN's internationally-agreed Convention on Biological Diversity as key insight into biodiversity.

A second index in the new Living Planet report calculates humanity's "ecological footprint", i.e. the scale at which it is using up natural resources. Currently, the global population is cutting down trees faster than they regrow, catching fish faster than the oceans can restock, pumping water from rivers and aquifers faster than rainfall can replenish them and emitting more climate-warming carbon dioxide than oceans and forests can absorb.

The report concludes that today's average global rate of consumption would need 1.5 planet Earths to sustain it. But four planets would be required to sustain US levels of consumption, or 2.5 Earths to match UK consumption levels.

The fastest decline among the animal populations was found in freshwater ecosystems, where numbers have plummeted by 75% since 1970. "Rivers are the bottom of the system," said Dave Tickner, *WWF's* chief freshwater adviser. "Whatever happens on the land, it all ends up in the rivers." For example, he said, tens of billions of tonnes of effluent are dumped in the Ganges in India every year. [...]

Also, by importing food and other goods produced via habitat destruction in developing nations, rich nations are "outsourcing" wildlife decline to those countries, said Norris. For example, a third of all the products of deforestation such as timber, beef and soya were exported to the EU between 1990 and 2008.

David Nussbaum, chief executive of *WWF-UK* said: "The scale of the destruction highlighted in this report should be a wake-up call for us all. [...] We all – politicians, businesses and people – have an interest, and a responsibility, to act to ensure we protect what we all value: a healthy future for both people and nature." (584 words)

Quelle: Damian Carrington, *The Guardian*, September 30, 2014, www.theguardian.com.

F | Further tasks

● **A task 4, p. 77**

1 Answer the questions in your own words as far as possible.
R

1. What do you understand by the term "the greenhouse effect"?
2. What are the main causes of CO_2 in the atmosphere?
3. What will happen if we continue to burn fossil fuels at the same rate as we are doing now?
4. What do you understand by the term "extreme weather conditions"?
5. How is *Bentley Motors* contributing to a better environment?

○ **B 1 task 2, p. 78**

2 This is what some people said after reading the advert. Report what they told you. Choose the correct words in brackets.

1. Ron: "I saw this advert on the Internet, too."

Example:
Ron said / told me that he had seen that advert on the Internet, too.

2. Julie: "My friend showed me the advert."
   Julie told me that (my / her) friend (showed / had shown) (me / her) the advert.
3. Sam: "I decided to give £2."
   Sam added that (I / he) (decided / had decided) to give £2.
4. Tom and Mark. "We donated money online."
   Tom and Mark told me that (we / they) (donated / had donated) money online.
5. Nick: "I filled in the form immediately."
   Nick said that (I / he) (filled / had filled) in the form immediately.
6. Jack: "I didn't know much about this problem."
   Jack remarked that (I / he) (didn't know / had not known) much about (this / that) problem.
7. Lisa and Sarah: "We have made the decision to give £5 a month.
   Lisa and Sarah pointed out that (we / they) (made the decision / had made the decision) to give £5 month.
8. Jenny: "I haven't checked out this website yet."
   Jenny told me that (I / she) (haven't checked / hasn't checked / hadn't checked) out (this / that) website yet.

● **C task 5, p. 81**

3 What food choices can we make to reduce CO_2? Use the key points to give a talk
P on the topic and explain your ideas. ▶ Präsentieren, S. 217

> **Food choices**
> eat foods produced locally – eat foods that are in season – choose foods that do not have packaging – if you can, grow your own food

Basic course > **Advanced course** > Exam course Ecology | **Unit 6**

E task 4, p. 84

4 Answer the questions in your own words. Do not just copy the prompts. For help see the information given below.

Help

1.	Why has the number of wild animals decreased by a half?	• kill them for food (line 5) • unsustainable numbers (lines 5–6) • polluting or destroying their habitats (lines 6–7) • human consumption (line 21) • deforestation (line 26) • cutting down trees faster (line 50) • catching fish faster (line 51) • pumping water … faster (lines 52–53) • emitting more climate-warming CO_2 (lines 54–55)
2.	According to *WWF*, how can the problem be solved?	• act now (line 22) • Earth must be protected (lines 24–25) • food and energy … produced sustainably (lines 26–27)
3.	What does our ecological footprint show us?	• scale at which it is using up natural resources (lines 48–49)
4.	Why have freshwater ecosystems become a major problem?	• rivers … bottom of the system (lines 66–67) • all ends up in the rivers (lines 69–70) • tens of billions of tonnes of effluent (lines 70–71)
5.	How do EU countries contribute to environmental damage?	• importing food and other goods (lines 73–74) • a third of all the products (lines 77–78) • timber, beef and soya (line 79)

E task 5, p. 84

5 Explain how the photos below refer to problems mentioned in the text "Earth has lost half its wildlife in the past 40 years" on p. 85.

87

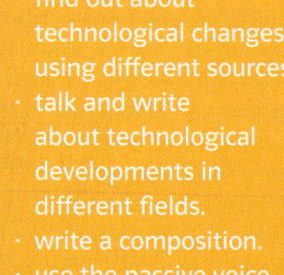

 457tn7

Unit 7
The present and future of technology

A | Getting started: Cleaner energy

Before reading

1 Describe the above photos.

2 Choose one of the types of energy in the photos and tell the class what you
P   already know about it. ► Fotos und Illustrationen, S. 211

3 Decide what types of renewable energy could be used in the following areas.
   Give reasons for your decision.

   1. A wet mountainous region
   2. A flat or mountainous high-wind area
   3. A dry, hot region
   4. An agricultural region near a big city

Understanding the text

4 Find out which energy sources in the photos are mentioned in the text,
R   "Scotland fossil-free by 2030?". ► Leseverstehen, S. 199

5 Explain who the people are and what they said in the text in your own words:
   ○ Task ► F 1, p. 98

   1. Ed Rose   2. Evelyn McTaggert   3. Georgia Henry

> **Help**
> solar power • wind power • water power • biomass

Basic course > **Advanced course** > Exam course   The present and future of technology | **Unit 7**

🔊 A2.12

Scotland – fossil-free by 2030?

More than a dozen new onshore wind farms and a couple of offshore wind projects are to receive financial backing from the UK government in an attempt to make UK energy
5   production more fossil-free.
   One area which has been designated for these plans is Scotland. According to several energy technology experts, a fossil-free Scotland is not only technically achievable but
10 would also prove a cheaper and safer option than fossil fuels such as oil, natural gas or coal. Although Scotland seems to have enough natural oil and gas in the North Sea, moving to fossil-free energy sources would benefit
15 the country in the long run. As one energy technology expert, Ed Rose, says: "These projects could create thousands of "green" jobs and give a massive boost to Scotland's homegrown energy. We are developing wind
20 and water power technology that can stand the difficult weather conditions in and around Scotland. Moreover, we can reduce our reliance on nuclear power and – as everybody knows – our oil resources are limited."
25   A report went as far as to say that it would be possible to introduce an energy policy based on the so-called "renewables" in Scotland by 2030. One only has to look at the potential Scotland has with its abundance of wind and wave
30 energy sources. Moreover, the government in Edinburgh believes that Scotland will soon be in a position to export substantial amounts of excess electricity to the rest of the UK, particularly if Scotland succeeds in making its
35 production of energy from alternative sources more efficient.

Of course, there are also objections to some of the plans. Conservationists point out that areas of outstanding beauty, in the Scottish Highlands for example, will be affected and 40 that birds and sea animals might suffer from onshore or offshore wind farms. A lot of tourists come to Scotland to enjoy the natural surroundings with its abundance of wildlife. All this would be in danger if the plans for 45 extensive wind farms went ahead. Moreover, people living near wind farms have to bear the noise of the turbines and the view of several high objects in their neighbourhood. This could lead to people leaving Scotland to live 50 elsewhere. Evelyn McTaggert, one of the wind project leaders, also admits that there are some technical problems which still have to be solved. She explains that when wind farms produce more energy than is needed, the energy often 55 gets lost because at the moment there are no ways to store it in Scotland. And as many bigger cities are situated further south, high-voltage power lines would have to be built above ground. Evelyn McTaggert realizes that the 60 construction of high-voltage power lines could cause protests from nearby villages or towns.
   Nevertheless, Georgia Henry, energy expert for an environmental party, says that all renewables should remain part of the 65 government's plans so that Scotland can reach its low-carbon emission goal by 2030. She maintains that by pursuing alternative forms of energy Scotland would become the UK's renewable powerhouse, providing clean energy 70 and at the same time encouraging further investment in Scotland.   *(516 words)*

Exam 6 **Mediation:** Ihre Klasse plant eine Klassenfahrt nach Schottland. Sie geben
M   Ihren Mitschülern mit Hilfe des Artikels auf Deutsch einen Überblick über die
        Entwicklung der Nutzung der Windenergie in Schottland. ▶ Mediation, S. 228

After reading

7 Make a list of the advantages and disadvantages of wind energy as mentioned
P   in the text. Use your list to talk about wind energy.

8 Compare the situation in your country / area with the situation in Scotland.
P

> **Help**
>
> On the one hand wind energy is …
> On the other hand it …

89

B | Grammar

B1 The future of energy

1 A lot of suggestions can be read in newspapers or heard in the news. Complete the suggestions in the passive voice. 'Must', 'should', 'can' or 'could' must be used at least once. ○ Help ▶ F2, p. 98

1. Use oil more carefully!

Example: Oil should be used more carefully.

2. Save energy!
3. Promote solar power and other renewable forms of energy!
4. Reduce energy consumption!
5. Make nuclear energy safer!
6. Use more biogas!
7. Make wind turbines more efficient!
8. Find new deposits of gas and oil!

> **Grammar box**
>
> **Passive voice**
> **Example: New technologies were developed.**
> Das Passiv wird gebildet mit einer Form von *to be* in der jeweiligen Zeit und der 3. Form des Verbs (Partizip Perfekt).
> **Example: Coal is transported to power plants by ship.**
> Der Ausführende kann mit *by* angehängt werden.
> **Example: Energy consumption must (should, can) be reduced.**
> Das Passiv kann auch mit Hilfsverben gebildet werden.
> ▶ p. 191

B2 How electricity is produced

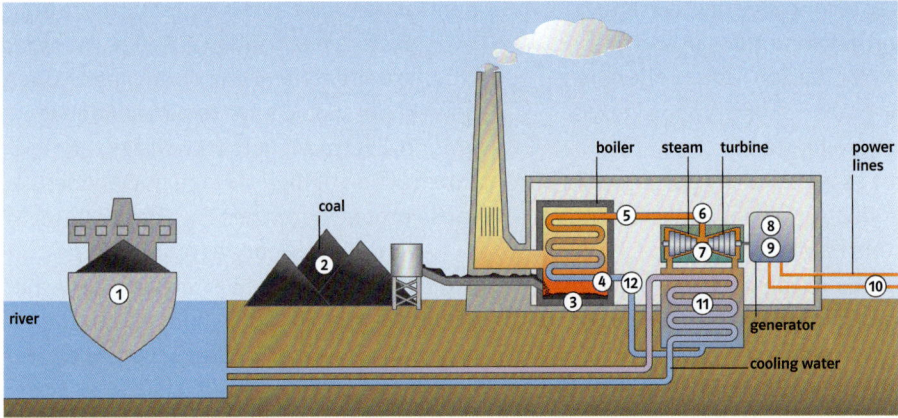

1 Describe how electricity is produced in coal-fired power stations.

1. coal / transport / to the coal-fired power plant / by ship

Example: Coal is transported to the coal-fired power plant by ship.

2. it / store / near power plant
3. coal / burn
4. water / heat
5. steam / produce
6. steam / lead / through turbines
7. blades of turbines / drive / by steam
8. magnets inside generators / move
9. electric energy / produce / in generators
10. it / send / into power lines
11. steam / cool down
12. water / use again

> ○ **Help**
>
> then • afterwards • later • finally • and so • in this way • next

2. Write a description of the process in a complete text. Connect the sentences with words from the *Help* box.

B3 Where were things made?

1 In your classroom you see lots of products such as T-shirts, sweaters, caps, school bags, smartphones, school books, glasses, earrings, pens, etc. Where were they made? Ask each other questions about products and answer them.

Example:
Student A: Where were your trainers made?
Student B: I think my trainers were made in Vietnam. (Or: I don't know where they were made.) And where were your glasses produced? ...

B4 A new wind farm

1 Complete the text about a new wind farm in Ainsworth, Nebraska. Use the passive voice in the right tense. The first example has been done for you.

Some years ago wind monitors **were put up** (1. put up) in different places around Nebraska. Soon it (2. find out) … that Ainsworth has wonderful winds. People in Ainsworth were surprised when their area (3. pick) …. First two small turbines (4. build) … north of Ainsworth in an area which (5. know) … for its horse thieves a hundred years ago. Today there is a large wind farm which (6. cannot, miss) … by visitors. When the project (7. finish) … a year ago a viewing platform (8. create) …. Power for nearly all of the homes in Ainsworth (9. can, generate) … by the wind farm today. The sound of a new era (10. can, hear) … and this is a sound that (11. create) … without burning coal. "A disadvantage is that wind farms (12. often build) … far from big cities in the last few years," says the mayor of Ainsworth. "Of course, not all questions (13. answer) … by wind energy in the future but it is a big step forward."

B5 Energy for transport

HOT 1 **Fallstudie:** Write a short report about the use of energy in transport from the past to the future. Think about steam engines and other inventions, the transport situation today and ideas for the future. Use the passive voice at least five times and the words in the *Help* box. ○ Task ▶ F 3, p. 98

> **Help**
>
> engine • steam • diesel • petrol • electric motor • hybrid car • biodiesel • biofuels • solar power • hydrogen

C | Reading: Tidal lagoon power

Facts

The Severn Estuary between Wales and England has the second highest tidal range in the world. This has led the government to consider a project which would create the largest power-generating lagoon in the world.

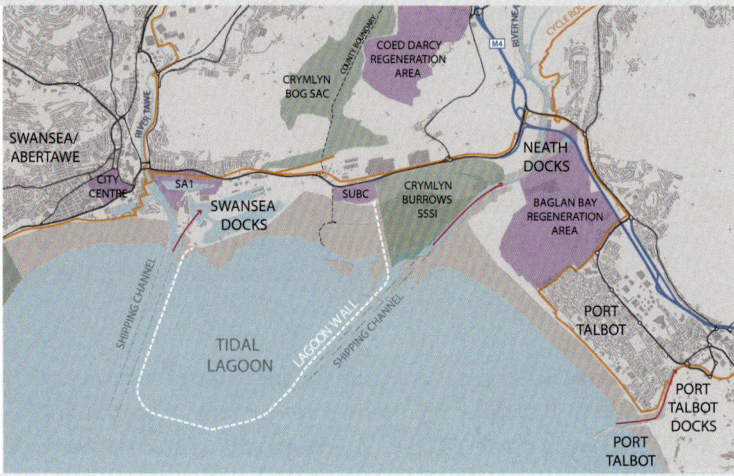

Before reading

1 Look at the *Facts* box above and describe the Swansea Bay Tidal Lagoon project.

P

A2.13

A Rahul Chopra, technologist: "A full-scale tidal lagoon programme would give the UK a great opportunity to generate electricity from our massive tidal range at a cost comparable to using fossil fuels or nuclear power. We must take advantage of the tide as a clean, carbon-free sustainable resource. And the technology involved is relatively simple. We don't need to split the atom here. It just involves installing a few turbines that would be used in a hydro-electric plant and building a protective breakwater to create a lagoon. The area which would be needed is only about 12 square kilometres. This project in South Wales is only just the beginning of a new era in the use of energy in the UK." (120 words)

B Penny Skinner, environmentalist: "We at 'Friends of the Earth' welcome the fact that Wales intends to put an emphasis on the use of clean renewable energy in the future. Nevertheless, such a project would have a major impact on the estuary and the wildlife here. Especially in the construction phase birds and animals will definitely be seriously disturbed by the noise and the construction work. Later, when the turbines are in operation there could be serious ecological consequences if wildlife is affected in a negative way. There are plenty of other ways to generate clean, sustainable energy without sacrificing our wildlife and areas of natural beauty." (106 words)

C David Davies, local politician: "This project would provide us in South Wales with massive amounts of sustainable energy, for over 150,000 houses for the next 150 years. Furthermore, this tidal lagoon will be the first of its kind in the world and that will make a really positive statement for the future of Welsh industry. And we shouldn't forget that it will make a big contribution to tackling the high levels of unemployment which exist at the moment." (78 words)

Basic course > **Advanced course** > Exam course   The present and future of technology | Unit 7

Understanding the texts

2 Do the following tasks. ▶ Leseverstehen, S. 199
R
1. Read what Rahul Chopra says about the project and describe details of the plan.
2. Read what the other people say. Decide who is for the project and who is against, and list their arguments.

3 **Mediation:** Für einen Bericht in Ihrer Umweltgruppe über alternative
M Energiequellen stellen Sie die Vor- und Nachteile des Projektes auf Deutsch gegenüber. ▶ Mediation, S. 228

TRAINING SKILLS – How to write a composition II

After reading

4 Is sustainable energy a real alternative? Write a composition in about 150 words using the following steps: ● Task ▶ F 4, p. 99

1. Write an introduction to the topic.

   Example:
   Today there is a lot of discussion about sustainable energy. Technologists have made it possible to use sustainable energy sources, such as solar, wind and tidal power.

2. List arguments for and against the use of sustainable energy sources. The prompts below may help you.

   enough land – relatively cheap – CO_2 – easy to produce – free resources – expensive technology – environmentally friendly – dangerous – renewable – exhaustible – problems with waste – emissions – dependent – climate changes – environmental problems – countryside – climate change – safe – clean – (in) dependent – stable democratic states – not always available

For	Against
environmentally friendly	…

3. Write sentences using connectives from *Help* box 1.

   Example:
   On the one hand technologists have created a way of generating electricity in a more environmentally friendly way…

4. Draw conclusions from the arguments above and state your point of view. The words in *Help* box 2 may help you.

   Example:
   In conclusion I would say that sustainable energy can…

○ **Help 1**

firstly • secondly • in addition • moreover • on the one hand • on the other hand • by / in contrast • however • although • next • then • because • therefore • not only … but also • finally

○ **Help 2**

in conclusion • as a result • in my opinion • in my view • my opinion is • in short • on the whole • personally I think

93

D | Practice

D1 Medical technology

1 Match the photos with the headings in the box below.

> surgery – medicine – examinations – disabilities – medical equipment – artificial insemination

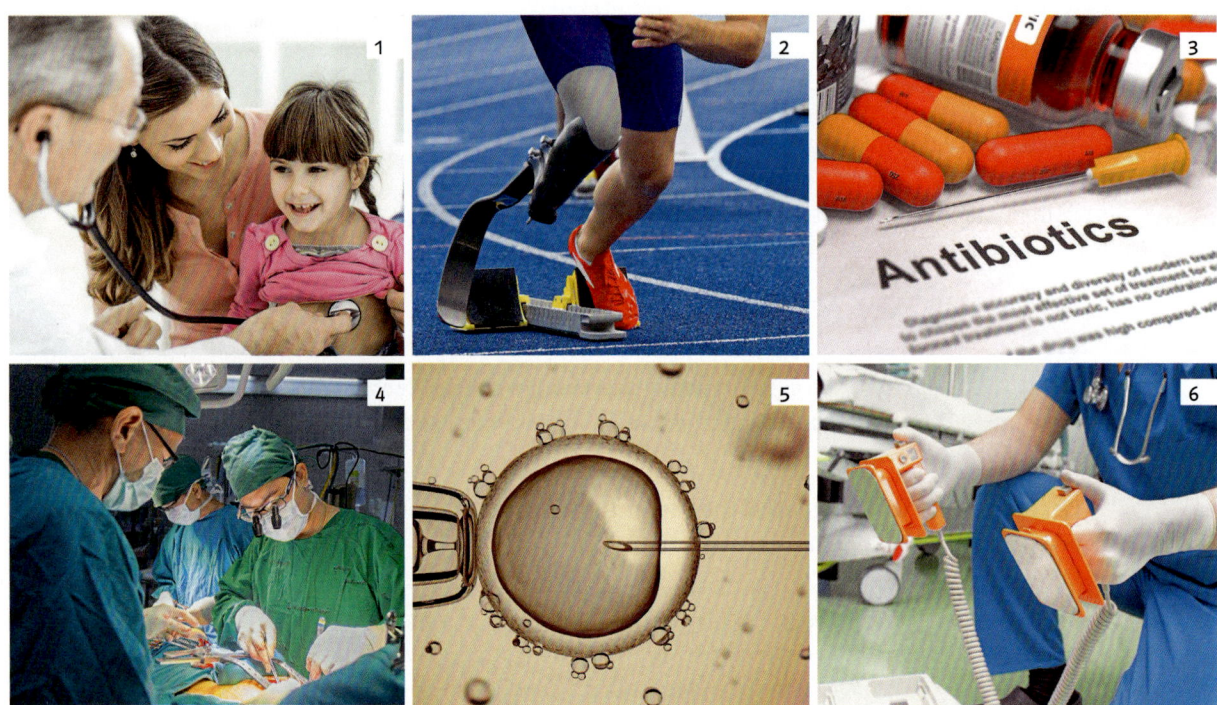

2 Outline in a few sentences how medical technology has developed over the years. Refer to the above photos and the *Help* box on the right in your answer.

> **Help**
>
> antibiotics • artificial body parts • defibrillator • operation • X-ray • ultrasound • organ transplant • vaccine

D2 Genetic engineering

Exam 1 **Hörverstehen:** Hören Sie dem Radiointerview aufmerksam zu und bearbeiten Sie die folgenden Aufgaben.
A2.14

1. Finden Sie heraus, wer spricht – Name und Arbeitsplatz.
2. Finden Sie heraus, über welche Themen die Vortragende spricht.

2 Hören Sie die Aufnahme noch einmal an, um die folgenden Fragen zu beantworten.
A2.14

1. Wie viele Babys sind schon durch künstliche Befruchtung gezeugt worden?
2. Was kann man durch bestimmte Tests an Embryos erkennen?
3. Was wissen zukünftige Eltern schon über die Gentechnologie?
4. Warum ist die Ärztin skeptisch im Hinblick auf diese Entwicklung?

D3 Do you always get what you want?

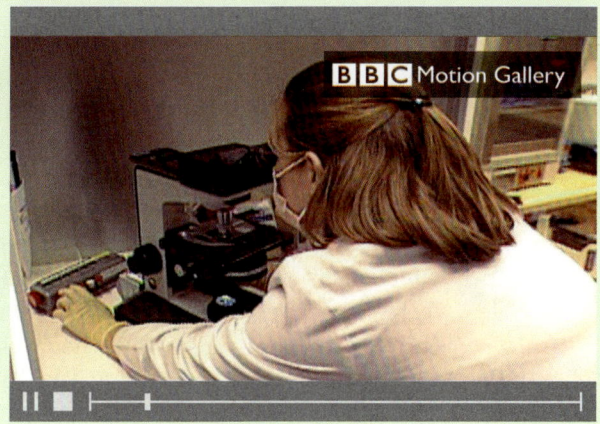

Before watching

1. Describe the photo.
   ▶ Fotos und Illustrationen, S. 211

2. Outline what you expect to see in the film.

While watching

3. Watch the film and check if your ideas in task 2 were right. ▶ Hör-Seh-Verstehen, S. 197

4. Watch the film again and do the following tasks:

   1. Complete the following table on a separate sheet of paper.

	Couple 1	Couple 2	Couple 3
1. First names of the couples			
2. Number of boys in their family			
3. Number of girls in their family			
4. Reasons for choosing the gender			

   2. Name the factors the institute takes into consideration when agreeing to help couples.

D4 Designer babies: How far should we go?

1. Do the following tasks in groups. ● Task ▶ F5, p. 99

   1. Collect the positive and negative aspects of creating "designer babies". Refer to the material on these two pages.
   2. In your teams discuss the positive and negative aspects of the introduction of "designer babies" in human genetic engineering. Part of the team are convinced of the positive aspects and the others are critical of the developments. At the end of the discussion you should try to reach a compromise. The words in the box may help you to argue.

2. **Materialgestützter Aufsatz:** Write a composition on the topic "Designer babies: How far should we go?" Explain arguments for and against designing babies according to parents' wishes and then state your own point of view.
   ▶ Materialgestützter Aufsatz, S. 199

Help

In my opinion ...
Another important argument is ...
That's not quite correct.
You're wrong there.
Hold on. I think ...
I'm sorry but ...
I must contradict you there.
Are you seriously saying that ...?
I partly agree ...
I suggest that we ...
What do you think about ...?

E | Reading +: Genetically-modified food

Before reading

1. Think of ways in which we could try to solve the problem of world hunger.

There's no choice: we must grow GM crops now

A Feeding the swelling numbers of people on our planet is one of the most serious challenges facing our leaders today. By 2050, it is likely Earth's population will have reached 9 billion.
5 Finding food for such numbers will not be easy. Science will not solve the problem on its own, of course, but clearly it has a key role to play. Without new technologies, future generations will starve. It is as straightforward as that. [...]

10 **B** At present, only one GM crop is grown commercially in Europe – a type of GM maize grown mostly in Spain. EU red tape has blocked the introduction of all others despite the fact that many offer rich environmental and
15 nutritional rewards compared with the growing of conventionally bred varieties.

C The situation is unacceptable, a point that was stressed last week by a group of government science advisers who warned that European
20 rules covering the growing of GM crops are no longer fit for purpose. They urged that Britain should be allowed to decide for itself whether genetically modified crops should be grown in the UK. The many benefits to be gained, in terms
25 of sustainable food production, far outweigh any perceived dangers, stated the report to the *Council for Science and Technology (CST)*, which advises David Cameron on scientific developments. [...]

30 **D** The report, prepared by leading UK plant researchers, is to be warmly welcomed. It is now 30 years since GM crops were first developed and their introduction debated in this country. The science has matured since then but
35 campaigners' responses to it have not. Scientific ignorance and bureaucratic inertia continue to hold the upper hand and over the decades have blocked the introduction of a swath of promising projects: plants that can boost vitamin levels in
40 our food, that can reduce farmers' reliance on pesticides, and that can increase yields for three decades. To repeat the point: this situation is unacceptable.

E We have a great deal to gain from growing
45 GM crops. They offer humanity a way to improve food productivity without having to make further inroads into our planet's wild places to create more fields for farmers. The position was summed up by Sir Mark Wolpert, the
50 government chief scientist last week, when debating the *CST's* report. "The challenge is to get more from existing land in a sustainable way or face the alternative, which is that people will go unfed, or we'll have to bring more wilderness
55 land into cultivation." From that perspective, the case for GM crops is unanswerable. [...]

F The world is going to find itself under massive strain to provide water, energy and food for its people. Already, almost a billion people are
60 suffering from serious food shortages and face starvation and in the next couple of decades there will be a worsening of that problem unless we take effective action now.

G To do that, we need to deploy the very
65 best, most productive technologies that are available – and given that the genetic modification of crops is probably the most powerful of all such techniques, it is clear Britain needs to act now to smooth the path for its
70 deployment. After 30 years, it is time to take GM crops to the nation. (547 words)

Quelle: *The Guardian*, March 16, 2014, www.theguardian.com.

Basic course > **Advanced course** > Exam course   The present and future of technology | **Unit 7**

Understanding the text

2 Do the following tasks on the text. ○ Help ▶ F 6, p. 99 ▶ Leseverstehen, S. 199
R
1. Find headings that sum up the main ideas in each paragraph.
2. Describe the food problems we are facing now and will face in the near future.
3. Explain what has stopped the introduction of GM crops in Europe.
4. Sum up the reasons why the author welcomes the report by plant researchers.
5. Explain why, according to the author, we should act now.

3 **Mediation:** Bei der Vorbereitung eines Vortrags über Biogenetik haben Sie den
M   Artikel auf S. 96 entdeckt. Fassen Sie die darin beschriebenen relevanten Punkte
    auf Deutsch zusammen. ▶ Mediation, S. 228

After reading

4 Read the statements 1–8 about the development and growing of GM crops. Then
R   match the statements with headings A–D.

> A. Danger to health   C. The environment at risk
> B. Ethical worries   D. Profits only for big agricultural companies

1. "A potential danger is that the bacteria in our stomachs could pick up antibiotic resistant genes found in many GM foodstuffs."
2. "By allowing GM crops we will put local farmers out of business. They will not be able to compete with the big farms that grow GM crops. Only big business companies will profit because they will have the patent on the GM crops."
3. "By introducing GM crops we are starting an uncontrolled experiment with unknown consequences for our ecosystem."
4. "Changing the genetic make-up of plants is unnatural. It takes nature millions of years to make genetic changes. What right do we have to make such changes overnight?"
5. "Developing and growing GM crops is immoral because it is against religious principles governing the relationship between humanity and nature. If you are keeping kosher, how do you know there are no pig genes in the tomato you are eating?"
6. "Farmers in developing countries cannot afford to grow GM crops. The gap between rich and poor countries will get wider."
7. "One big worry is that GM crops could harm wildlife. We could lose useful species such as bees and butterflies."
8. "Some people are allergic to certain foods. GM crops may contain genes introduced from unrelated species, for example, a fish gene can be put into a plant. This increases the possibility that GM crops may contain allergenic substances."

5 **Materialgestützter Aufsatz:** Write a composition on the following question, using
P   knowledge you have gained in this unit. Use arguments for and against and express
    your own opinion. ▶ Materialgestützter Aufsatz, S. 199

"Growing GM crops – a necessity or a big mistake?"

F | Further tasks

A task 5, p. 88

1 Find the most suitable options according to the text. More than one answer can be true.

1. In the future Scotland intends to use more energy from …
   a) the offshore oil.
   b) nuclear power stations.
   c) renewable sources.
   d) coal.

2. In Scotland you can find …
   a) fewer onshore wind farms than offshore wind farm projects.
   b) a potential to use the wind and the sea to produce energy.
   c) onshore and offshore wind farms.
   d) oil and gas in the North Sea.

3. Scotland has a lot of …
   a) sheep.
   b) wind.
   c) sunshine.
   d) energy sources which are fossil-based.

4. Increasing the production of renewable energy in Scotland will…
   a) encourage more companies to invest in Scotland.
   b) be expensive and dangerous.
   c) reduce carbon emissions.
   d) provide Scotland with more jobs.

B 1 task 1, p. 90

2 A lot of suggestions can be read in newspapers or heard in the news. Complete the suggestions in the passive voice. 'Must', 'should', 'can' or 'could' must be used at least once. ▶ Passive voice, S. 191

1. Use oil more carefully!	**Example: Oil should be used more carefully.**
2. Save energy!	Energy …
3. Promote solar power and other renewable forms of energy!	Solar power and other renewable forms of energy …
4. Reduce energy consumption.	Energy consumption …
5. Make nuclear energy safer!	Nuclear energy …
6. Use more biogas!	More biogas …
7. Make wind turbines more efficient!	Wind turbines …
8. Find new deposits of gas and oil!	New deposits of gas and oil …

B 5 task 1, p. 91

3 Choose one interesting product (for example a car, a T-shirt, fish fingers) and describe its production process. Information from the Internet can help you. Use the passive voice at least five times in your description.

Basic course > **Advanced course** > Exam course   The present and future of technology | **Unit 7**

C task 4, p. 93

4 **P** You visited your partner college in Swansea (South Wales) last year and you have just heard about the project. Write to your exchange partner asking how he/she feels about it. Tell him/her what you know about the project and give your view of it. ▶ Persönliche Briefe und E-Mails, S. 210

D 4 task 1, p. 95

5 **M** An English-speaking friend of yours is interested in the current discussion about advances in human genetic engineering. Give him or her a summary of the main ideas in the commentary about genetic engineering. ▶ Mediation, S. 228

SCHÖNE NEUE WELT?

Ein Kommentar von Wilhelm Butterweck

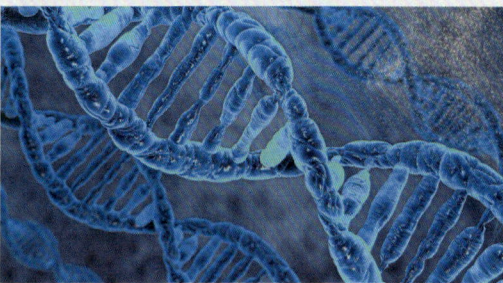

Bekanntlich ist es Wissenschaftlern vor einiger Zeit gelungen, gentechnisch veränderte menschliche Embryos zu erzeugen und das Verfahren wird in vielen Ländern unter unter-
5 schiedlichen gesetzlichen Rahmenbedingungen angewendet. Dies hat die kontroverse Debatte um die Sicherheit und die ethischen Aspekte von genetischen Eingriffen wiederbelebt, die das Potenzial haben, Erbkrankheiten bei Neu-
10 geborenen zu verhindern.

Kritische Wissenschaftler mahnen allerdings, dass die gentechnische Veränderung der DNA eines menschlichen Embryos nicht nur diesen einzelnen Menschen betrifft, sondern auch
15 Auswirkungen auf seine Kinder und Kindeskinder hat. David Robson, einer der führenden Wissenschaftler auf diesem Gebiet meint, dass die Entwicklung schon lange erwartet worden ist. Ihm war von Anfang an klar, dass die neuen medizinischen Technologien auch am Menschen 20 eingesetzt werden würden und dass dies bald geschehen würde.

Natürlich kann man argumentieren, dass es große Vorteile hat, wenn man genetisch bedingte Krankheiten verhindern kann, aber wir wissen 25 nicht, ob das Verfahren wirklich sicher ist und welche Folgen es in Zukunft haben wird. Und wann kommt der Tag, dass wir nur noch manipulierte Kinder auf die Welt bringen, weil wir ja in der Lage sind, die Haar- und Augenfarbe, 30 die Größe oder sogar die Intelligenz des Kindes beeinflussen zu können? (199 Wörter)

E task 2, p. 97

6 **R** Match the headings 1–7 with the suitable paragraphs of the article, "There's no choice: we must grow GM crops now" on p. 96.

1. British experts' arguments in favour of GM crops
2. The author's positive attitude towards GM crops
3. Restrictions of GM crops in the EU
4. Growing world population
5. Call for action to prevent future food problems
6. Genetic modification of crops as the most suitable technology
7. Two alternatives for the future

Unit 8
The service industry

In this unit you will learn to ...
- use different sources to find out about the service industry.
- talk and write about services and the service industry.
- point out different aspects of the service industry and explain its impact on people and the environment.
- do reading comprehension tasks.
- use conditional clauses.

 bh36ja

A | Getting started

A1 Working in different sectors

1 Name and describe the jobs in the photos.
P

2 Match the jobs above with the following sectors of the economy:

  1. Agriculture   2. Industry   3. Services

3 In which of the three sectors would you like to work? Say why.

4 Describe and analyze the graph.   ○ Help   ▶ F1, p. 110   ▶ Diagramme, S. 215
P

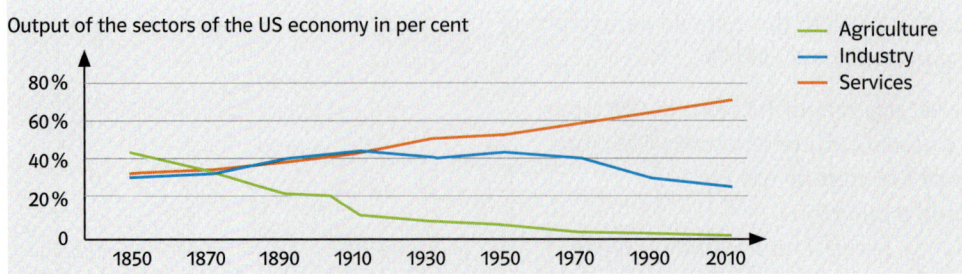

5 What jobs seem to have a better future than others? Give reasons.

A2 Work in the service sector

 A2.15

Careers in tourism and leisure by Alice Woods

Normally summer is the perfect time of year to relax and enjoy the holidays. Millions of holiday makers fly abroad or take the ferry to the Continent, while others prefer to stay on
5 the coast in the south west of England or in the Lake District. But for a certain kind of people it is the busiest time of the year: for people who work in tourism and leisure.

This sector has been enjoying a boom in the
10 last few decades. Three in ten of all additional jobs in the UK have been created by the tourist industry. There are a lot of employment opportunities in Britain but working in tourism can, of course, mean the chance to travel or
15 even live abroad. These job opportunities are not only limited to tour guides or club representatives, people also have a chance to work in a wide range of fields – from marketing events to hotel management.
20 Applicants do not necessarily need a degree but can also do training on the job. Of course, it helps if you already have some experience from part-time jobs or former temporary jobs in the summer holidays. Employees are expected
25 to deal with all kinds of tourists so employers look for outstanding people skills. If you want to be successful in your job, you must be flexible, communicative and able to work in a team. As Norman Waits, managing director of a leading
30 tour operator puts it: "Our customers always come first for us so we look for employees with a passion for our product and our service. We make sure that our employees get to know all areas of our company. You see, many of our
35 leading managers worked their way up from the bottom."

Pawan Durani who has just started his on-the-job training is sure that he has made the right choice: "Tourism is a booming
40 industry where dedicated people can make a lot of money. The travel industry is really exciting and fun. And for me one of the best things is that I have the chance to travel. I've already made some orientation visits to the
45 Far East and to Central America as we have to learn about various destinations all over the world. So, as you can see, the on-the-job training is not only theory but a real practical experience!" (397 words)

Understanding the text

1 Correct the statements according to the text. • Task ▶ F 2, p. 110
R
1. In the summertime everyone can relax and go on holiday.
2. 30 % of all jobs in Britain are in the tourist industry.
3. All employees in the tourist industry work as tour guides or club representatives in Britain.
4. The most important qualification for applicants is experience in the travel and tourism sector.
5. Pawan Durani has been to the Far East and Central America with his family.

2 **Mediation:** Für einen Freund, der sich für eine Stelle in der Tourismusbranche
M interessiert, fassen Sie die wesentlichen Aussagen des Textes über die Anforderungen und die Möglichkeiten in dieser Branche auf Deutsch zusammen. ▶ Mediation, S. 228

After reading

3 Describe your dream job in the travel and tourist industry.
P

B | Grammar

B1 Sightseeing quiz

1 Match the following sights with the correct cities and countries.

Sights	Cities	Countries
Red Square	Paris	USA
Opera House	London	Australia
Ying Sin Koon Temple	Berlin	China
White House	New York City	France
Brandenburg Gate	Washington D.C.	Russia
Statue of Liberty	Sydney	Britain
Eiffel Tower	Moscow	Germany
Tower Bridge	Hong Kong	USA

2 Check if your partner's solutions are correct.

Example: Student A: What will you see if you go to Paris in France?
Student B: If I go to Paris, I will see the Eiffel Tower.

B2 Tourism and the environment

1 What would happen if …? Complete the suggestions for a better environment using the correct forms of the verbs in brackets. ○ Help ▶ F 3, p. 110

1. If people **(use)** public transport more, they **(save)** energy.

   Example:
   If people used public transport more, they would save energy.

2. If flights (be) more expensive, people (fly) less.
3. People (not travel) so far or so often if they (think) more about the environment.
4. If fuel (be) more expensive, people (not use) their cars so much.
5. Visitors (do) sightseeing by bike if cities (have) more bikes for hire.
6. If the transport of goods by ship (be) faster, more goods (be delivered) by ship.
7. If the beaches (have) some more bins, the tourists (not drop) so much litter.
8. If the guests (not want) fresh towels every day, the hotels (save) a lot of water.

Grammar box

Conditional Type 1
Example: If you travel to New York, you will see the Statue of Liberty.
Present simple im *if*-Satz – Zukunft mit *will* im Hauptsatz

Conditional Type 2
Example: If I had the money, I would travel around the world.
Past simple im *if*-Satz – *Conditional* mit *would* im Hauptsatz

Conditional Type 3
Example: If I had known better, I would have stayed at home.
Past perfect im *if*-Satz – *Conditional* mit *would have* im Hauptsatz
▶ p. 190

B3 What would you do if …?

1

Now use your imagination. Think about things you would do if …

Example:
If I had my own plane, I would fly to the United States whenever I liked.

1. If I were a travel agent, …
2. If my parents owned a house on Hawaii, …
3. If my friend asked me to go on holiday to Majorca, …
4. If I spoke several languages, …
5. If I won the lottery, …

B4 After the holidays

1

Jennifer and Carl, a newly married couple, have come back from their honeymoon in Ireland. They had some problems during the trip and now they are having an argument. Complete the dialogue with the highlighted verbs.

Jennifer: Before we can watch TV we must unpack all of our bags and put the washing machine on.

Carl: Well, if you **hadn't taken** so many clothes on holiday, we **wouldn't have** needed so many suitcases.

Jennifer: Oh come on, I needed those pretty dresses, otherwise we wouldn't have got into those trendy discos. If you (1. not speak) … to that girl in the bar, I (2. not be) … jealous and then we (3. not have) … a big argument and we (4. have) … a perfect trip.

Carl: You always blame me if anything goes wrong. If you (5. book) … a holiday to Majorca instead of Ireland, we (6. have) … a wonderful time in the sun and we (7. relax) … more.

Jennifer: Well, I asked you and you didn't want me to change the flight. But it (8. be) … more relaxing if you (9. take) … your driving licence. Then I (10. not drive) … the car and the accident (11. not happen).

Carl: Oh, never mind. If I (12. not marry) … you, I (13. not have) … so much fun.

Unit 8 | The service industry

TRAINING SKILLS – How to answer questions on a text

C | Reading: Mass tourism

Before reading

1 Look at the heading of the text. What do you think the text is about?

Example: The heading could mean that ...

🔘 A2.16

IT'S NOT ONLY SUNSHINE AND FUN

A After World War II not only the number of cars, houses and consumer goods exploded in size but also international tourism grew significantly. Now mass tourism has reached
5   every remote part of the world bringing money, jobs, hotels and airports. With cheap hotels and flights at hand millions of travellers cover long distances in each and every direction in order to find new attractions. In
10 many countries and regions, tourism is the main source of employment and income today with worldwide revenues from tourism amounting to about US $ 2 trillion per year!

B However we do not need to travel far in
15 order to see the problems this enormous rise in mass tourism has caused. In Spain, the world's second most popular tourist destination, the effects are obvious. The combination of high tourist activity on the
20 one hand and agriculture on the other have led to massive drinking water shortages. In some coastal areas population figures are ten times higher in the peak season in summer compared to the relatively quiet
25 wintertime. Hundreds of litres of drinking water are consumed by each tourist per day, and not only for drinking or preparing food, but also for showers and swimming-pools. The number of golf courses has risen enormously
30 and these require millions of litres of water to stay green in the summertime. Moreover intensive agriculture also reduces the reserves of drinking water in many areas. As there is little rainfall in Spain this pressure on
35 water supplies leads to falling groundwater levels. When these levels sink seawater replaces groundwater in coastal areas and contaminates wells and farmland.

C Another effect of the increase in mass
40 tourism is massive air pollution. A study says that one transatlantic return flight alone produces about half the CO_2 emissions that an average person usually produces in one year! Flights to popular tourist destinations have become so cheap that millions of tourists from
45 Britain or Germany just hop onto a plane to the south of Spain or Majorca every summer or book long-distance flights to Thailand or the Caribbean. The CO_2 emissions from holiday air travel contribute to global warming which
50 among other effects causes a rise in sea levels. And ironically, this rise puts all the coastal areas worldwide at risk including popular coastal tourist resorts.

D These are just two examples of how mass
55 tourism leads us in the wrong direction. So what can we do? Well, the first step is to think before planning your holiday and to care what effect it might have. Do not only look for a maximum of pleasure and a minimum
60 of costs. The real cost of your holiday is much higher than you think if you consider the effect of your journey on the local people and the environment. Do local people really profit from my stay or am I supporting international
65 investors? Will I really get to know local people and their culture or will I live in a tourist ghetto? Am I helping to harm the environment or am I treating it with respect? Of course, holidays can mean sunshine and fun. But planning your
70 holiday more thoughtfully could mean that you care. (528 words)

Basic course > **Advanced course** > Exam course   The service industry | **Unit 8**

Understanding the text

2 Read the text on p. 104 carefully.
R

3 Summarize the text in a few sentences to make sure that you have understood the main points. ○ Task ▶ F 4, p. 111

> **Example:** The text is about the enormous rise in tourism since World War II and its effect on tourist resorts. On the one hand mass tourism brings money and jobs but on the other hand …

4 Read the questions.
1. How has tourism developed since the Second World War?
2. What are the positive effects of mass tourism?
3. How does mass tourism affect water consumption and supplies in holiday resorts?
4. What are the effects of holiday air travel on the environment?
5. How should we react to the negative effects of mass tourism?

5 Scan the text and note the lines where you can find information for the answers.

> **Example for question 1:** Lines 3–4, 6–9

6 Look up all the unknown words which are important for your answer.

> **Example for question 1:** remote (line 5)

> **remote**, *adj*: 1. A place that is remote is a long way from where people live. 2. If you describe someone as being remote you mean that the person is not friendly.

7 Decide which explanation is the most suitable according to the text.

> **Example for question 1:** The first explanation is the most suitable.

8 Write down key words that you can use in your answer.

> **Example for question 1:** tourism has grown, cheap, far-away places

9 Answer the questions using your own words as much as possible.
– You may use the question as an introduction in your answer.
– Give and rephrase the main facts using your key words.
– Always write full sentences.

> **Example for question 1:** Since World War II international tourism has grown very quickly. It has become relatively cheap to travel on holiday, even to far-away places.

10 Check your answer.

---

11 **Mediation:** Zu Hause in Ihrer Familie planen Sie, wie Sie Ihren nächsten Urlaub
M verbringen wollen. Stellen Sie auf der Grundlage des Textes Argumente dar, welche Probleme der Massentourismus mit sich bringen kann und worauf man bei der Planung seines Urlaubs achten sollte. ▶ Mediation, S. 228

Unit 8 | The service industry

D | Practice

D1 Working in the sport and fitness industry

Before listening

1 Do you go to a fitness centre or health club? Talk about your experiences.

While listening

Exam 2 **Hörverstehen:** Hören Sie den drei Sprechern zu und ergänzen Sie die
R folgenden Aussagen. ▶ Hörverstehen, S. 196
A2.17

1. Das Gehalt der angestellten Trainer richtet sich nach …
2. Wenn man als Trainer erfolgreich sein möchte, muss man …
3. Als selbstständiger Fitnesstrainer benötigt man außerdem …
4. Man muss allerdings nicht besonders …
5. Als selbstständiger Trainer bezahlt man allerdings …
6. Das Einkommen selbstständiger Trainer richtet sich danach, …
7. Nachdem Jemima Scott studiert hatte, musste sie zuerst …
8. Für die Zukunft plant Jemima eine Tätigkeit in …
9. Interessierte Hörer können …

After listening

3 Would you like to work as a personal trainer in a fitness centre? List the
P advantages and disadvantages and state your point of view.

D2 6 ways to stay healthy and fit

Less than 5 % of adults get at least 30 minutes of exercise each day, and only a few more manage to meet the recommended weekly minimum of 150 minutes of exercise. It is not always easy to fit training into a busy schedule but the following easy tips may help you to lead a healthier, happier life.

1. Get enough sleep.
2. Eat a healthy breakfast and fresh fruit each day.
3. Drink plenty of water.
4. Reduce stress, take breaks.
5. Go out for a walk or go jogging.
6. Show your emotions.

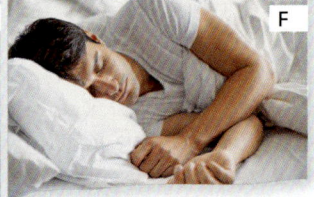

Basic course > **Advanced course** > Exam course · The service industry | **Unit 8**

1
R
Match the photos with the tips. Say why you think they match.

2
P
Choose one tip that is best for you. Explain to the class why you think that this tip could help you to stay healthy and fit.

3
P

Work in pairs. Write a short information brochure on healthy living aimed at young people. Think of some more practical tips.

D3 Physical activity and fitness

Before watching

1
P
V10
Describe the photo on the right and the photo at the top of p. 106. Compare the advantages and disadvantages of doing exercise in a fitness centre and in the open air.
▶ Fotos und Illustrationen, S. 211

While watching

2
R
Watch the film and find out its main message.
○ Task ▶ F 5, p. 111
▶ Hör-Seh-Verstehen, S. 197

3
Watch the film again. Match the people on the left with the statements a)–h).

1. Middle-aged woman at gym
2. Young woman at gym
3. Young man at gym
4. Health education expert
5. Young woman walking
6. Young man walking
7. Elderly woman walking
8. Reporter

a) I can easily fit my workout into my daily routine.
b) I walk every morning.
c) The new gym is expensive, walking is cheap.
d) Exercise is very important, otherwise I would not be able to move.
e) Crash diets don't work. Long-term exercise is the key to good health.
f) Workouts at the fitness centre can be boring.
g) When you've done training for a month it gets easier.
h) 50 % give up within half a year.

After watching

4
"People's desire to stay fit and healthy will create many more jobs in the leisure sector." Discuss. ○ Task ▶ F 6, p. 111

107

E | Reading +: Serving people

Before reading

1. What is the minimum wage in your country?

2. In what sectors do you think people receive minimum wages?

Living on $2.13 an hour and tips: the harsh inequality of the service industry

In most US states, 'tipped-minimum wage' can be shockingly low even before taxes, and women most often pay the price

Imagine that your pay depended on the mood of your clients, or on whether all your colleagues and superiors did their jobs well. Food industry workers like Nakima Jones don't have to imagine this – for them, income instability is a daily reality. Jones is one of 10 million Americans working in food and drink establishments throughout the nation. She knows what it's like to depend on customers for her rent and grocery money.

Jones, who was born and raised in New York City, has been working on and off in the restaurant industry since she was 16 years old. Jones recalled some of the hardships of working for tips this week in a panel [...], which focused on surviving on pay of less than $5 an hour. Among the obstacles she faced were an ever-changing schedule, double shifts and even the fear of going to the bathroom, as she didn't want to risk giving customers a reason to say she had been inattentive.

Since 1996, the federal tipped-minimum wage for food workers like Jones has been $2.13. So far, only seven states have passed legislation eliminating this kind of sub-wage, requiring all workers to be paid a statewide minimum wage. Some states have taken steps to increase the tipped wage slightly. For example, New York restaurant workers are now paid $5 an hour. Yet many states still pay their food industry workers less than $3 an hour.

This tipped-minimum wage policy is basically the restaurant industry asking its customers to pay its workers, says Saru Jayaraman, co-director of Restaurant Opportunities Centers United, also known as ROC-United, and author of *Behind the Kitchen Door*.

"When you earn a wage of $2 or $5, you don't actually earn a wage at all. Your wage is so low it goes entirely to taxes and you get a pay stub that says 'This is not a paycheck'. It says '$0'. And you live off of your tips," explains Jayaraman. Restaurant workers are also required by law to claim their tips as income. The tax on their combined income – hourly wage plus tips – is considerably more than what they would pay on their hourly pay.

Relying mostly on tips for one's income is not just an issue of income instability, but also that of job insecurity that comes with having a seasonal job. "When you live off of tips, your rent and your bills don't go up and down, but your income does. It varies day to day, week to week, month to month, year to year," says Jayaraman. "You don't actually have an income. In fact, you are interviewing for your job every time a new customer sits down."

That kind of job insecurity is even harder on mothers as they have to work around an ever-changing schedule to juggle doing their job and taking care of their kids.

A women's issue, a family issue

[...] Actually, 70 % of tipped workers are women, who work at the iHop and Applebee's and Olive Garden and Red Lobster. They suffer from three times the poverty rate of the rest of the

US workforce. They use food stamps at double the rate of the rest of the US workforce, which means that the women who put food on our tables in America cannot actually afford to eat themselves. [...]

The change needs to come within the restaurant industry, says Catherine May Saillard, owner of ICI restaurant in Brooklyn. One way to do so is to "change the way people think about leadership and authority within restaurant setting" and to get more women in the leadership positions.

"Whenever I place an ad to look for a chef, out of a 100 résumés, I would have five from women. I don't think that women cook less or not as well as men," she explains. "If I place an ad for a manager position, out of a 100 résumés, I would have two that would be women. And if I place an ad for a part-time brunch server, then I would have 95 women and five men."

While women made up 66% of tipped employees between 2010 to 2012, men only made up 34%, according to a report by ROC-United. In management, those numbers were reversed, with women making up just 38% and men making up 62%.

"I strongly support the raising [of] the minimum tipped wage," Saillard says. "I could fight against it, because that is money that is going to come out of my pocket, but I think the increase is fair." (783 words)

Quelle: Jana Kasperkevic, *The Guardian*, January 19, 2014, www.theguardian.com.

Understanding the text

3 Match the statements with one of the people mentioned in the text: Nakima Jones, Saru Jayaraman, Catherine May Saillard.
○ Task ▶ F 7, p. 111; ● Task ▶ F 8, p. 111; ▶ Leseverstehen, S. 199

1. "Most of the applicants for the well-paid jobs are men."
2. "Workers can never be sure how much they will earn the next day."
3. "I have no fixed working hours."
4. "Restaurant workers have to pay taxes on their tips."
5. "My income depends on the goodwill of our guests."
6. "Although I will have to pay for it I think a rise in minimum wages would be fair."

4 Compare the situation of workers in cafés and restaurants in the USA and in your country. Make a list of similarities and differences and present it in class.

5 **Mediation:** Im Rahmen Ihres Unterrichts sprechen Sie über Mindestlöhne und die Benachteiligung von berufstätigen Frauen. Mithilfe des Textes auf S. 108 und 109 bereiten Sie auf Deutsch einen Bericht über die Situation in den Vereinigten Staaten vor. ▶ Mediation, S. 228

After reading

6 Why do you think it is that mostly women are poorly paid in the food industry? Find reasons and make suggestions on how this situation can be changed.

7 **Rollenspiel:** Work in pairs. Student A is the owner of "Stud's", a large chain of cafés. See role card A on p. 174. Student B represents the employees who are mostly women. See role card B on p. 174. Negotiate the wages and working conditions. First state your point of view, then discuss and come to a reasonable agreement.

F | Further tasks

1. A 1 task 4, p. 100

Describe and analyze the graph. The phrases in the *Help* box can help you.

Output of the sectors of the US economy in per cent

[Graph showing Agriculture, Industry, Services from 1850 to 2010, with y-axis from 0 to 80%]

Help

The chart shows how the output of the different sectors of the US economy developed from …
The output of the agricultural sector decreased …
The share of the industrial sector first … until 1910, then remained relatively …
Since 1970 its share …
The only sector that saw a steady increase was …
Its share …
In conclusion you can say that the service sector …

2. A 2 task 1, p. 101

Answer the questions on the text "Careers in tourism and leisure" on p. 101 using your own words as much as possible.

1. What kind of people have to work hardest during the summer?
2. In which areas of the tourist industry are jobs available?
3. What qualifications should someone have if they want to start a career in the tourist industry?
4. What are the advantages of a career in the tourist industry according to Pawan Durani?

3. B 2 task 1, p. 102

Match the beginning of each sentence with a suitable ending and fill in the correct form of the verb.

1. If we depart at eight o'clock,
2. If he wants good service,
3. They will not arrive on time
4. If you want to save money,
5. When will we arrive
6. You will pay £10 extra
7. Where will Mary spend her holidays
8. If Jennifer and Carl decide to travel next month,

a) he (pay) more for his air ticket.
b) if they (not catch) their taxi.
c) they (only stay) for a few days.
d) if she (not want) to stay at home?
e) it (be) better to look online for a cheap flight.
f) if we (depart) at half past five?
g) we (arrive) at 10.
h) if you (check in) a suitcase.

Basic course > **Advanced course** > Exam course   The service industry | **Unit 8**

○ **C task 3, p. 105**

4   Match the headings with a suitable paragraph of the text "It's not only
R   sunshine and fun" on p. 104. Two headings do not match.

1. Negative effect on water supply
2. Careful planning necessary
3. Happy holidays in the sun
4. Tourist industry on the rise
5. High population figures
6. Air pollution and global warming

○ **D 3 task 2, p. 107**

5   Watch the film and say which of the statements below describes its main
R   message best..
V10
1. Too many people are overweight.
2. Go to a fitness centre regularly.
3. Long-term exercise is the key to good health.

○ **D 3 task 4, p. 107**

6   Refer to the statements in task 4 on p. 107 and give a summary of the film.

○ **E task 3, p. 109**

7   Decide if the following statements are true or false according to the text
R   "Living on $2.13 an hour and tips: the harsh inequality of the service industry" on
       pp. 108–109.

1. Nakima Jones gets a fixed pay.
2. 10 million US-citizens work in bars, cafés, restaurants etc.
3. Nakima does not have fixed working hours.
4. The minimum pay in all American states is $2.13.
5. The pay is so low that in fact customers provide most of the restaurant workers' income with their tips.
6. As restaurant workers depend on tips to earn a living they never know if they will be able to pay their rent.
7. It is especially difficult for working mothers to combine a job and a family.
8. Most restaurant workers who depend on tips are white men.
9. Only a few women apply for jobs as chefs or restaurant managers.

● **E task 3, p. 109**

8   Give reasons why the statements in task **7** above are true or false. Correct the
       false statements.

In this unit you will learn to ...
· welcome someone formally.
· deal with guests.
· show someone around a workplace.
· deal with intercultural differences.

Unit C

 8eq7fv

Cross-cultural communication at work:
Working in London

A | Starting work

Before listening

1 Bastian Topp from Stuttgart is starting his work placement at the Hotel Victoria in London. Kate Huggins, the general manager, welcomes him. Read the dialogue and find out how people greet each other when they meet for the first time.

 A2.18

Kate:	Hello there. What can I do for you?
Bastian:	Good morning. I'm Bastian Topp from Germany. I'd like to speak to Ms Huggins, please.
Kate:	You're lucky. That's me. Pleased to meet you, Bastian.
5 Bastian:	Pleased to meet you, too, Ms Huggins.
Kate:	Please call me Kate. First of all I'd like to introduce you to Luke Shaw, here. You'll be working with him a lot.
Luke:	Nice to meet you, Bastian.
Bastian:	Nice to meet you, too, Luke.
10 Kate:	Well, Luke, would you mind showing Bastian around the hotel? I'll get someone to cover for you on reception.
Luke:	I'd be glad to. Well let's start. Just follow me please, Bastian.

(103 words)

Basic course > **Advanced course** > Exam course · Working in London | **Unit C**

While listening

2
R
A2.19

Luke takes Bastian on a tour of the hotel. Listen to what Luke says and follow their route on the plan of the hotel below. Find out which rooms they enter.
▶ Hörverstehen, S. 196

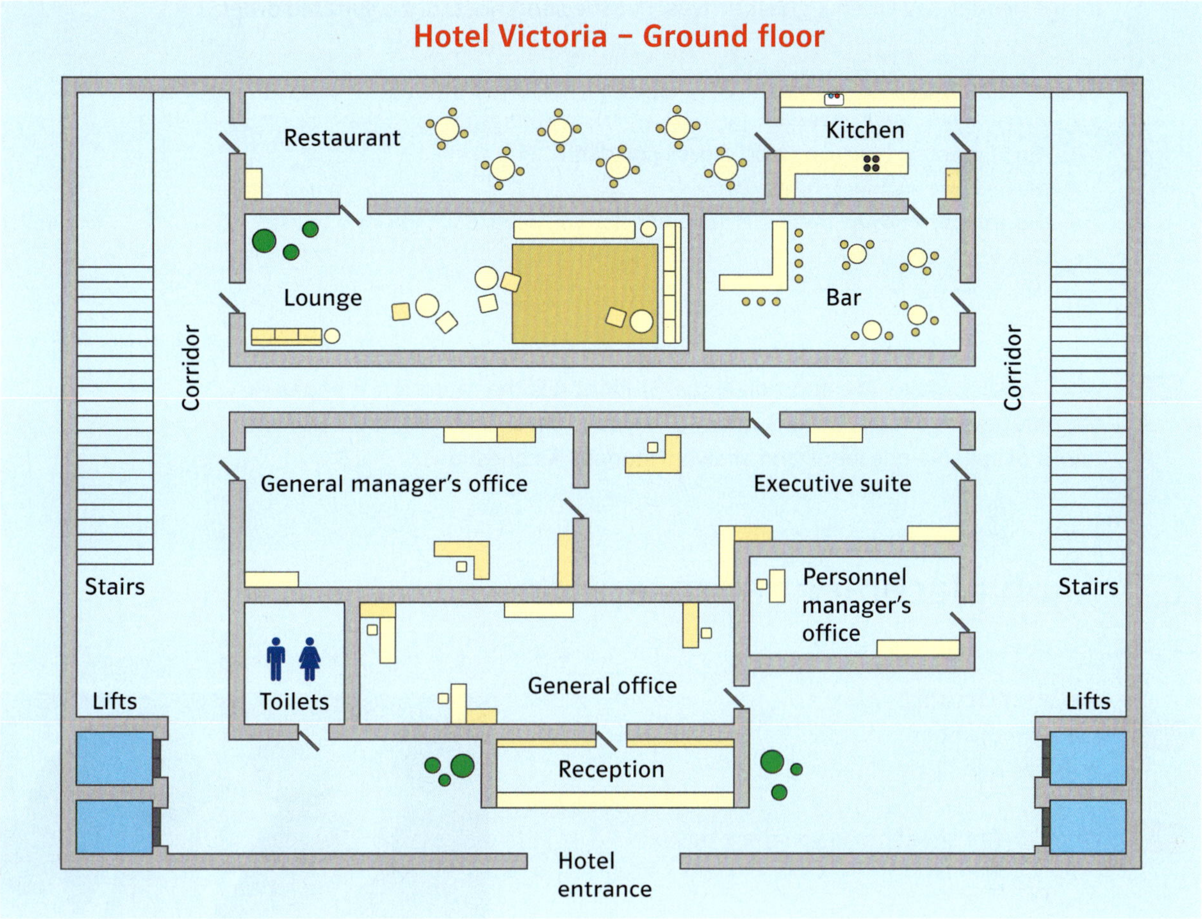

Hotel Victoria – Ground floor

3
A2.19

Hörverstehen: Hören Sie die Führung durch das Hotel ein zweites Mal und beantworten Sie die Verständnisfragen in ganzen Sätzen auf Deutsch.
▶ Hörverstehen, S. 196

1. Wo wird Bastian in den ersten Wochen arbeiten?
2. Wofür wird die „Executive Suite" benutzt?
3. Was findet ab und zu im Büro der Geschäftsführerin statt?
4. Warum ist das Restaurant momentan leer?
5. Warum führt Luke Bastian in die „Millennium Bar"?

After listening

4
I

Work with a partner. Student A is a sales representative for local fish products. He/she has arrived at the hotel and wants to talk to the head chef. Student B works on reception and gives directions to the kitchen using the plan of the hotel. Use the *Help* box on the right.

Help

Turn right / left
Go straight on / ahead
Go through
Go down / up / over
there
on your right / left

113

B | Welcoming guests

1 Bastian is on duty at reception. In the box below you can find a number of things he may say when a guest arrives. Put the sentences into a suitable order.

> 1. One moment, please. I'll check the computer. You're in room 421.
> 2. What's your name, please?
> 3. Good evening. How can I help you, sir / madam?
> 4. Have a nice evening, sir / madam.
> 5. Here's your key. And if there is anything else you need, don't hesitate to ask.
> 6. The lift is on the right.
> 7. That's on the fourth floor.

2 Work in pairs. Make up a short dialogue. Student A is the receptionist and uses the phrases in the box above. Student B wants to check in to the hotel. He / she thinks of suitable questions and answers student A's questions.

C | A job placement at reception

Before watching

1 Describe the photo.
▶ Fotos und Illustrationen, S. 211

2 What kind of situation do you think this is?

While watching

3 Watch the film again and find out the following information:
▶ Hör-Seh-Verstehen, S. 197

1. the departments which the new trainee will get to know
2. the caller's family name
3. the date of his arrival
4. the number of nights he wants to stay at the hotel
5. the type of room he wants to book
6. the name of his credit card

After watching

4 Describe the difficulties that you had when you started a job placement or a part-time job.

D | Cross-cultural misunderstandings

1 Describe what is happening in the cartoon and explain what cultural misunderstandings arise in this situation.
► Fotos und Illustrationen, S. 211

2 Luke tells Bastian how to deal with guests and gives some examples of cross-cultural misunderstandings that could arise with international guests. Explain what has gone wrong in the following situations.

1. A local businessman arranged a business lunch for a group of Muslim business partners at the hotel. The partners were not pleased with the invitation. The lunch had to be cancelled at short notice.
2. Luke's girlfriend Alisha, a sportswear representative, was in a restaurant in Brazil last year. She wanted to tell the waiter that the food was good. She used her thumb and forefinger to make a circle to show appreciation. The waiter didn't appreciate that at all and told her to leave the restaurant.
3. While Luke's brother, Steve, was on a promotion trip in Saudi Arabia he had a lot of brochures in his right hand and so he gave his Arab business partner his left hand as a greeting. The atmosphere changed and the promotion tour went very badly.
4. While Luke was studying Spanish in Mexico, he once asked a single Mexican woman if a situation had made her *"embarasada"*. She reacted in a strange way and left without saying goodbye.

E | Checking out and saying goodbye

1 Mr Rooney wants to check out. What do people say in this situation? Read the dialogue and fill in the gaps.

Mr Rooney:	Good morning. We'd like to check out, please.
Receptionist:	Good morning. Which (1) … were you in, (2) …?
Mr Rooney:	I was in 307.
Receptionist:	Let me look in the (3) … One moment, (4) … . Well that's £210 for 3 nights. Did you take anything from the (5) …?
Mr Rooney:	No, I didn't. I had a drink in the hotel bar last night.
Receptionist:	Fine. That's £210 then. How would you (6) … to pay, sir?
Mr Rooney:	Do you accept this credit card?
Receptionist:	Of (7) …, sir.

2 Work in pairs and continue the dialogue. Student A is the receptionist. Student B is Mr Rooney. The phrases in the box may help you.

○ **Help**
- I hope that you enjoyed your stay with us.
- Do you need help … (with your luggage / …)?
- Can I get you … (a taxi / …)?
- Have a good journey.
- Take care.
- Hope to see you again soon.
- Good bye.

In this unit you will learn to ...
- do research on various aspects of migration and globalization from different sources.
- talk and write about migration and globalization.
- do a mediation task.
- use the infinitive and the gerund.

 3b69yp

Unit 9
Living and working in a globalized world

A | Getting started: Migrant workers

Before reading

1 **P** Describe the illustrations. ▶ Fotos und Illustrationen, S. 211

2 What do you think the slogans want to express?

Understanding the texts

3 **R** Read the comments in the British online magazine "What's your story?" and do the following tasks in complete sentences.
○ Task ▶ F1, p. 126; ● Task ▶ F2, p. 126 ▶ Leseverstehen, S. 199

1. Explain the difference between "expats" and "immigrants".
2. Explain how immigrants contribute to the financial situation of the country.
3. Give reasons why Derek emigrated from the UK.
4. Describe some of the immigrants' negative experiences.

Exam **4** **M** **Mediation:** In Ihrer Jugendgruppe ist eine Veranstaltung zum Thema „Einwanderung in Deutschland" geplant. Zur Vorbereitung darauf fassen Sie die wesentlichen Aussagen der Einwanderer in den Online-Kommentaren auf Deutsch zusammen. ▶ Mediation, S. 228

Basic course > **Advanced course** > Exam course   Living and working in a globalized world | **Unit 9**

www.yourstoryboard.co....uk

What's your story? 78 comments

Mavuna You would expect that all people who go to work outside their country are called the same. But that's not true. People from Africa – like me – are called immigrants. People from Arab or Asian countries are called immigrants, too. However, Brits who leave their country to work abroad are expatriates or expats for short. So it depends on the colour of your skin if you are an immigrant or an expat. (72 words)

Marek First I came here from Poland without my family. I just wanted to see if it was possible to earn enough money to make a living for me and my family. They arrived in England two years later and we left everything behind us – our friends, our house and the rest of the family. But we are happy to be here and we have found a new home. We love the people here and the country and we hope that our children will have a good future. (88 words)

Derek I left Wales five years ago and started a job in Germany. You know, the job situation in my home country is terrible. My pay in Germany as a building worker is excellent and the living conditions are better than in Wales. Whenever I come back to my home town I feel that time has stood still. (57 words)

Davu Why does everybody here think that people only migrate to Britain because they want to live on state benefits? A few people may do so but the majority of immigrants come here to work. They work hard and pay taxes and national insurance contributions. It does not seem clear to the average British person that the amount of taxes that we immigrants pay is much higher than the amount of benefits that we receive. (75 words)

Bahati When I came here from Canada I did not know how much racism I would experience here in the UK. People are always nice to me when they hear me on the telephone. They like my Canadian accent but as soon as they see my brown skin they call me "Paki" or make monkey noises at me. When I try to talk about these things with friends they won't listen. They don't see a race problem in Britain. So I don't go out any more because I feel uncomfortable and unsafe. (91 words)

Adna You can meet people with prejudices wherever you live – not only in the UK. And I know what I am talking about – I have been to many places. But to me the most important thing is that I am accepted by my friends and my colleagues. They don't care about my nationality or the colour of my skin. (58 words)

After reading

5 In 2011 most foreign-born people in the UK came from India (684,000), Poland (521,000), Pakistan (419,000), the Republic of Ireland (398,000) and from Germany (290,000).
What reasons could people from these countries have when they decided to emigrate to the UK?

6 Would you be willing to work or study abroad? Where would you like to live? What would life be like? Prepare a short talk and tell the class. ► Präsentieren, S. 217

Unit 9 | Living and working in a globalized world

B | Grammar

1 Sam, a student in New Zealand, is spending a year in London in the UK as part of his course. His tutor gives him a list of things to do before he leaves. Report what the tutor wants Sam to do as in the example. The verbs in the box may help you.

Example: Sam's tutor told him / advised him to send an e-mail to Mr Wilkins in London.

read – find out – write – **send** – check – contact

Checklist
1. e-mail to Mr Wilkins, your tutor in London
2. letter to your host family
3. courses at the college
4. flights to London
5. company where students do their work placements in London
6. more about the British way of life

2 Sam has received an e-mail back from London. Complete the e-mail using the correct form of the verbs below. ● Task ▶ F 3, p. 126

let – **expect** – make – want – ask – expect

From: studentadvice@london-uni.ac....uk
To: sam_80@wellingtoninstitute.nz
Subject: Student visit
Date: Tue. 8 Sept. 20 ...

Dear Sam,

We want to give you an idea of what we (1) **expect** you to do during your stay.
Your tutors have (2) ... us to develop a work plan for you. They (3) ... you to do
a work placement in a company two days a week.
5 You will spend the rest of the week at college. The college (4) ... you to give a
presentation about life in New Zealand and how it differs from the British way
of life. So you see, it's not a holiday! We (5) ... you work hard. But we will (6) ...
you go early on Fridays so that you can see as much of London as possible.
We look forward to meeting you soon.

10 Regards,
Cathy Jackson
Student Advisor London University

Grammar box

Infinitive with 'to'
Example: He told her to send an e-mail.
Nach bestimmten Verben (*ask, tell, advise, expect, etc.*)

Infinitive without 'to"
Example: Please let me go.
Als Objekt nach *make* und *let*
▶ p. 191

Gerund
Example: Julie loves reading.
Nach bestimmten Verben (*enjoy, like, dislike, hate, prefer etc.*)
Example: Julie is interested in reading love stories.
Nach Verben, Adjektiven, Substantiven mit Präpositionen
▶ p. 192

Basic course > **Advanced course** > Exam course   Living and working in a globalized world | **Unit 9**

3 Sam has arrived in London and has already made two new friends, Julie and Marvin. You can see below what they like and don't like doing.

1. Work in pairs. Play the roles of Julie and Marvin. Tell each other about your likes and dislikes. Use the words in the box on the right.

   Example: Julie: I enjoy reading love stories.

Julie

Marvin

like ⊕
enjoy ⊕⊕
love ⊕⊕⊕

dislike ⊖
not enjoy ⊖⊖
hate ⊖⊖⊖

likes	doesn't like	likes	doesn't like
love stories ⊕⊕	sport on TV ⊖⊖	football ⊕⊕⊕	cricket ⊖⊖
discos ⊕	fantasy novels ⊖	cinema ⊕	fast food ⊖⊖⊖
restaurant ⊕⊕⊕	tennis ⊖⊖⊖	pop music ⊕⊕	TV ⊖

2. What do they prefer doing?

   Example: Julie prefers reading love stories to fantasy novels.

4 Match each phrase with the correct preposition. Then make sentences.

Example: I'm interested in playing … / in listening to … / in reading …

1. be interested – 2. be good – 3. be tired – 4. be afraid – 5. look forward – 6. succeed – 7. apologize

in – to – in – of – for – of – at

5 Sam's work placement is at a logistics company. When he arrives there, he is given a list of guidelines for new employees. Use the prepositions and verbs to complete the guidelines.

at – at – before – for – in – in – of – to

persuade – have – ask – make – **help** – work – discuss – speak

- We are good **at** (1) **helping** customers with their logistic problems. A lot of our work is done on the phone, so remember to be polite. You must also be interested … (2) … customers about their specific problems.
- Very often our phone lines are busy, so, first you should apologize to callers … (3) … to wait … (4) … to you.
- Remember we have to succeed … (5) … them that we can solve their logistic problems. So, you have to be good … (6) … their problems.
- At first the work can be difficult, but don't be afraid … (7) … small mistakes. In this way you will learn. We look forward … (8) … with you.

C | Reading: Profits or ethics?

Before reading

1 Look at the picture and describe the situation. In what countries can you find working conditions like the ones shown?

2 Look at the beginning of the text and find out what country it refers to.

🔊 A2.21

£3 per hour! A fair deal?

Decades ago, the British textile industry declined and the manufacturing companies left for South-east Asia. In the last few years however, we have been able to hear the sound
5 of thousands of sewing machines again – in small garment factories and workshops around Britain. But "Made in Britain" is not what we might expect, according to a new report of exploitation inside the East Midlands
10 garment industry.

The report reveals that there are about 12,000 employees in this sector. From this workforce 75–90 % are paid £3 per hour. This is less than half of the legal minimum wage.
15 On top of that it details workplace practices including: inadequate health and safety standards, bullying, a lack of toilet breaks, no maternity pay and no real employment contracts.

20 One fashion designer describes the work in a factory where clothes for UK street retailers are produced within weeks. "I tried to do the women's work in one of the factories for a day. You won't believe how hard this was for me.
25 I couldn't stand it! And these women work there day in day out. Through talking to them we found out that many of them were paid even less than £3 per hour," she said. "This factory was one of the better ones, yet it had no
30 contracts, paid less than the minimum wage, health and safety standards were not observed and the employees did not know about their legal rights." The designer quit her job when her company gave an order to one of the
35 "factories" at the back of a house. "And when I say a 'factory', it was just a shed," she said. "The culture of buying and selling is connected to the 'race to the bottom'. How cheaply can I get this?"

According to the report, the workers are
40 mostly women – largely from South-east Asia or from Eastern Europe. "They are not forced to work there," says Dr Doug McLean, one of the researchers for the report. "But as long as these women do not speak English properly
45 they cannot get better jobs in other sectors. They are glad that they can contribute to the family income. So although the jobs in these backyard factories are poorly paid and violate the workers' rights, they are also sought after."
50 For the public, however, the workers remain invisible. "If you get something cheap, there is a reason for that," says McLean. "What has made it so cheap? Ultimately, businesses need to cut their costs, and where do they cut them – it's
55 usually the labour costs."

"Of course, this is not only a British but also a European and even a worldwide problem. Romanian migrants work on Hungarian fields for one pound an hour, undocumented
60 Nigerians in Belgium work in the cleaning or building industry. More and more women are travelling abroad as unskilled migrant workers to earn money for their families. Thousands of South-east Asian women work in other
65 countries doing jobs in the household with no rights at all. They send what little they earn to their families and hope that one day their children will be better off!" (520 words)

Basic course > **Advanced course** > Exam course   Living and working in a globalized world | **Unit 9**

TRAINING SKILLS – How to do mediation exercises

Understanding the text

3
M
Im Rahmen eines Schulprojekts zur Globalisierung soll die Lage der Fabrikarbeiterinnen in der Bekleidungsindustrie weltweit dargestellt werden. Als Beispiel für Missstände in Industrieländern erstellen Sie einen Beitrag über Großbritannien. Dazu entnehmen Sie dem Artikel wichtige Informationen. Formulieren Sie ganze deutsche Sätze. ► Mediation, S. 228

1. Read the text to get a general impression of it.
2. Read the task carefully and find out what text type you are supposed to produce and for whom, and which language you must use.

   Example: Text type: Report – Addressee: Other students – Language: German

3. Read the text again. While reading the text, note down the information you need to do the task. Select only the relevant points.

   Example: First paragraph: small garment factories, in Britain

4. Arrange the information you noted down. A word web can help you.

   Example:

   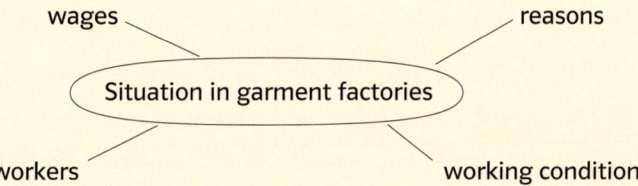

5. Summarize the most important details in the target language (here: German).

   Example: Situation in den Textilfabriken in Großbritannien, Arbeitsbedingungen, Löhne, Arbeitskräfte, Gründe für diese Zustände

6. Start with an appropriate introduction.

   Example: Nicht nur in den Entwicklungsländern kann die Lage von Fabrikarbeiterinnen äußerst schlecht sein.

7. Write your text referring to your word web. Always remember your addressee.
8. Do not forget that a mediation exercise is not a translation. Do not translate.
9. In the end check your text (structure, language, spelling).

After reading

Exam **4**
M
Mediation: Für Ihr Schulprojekt informieren Sie sich über die Lage der Fabrikarbeiterinnen in der Bekleidungsindustrie in Südostasien. Suchen Sie dazu einen geeigneten Artikel in englischsprachigen Zeitungen – z. B. *The Guardian*, *The Times*, *USA Today* – und entnehmen Sie diesem die notwendigen Informationen. Formulieren Sie ganze deutsche Sätze.
► Mediation, S. 228

○ Help

Key words
name of a country e.g. Pakistan, Bangladesh, Vietnam • clothes • working conditions • factory

D | Practice

D1 Who is to blame?

Before listening

1
P

Look at the picture and describe the situation. ▶ Fotos und Illustrationen, S. 211

While listening

Exam 2
R
◉ A2.22

Hörverstehen: Hören Sie der Sprecherin zu und ergänzen Sie die folgenden Aussagen auf Deutsch. ▶ Hörverstehen, S. 196

1. Die Herstellung von Konfektionskleidung in Bangladesch hat …
2. Diese Branche beschäftigt heutzutage …
3. Den größten Anteil der Belegschaft bilden …
4. Die Fabrikgebäude sind nicht geeignet für …
5. Es sind schon mehrere schwere Unglücke passiert, weil …
6. Weitere ungelöste Probleme in der Textilindustrie sind …
7. Auf dem Weg zur Arbeit sah die Kommentatorin, dass die Bekleidungsgeschäfte …
8. Die Ware stammte aus …
9. Mit ihrem letzten Satz möchte die Kommentatorin ausdrücken, dass sich das Verbraucherverhalten …

After listening

3 Check the clothes and shoes that you are wearing to find out where they were produced.

4 Point out why most of your clothes and shoes come from these places although high transport costs are involved.

5 By referring to the podcast point out who you feel is responsible for the poor situation of the workers in Asia.

D2 Helping the poor in the Third World

1
P

Describe and analyze the cartoon.
○ Help ▶ F 4, p. 126 ▶ Karikaturen, S. 214

"OF COURSE I SUPPORT POOR CHILDREN. THAT'S WHY I BOUGHT THIS DRESS, HANDMADE BY A 12-YEARS OLD INDIAN GIRL THAT EARNS ONLY 30 CENTS A DAY."

Basic course > **Advanced course** > Exam course   Living and working in a globalized world | **Unit 9**

D3 Emerging markets: India

Before watching

1 Interview each other to find out what you already know about India. Tell the class about your findings.

While watching

2  Watch the film and find the missing information.
▶ Hör-Seh-Verstehen, S. 197

1. Name of India's software giant
2. Number of employees 12 years ago
3. Number of employees today
4. Facilities for employees
5. India has the … largest software industry.
6. The female interviewee has a … job at the company.
7. Increasing numbers of young … are coming to India.
8. Eric now works in India for …
9. He is already doing …
10. Statement by the Indian businessman: "The future …

D4 What does globalization mean to us?

> Globalization enables countries to move closer to each other. People
> from different countries are able to live and work together. Companies
> and organizations can cooperate more easily. We can exchange goods,
> money and ideas faster and more cheaply than ever before. Modern
> 5 communication and technology, like the Internet, mobile phones or
> satellite TV help us in our daily lives. Globalization means that there is free
> movement of people, goods, money and ideas.

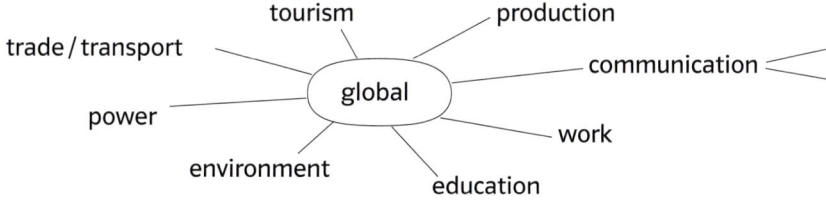

1 P Complete the word web using information from this unit and your own ideas. Think of positive and negative aspects of globalization. ○ Task ▶ F 5, p. 126

2 P Work in groups. Prepare a presentation about the advantages and disadvantages of globalization. Use the information you have found out above and any other ideas you may have. Then give your presentation in class.

Exam 3 P **Materialgestützter Aufsatz:** "The world is getting smaller." Use the information you have got so far and your own ideas to write a composition.
▶ Materialgestützter Aufsatz, S. 199

123

E | Reading +: We are the change!

Before reading

1 Describe the photo. What do you think the woman wants to express by the slogan?

Understanding the text

2 Read the text below and do the following tasks.
○ Task ▶ F 6, p. 127; ▶ Leseverstehen, S. 199

1. Explain the difference between fast fashion and slow fashion.
2. Point out the arguments against fast fashion given in the text.
3. Describe the aims of the management of *Arthur & Henry*.
4. Explain the quotation: "Fashion goes out of fashion. Style never."

Exam 3 **Mediation:** Sie wollen Ihre Freunde davon überzeugen, nicht ständig dem Trend nach billiger neuer Mode hinterherzulaufen. Führen Sie dazu anhand des Textes die Argumente an, die für einen nachhaltigen Umgang mit Kleidung sprechen. ▶ Mediation, S. 228

Not all Asian clothing factories are unethical

I've written a lot recently [...] about the slow but steady resurgence of the British fashion manufacturing industry. This rise has coincided with news of disasters, exploitation and abuse
5 of workers in clothing factories in Asia. [...]
   But there are those who produce products in Asia who are genuinely concerned about ethics and sustainability, about worker welfare and environmental issues. To consider this side
10 of the issue I contacted Clare Lissaman, the co-founder and director of *Arthur & Henry*, a business selling shirts and cotton scarves which have been ethically-made in India. "A couple of years ago we sat in a pub garden and tried to
15 write down what an 'ethical fashion business' would entail," she says. "It got complicated, backs of envelopes were used and everything. "They found that there were many questions that would need to be considered. Lissaman
20 continues: "Was local production ethically superior to distant production? The carbon footprint of local [production] is lower, isn't it? Well, where do all the materials come from in the first place? Is it better to create a job in
25 Wales or Bangalore? What about the ethics of producing 'fast fashion' – isn't it fundamentally wrong to produce a T-shirt that is only going to be worn once before being thrown away, but what if the production of said T-shirt gives somebody a job so that they can feed their 30 children? The point here is that all too often today the job making that cheap T-shirt does not enable them to keep themselves, let alone their children."
   After much discussion, Lissaman and her 35 colleagues came to the following tentative conclusions: 1) "Fast fashion" is fundamentally wrong. Even regardless of labour standards and environmental concerns, throwing something away before it has reached the end of its useful 40 life is a waste of the earth's resource[s] and human endeavour. We all do it to a certain extent, but that doesn't make it right. 2) Fast fashion is practically wrong. The demands of the industry that requires low costs and rapid 45 turn-around times generate an industry that pays people very badly, gives them near zero job security, is damaging to the environment and leads to disasters such as the Rana Plaza building collapse in Bangladesh which killed 50 1,100 people, mainly garment workers.

So they decided that they, "would build a business based around 'slow fashion' and the spirit of Coco Chanel – 'Fashion, you see, goes out of fashion. Style never.' That business was *Arthur & Henry*. Nothing would make us happier than somebody wearing one of our shirts to the office until the cuffs start to fray, then rolling the sleeves up at the weekends, then migrating it into a gardening shirt, then finally turning it into rags. Every ounce of usefulness has been extracted from all the effort put into its production, from farmer to tailor, from miller to shop assistant."

They also decided that, when running the business, they would treat people decently. Not just the farmers who grow the cotton, or the mill workers who turn it into fabric, but everybody else who works in the business and all of their customers as well.

"Our goal isn't monochrome," says Lissaman. "Yes, success to us means making money – that, after all, is a degree of proof that what we are doing is working and sustainable – but success also comes in other forms; the money we raise for charity (1% of turnover); minimising any damage we do to the environment (our cotton is organic, our garments now GOTS* certified for the whole of their production); maximising benefit to workers.

"We treat our suppliers well, paying a decent price so they can pay decent wages. We talk with our tailors and cutters and finishers. We treat them as the skilled human beings they are, not just numbers behind a sewing machine. We produce in India because it's close to the cotton growing, the fabric weaving, but also because around a quarter of Indians live below the poverty line. They need decent work. If others copy us and join the market for ethical menswear, that, too, we shall treat as a success".

[…] Despite her strongly held views, Lissaman doesn't like to preach. "We are in the shirt business, […] let's just make some fantastic clothes and accessories […] but everybody deserves a decent life". (734 words)

*The Global Organic Textile Standard (GOTS) is the worldwide leading textile processing standard for organic fibres, including ecological and social criteria.

Quelle: David Evans, *The Guardian*, November 14, 2014, www.guardian.com.

After reading

4 Which of the comments do you agree with most? Say why.

1. If we do not buy these clothes, the workers will lose their jobs.

2. The governments in Asian countries are responsible for their citizens. They have to introduce laws which protect the workers.

3. Producers in Asia have to exploit workers because American and European fashion brands force them to produce as cheaply as possible.

4. It is our fault. The consumers can easily stop buying these clothes.

5. Most consumers in western countries buy cheap clothes because they can't afford more expensive high-quality fashion.

5 Would you personally be willing to support the idea of 'slow fashion' and buy fewer clothes which are more expensive but last longer? State your point of view and give reasons.

F | Further tasks

1 — A task 3, p. 116
R

Read the comments and match them with six of these headings.

1. We feel at home.
2. The UK benefits from immigrants!
3. Why are only white people expats?
4. I suffer from the working conditions here.
5. Black isn't beautiful in the UK.
6. Other countries make good offers, too.
7. Many people only live on benefits.
8. I don't care about prejudices.

2 — A task 3, p. 116
R

1. Describe Arzu's path in life.
2. Explain why Arzu came to Britain and why she stayed.

> **Arzu:** "Life as a female teenager in my home country was terrible. I was oppressed by my father and wasn't able to decide about my future. My father had already chosen a husband
> 5 for me but I wanted to take charge of my own life. With the help of friends I managed to flee, which was very risky. I arrived in Paris where I felt alone because I couldn't speak the language and had no family or friends there. At last I
> 10 found a job so I was able to save some money until I could start my studies at university. During my first holiday in Britain I met my husband. We got married and I stayed in London with him. Today we have two beautiful children who were born here. They are British. I have a 15 good job now and I pay taxes. I did not come to the UK for benefits – I wanted freedom and safety. You cannot imagine how important it is to live in a free country. I am glad and thankful that my children can grow up here. But I am still 20 worried that my father could find me and the children." (196 words)

3 — B task 2, p. 118
P

Prepare a short leaflet for exchange students from Britain in which you tell them about the rules at your college. Use the verbs in the box.

| let – expect – make – want – ask |

4 — D 2 task 1, p. 122
P

Describe and analyze the cartoon on p. 122. Use the words in the *Help* box.

○ Help

The cartoon shows …	elegant ladies – expensive dress – sofa – glass of champagne
The caption reads …	
The cartoonist wants to point out …	wealthy people in developed countries – good feeling – although – fraction of the money

5 — D 4 task 1, p. 123

The following phrases can help you to complete the word web.

- bad working conditions in developing countries
- chance to get to know other cultures
- jobs lost in industrialized countries
- low wages in developing countries

- bad working conditions in developing countries
- chance to get to know other cultures
- chance to study abroad / chance to work abroad
- data collected by Internet service providers
- destruction of many areas in developing countries
- access to information from all parts of the world
- international brands replace local products

- jobs lost in industrialized countries
- low wages in developing countries
- many possibilities to learn foreign languages
- big companies influence political decisions
- transport of goods / tourism increase pollution
- products from far-away countries available
- the Internet connects people all over the world

E task 2, p. 124

1. Explain the difference between fast fashion and slow fashion.
2. Point out arguments against fast fashion and say why clothes should not go into landfill sites.

Clothes join rubbish of our throwaway society

Britain has become such a throwaway society that one in three councils is now collecting clothes along with rubbish.

Caroline Lucas, the Green MP said: 'We have become a very throwaway society because the cost of things do(es) not reflect the labour or the true costs that have gone into them.'

In an age of "fast fashion", 1.5 million tons of clothes and textiles go straight into landfill sites in Britain every year. Oxfam said that 9,513 garments were thrown into landfill every five minutes, totalling one billion items per year and the equivalent of one in four garments sold. While every other type of landfill waste is reducing, textiles has risen.

The *Waste and Resources Action Programme (Wrap)*, a Government agency in charge of reducing waste, said 31 per cent of councils had now introduced collections for textile recycling, up from a handful a decade ago. The trend has been dubbed the "*Primark* effect"; however it is not just cheap clothes that are being discarded. Charity shops are receiving designer brands and good quality high street labels that have hardly been worn. Recent donations to the Trinity Hospice in Victoria, London, have included *Versace* and *Dolce and Gabanna*.

Caroline Lucas, the Green MP, said that people no longer knew how to mend clothes and it was cheaper to buy a new dress than to pay to get it mended. She urged shoppers to think about the labour and environmental impact behind clothing before buying new things and to reuse and recycle. "We have become a very throwaway society because the cost of things do(es) not reflect the labour or the true costs that have gone into them."

Safia Minney, the founder of *People Tree*, a fair trade fashion retailer, today addresses the *Telegraph Hay Festival* about the need for a return to "slow fashion", where people buy clothes to last and dispose of them responsibly. "We need to consume less fashion and wear our clothes for longer, while the fabrics and clothes we do buy need to have more 'value added' – benefiting not only the farmers but also as many artisans as possible in its transformation to clothing."

Wrap has started to encourage more councils to collect textiles for recycling. About 60 per cent of clothing sent for recycling is sold to other countries for reuse, mostly Africa and Eastern Europe, while 35 per cent is reused as mattress stuffing or insulation. Less than five per cent is of such low quality it is sent to landfill. Textile recycling is said to be worth around £250 million every year to the British economy. […] (442 words)

Quelle: Louise Gray, May 31, 2012, *The Telegraph*, www.telegraph.co.uk.

In this unit you will learn to ...
- find out about human rights, their development and their abuse.
- talk and write about various aspects of human rights.
- research civil rights and political participation in the UK.
- write a material-based composition.
- use the present and past participle.

 h7fj8p

Unit 10
International organizations and politics

A | Getting started: Our needs and our rights

Before reading

1 **P** Describe the photos above.

2 The photos show some of the basic needs of human beings. Match the photos with the appropriate words in the box. Two words do not fit. ▶ Fotos und Illustrationen, S. 211

> education – health care – clean water – shelter – clothing – nutritious food

3 These basic needs of human beings are also examples of human rights. Outline other human rights.

🌐 **Internet key words:** The Universal Declaration of Human Rights

Understanding the text

4 **R** Read the text on p. 129 and find headings for each paragraph. Then write down key words for each of the headings. ⭕ Help ▶ F1, p. 138; ▶ Leseverstehen, S. 199

128

A3.1

Are we all born equal and free?

A People's understanding of human rights is continually developing. That is why there is no universally agreed definition. However, human rights may be generally defined as those rights, which humans inherit by birth, which cannot be purchased or earned or loaned or denied and without which we cannot live as human beings. They are built on our demand for a life in dignity, respect and protection. For example, the right to have whatever you need so that you are not hungry, have clothes and a place to live not only means that every human being is entitled to enough food, clothes and shelter, but that the government has a responsibility to provide these things for its citizens.

B When talking about human rights we usually refer to values that the nations of the world have agreed upon. These have been set down in many international agreements. The most important document is the *Universal Declaration of Human Rights (UDHR)* adopted by the United Nations in 1948. The *UDHR* serves as a basis for the international protection of human rights and is a common statement of shared goals by the member states of the *UN*.

C In European law human rights are often divided into three generations: First generation human rights refer to classic human rights, e.g. rights to freedom and political participation. We should all enjoy freedom of speech and equality before the law. Second generation human rights are related to economic, social and cultural rights, for example the right to education, the right to work and the right to social security. Third generation human rights are also called solidarity rights because they cannot be applied only to individuals but must be seen collectively. The right to peace and the right to self-determination are examples of third generation human rights.

D However, the existence of the *UDHR* does not mean that human rights are not violated anymore. There are still countries where people are discriminated against because they belong to an ethnic, religious or political minority. In some countries these people are even tortured or killed. So, although the *Declaration* has great moral standing and influence it is still not really binding for many states and their governments. Nevertheless, human rights violations are monitored by the *UN* and also by non-governmental organizations (NGOs) like *Human Rights Watch* or *Amnesty International* who put pressure on governments that abuse human rights. (405 words)

---

5 Use your notes from task **4** to give a summary of the text.

 6 **Mediation:** Sie planen einen Infostand zum Thema Menschenrechte für das Sommerfest Ihrer Schule. Bereiten Sie anhand des Textes Plakate auf Deutsch vor.
▶ Mediation, S. 228

After reading

 7 Find out about one of the organizations of the UN or about an NGO on the Internet and present your results in class.

 Internet key words: UN e.g. UNESCO – UNICEF – WHO – World Food Programme, **NGOs** e.g. Human Rights Watch – Amnesty International – *Médecins sans frontières* – Oxfam

---

Facts

The United Nations
Membership: 193 member countries
Headquarters: New York City
Tasks: maintain international peace, protect human rights, deliver humanitarian aid

Non-governmental organizations (NGOs)
Organization: neither part of a government nor a profit-oriented business
Members: people who share interests which are often humanitarian

B | Grammar

B1 Human Rights Friendly Schools

1 Replace the highlighted words with a present participle (ing-form) or past participle (third form of the verb).

Example: **A non-governmental human rights organization called *Amnesty International* has established the project "Human Rights Friendly Schools", because...**

A non-governmental human rights organization (1. which is called) ... *Amnesty International* has established the project "Human Rights Friendly Schools" because they wanted to integrate human rights and principles into all areas of school life. The students (2. who study) ... at a HR friendly school are taught on the principles of equality, respect and participation. The school curriculum (3. which includes) ... courses on human rights encourages young people to put human rights into practice every day. A project (4. which enables) ... young people to know their human rights, integrates global principles in the Universal Declaration on Human Rights into key areas of school life such as the curriculum and school environment. Students (5. who attend) ... Accra High School in Ghana have made human rights an important part of school life. After they had agreed on general aims (6. which promote) ... a democratic environment, they integrated new teaching methods and rules for responsible behaviour inside and outside the classroom. A human rights garden (7. which is maintained) by students and staff is just one example of a space where openness, tolerance and communication are supported.

B2 UNICEF

1 Rewrite the statements about *UNICEF*, a well-known aid organization for children, using participles and gerunds as in the examples.

1. Because the *UN* wanted to help children in need following World War II, they founded *UNICEF*.

    Example: **Wanting to help children in need following World War II the UN founded UNICEF.**

> **Grammar box**
>
> **Gerund**
> **Example: After speaking to me Liz went home.**
> Zur Verkürzung von Sätzen nach *after* und *before*.
> ▶ p. 197
>
> **Present participle**
> **Example: Wanting to help children she founded a new organization.**
> Zur Verkürzung von Sätzen mit *because, as, while, when*
> **Example: Every day you can see lots of people (who are) visiting the UN buildings.**
> Zur Verkürzung von Relativsätzen im Aktiv
> ▶ p. 197
>
> **Past participle**
> **Example: There are lots of restaurants (which were) built for tourists.**
> Zur Verkürzung von Relativsätzen im Passiv
> ▶ p. 197

2. After the *UN* had established the *United Nations International Children's Emergency Fund* in 1949, they could give food and clothes to children in need.

   Example: **After establishing the *United Nations International Children's Emergency Fund* in 1949, the *UN* could give food and clothes to children in need.**

3. Before *UNICEF* helped children with long-term projects, they had only carried out short-term projects, like giving them clothes and food.
4. Because *UNICEF* wanted to help children to a better life, they tried to improve their chances of a good education.
5. After they had organized projects to educate the children, *UNICEF* then started to train the teachers.
6. Because the Nobel Prize committee knew that *UNICEF* had carried out so many successful projects to help children all over the world, they gave *UNICEF* the Nobel Peace Prize in 1965.
7. As *UNICEF* saw that many children in developing countries were dying, they increased the aid given to them in the 1970s.
8. Because many children live in war zones nowadays, they need help from organizations like *UNICEF*.

B3 Food aid for Belarus

Work in pairs and complete the interview using the infinitive or the -ing form of the verb in brackets. The first examples have been done for you.

Radio Livestation has created a series called "About your neighbour". Presenter Carlo Cardoso is interviewing Rita Swanson.

Carlo: Hello and welcome to our show "About your neighbour". Today we are going to talk about **helping** (1. help) our neighbours and for that reason I have invited Rita Swanson, who has organized an aid project called "Food aid for Belarus".

Rita: Thank you for **inviting** (2. invite) me. I really want **to tell** (3. tell) your listeners about our successful aid project for Belarus and I would like **to say** (4. say) thanks for the money we were able **to collect** (5. collect).

Carlo: Before (6. tell) … us about your trip I would like (7. know) … how you got the idea of (8. help) … people in Belarus?

Rita: Well, one of my friends comes from Belarus and some of her relatives still live there. One day while (9. have) … lunch she told me about them and how the government has failed (10. help) … them. So I decided (11. collect) … money. I have always enjoyed (12. help) … people.

Carlo: How did you arrange (13. get) … the food to Belarus?

Rita: After (14. hear) … that it is difficult to take food over the border we wanted (15. avoid, drive) … there. So we decided (16. take) … money there and (17. buy) … the food in Belarus.

Carlo: You made over £ 5,000. How did you succeed in (18. get) … so much money?

Rita: Instead of just (19. tell) … people about the project I also showed them photos of smiling children who had received food aid. That worked really well. And I hope (20. be able, do) … this project again next year.

Carlo: Thank you for (21. tell) … us about your project, Rita, and good luck with it next year.

C | Reading: Human rights and mass surveillance

Exam 1 Read the task carefully. ▶ Materialgestützter Aufsatz, S. 199

Task: We all like to keep our private lives private. This is a basic human right. Discuss how mass surveillance conflicts with the human right to privacy.

2 Look at the material to get a first impression of the topic and sources.

1

CONCERN ABOUT THE GOVERNMENT'S ANTI-TERRORISM POLICIES IN THE US (%)
— Not gone far enough to protect country
— Gone too far restricting civil liberties

49, 55, 58, 47, 47, 50, 49
29, 26, 27, 32, 35, 35, 37
04 05 06 07 08 09 10 11 12 13 14 15

"Now that everyone's street is online, we're mapping interiors."

3

Mass surveillance is fundamental threat to human rights, says European report

Europe's top rights body has said mass surveillance practices are a fundamental threat to human rights and violate the right to privacy enshrined in European law.
  The parliamentary assembly of the Council of Europe says in a report that it is "deeply concerned" by the "far-reaching, technologically advanced systems" used by the US and UK to collect, store and analyse the data of private citizens. [...]
  US-UK operations encompass "numerous persons against whom there is no ground for suspicion of any wrongdoing," it adds. [...]
  It says the assembly is deeply worried by the fact that intelligence agencies have deliberately weakened internet security by creating back doors and systematically exploiting weakness in security standards and implementation. Back doors can easily be exploited by "terrorists and cyber-terrorists or other criminals", it says, calling for a greater use of encryption. [...]
  The assembly acknowledges there is a need for "effective targeted surveillance of suspected terrorists and organised criminals". But citing independent reviews carried out in the US, it says there is little evidence that mass surveillance has stopped terrorist attacks. [...] (186 words)

Quelle: Luke Harding, *The Guardian*, 26.01.2015, www.theguardian.com.

Basic course > **Advanced course** > Exam course   International organizations and politics | **Unit 10**

DER GROSSE BRUDER MACHT PAUSE

4

[…] Zum ersten Mal seit beinahe 14 Jahren können die Amerikaner am Montag mit ihren Freunden, Großeltern oder Liebhabern telefonieren, ohne dass der Staat die Verbindungsdaten automatisch abspeichert. […] Zum ersten Mal seit 2001 ist der Staat nicht allwissend. Das Weiße Haus nennt dies noch am Sonntagabend „unverantwortlich". […]

Die Geschichte dieses Sinneswandels beginnt mit Edward Snowden. Im Sommer vor zwei Jahren enthüllt der Whistleblower, wie maßlos die *National Security Agency (NSA)* Telefon und Internet überwacht. […]

Ein halbes Jahr nach den Snowden-Enthüllungen legt Präsident Obama Anfang 2014 Reformideen vor. Während er an der Spionagepraxis im Ausland kaum etwas ändert, kommt er immerhin seinen eigenen Bürgern entgegen: […] Künftig soll nicht mehr die *NSA* sämtliche Verbindungsdaten speichern, sondern die Telefongesellschaften. Möchte der Staat wissen, mit wem ein Verdächtiger telefoniert hat, muss er sich einen Gerichtsbeschluss besorgen und die Daten bei diesen Firmen anfordern. […] (142 words)

Quelle: Nicolas Richter, *Süddeutsche Zeitung*, 1. Juni, 2015, www.sueddeutsche.de.

5

"But governmental surveillance is not about the government collecting the information you're sharing publicly and willingly; it's about collecting the information you don't think you're sharing at all, such as the online searches you do on search engines … or private emails or text messages … […]"

Mikko Hyppönen, computer security expert, www.huffingtonpost.com/tedtalks, February 4, 2014.

---

3 Summarize the main ideas of each piece of information given. ○ Help ▶ F2, p. 138

Example: Material 1: The diagram shows what Americans think about government anti-terrorism policies. In 2004 …

4 Decide how relevant this information is and choose three pieces of information.

5 Analyze the material you have chosen carefully. Take notes.

Example: 2015 US survey; not enough is being done to protect the country (49%); authorities have gone too far in restricting human rights (37%)

6 Find an introduction to your composition.

Example: Whether it is carried out by the government or by private firms, surveillance has always been a controversial and emotional topic but it has become more controversial since Edward Snowden revealed …

7 Write your complete composition. Use typical phrases to introduce, connect or finish your statements. Check your text. ▶ Bindewörter, S. 237

○ **Help**

Today there is a lot of discussion about…
Today many people are worried about…
Firstly…, secondly…, finally…
In addition…
That's why…
Therefore…
On the one hand… on the other hand…
In conclusion…
All in all…
In my opinion…

D | Practice

D1 Changes in civil rights in the UK

Before listening

1 Match the dates with the developments in civil rights below.

1215 – 1776 – 1789 – 1948 – 1953

1. European Convention for the Protection of Human Rights and Fundamental Freedoms
2. French Revolution – Declaration of the Rights of Man and of the Citizen
3. Magna Carta in England (see *Facts*)
4. Declaration of Independence of the United States of America
5. United Nations – Universal Declaration of Human Rights

While listening

Exam 2 R ⊙ A3.2

Hörverstehen: Sie hören einen Radiobeitrag über die historische Entwicklung der Bürgerrechte im Vereinigten Königreich. Hören Sie aufmerksam zu und vervollständigen Sie auf Deutsch die untenstehenden Sätze mit Informationen aus dem Beitrag. ○ Help ▶ F 3, p. 139

1. Simon Rosenberg stellt sein Buch vor anlässlich des …
2. Bürgerrechte sind Rechte und Freiheiten, die …
3. Als Beispiele für Bürgerrechte nennt Rosenberg …
4. Die Bürgerrechte sollen nicht nur die Regierung davon abhalten, ihre Macht zu missbrauchen, sondern auch …
5. Statt des Grundgesetzes besitzt das Vereinigte Königreich …
6. Im Vereinigten Königreich bestehen die Bürgerrechte aus …
7. Als Beispiel für die Entwicklung eines Bürgerrechts nennt Rosenberg die Entwicklung des …
8. Bis zu Beginn des 19. Jahrhunderts war das Recht, an Wahlen teilzunehmen, abhängig von zwei Faktoren: …
9. Frauen war es erst in diesem Jahr gestattet zu wählen …
10. Momentan gibt es eine Debatte darüber, …

D2 Have your say – political participation in the UK

1 P Describe how parliamentary democracy works in the UK by referring to the chart on p. 135. ○ Help ▶ F 4, p. 139

> **Cross-cultural tips**
>
> **Prime Minister** = Head of government, but not head of state (UK, Australia)
> **Chancellor** = Head of government, but not head of state (Germany)
> **President (in a presidential system)** = Head of government and head of state (USA)
> **President (in a parliamentary system)** = Head of state, but not head of government (Germany)

Facts

Magna Carta
In 1215 King John of England agreed to this charter in order to put an end to a war between the king and some rebel barons. Most famous clause: "No man shall be arrested or imprisoned except by the judgment of their equals and by the law of the land. To no one will we sell, to no one deny or delay right or justice." Magna Carta has greatly influenced modern western democracy and can be found in documents such as the Declaration of Independence of the United States of America.

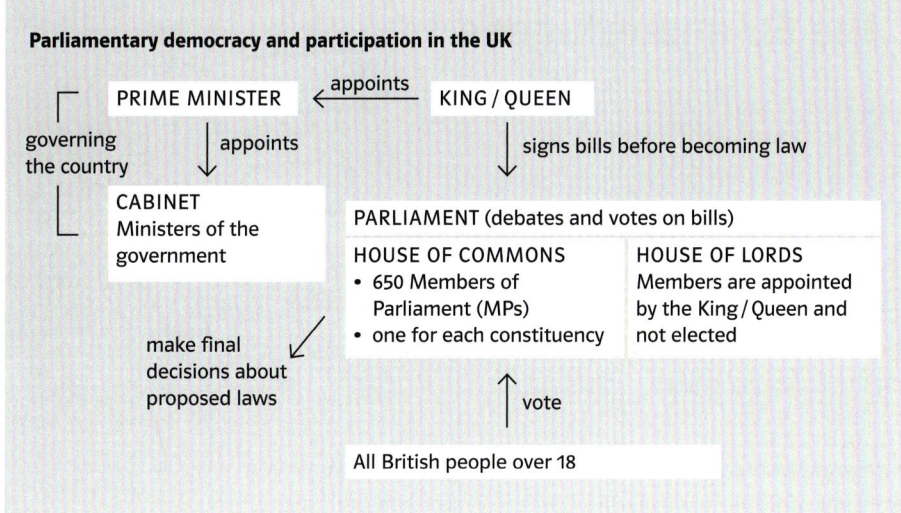

D3 Prime Minister's Question Time

Before watching

1 Describe the photo and say in what way the hall of the House of Commons and the hall of the Bundestag are different. ▶ Fotos und Illustrationen, S. 211

While watching

2 Watch the film and answer the following questions. ▶ Hör-Seh-Verstehen, S. 197

1. Who is Jeremy Corbyn?
2. Why does he thank the Speaker first?
3. What do people criticize about Prime Minister's question time and parliament?
4. What do people wish to be different in the future?
5. Why has Mr Corbyn sent an email to thousands of people?
6. How many people have replied to his email?
7. Who is the second speaker?
8. What does he think about changing Prime Minister's question time?
9. What other topic does the second speaker talk about?

After watching

3 Why do you think several MPs stand up after each speaker ends his speech?

D4 Debate – Should the voting age be lowered to 16?

1 In groups prepare for the roles of proposers and opponents. Then hold the debate. In the end vote for or against the motion. ▶ Debatte, S. 221

E | Reading +: The EU and refugees

Before reading

1 Analyze the cartoon. ▶ Karikaturen, S. 214
P

2 Explain the expression "Fortress Europe" by referring to the cartoon.

Understanding the text

3 Read the text and do the following tasks.
R ▶ Leseverstehen, S. 199

1. Describe what happened in the Mediterranean according to the text.
2. Summarize the content of the letter to David Cameron, the British Prime Minister, written by 19 charities.
3. Outline the Italian policy.
4. Describe the measures discussed at a meeting of EU ministers.
5. Point out the UN human rights chief's criticism of the EU's position.

EUROPE A FORTRESS? WHAT ARE YOU TALKING ABOUT?!
CAN'T YOU SEE – THE DOOR IS OPEN WIDE!

MIGRANT BOAT DISASTER: Leading aid and human rights groups accuse Britain of fuelling refugee crisis

19 charities have signed an open letter to David Cameron on the issue

Leading aid and human rights groups have accused Britain of fuelling the crisis which has led to mass drownings in the Mediterranean by providing no legal means for refugees to reach
5 safety and helping to build the walls of "fortress Europe".

In an open letter to David Cameron published by *The Independent*, a coalition of 19 charities calls on the UK to ensure that a fully resourced
10 search-and-rescue mission is re-established to prevent tragedies such as the deaths of at least 700 migrants off the island of Lampedusa over the weekend.

The organisations, led by the *British Refugee*
15 *Council*, *Amnesty International* and *Oxfam*, condemn Britain's failure to offer an "asylum visa" to those fleeing conflict zones such as Syria and declare that EU immigration policies have had "deadly results". They warn: "The solution can
20 never be to watch on while desperate people drown. Until safer ways to seek refuge are found,

more people will be forced into the hands of smugglers… Building the walls of fortress Europe has had deadly results." […]

Mr Cameron […] lay(s) the blame for the 25
deaths of hundreds of migrants on the capsized fishing boat on "appalling human traffickers". A Bangladeshi survivor of the disaster claimed yesterday there had been 900 on board the

vessel while Italian investigators said it
appeared that many of its passengers had been
locked inside the hull by the smugglers. [...]

As Italy and Malta announced they were
working on the rescue of up to three more
35 vessels [...] after new distress calls were
received, it emerged that the Italian authorities
are considering military action against the
traffickers. The Italian premier Matteo Renzi,
who discussed the migrant crisis with Mr
40 Cameron over the phone yesterday, is even
considering sinking the smugglers' vessels in
Libyan harbours before they can take to sea,
according to media reports.

The Foreign Secretary Philip Hammond and
45 Home Secretary Theresa May have held a
meeting of their EU opposites in Luxembourg
to discuss immediate measures to deal with
the situation in Libya. A 10-point plan to tackle
the crisis agreed by EU ministers yesterday
50 included boosting patrols with greater "financial
resources" and a systematic effort "to capture
and destroy" boats used by smugglers.

But as boats arrived in Malta and the Sicilian
city of Catania bringing the dead from Sunday's
55 disaster, high-level condemnation continued
of the EU's approach to controlling the tide of
migrants trying to reach the shores of Italy and
Greece. *Save the Children* said the death toll of
migrants in recent days should be compared
to the sinking of the Titanic and was 31 times
60 the number killed in the sinking of the Costa
Concordia.

An EU-funded, Italian-led operation, *Mare
Nostrum*, which pulled more than 150,000 people
from the Mediterranean in 2014, was replaced
65 last year with a much smaller scheme, known
as Operation Triton, amid concern that the more
comprehensive emergency cover was acting [as]
a "pull factor" for migrants. [...]

Zeid Ra'ad al-Hussein, the *UN's* human rights
70 chief, described the *EU* position as "callous" and
called on the bloc to adopt a "more courageous"
approach by opening legal channels to enable
migrants to enter. In a statement, Mr Hussein
said: "Europe is turning its back on some of the
75 most vulnerable migrants in the world and risks
turning the Mediterranean into a vast cemetery."

He added that *EU* policy consisted of "short-
sighted, short-term political reactions pandering
to the xenophobic populist movements that
80 have poisoned public opinion".

The signatories to the letter said *EU* nations
had to look again at opening their doors to
the refugee tide. The letter said: "The gloomy
backdrop to the tragedy is that there is a lack
85 of safe and legal ways for refugees to access
protection in Europe." (729 words)

Quelle: Cahal Milmo, Michael Day, *The Independent*, April 20, 2015, www.independent.co.uk.

4 Mediation: Sie möchten darüber aufklären, welche Möglichkeiten die EU hat, um in Zukunft mit der Flüchtlingsproblematik im Mittelmeer umzugehen. Fassen Sie hierzu die im Text angesprochenen möglichen Maßnahmen der EU zusammen. ▶ Mediation, S. 228

After reading

5 Materialgestützter Aufsatz: As all states of the EU have adopted the *Universal Declaration on Human Rights*, they have a responsibility to save refugees in the Mediterranean. Discuss the European migration policy taking into account the material on these two pages.
● Task ▶ F 5, p. 139 ▶ Materialgestützter Aufsatz, S. 199

F | Further tasks

A task 4, p. 128

1 Read the text on p. 129 and match the paragraphs (A–D) with the headings (1–4) and the key points (I–IV) below.

Headings
1. Violations of human rights
2. Attempt to define human rights
3. Agreement on what human rights are
4. Classification of human rights

Key points
I untouchable basic rights – government's duty – help people to live a dignified life
II division of human rights: first, second, third generation rights
III human rights violations – UN and NGO monitoring of discrimination
IV collective international agreements – adopted by majority of states in the world

C task 3, p. 133

2 Summarize the main ideas of each piece of information given. The following prompts can help you.

Help

Material 1	• concern – worry about a situation • civil liberty – a person's right to think, say and do what they want (as long as they respect others)
Material 2	• interior – the inner part of a house • to map – to make a map of • mount – used to hold the cameras
Material 3	• surveillance – watching someone • threat – possibility that s.th. unpleasant will happen • to violate – not to respect, to damage • enshrined – contained in and protected by • to encompass – to include • suspicion – feeling somebody could be guilty of a crime • deliberately – planned, done on purpose • to exploit – to make use of • implementation – carrying out, putting into practice • encryption – way to translate data into a secret code • to cite – to say or write the words of somebody else • evidence – s.th. that shows that it is true
Material 4	• irresponsible – without a sense of responsibility • whistleblower – s.o. who tells police or reporters s.th. that has been a secret • to monitor s.th. – to watch and listen to s.th. over a period of time • connection data – details about online activities or phone calls • suspect – s.o. who is believed to be guilty of a crime • court order – statement from a court to allow surveillance

D 1 task 2, p. 134

Sie hören einen Radiobeitrag über die historische Entwicklung der Bürgerrechte im Vereinigten Königreich. Hören Sie aufmerksam zu und vervollständigen Sie auf Deutsch die untenstehenden Sätze mit Informationen aus dem Beitrag.

1. Simon Rosenberg stellt sein Buch vor anlässlich des … Jahrestages der Magna Carta.
2. Bürgerrechte sind Rechte und Freiheiten, die von einem bestimmten Staat gewährleistet werden und die Teilhabe der Bürger …
3. Als Beispiele für Bürgerrechte nennt Rosenberg das Wahlrecht, persönliches Freiheitsrecht, die Freiheit der Meinungsäußerung und …
4. Die Bürgerrechte sollen nicht nur die Regierung davon abhalten, ihre Macht zu missbrauchen, sondern auch die Bürger schützen vor …
5. Während Deutschland das Grundgesetz hat, besitzt das Vereinigte Königreich keine …
6. Im Vereinigten Königreich bestehen die Bürgerrechte aus einzelnen Gesetzen und …
7. Als Beispiel für die Entwicklung eines Bürgerrechts nennt Rosenberg die Entwicklung des …
8. Bis zu Beginn des 19. Jahrhunderts war das Recht, an Wahlen teilzunehmen, abhängig von zwei Faktoren: Geschlecht und …
9. Frauen war es im Vereinigten Königreich erst in diesem Jahr gestattet zu wählen …
10. Auch heute noch entwickelt sich das Wahlrecht. Momentan gibt es eine Debatte darüber, das Wahlalter von 18 Jahren …

D 2 task 1, p. 134

Describe how parliamentary democracy works in the UK referring to the chart on p. 135.

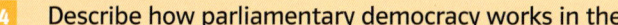

The graph shows (1) … in the UK. Citizens are allowed to vote at (2) … In elections voters elect (3) … who represent the citizens' interests in the House (4) … , one of the two chambers of the British (5) … There is one MP for each (6) … . The second chamber is the House (7) … The members of the House of Lords are not (8) … , instead they are appointed by (9) … Both chambers of the House of Parliament have debates about (10) … , which are also called (11) …, and make (12) … about those laws. The King or Queen must (13) … before they become law. The government of the UK consists of (14) … The Cabinet is appointed by (15) … and comprises all the important (16) … , e.g. Secretary of State for Defence.

E task 5, p. 137

Write a letter or e-mail to the editor of *The Independent* stating your point of view on the article about the migrant boat disaster. ▶ Leserbriefe, S. 208

Unit 11

qv66vm

Exam course:
Young people – leisure and health

A | Hörverstehen

Aufgabe 1a: Satzergänzungen

Has technology changed our children into inactive loafers?
In der Nachrichtensendung „Science at Six" wird über den Einfluss von Technologien auf das Verhalten von Kindern und Jugendlichen berichtet. Dazu wurden Menschen aus unterschiedlichen Bereichen befragt, die ihre Meinung zu dem Thema äußern.

Hören Sie den ersten zwei Beiträgen aufmerksam zu und vervollständigen Sie auf Deutsch die unten stehenden Sätze.

1. Die Mutter ist besorgt, weil …
2. Die Freizeitaktivitäten ihrer drei Kinder beschränken sich auf …
3. Der Sportlehrer glaubt, dass Technologien eingesetzt werden können, um …
4. Der Sportlehrer gibt drei Beispiele für Anwendungssoftware, nämlich …

Aufgabe 1b: Offene Fragen

Hören Sie zwei weiteren Beiträgen aufmerksam zu und beantworten Sie die unten stehenden Fragen auf Deutsch.

1. Aus welchem Grund kommen junge Patienten in die Praxis des Physiotherapeuten?
2. Welche Ursachen nennt der Physiotherapeut für die gesundheitlichen Probleme der Jugendlichen?
3. Was empfiehlt der Physiotherapeut als Gegenmaßnahme?
4. Welche sozialen Medien nutzt Marco?
5. Was meint Marco mit seiner Aussage: "It's all a matter of balance."?

B | Leseverstehen

Aufgabe 2: Mediation

In Ihrem Freundeskreis gibt es immer mehr junge Frauen und Männer, die sich Sorgen um ihre Figur machen.

Sie haben den folgenden Artikel gelesen und informieren Ihre Freunde über die dort vorgestellte Umfrage über die Entwicklungen und Gründe unter Jugendlichen, abnehmen zu wollen.

Teenage girls are skipping meals as weight anxiety soars

Two-thirds of girls in their mid-teens want to be thinner, and self-esteem continues to fall.

Two in three girls aged 14 and 15 say they want to lose weight, according to an annual survey of 78,000 teenagers, which reveals a startling increase in recent years in teenage girls who are anxious about their size.

The percentage of girls in their mid-teens who say they are overweight shot up from 56% in 2009 to 64% in 2014. Among 14- and 15-year-old males, 29% said they also wanted to slim down. A similar survey carried out in 1991 found that 54% of female pupils and 22% of males "would like to lose weight".

The Schools Health Education Unit (SHEU), which works with local authorities to monitor the health and lifestyles of pupils, said a worryingly high proportion of those girls who felt they should be slimmer were acting on their anxieties, with 17% saying they ate no breakfast and one in four (24%) missing lunch.

Dr David Regis, research manager at the SHEU, which has been carrying out mass surveys for local authorities since 1977, said: "We have looked at correlations with how these youngsters who say they want to lose weight actually eat. Are they just agonising, or taking steps to lose weight? We certainly find that they are avoiding high-calorie foods and skipping meals, which is never the best way to lose weight anyway."

Regis said he was also alarmed by the number of younger girls who were unhappy with their weight. Half (51%) of 12- and 13-year-old females said they wanted to lose weight, up from 44% in 1991. Nearly a third (31%) of 10- and 11-year-olds also said they would like to slim down, up from 26% in 1991. [...]

The survey results emerge as parts of the media and some major retailers have, once again, come under fire for promoting unrealistic and unhealthy body shapes [...]. Last week the clothes giant *Topshop* agreed to stop using very tall and skinny mannequins after Laura Berry, 25, complained on *Facebook* that they had "ridiculous" proportions. The post has attracted more than 5,000 "likes", and hundreds replied on *Topshop's Facebook* page in a sign of growing anger at the manner in which women are made to feel insecure.

The SHEU survey revealed last year that, more generally, self-esteem of teenage girls had fallen significantly since the start of the most recent economic downturn. After consistent year-on-year increases since the early 1990s in the number of young people scoring in the highest bracket of self-esteem, a sudden and dramatic change occurred after 2007. From a peak that year, when 41% of 14- and 15-year-old girls reported high self-esteem, that figure had fallen to 33%.

This year's survey shows that this trend has continued, with just 26% now evaluating themselves as having high self-esteem.

"Youngsters are feeling less comfortable in several areas of their lives, with lower self-esteem, and perhaps alongside that is less body confidence," Regis said. "It is a well rehearsed argument, but there is an over-representation in the media of a particular selection of body types and a lack of representation and celebration of more realistic and no less healthy body types."

Angela Balding, survey manager at the Schools Health Education Unit, said the evidence suggested there was a correlation with the use of social media, which may be acting as an echo chamber for existing worries.

"We mentioned last year that the rising trend of self-esteem from 1997-2007 stopped in 2008, and the figures we are seeing for high self-esteem in 2014 have fallen again since last year, especially for girls.

"The 2008 date coincides with the economic recession, so that's a plausible explanation – but we are also aware of new pressures about being online and spending so much time on social media.

"Social media can be a source of social anxiety [...]. For example, the Year 10 girls [14 and 15 years old] who spent three-plus hours messaging online were more likely to say someone they didn't know in person had asked to meet them, and they report more exposure to other undesirable online behaviours." (694 Wörter)

Quelle: Daniel Boffey, *The Guardian*, www.theguardian.com, 2 August 2015.

C | Textproduktion

Aufgabe 3: Materialgestützter Aufsatz

Write a composition about the following topic.
- Use the information of at least three of the given materials.
- Name which ones you are using.
- Make use of your own ideas.
- Do not write three separate compositions but one covering all the materials chosen.

Discuss the impact that taking drugs, smoking and drinking alcohol can have on young people's health. Present strategies outlining how their abuse can be reduced. State your point of view.

1

Keine E-Shisha unter 18 – ob mit Nikotin oder ohne

Elektrische Verdampfer mit Himbeer- und Schokogeschmack sind bei Jugendlichen beliebt. Doch auch die nikotinfreien Produkte sind gesundheitsgefährdend. Sie dürfen künftig erst ab 18 geraucht werden.

Die Bundesregierung will den Verkauf von E-Zigaretten und E-Shishas an Kinder und Jugendliche unter 18 Jahren so schnell wie möglich verbieten. Entsprechende Pläne stellten Bundesfamilienministerin Schwesig (SPD) und Bundesernährungsminister Christian Schmidt (CSU) am Donnerstag in Berlin vor. Das Verbot soll für E-Produkte mit und ohne Nikotin gelten.

E-Zigaretten und E-Shishas würden oft als gesunde Alternative zum Tabakrauchen angepriesen, sagte Schwesig. „Sie gelten als cool und angesagt. Aber selbst wenn sie nur nach Mango und Schokolade schmecken, sind sie nicht harmlos, selbst ohne Nikotin. Deshalb gehören sie nicht in Hände von Kindern und Jugendlichen und müssen verboten werden."

36 Prozent aller 12- bis 17-Jährigen haben die nikotinfreien E-Produkte schon einmal ausprobiert, etwa 534 000 [...] Mädchen und Jungen in Deutschland vernebeln sich regelmäßig mit dem vermeintlich harmlosen Dampf.

Studien des Bundesinstituts für Risikobewertung, des Deutschen Krebsforschungszentrums und der Bundeszentrale für gesundheitliche Aufklärung hätten nun aber ergeben, dass beim Dampfen sowohl von nikotinhaltigen als auch nikotinfreien E-Zigaretten Carbonylverbindungen entstehen, die Krebs auslösen könnten, sagten die Minister.

Außerdem enthielten die Aerosole von E-Zigaretten und E-Shishas feine und ultrafeine Partikel. Eine chronische Schädigung durch diese Partikel wirkt sich besonders in der Wachstumsphase aus und beeinträchtigt bei Kindern die Lungenentwicklung. [...]

Gefährlich seien die E-Produkte allein schon deshalb, weil sie einen „Gateway-Effekt" haben könnten, Kinder und Jugendliche das Rauchen also quasi „erlernen" könnten, sagte Schmidt. Er zog dabei auch Parallelen zu der Diskussion um Alcopops. Auch hier habe der süße Geschmack den Akoholgeschmack überdeckt, was die Produkte harmloser erscheinen ließ. [...]

(274 Wörter)

Quelle: Sabine Menkens, www.welt.de, 23. April 2015.

Binge drinking as a teenager can damage the brain for LIFE: Alcohol triggers changes to the regions affecting memory and learning

Teenagers who regularly drink alcohol could be doing irreparable damage to the parts of the brain that control memory and learning, scientists warn

Binge drinking as a teenager causes long-lasting changes to the regions of the brain that control learning and memory.

A new study has shown that alcohol exposure during adolescence, before the brain is fully developed, can result in abnormalities that have enduring […] effects on a person's behaviour.

And scientists warn alcohol could also slow down emotional maturity.

Dr Mary-Louise Risher, at Duke University, said: "In the eyes of the law, once people reach the age of 18, they are considered adult.

But the brain continues to mature and refine all the way into the mid 20s. It's important for young people to know that when they drink heavily during this period of development, there could be changes occurring that have a lasting impact on memory and other cognitive functions." […]

Professor Swartzwelder, added: "Something happens during adolescent alcohol exposure that changes the way the hippocampus and other regions of the brain function and how the cells actually look."

[…]

Dr Risher said this immature quality of the brain cells might be associated with behavioural immaturity.

"It's quite possible that alcohol disrupts the maturation process, which can affect these cognitive function[s] later on," she said.

"That's something we are eager to explore in ongoing studies." […]

(252 words)

Quelle: Lizzie Parry, *The Daily Mail*, www.dailymail.co.uk, 27 April 2015.

1. "Several professional athletes have wrongly taught many young Americans by example that the only way to succeed in sports is to take steroids."

US American politician

2. "It is 10 years since I used drugs or drank alcohol and my life has improved immeasurably. I have a job, a house, a cat, good friendships and generally a bright outlook. The price of this is constant vigilance because the disease of addiction is not rational."

Russell Edward Brand, English comedian and actor, www.theguardian.com, 9 March, 2013.

3. "Healthy, happy people bond with other humans. But if you can't do that because you're so traumatised by your childhood that you can't trust people, you may well bond with a drug instead."

Johann Hari, British journalist and author, www.theguardian.com, 2 January, 2015.

Whether pupils' friends or families smoke

The chart below, based on data from the Health and Social Care Information Centre, illustrates whether any of pupils' friends or family members smoked cigarettes.

Smokers pupils know, by smoking status

Whether friends or family members smoke, by age

ALL PUPILS 2012						
Friends / family smoke Age	11 years	12 years	13 years	14 years	15 years	Total
	%	%	%	%	%	%
Any friends	20	32	53	69	82	55
My boyfriend or girlfriend	1	1	3	5	9	4
Some friends of my own age	8	19	41	63	77	45
Some friends older than me	17	24	39	52	62	41
Some friends younger than me	2	4	12	24	38	18
Any family members	67	66	68	69	70	68
My mother, father or step-parent	31	31	34	32	34	32
My brother or sister	7	10	15	16	19	14
Other relatives	49	51	52	55	56	53
None of my friends / family smoke	28	26	17	12	8	17

Percentages total more than 100 because pupils could give more than one answer.

Quelle: Nach Health and Social Care Information Centre, UK.

Unit 12

Exam course:
Modern media and advertising

c559vf

A | Hörverstehen

A3.5 Aufgabe 1a: Satzergänzungen

Es haben vor Kurzem verschiedene Untersuchungen zur Nutzung der sogenannten „Neuen Medien" stattgefunden, deren Ergebnisse in einer Wissenschaftssendung im Radio präsentiert werden.

Hören Sie zwei Experten aufmerksam zu und ergänzen Sie die folgenden Aussagen in Stichworten auf Deutsch.

Expertin A
1. 74% der jungen Leute nutzen das Smartphone in der folgenden Weise: …
2. Besondere Gefahr bedeutet das folgende Verhalten: …
3. Trotzdem ziehen zwei Drittel der jungen Leute das Folgende den sozialen Medien vor: …

Experte B
4. Junge Leute gehen heute im Vergleich zu vor 10 Jahren um so viel Prozent häufiger ins Internet: …
5. Der Anteil der Erwachsenen, die das Internet nutzen, ist in dieser Zeit auf den folgenden Wert gestiegen: …
6. Dieser Anteil von Internet-Nutzern nutzt heute auch die sozialen Medien: …

Aufgabe 1b: Offene Fragen

Zwei weitere Experten äußern sich zur Mediennutzung. Hören Sie diesen aufmerksam zu und beantworten Sie die folgenden Fragen auf Deutsch.

Expertin C
1. Welches ist für junge Leute der wichtigste Grund für die Nutzung der sozialen Medien?
2. Zu welchem Zweck nutzen drei Viertel der jungen Menschen die sozialen Medien?

Experte D
3. Wie gehen etwa 70% der Internetnutzer mit ihren privaten Daten um?
4. Auf welche Weise benutzen zwei Drittel der Internetnutzer ihr Passwort?
5. Wie reagiert mehr als die Hälfte der Internetnutzer auf Nachrichten über Hacker?

B | Leseverstehen

Aufgabe 2: Mediation

Unter Ihren Freunden ist eine Diskussion über mögliche Gefahren der sozialen Medien entbrannt.
Sie haben den folgenden Artikel gelesen und informieren Ihre Freunde anhand des Beispiels von Ellie Nudd über die Formen und die Folgen des Mobbings in den sozialen Medien.

CYBERBULLYING: How anonymous attacks changed me for ever

Caught in the web: Ellie Nudd was 17 when she joined a social networking site. She made a profile, and then her torment began.

Ellie Nudd was a typical teenager, studying for A-levels in English, sociology and business in her hometown of Colchester. Now aged 21, she describes her younger self as "open and trusting", someone who found it easy to make friends.

Soon after joining the social networking site *Formspring* at the age of 17, she recalls, all that changed: "At the time, it was the latest site; everyone at my school had it. It was one of those sites where you can make your profile public or private, and comments can be made anonymously or you can leave your name."

She made a profile, which anyone could see. It was, she says, the start of a period of bullying that would scar her life for ever. "In the beginning, it was comments about my appearance. These were public comments that everyone could see: they wrote about how I looked, where I worked. They knew what car I drove, they knew everything about me."

The scariest part, she reflects four years later, was "this was clearly [being done by] someone I knew, but I knew nothing about them".

With the anonymity the site gave her abuser or abusers, Ellie had no way of knowing if it was a so-called friend or people she worked with. "It could have been anyone; it was obvious it was someone I was seeing every day."

Over a period of months, Ellie adds, "it escalated to death threats. Towards the end, the messages were very aggressive and personal. They were kind of stalkerish, too, pointing to other comments I'd made on a different networking site, or for instance if I drove over a bridge one day they would write, 'Next time you cross that bridge, you're going to crash.'"

The impact on her life was devastating. "It followed me everywhere. I'm not saying [online bullying] is worse than any other kind of bullying, but if you're being bullied face to face, you can at least get away from it at home."

At the time, Ellie was "too embarrassed" to tell her family what was happening. "It sounds silly, but I felt like I must have done something wrong to deserve it. It is hard to say to someone, 'I'm being bullied and I need help.'

"I didn't tell my family for a long time, but my friends obviously saw the comments with their own eyes. It was difficult for them; at first, they would say 'it's just words'. But it's not as simple as that. That was the most frustrating thing that everyone around me didn't seem to understand."

Ellie says the whole time this was going on she never engaged with the bullies, and yet they carried on. Why did she not just stop looking at the comments? Or leave the site altogether? "Because it was a public site, others could still see the messages being left. I had to keep looking at the site, I couldn't stop. To tell a 17-year-old to stop using a social network, it's not going to happen. For me, it was impossible. Weird as it sounds, I wanted to see it. Everyone else could read it; I wanted to see it, too."

The reverberations of the abuse, Ellie recalls, were widely felt: "It really affected my concentration; there were times in class when I was very emotional and couldn't focus. I couldn't trust anyone." She felt "frustrated" and "angry" that these people thought they could harass her with total impunity. "They knew they could get away with it."

Finally, after several months of fearing for her life, Ellie went to the police. "They took over my profile, and for my own wellbeing they told me to stop using the site. Since then my account has been shut down." Yet the police were never able to find out who was responsible. "In the site's terms and conditions, it said [the owners] would release the names [of anyone making salacious comments], but because it was a foreign company [who owned the site], the British police couldn't get any response from them."

Even now, Ellie says, not knowing who was behind the cyberbullying "still influences the way I look at the world and how I view new people who come into my life".

"Four years ago, I was very open to meeting new people, and I found it easy to talk to people and get to know them. Now I'm very closed off and guarded. I've got a very close circle of people around me, but I find it hard to trust and open up to new people."

Ellie has just finished a degree in Criminology and is about to start her master's. She still uses social networking sites, but has learnt to keep them "really private".

"Now I know exactly who is in my network. It is not something you ever really get over. It takes only seconds to type something on a computer, but for those on the other side it sticks with you for the rest of your life." (871 Wörter)

Quelle: Charlotte Philby, *The Independent*, 10 August 2014, http://www.independent.co.uk.

C | Textproduktion

Aufgabe 3: Materialgestützter Aufsatz

Write a composition about the following topic.
- Use the information of at least three of the given materials.
- Name which ones you are using.
- Make use of your own ideas.
- Do not write three separate compositions but one covering all the materials chosen.

Many people say that advertising that targets children and teenagers should be banned on TV and radio, as well as on social media. Discuss the pros and cons of a ban and state your point of view.

1

WIE GEFÄHRLICH WERBUNG FÜR KINDER IST

Viele Eltern fürchten, dass Werbung gefährlich für Kinder ist. Aber Werbung und Kinder muss nicht zu Konflikten führen, wenn die Eltern den Kindern helfen, Werbung und Wirklichkeit zu unterscheiden.

Kinderwerbung verbieten?
Stefan Aufenanger, Professor für Medienpädagogik an der Uni Mainz, hält dagegen: „In Deutschland wird die Wirkung von Werbung überschätzt", sagt er. Natürlich weckt die Werbung Wünsche; nicht nur bei Kindern. Das ist schließlich Zweck des Ganzen. Die Hersteller geben jährlich mehr als 20 Milliarden Euro aus, damit wir glauben, ihre Produkte würden uns froh oder schlank machen. Das ist nicht immer ganz ehrlich und manchmal irreführend. „Aber beschützen müssen wir unsere Kinder davor nicht.", sagt Aufenanger. Eher aufkären.

„Kinder stehen Werbebotschaften umso kritischer gegenüber, je mehr sie darüber wissen, was Werbung will und mit welchen Tricks sie arbeitet." Statt also Werbung zu verteufeln, sollten wir sie als das sehen, was sie ist: ein Teil unserer Kultur, der unsere Welt bunt macht. Wenn Werbung gut gemacht ist, finden wir sie lustig, ist sie schlecht, finden wir sie langweilig. Dann ist ihr Einfluss aber gleich null. Das wissen die Werber und geben sich daher Mühe, Werbung zu erfinden, die uns anspricht.

Dabei sind Kinder als Zielgruppe besonders interessant, schließlich sind sie nicht nur die Kunden von morgen. […]

Problem: versteckte Werbung
Um mit Werbung umgehen zu lernen, müssen Kinder sie erst einmal erkennen. Bei Fernsehspots schaffen das schon Sechsjährige, sagt Stefan Aufenanger. Dabei helfen das laute „Jetzt kommt Werbung!" das die Spots im Kinderprogramm ankündigt und das Verschwinden des Senderlogos oben rechts in der Ecke des Bildschirms. […]

Problematisch findet Stefan Aufenanger Werbeformen, die uns auf den ersten Blick gar nichts verkaufen wollen. Zum Beispiel werden Computerspiele von Firmen gesponsert, deren Produkte dann darin vorkommen. „Bei den Autorennen fahren längst echte Automarken mit, bei Sportspielen ist die Bandenwerbung im Stadion echt", sagt Aufenanger. „Die Werbung ist so subtil, dass auch Erwachsene sie oft nicht durchschauen. Aber die Marken prägen sich ein."

Auch werden viele der von Kids begehrten Klamotten erst zu „Must-Haves" weil Promis sie tragen. „So werden Sachen ohne Kampagne cool", so der Professor.

(350 Wörter)

Quelle: www.familie.de

"Actually, Mama was her third word. *Buy Now* were her first two."

Marketing and advertising to children

In today's complex commercial world, children are increasingly recognized and behaving as an independent consumer group. With discretionary income to spend and influence on family purchases, children are a market force on the rise and consequently, a target audience for marketing and advertisements. [...]

5 Child- and youth-targeted marketing is more than just commercials in traditional media channels. Children today have access to countless media outlets that are far more difficult to monitor than radio or television. Marketing to children has expanded to include messaging at points of sale, children's clubs, sporting events, concerts, websites, social networking sites and even in schools. Marketing messages may introduce children to
10 inappropriate content like violence, sexualization and unrealistic body images. [...]

Marketing and advertising to children and young people can be an important aspect of a business strategy, yet children's rights such as the right to health, the right to non-discrimination or the right to be protected, must be at the core of considering any such marketing and advertising campaign. Unfortunately, self-regulatory initiatives are
15 insufficient to guarantee that the impact of advertising on children is not harmful, which is why complementary action by governments and international organizations is important.

It is only by working together and combining the efforts of governments, business and other stakeholders that we can start shaping marketing and advertising practices as a positive contribution for our children today and future generations. (250 Wörter)

Quelle: Bo Viktor Nylund, senior adviser, corporate social responsibility at UNICEF, www.theguardian.com.

4

1 "Doing business without advertising is like winking at a girl in the dark. You know what you are doing, but nobody else does."

Steuart Henderson Britt, author, *New York Herald Tribune*, October 30, 1956.

2 "Almost all children under 11 depend on their parents for money. So advertising makes heavy use of "pester power", as it is more effective than targeting parents directly. Yet a civilised society should require advertisers to sell to parents, not to children."

Jonathan Kent, co-founder *Leave Our Kids Alone*, www.telegraph.co.uk, April 11, 2013.

5

Marketing to college students

The chart below, based on data from *Barnes & Noble College Marketing*, illustrates the advertising methods that college students believe they are most influenced by.

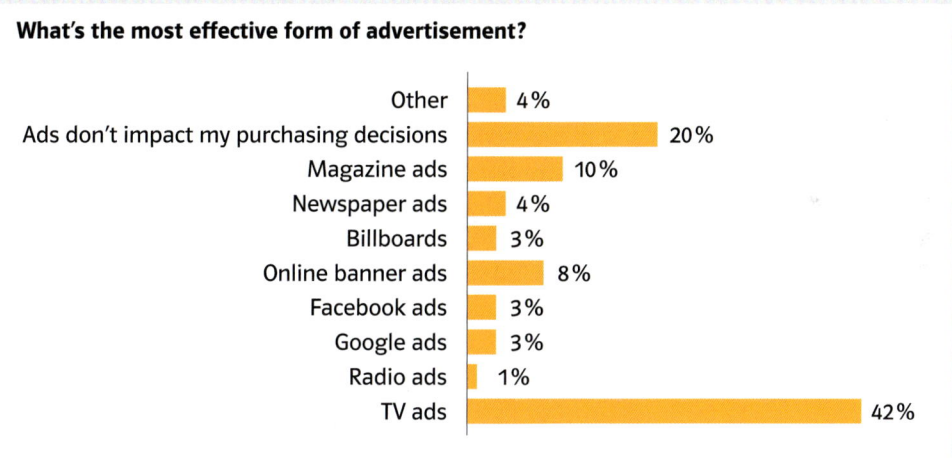

What's the most effective form of advertisement?

Category	Percentage
Other	4%
Ads don't impact my purchasing decisions	20%
Magazine ads	10%
Newspaper ads	4%
Billboards	3%
Online banner ads	8%
Facebook ads	3%
Google ads	3%
Radio ads	1%
TV ads	42%

Quelle: Nach www.bncollegemarketing.com.

Unit 13

Exam course:
Young people and society

n8iy9q

A | Hörverstehen

A3.7 Aufgabe 1a: Offene Fragen

Vor kurzem sind in den britischen Medien verschiedene Programme über die Situation junger Menschen in Großbritannien ausgestrahlt worden.
Hören Sie den Sprechern zu, die jeweils ihre persönlichen Erfahrungen präsentieren, und bearbeiten Sie die folgenden Aufgaben in Stichpunkten auf Deutsch.

1. Nennen Sie zwei Personengruppen, die insbesondere von Adam erwähnt werden, weil sie nicht wissen, wie es in den Armenvierteln aussieht.
2. Nennen Sie fünf von Adam erwähnte Verbrechensarten, die häufig in den ärmeren Vierteln vorkommen.
3. Erläutern Sie laut Adam drei Tätigkeiten, die junge Menschen in solchen Vierteln aus Langeweile tun.
4. Nennen Sie laut Rachel die drei Vorurteile, die die meisten Menschen haben, wenn sie über Obdachlose reden.
5. Beschreiben Sie die Heime, in denen Obdachlose wohnen.
6. Geben Sie laut Rachel zwei Gründe, warum junge Menschen obdachlos werden.

Basic course > Advanced course > **Exam course**　　　　　　　　　　　Young people and society | **Unit 13**

⊙ A3.8　**Aufgabe 1b: Satzergänzungen**

Radio Newcastle hat Teenager zum Thema „Junge Menschen in der Gesellschaft"
ins Studio eingeladen.
Hören Sie aufmeksam zu, was Alexandra sagt und vervollständigen Sie auf Deutsch
die unten stehenden Sätze. Entnehmen Sie den Aussagen je zwei Aspekte.

1. Laut Alexandra meinen die meisten Menschen bezüglich Studenten, dass sie …
2. Die Tatsache, dass viele Firmen in Nordengland schließen, hat eine negative
   Auswirkung auf die Studenten dort, weil …
3. Langfristig ist Alexandra der Meinung, dass ärmere Studenten besonders
   benachteiligt sind, da …

B | Leseverstehen

Aufgabe 2: Mediation

Unter Ihren Freunden ist eine Diskussion über die Rechte der Menschen mit
Behinderungen in der Gesellschaft entbrannt.
Sie haben den folgenden Artikel gelesen und informieren Ihre Freunde anhand des
Beispiels von Sarah Merriman über die Kampagne der jugendlichen Behinderten in
Großbritannien.

Young people with disabilities campaign for the right to learn

In June, my daughter attended a
demonstration outside the houses of
parliament. Sarah, who has Down's
syndrome, travelled by coach from
5　Somerset with fellow students and staff
from her college, where she met 80 other
young people to launch a campaign
highlighting the need for educational
equality for people with disabilities.
10　　Sarah has been lucky. Having been
well supported by the London borough
of Haringey, she attended a mainstream
school, a sixth-form college and recently
graduated from Foxes Academy – a
15　residential catering college and training
hotel for young people with learning
disabilities. She hopes to become a
waitress. But not every young person
with physical or learning disabilities is so
20　fortunate; many face a postcode lottery,
particularly when it comes to post-16
education.
　　There are about 70 specialist further
education colleges in the UK – most offering
residential care – but places can cost more　25
than £30,000 a year, and over £150,000 for
students with complex needs. Many young
people and their families face a long battle
to secure funding for their child to attend
such a college – particularly (as is often the　30
case) when the one that best serves their
needs is in another local authority.
　　Young people with physical or learning
disabilities face particular challenges and
difficulties with education and employment.　35
While it may be possible for them to work
and live independently, they sometimes
take longer to learn new skills and need
support in doing so. Specialist colleges do
a huge amount of work in helping young　40

people to prepare for the next steps in their lives.

During her three years as a student at Foxes Academy, Sarah worked in the training hotel, learning skills such as food hygiene, housekeeping and cooking, while living independently in supported housing with seven other "learners". She is aware she has been lucky, and now wants to help other young people in her situation.

That is why Sarah and her friends are supporting the A Right Not a Fight campaign, which calls for students with a physical or learning disability to have the choices most young people take for granted – such as choosing a further education college that best meets their needs. The idea for the campaign was developed by a group of student representatives who attend specialist colleges. […]

While the aspirations of the Children and Families Act – greater educational choice for students with a learning difficulty or disability, encouragement of education, up to the age of 25, and closer working between health, education and social care professionals – are spot on, those working in the sector fear recent changes to funding arrangements for school-leavers with high levels of need will prevent young people and their families from making the most of the opportunities promised. […]

Sarah and her friends do not want to be reliant on benefits. They want, like everyone else, to be given the chance to prove themselves in the workplace. And this is deeply embedded in the ethos of Foxes Academy, where 88% of learners have found employment on leaving and 85% are living semi-independently. […]

We have come a long way from the days when children with Down's syndrome were written off at birth, denied an education when children and deprived of some medical interventions as adults. As Sarah's experience has shown, there is now the opportunity of a life fulfilled, and specialist colleges have a vital role to play. They empower young people with learning difficulties or disabilities to take control of their lives – particularly in the residential setting where living away from home prepares them for life beyond the family home. This arrangement is, after all, the norm for most university students in halls of residence and shared houses.

Apart from the experience of living communally and making many friends, Sarah has also found love at Foxes – her long-term boyfriend, Daniel, who has autism, is a delightful young man and a true athlete. He has been selected for the Great Britain's Special Olympic cycling team. […]

It was impossible not to be moved by the dignity, confidence and earnestness of the students outside Westminster as they talked proudly of their achievements and their hopes for the future. […] (695 Wörter)

Quelle: Andy Merriman, *The Guardian*, www.theguardian.com, 19 August 2014.

C | Textproduktion

Aufgabe 3: Materialgestützter Aufsatz

Write a composition about the following topic.
- Use the information of at least three of the materials.
- Name which ones you are using.
- Make use of your own ideas.
- Do not write three separate compositions but one covering all the materials chosen.

There has been a lot of discussion about developments in racial equality in the United States over the last fifty years, and how things have changed for young people in particular.

Discuss the situation in the United States and state your point of view.

1

USA: Abschied vom Traum einer postrassistischen Gesellschaft

LZ Granderson fühlte sich schmerzlich in die sechziger Jahre zurückversetzt, als er zu Beginn der Woche die Bilder aus der Kleinstadt Ferguson im US-Bundesstaat Missouri
5 sah. […] Der afroamerikanische Kommentator für den Nachrichtensender CNN war nicht der Einzige in den USA, der während der Ereignisse der vergangenen Tage an die schwersten Zeiten des Kampfes für Bürger-
10 rechte für schwarze Amerikaner vor fast 50 Jahren denken musste. Nach dem Tod des unbewaffneten schwarzen Jugendlichen Michael Brown durch eine Polizeikugel am vergangenen Sonntag macht sich in Ame-
15 rika zunehmend das Gefühl breit, dass sich an der Lage der Schwarzen im Land seit den Tagen von Martin Luther King fundamental nichts geändert hat. […]

    Offiziell ist die Ursache von Browns Tod
20 noch nicht geklärt. Die beteiligten Polizisten behaupten, eine Pistole sei während eines Handgemenges der Beamten mit Brown versehentlich losgegangen. Dorian Johnson, der Freund und Begleiter Browns an jenem
25 Abend, hat jedoch eine dramatisch andere Version der Ereignisse. […] als ein Beamter dann versuchte, Brown in den Polizeiwagen zu zerren, riss dieser sich los und begann

wegzulaufen. Daraufhin eröffnete der Poli-
30 zist, dessen Identität bislang nicht preisgegeben wird, das Feuer. Als Brown von den tödlichen Schüssen getroffen wurde, habe er laut Johnson bereits die Arme in die Luft gestreckt gehabt, um sich zu ergeben.

    Die Demonstrationen in Ferguson und in
35 den gesamten USA, wo sich auf den Straßen vieler Städte der Zorn über den Vorfall Bahn bricht, neigen offensichtlich dazu, Johnsons Version zu glauben. Und das aus gutem Grund: Allein die Ereignisse der vergange-
40 nen Wochen zeigen einen tief verwurzelten institutionellen Rassismus der amerikanischen Ordnungskräfte. […] (264 Wörter)

Quelle: Sebastian Moll, New York, *Zeit online*, www.zeit.de, 30. Juli 2015.

Ferguson, 11 days on: "We're sitting on a powder keg"

The killing of Michael Brown by a police officer in Ferguson has sparked violent confrontations and shattered any illusions of racial harmony in Barack Obama's US. [...]

The notion may have taken hold among some elites on America's coasts and European capitals that the US led by Barack Obama has entered some kind of cheerful post-racial era; that the new challenge, after the great recession, is colour-blind income inequality. Yet 50 years after the passage of the Civil Rights Act, and six after the election of the first African-American US president, hundreds of young black men this month have taken to the streets of a midwestern suburb to deliver a cathartic roar against the overwhelmingly white authorities that they blame not only for murdering their friend, but for ruining their lives.

Brown, who was unarmed, was shot dead by Officer Darren Wilson, who is white, in sharply disputed circumstances. [...]

The complaints of young black men in Ferguson are borne out painfully by the official statistics. Figures published last year by Missouri's attorney general showed that seven black drivers were stopped by police in the town for every white driver, and that 12 times as many searches were carried out on black drivers as white, despite searches of white people being far more likely to turn up something illegal. [...]

The penalties issued for minor offences uncovered during these stops make up almost a quarter of the town's annual revenues, leading to resentment that poorer residents are being milked to fund the salaries of white bureaucrats. [...]

It matters that the authorities imposing this regime do not resemble the community they police. While the town's population is 67% black, 50 of Ferguson's 53 police officers – 94% – are white. Ferguson is led by a white mayor, James Knowles, who since the crisis erupted has relentlessly defended his police officers. Five of the city's six councillors are white and only one is black. [...] (327 words)

Quelle: *The Guardian*, www.theguardian.com, 20 August 2014.

---

1. "At the heart of the problem of racism is the fact that the United States is a racially divided nation where extreme racial inequality continues to persist."

Jonathan Kozol, Savage *Inequalities: Children in America's Schools*, NY: Crown Publishers, 1991.

2. "Hip-hop has done more than any leader, politician or anyone to improve race relations. This generation is the least racist generation."

Jay-Z (musician, rapper), *Best Life* magazine, March 20, 2009.

What do you do to mark Martin Luther King Jr. Day?

4

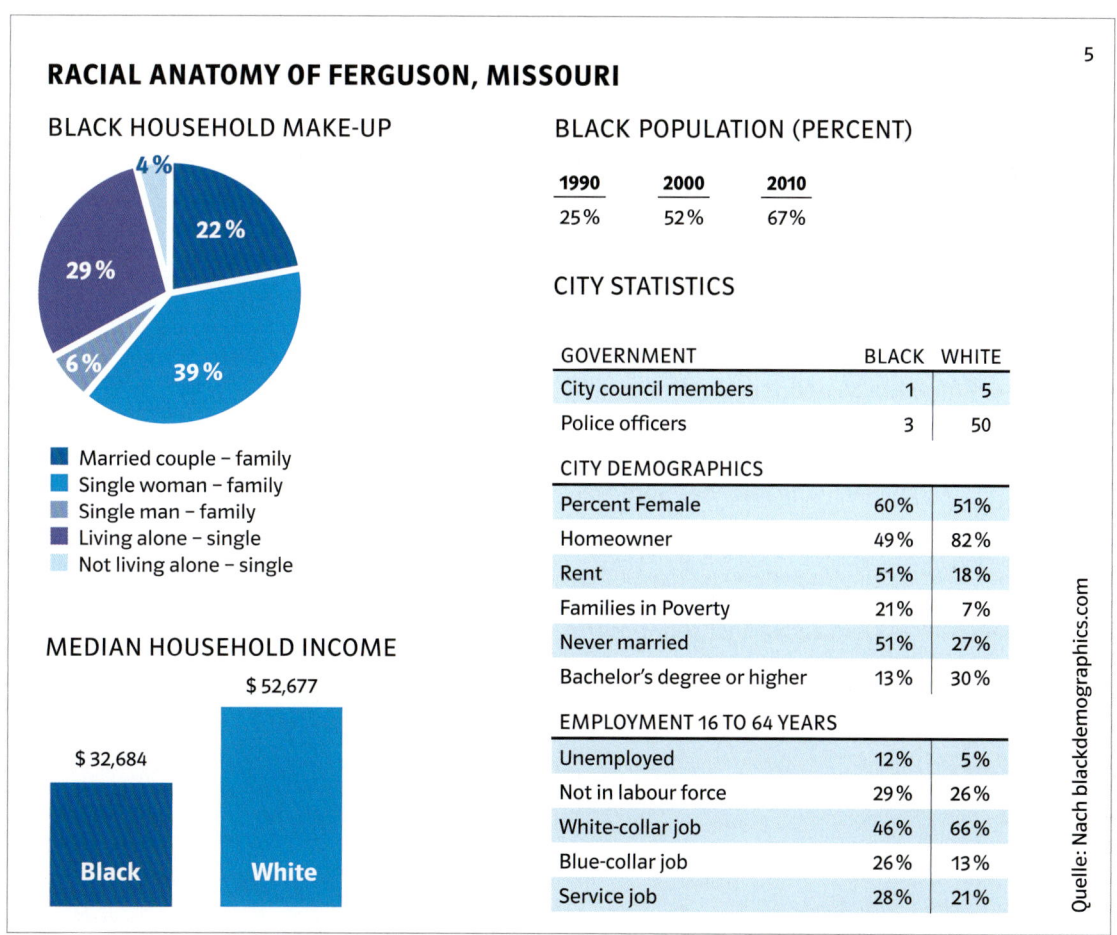

5

RACIAL ANATOMY OF FERGUSON, MISSOURI

BLACK HOUSEHOLD MAKE-UP

- 39 % Married couple – family
- 22 % Single woman – family
- 6 % Single man – family
- 29 % Living alone – single
- 4 % Not living alone – single

BLACK POPULATION (PERCENT)

1990	2000	2010
25 %	52 %	67 %

CITY STATISTICS

GOVERNMENT	BLACK	WHITE
City council members	1	5
Police officers	3	50

CITY DEMOGRAPHICS		
Percent Female	60 %	51 %
Homeowner	49 %	82 %
Rent	51 %	18 %
Families in Poverty	21 %	7 %
Never married	51 %	27 %
Bachelor's degree or higher	13 %	30 %

EMPLOYMENT 16 TO 64 YEARS		
Unemployed	12 %	5 %
Not in labour force	29 %	26 %
White-collar job	46 %	66 %
Blue-collar job	26 %	13 %
Service job	28 %	21 %

MEDIAN HOUSEHOLD INCOME

- Black: $ 32,684
- White: $ 52,677

Quelle: Nach blackdemographics.com

Unit 14

Exam course:
Technology, energy and environment

3qa8uw

A | Hörverstehen

A3.9 Aufgabe 1a: Satzergänzungen

In einem Bericht im Radio wird über eine aktuelle Kampagne zum Umweltschutz berichtet. Dabei kommen auch einige der Aktivisten zu Wort.

Hören Sie aufmerksam zu und vervollständigen Sie auf Deutsch die unten stehenden Sätze. Entnehmen Sie den Aussagen je zwei Aspekte.

Sprecher	1. Nach Angaben des Sprechers haben sich die Demonstranten versammelt, um …
Junge Frau	2. Die junge Frau ist der Überzeugung, dass …
Älterer Mann	3. Der Landwirt ist sehr besorgt, denn …

Basic course > Advanced course > **Exam course** Technology, energy and environment | **Unit 14**

🔊 A3.10 **Aufgabe 1 b: Offene Fragen**

In einer Reportage hören Sie zwei weitere Aktivisten, die ihre Teilnahme an der Kampagne zum Umweltschutz begründen. Hören Sie ihnen aufmerksam zu und bearbeiten Sie auf Deutsch die unten stehenden Aufgaben.

Ältere Frau
1. Nennen Sie zwei von dieser Frau angesprochene Auswirkungen des Klimawandels insbesondere auf Entwicklungsländer.

Junger Mann
2. Erläutern Sie drei Aspekte in den Ansichten des jungen Mannes, die unsere Verantwortung für den Schutz der Umwelt deutlich machen.

B | Leseverstehen

Aufgabe 2: Mediation

Sie sind Mitglied einer Umweltgruppe in Ihrer Heimatstadt. Sie haben den Zeitungsbericht über das *Global Apollo Programme* gelesen und stellen die wesentlichen Informationen dieses Berichts für Ihre Gruppe schriftlich zusammen.

Plan launched to prevent critical climate change by making green energy cheaper than coal

[…] Scientists and economists have joined forces to launch a global research initiative to make green energy cheaper than coal within 10 years, a target they believe is
5 critical to avoid dangerous climate change. They have compared the goal to the Apollo programme of the 1960s when the United States stated that it would put a man on the Moon by the end of the decade.
10   Leading academics […] said that the world cannot be saved from global warming unless coal – the dirtiest fossil fuel – is put out of business. They have called the plan the Global Apollo Programme and hope
15 to recruit countries from around the world in an international commitment to boost research and development into key areas of renewable energy, storage and electricity transmission.

20   By 2025, they hope the research will mean that wind, solar and other forms of green energy will be able to undercut the cost of burning coal to generate power, making it feasible to keep within the critical
25 2C* increase in global temperatures needed to prevent dangerous climate change.
    "It all starts with this climate-change risk we're facing. It's a looming catastrophe that I think can be avoided," said Sir David, one
30 of the architects of the programme who has been a long-term advocate of moving away from fossil fuels towards a "decarbonised" economy.
    "This is a massively important global
35 opportunity and we need to commit ourselves to action," Sir David said at the programme's launch yesterday at the Royal Society in London. "To stay below 2C is

*2 degrees Celsius

going to be very challenging. We need to treat this as an extremely urgent problem. If we delay the progress towards that required pathway it will become far more painful to do so in the future," he added.

The Global Apollo report [...] states that there is a "shocking underspend" on global research and development aimed at renewable energy – amounting to just 2 per cent of total global public funding on research. This needs to be boosted from $6bn (£4bn) a year to at least $15bn a year, the report says.

This would amount to each participating country spending 0.02 per cent of its gross domestic product in order to join the Global Apollo consortium and reap the fruits of the research, said Lord Layard, emeritus professor of economics at the London School of Economics.

"This challenge is at least as big as the challenge of putting a man on the Moon .... We believe that is an absolute minimum to crack this problem. The good news is that we are seeing this technological progress. The bad news is that it's simply not fast enough," Lord Layard said.

Lord Stern, who headed a major government review into the economics of climate change, said that the current cost of coal is about $50 a ton, although the true costs in terms of environmental damage and impact in human health is probably nearer to $200 a ton.

The next 20 years will see major changes to the way people around the world live, which presents problems as well as opportunities for new technological breakthroughs that will make renewable energy more competitive, Lord Stern said. "How we build our cities and our transport, and how we build our energy systems over the next 20 or so will fundamentally determine our chances of holding to within 2C," he said. "This is an idea whose time has come. Indeed this is an idea that cannot be postponed."

World leaders agreed in 2010 that it was important to limit global temperature increases to 2C which would mean keeping atmospheric carbon dioxide concentrations to within 450 parts per million.

However, the burning of fossil fuels, and coal-fired power stations in particular, has resulted in carbon dioxide emissions continuing to increase, with concentrations reaching 400ppm with no signs of abating. Meanwhile, global energy demands are expected to rise by a further third by 2035.

"The average temperature is already 0.8C above the pre-industrial level," the Global Apollo report says.

"If it rises to over 2C above that level, there will be serious environmental consequences for billions of people – including increased droughts, floods and storms. Millions will lose their livelihood and have to migrate," it says. [...] (710 words)

Quelle: Steve Connor, *The Independent*, www.independent.co.uk, June 2 2015.

C | Textproduktion

Aufgabe 3: Materialgestützter Aufsatz

Write a composition about the following topic.
- Use the information of at least three of the given materials.
- Name which ones you are using.
- Make use of your own ideas.
- Do not write three separate compositions but one covering all the materials chosen.

On the one hand the media often report on new technological developments and their potential benefits, on the other hand we hear about disasters and dangers caused by this new technology.

Discuss how we should deal with the opportunities and the risks of new technology.

1

IMMER GRÖSSERE RISIKEN FÜR MENSCH UND UMWELT

Seit den siebziger Jahren ist es vorbei mit jenem naiven Fortschrittsoptimismus der ersten Nachkriegsjahrzehnte, der jede neue technische Errungenschaft als einen weiteren Schritt in eine schöne neue Welt betrachtete. Hoffnungen auf eine Welt, in der dank der Technik die Probleme der Ernährung, Arbeit und Armut schließlich beseitigt wären, erwiesen sich als Illusion.

Heute formen vielmehr oft Katastrophenmeldungen das Bild der Technik […] – immer mehr Menschen begreifen diese Ereignisse als Warnzeichen einer Entwicklung, die fortwährend größere Risiken für Mensch und Umwelt hervorbringt. Und zunehmend weniger Bürger schätzen den Nutzen, der ihnen hier erwächst, so hoch ein, dass ihnen diese Risiken in ihrer Gesamtheit noch vertretbar erscheinen.

Dabei wird von kaum jemandem ernsthaft bestritten, dass der technische Fortschritt in der Vergangenheit erhebliche Vorteile mit sich gebracht hat. Die Lebenserwartung stieg, privater Wohlstand mehrte sich, die Menschen erlebten mehr persönliche Freiheit.

Allerdings profitiert die Menschheit von diesen Segnungen der Technik in unterschiedlichem Maß; so haben viele Menschen der Dritten Welt bislang oft nur die Schattenseiten des Fortschritts erfahren.

Und auch in den hochindustrialisierten Ländern ist in den letzten Jahrzehnten immer deutlicher geworden, dass neue Technologien nicht immer die Lösung bisheriger Probleme sind, sondern auch Gefahren mit sich bringen. […] Was in der Feuerung eines einzelnen Heizkessels als harmlos erscheint, kann bei millionenfacher Anwendung zur globalen Gefahr werden.

Je deutlicher diese Zweischneidigkeit der technischen Entwicklung im Bewußtsein der Menschen Konturen gewinnt, desto lauter wird der Ruf nach einer sozial und ökologisch verantwortbaren Nutzung des technischen Fortschritts. (246 Wörter)

Quelle: Meinolf Dierkes, www.spiegel.de, 16. Februar, 1987.

"The end is neigh" (= near)

Technology has created more jobs than it has destroyed, says 140 years of data

Study of census results in England and Wales since 1871 finds rise of machines has been a job creator rather than making working humans obsolete

[...] The battle between man and machines goes back centuries. Are they taking our jobs? Or are they merely easing our workload? [...] Going back over past jobs figures paints a more balanced picture, say authors Ian Stewart, Debapratim De and Alex Cole.

"The dominant trend is of contracting employment in agriculture and manufacturing being more than offset by rapid growth in the caring, creative, technology and business services sectors," they write. "Machines will take on more repetitive and laborious tasks, but seem no closer to eliminating the need for human labour than at any time in the last 150 years."

In some sectors, technology has quite clearly cost jobs, but Stewart and his colleagues question whether they are really jobs we would want to hold on to. Technology directly substitutes human muscle power and, in so doing, raises productivity and shrinks employment. [...]

The report cites a "profound shift", with labour switching from its historic role, as a source of raw power, to the care, education and provision of services to others. It found a 909% rise in nursing auxiliaries and assistants over the last two decades. Analysis of the UK Labour Force Survey from the Office for National Statistics suggest the number of these workers soared from 29,743 to 300,201 between 1992 and 2014. [...]

In some sectors – including medicine, education and professional services – technology has raised productivity and employment has risen at the same time, says the report. [...] Technological progress has cut the prices of essentials, such as food, and the price of bigger household items such as TVs and kitchen appliances. The real price of cars in the UK has halved in the last 25 years, notes Stewart. That leaves more money to spend on leisure, and creates new demand and new jobs. [...]

(332 words)

Quelle: Katie Allen, *The Guardian*, www.the guardian.com, 18 August 2015.

4

1 "… imagine if trees gave off Wi-Fi signals. We would be planting so many trees and we'd probably save the planet too. Too bad they only produce the oxygen we breathe."

www.progressio.org.uk , February 5, 2014.

2 "What new technology does is create new opportunities to do a job that customers want done."

Tim o'Reilly, futurist and software pioneer, readwrite.com, November 17, 2004.

3 "I've come up with a set of rules that describe our reactions to technologies:
  1. Anything that is in the world when you're born is normal and ordinary and is just a natural part of the way the world works.
  2. Anything that's invented between when you're fifteen and thirty-five is new and exciting and revolutionary and you can probably get a career in it.
  3. Anything invented after you're thirty-five is against the natural order of things."

Douglas Adams, author, *The salmon of doubt: Hitchhiking the galaxy one last time*, William Heinemann Ltd., 2002.

5

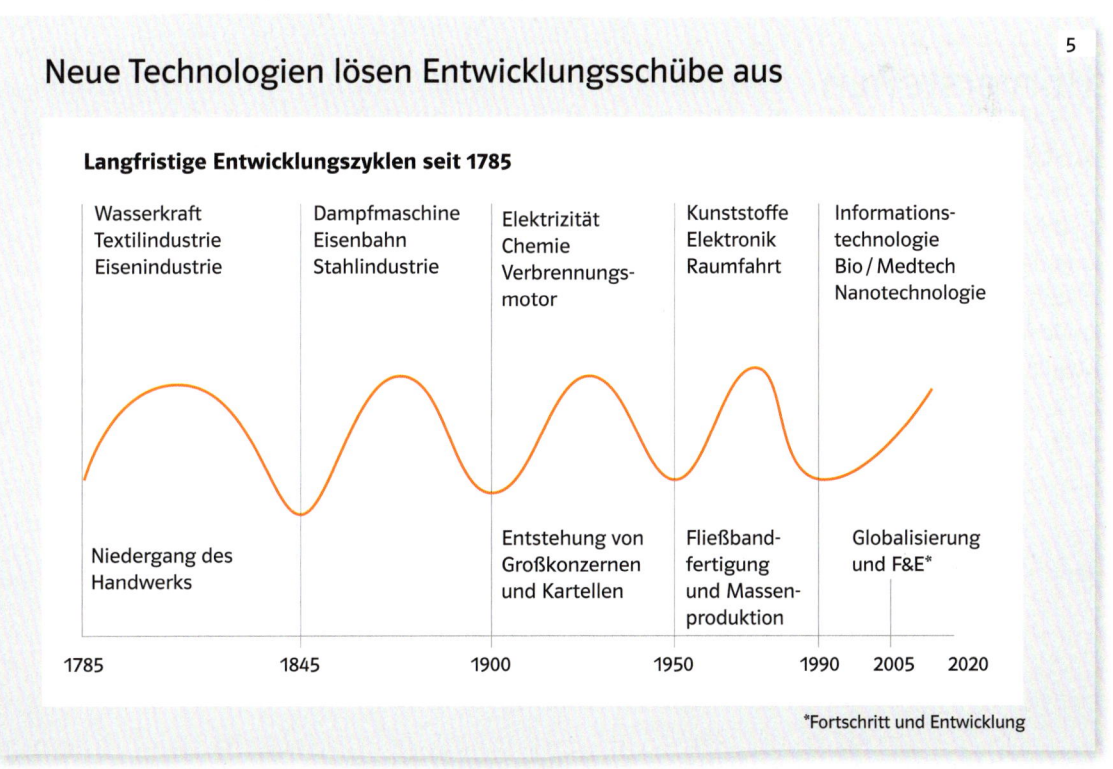

Unit 15
Exam course:
Globalization and migration

y9xn2a

A | Hörverstehen

A3.11 Aufgabe 1a: Offene Fragen

In der letzten Zeit ist eine Diskussion über die Auswirkungen der Globalisierung und damit verbundene Migration entbrannt.
Hören Sie den Sprechern zu, die jeweils über ihre Erfahrungen in Großbritannien berichten, und bearbeiten Sie die folgenden Aufgaben in Stichpunkten auf Deutsch.

Bob
1. Nennen Sie zwei Gründe, warum Bob nach Wales auswanderte.
2. Beschreiben Sie zwei Auswirkungen der neuen Migration, die Bob erwähnt.

Jana
3. Nennen Sie zwei Entwicklungen in der Migration zwischen Polen und Großbritannien in den letzten Jahren.
4. Beschreiben Sie drei Dinge, die Jana während ihrer Zeit in Schottland zu schätzen gelernt hat.

🔊 A3.12 **Aufgabe 1 b: Satzergänzungen**

Ein Flüchtling berichtet über seine Erfahrungen. Hören Sie aufmerksam zu und ergänzen Sie die folgenden Sätze auf Deutsch.

1. Als der Krieg begann, hat Mustafas Familie …
2. In Mustafas Heimatland ging es der Familie vergleichsweise gut, weil …
3. Nachdem Großbritannien die Familie als Flüchtlinge anerkannt hatte, entschied die Familie…
4. Die Familie erhielt eine Unterkunft in Bradford in Nordengland, weil …
5. Die Familie hat inzwischen eine kleine Wohnung gefunden, da…
6. Seine Brüder lernen schnell Englisch, denn …
7. Mustafas Mutter ist aus zwei Gründen unglücklich und einsam, weil …
8. Mustafa hofft, eines Tages eine Arbeit zu finden, bei der er …

B | Leseverstehen

Aufgabe 2: Mediation

Unter Ihren Freunden ist eine Diskussion entbrannt über die Art und Weise, wie modische Kleidung für junge Menschen hergestellt wird.

Sie haben den folgenden Artikel gelesen und informieren Ihre Freunde anhand des Zeitungsartikels über die Situation der Frauen in der Textilindustrie in einigen Entwicklungsländern und über Möglichkeiten der Verbesserung der Arbeits- und Lebenssituation dort.

IMPROVING CONDITIONS FOR WOMEN HAS A DOMINO EFFECT

Providing training, healthcare and childcare to female workers has an impact that stretches beyond the factory floor

The world's clothes are mostly made by women. Typically, these workers are young, with limited education and live in developing countries. It has been well documented that working conditions across garment industries are in much need of improvement. Yet these jobs are important. In their world, paid factory work can provide a better alternative than other options available such as unpaid family agriculture or domestic work. But is this work a catalyst for female empowerment or a better life for women?

Better Work, a joint project of the International Labour Organization (ILO) and the International Finance Corporation (IFC), has a presence in more than 900 garment factories employing one million workers across Cambodia, Vietnam, Lesotho, Nicaragua, Haiti, Jordan and Indonesia with a programme in Bangladesh on the way.

Our latest research from Vietnam shows that a garment job for a woman is a positive development but does not necessarily result in empowerment or even equality. Recent years have seen significant and sustained improvements in Vietnamese industrial conditions but, as is often the case, improvements for women are lagging behind.

Around 80% of Vietnam's 700,000 factory workers are women. Women tend to be sewers and helpers, while men are usually in higher paid occupations working as cutters and mechanics. Men are three times more likely than women to be supervisors. [...]

Women tend to work longer hours than men and are less likely to be promoted or receive training, even when they have been working at the factory longer than men. Women are also in poorer health, and women's average hourly wages (excluding bonuses) are just 85% of men's. Female garment workers also reported less leisure time than men, because gender dynamics at home remain the same; women are working full time while retaining full time responsibilities in the home.

These findings are disappointing but also pave the way for an enormous development opportunity. Providing good conditions for women at work has an impact that stretches significantly beyond the factory floor. IMF research finds that some countries miss out on up to 27% growth per capita due to gender gaps in the labour market. Improved working conditions for women have a domino effect, leading to greater investments in children's health and education and household income. In Vietnam, for example, family remittances from workers in the factories where we work are increasing over time: 70% of workers send money to family members, and women send home 24% more than men.

Improving the livelihoods of garment workers is the right thing for the industry to do. But ultimately factory work will not be empowering for women workers unless the disadvantages they face are tackled head on. Paid work can and should create opportunities for women to realise their rights, express their voice and develop their skills.

We know what works. A considerable share of the female garment workforce have young children and appropriate childcare and health facilities can provide them with essential support and make business sense. One factory in Vietnam which established a kindergarten and health clinic for workers found that the investment reduced staff turnover and absenteeism, contributed to a fall in industrial disputes, saved costs and sustained productivity over several years.

Women need access to independent workers organisations that can empower them and represent their choices and interests in the workplace. Trade unions must be able to form, organise and to bargain on behalf of workers. Barriers that prevent them from doing so should be removed. By their own admission, workers organizations also have work to do to better represent women workers.

There is no doubt that there is a huge development and business opportunity to grasp by investing in good jobs for women and by providing women with the support they need to realise their rights and their full potential in the workplace. (658 words)

Quelle: Dan Rees, *The Guardian*, www.theguardian.com, 7 March 2014.

C | Textproduktion

Aufgabe 3: Materialgestützter Aufsatz

Write a composition about the following topic.
- Use the information of at least three of the given materials.
- Name which ones you are using.
- Make use of your own ideas.
- Do not write three separate compositions but one covering all the materials chosen.

The fairtrade movement tries to improve living and working conditions in developing countries.

Discuss the positive effects of the fairtrade movement and possible difficulties.

Scottish co-op launches Fairtrade football campaign

Glasgow-based *Bala Sport* aims to import Fairtrade footballs to combat low pay and dangerous conditions in Pakistan's football factories

A Scottish co-operative which aims to improve the lives of often exploited factory workers in Pakistan has launched a crowdfunding campaign to help it import thousands of Fairtrade footballs. [...]

The group, whose name means "ball" in Gaelic and "strength" in Punjabi, works with manufacturers in the northern Pakistani city of Sialkot, close to the border with the Indian state of Jammu and Kashmir, where around 70% of the world's hand-stitched footballs are made. [...]

But while ball-making is a pillar of Sialkot's economy (the town also specialises in making surgical instruments), the industry has long faced criticism over low pay and poor working conditions. [...]

Bala Sport's co-founder, Angus Coull, visited Sialkot in 2014. He said he'd found vast differences between factories. "We visited four factories producing balls under Fairtrade agreements. You could see that they had fire escapes, fire extinguishers, health and safety notices, proper ventilation and everything you'd expect to find in a UK factory. The workers had face masks and eye

protection. But when we went to another factory there was nothing like that. It was underground in the basement of a building, and the only ventilation was from holes in the ceiling."

Coull argued that in a sport where top players can earn tens of millions of pounds per year, governing bodies also had a clear moral responsibility to protect low-paid workers. [...]

Established in February 2015, *Bala Sport* pays a 10% premium on manufacturing costs designed to give workers' families access to healthcare and education. The group has already sold thousands of footballs around the country, Coull added, where there were only around 80 Fairtrade footballs in the whole of the UK when he started. (302 words)

Quelle: Owen Duffy, *The Guardian*, www.theguardian.com, 27 July 2015.

FAIRTRADE: WENN KAFFEE BITTER SCHMECKT

KEINE LANGFRISTIG POSITIVEN EFFEKTE

[...] Was nützt eine Idee, die gut gemeint, aber schlecht umgesetzt ist? So fanden kürzlich Wissenschaftler der University of London heraus, dass die Löhne in Betrieben in Uganda und Äthiopien ohne Fairtrade-Label zum Teil nicht nur ähnlich hoch, sondern sogar höher und die Arbeitsbedingungen besser waren. „Laut unseren Untersuchungen war Fairtrade kein effektiver Mechanismus, um das Leben der ärmsten Landbevölkerung, der angestellten Arbeiter, zu verbessern", sagte Studienautor Christopher Cramer dem *Guardian*.

Die Untersuchung, von Fairtrade heftig als unzulässig verallgemeinernd kritisiert, ist nicht die einzige dieser Art. Forscher der Universitäten Berkeley und San Diego untersuchten die Daten aus 13 Jahren von Kooperativen in Guatemala und fanden praktisch keinen langfristigen positiven Effekt. Ihr Fazit: Die wirtschaftlichen Vorteile werden durch die hohen Zertifizierungskosten wieder aufgefressen.

Fairtrade-Bauern erhalten einen Mindestpreis von aktuell 1,40 US-Dollar pro Pfund. Dazu kommt eine Prämie von 20 Cent, zum Teil noch ein Bio-Aufschlag von weiteren 0,30 Cent. Dieses Geld fließt, auch wenn der Weltmarktpreis niedriger ist. Ist der Börsenpreis höher, erhalten sie diesen. Um in den Genuss des Geldes zu kommen, müssen die Bauern aber erst einmal kräftig vorstrecken. Eine Antragsgebühr von 525 Euro wird fällig, danach eine Erstzertifizierungsgebühr von weiteren 2.250 Euro. Dank der (jährlich zu zahlenden) Gebühren würden die Bauern aber auch beraten, argumentiert Fairtrade-Deutschland-Chef Dieter Overath. So steige die Produktivität, wodurch die Bauern wieder profitieren. [...]

(228 Wörter)

Quelle: Axel Hansen, *Die Zeit*, www.zeit.de, 18. August 2014.

FAIRTRADE IN NUMBERS

2 OUT OF 3 PEOPLE UNDERSTAND THAT THE FAIRTRADE SYMBOL MEANS A BETTER DEAL FOR FARMERS AND WORKERS.

6 OUT OF 10 CONSUMERS BELIEVE THEIR SHOPPING CHOICES CAN HELP FARMERS AND WORKERS IN POORER COUNTRIES.

7.5 OUT OF 10 SHOPPERS BELIEVE INDEPENDENT CERTIFICATION IS THE BEST WAY TO VERIFY A PRODUCT'S ETHICAL CLAIMS.

1. "Please buy more fairtrade so you can keep remembering the farmers over here who grow the coffee."

Kagera Co-Operative Union Field officer, Olivia Mwombeki.

2. "No business which depends for existence on paying less than living wages to its workers has any right to continue in this country."

Franklin D. Roosevelt, American President 1933–1945, statement on the National Industrial Recovery Act, Presidential Library and Museum, June 16, 1933.

3. "Nobody wants to buy something that was made by exploiting somebody else."

Jerry Greenfield, co-founder of Ben&Jerry's ice cream, (Ben&Jerry's Builds on Its Social-Values Approach), *The New York Times*, November 16, 2010.

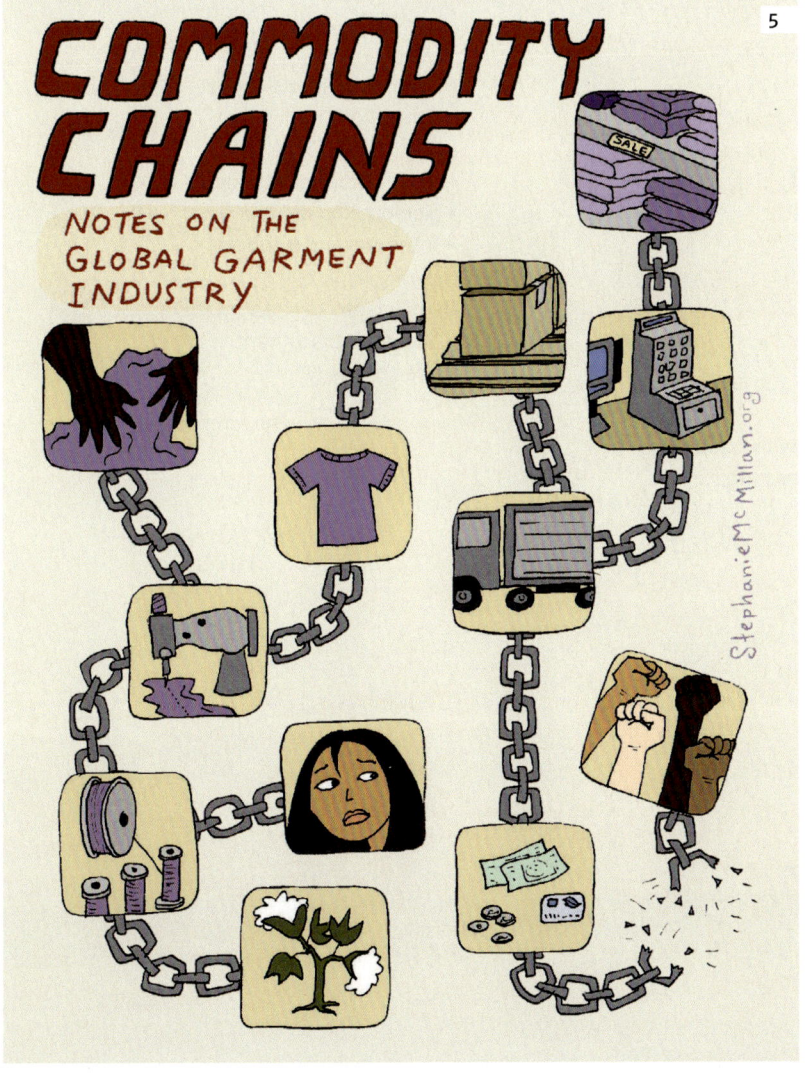

Role cards

Unit 1

Role card A C task 5, p. 13
Employee

Find out the following about the young European:
- their name
- their country of origin
- their reasons for coming to Britain
- their placements or jobs
- their part-time jobs
- how they like life in London
- their plans for the future

Unit 2

Role card A B 3 task 1, p. 23
Interviewer

1. When / born?
2. When / live / in Exeter?
3. How long / live / in London?
4. When / go to college?
5. What / do / then?
6. How long / be / a shop assistant at Morrisey's?
7. When / start / learning German?
8. How long / be interested / working with people?
9. When / hear / about the job advertisement?

Role card B B 3 task 1, p. 23
Linda Smith

1. Exeter / 1995
2. 1995 – 2011
3. since 2011
4. 2011 – 2013
5. customer service at R.S. Reynolds
6. since 2015
7. five years ago
8. always
9. last month

Unit 2

Role card A E 1 task 3, p. 29
Applicant

Think about the following:
- education
- work experience
- skills and qualifications
- personality and character
- interests and hobbies
- possible questions

Role card B E 1 task 3, p. 29
Employer

Prepare questions about:
- education
- work experience
- skills and qualifications
- personality and character
- interests and hobbies

Be prepared to say something about:
- the work placement
- the company

Unit A

Role card A — C task 4, p. 34
Bastian

- meldet sich
- erzählt, dass er ein Praktikum im Hotel Victoria in London macht
- erzählt, dass das Hotel Victoria für ihn ein Zimmer im Westward Boarding House gebucht hat
- fragt, ob er das Zimmer für die Zeit vom 1. August bis 31. August bekommen kann
- fragt, ob das Zimmer wirklich 30 Pfund pro Nacht kostet
- fragt, wie das Zimmer ausgestattet ist
- bucht das Zimmer endgültig
- nennt seine Daten und bedankt sich

Role card B — C task 4, p. 34
Ms Lisa Davies

- nimmt das Gespräch an
- erzählt, dass bei ihr oft junge Menschen wohnen, die ein Praktikum im Hotel Victoria machen
- bestätigt, dass ein Zimmer für ihn reserviert ist
- sagt zu, dass er das Zimmer in dieser Zeit haben kann
- bestätigt, dass das Zimmer 30 Pfund pro Nacht inklusive Frühstück kostet
- gibt Auskunft über die Ausstattung des Zimmers: Einzelzimmer, Tee- und Kaffeezubereitung im Zimmer möglich, Fernseher
- bestätigt die Buchung und erfragt Daten des Anrufers (Name, E-Mail Adresse, Handynummer)

Unit 3

Role card A — C 2 task 2, p. 41
Salesperson

You have a part-time job in a German department store. Your job is to persuade customers to buy. Sometimes English-speaking customers come to the store.
Think about:
- the advantages of the product
- how it compares with other products on the market
- its price

Be prepared to tell the customer where and how the product was made.

Role card B — C 2 task 2, p. 41
Customer

You are a well-informed customer who asks critical questions. You can only speak English.
Ask the salesperson about:
- possible advantages and disadvantages of the product
- the quality of the product
- the place of production
- the conditions of production
- other better prices and offers

Unit 3

Role card A — E task 5, p. 44
Student

You are not sure about the ban.
Possible arguments:
- information
- entertainment
- waste of time
- spend too much money

Role cards

Unit 3

Role card B — E task 5, p. 44
Company representative

You sell products to children and teenagers.
Possible arguments:
- information about new products
- children want to have a choice
- new jobs are created

Role card C — E task 5, p. 44
Parent

You are against this type of advertising.
Possible arguments:
- manipulation
- waste of money
- dangers (ads for alcohol, cigarettes, etc.)

Unit 4

Role card A — D 3 task 1, p. 55
Student

A smartphone is a must-have for you, both outside college and at college. You want to keep in contact with your friends. You sometimes look up useful things in class on your smartphone.

Role card B — D 3 task 1, p. 55
Head teacher

You are the host in this discussion. You have invited parents to the college to inform them about the trouble with smartphones and to find a solution to the problem.
You describe the current situation and the problems that have arisen with the growing use of smartphones.

Unit 4

Role card C — D 3 task 1, p. 55
Parent

You want your son/daughter to take a smartphone to college so that he/she can reach you, and you can reach him/her in case of an emergency or an accident.
On the other hand you fear that young people use their smartphones and tablets far too much, not only at college.

Role card D — D 3 task 1, p. 55
Police officer

You give information about the misuse of smartphones and social media, and the risks for young people.
You want schools to teach young people how to handle modern media properly.

Unit 5

Role card A — D 2 task 3, p. 67
College student

You
- are a student at a college in Greenwich
- have little money
- want to know about the possibility of renting a room only
- live alone and feel lonely
- have no family or friends in Greenwich

Talk about
- your interests and hobbies
- your personality / character
- how you can contribute to the community

Unit 5

Role card B — D 2 task 3, p. 67
Resident

Prepare questions about
- reasons for application
- personality / character
- contribution to community

Talk about
- yourself and your family
- the different groups of residents
- life in the community
- what the community can offer

Unit B

Role card A — B task 2, p. 73
Wirtin (Ms Davies)

- fragt, ob sie beim Gepäck behilflich sein kann
- fragt, wie lange die Reise gedauert hat
- sagt, sie versteht, dass er müde ist
- zeigt ihm das Zimmer
- sagt, Bastian soll nicht zögern zu fragen, wenn er Hilfe braucht
- sagt, dass das Frühstück von 8 Uhr bis 9 Uhr serviert wird
- wünscht eine gute Nacht

Role card B — B task 2, p. 73
Bastian

- bedankt sich und sagt, dass er sein Gepäck allein tragen kann
- antwortet, dass er ca. 14 Stunden gebraucht hat
- bestätigt, dass er müde ist
- sagt, dass ihm das Zimmer gefällt
- bedankt sich und verspricht zu fragen, wenn er Hilfe braucht
- freut sich auf das englische Frühstück
- bedankt sich und wünscht eine gute Nacht

Unit B

Role card A — D task 3, p. 75
Bedienung

- fragt, was der Gast zum Frühstück haben möchte
- nimmt die Bestellung an und fragt, was der Gast trinken möchte
- sagt, dass er / sie das Frühstück sofort bringt

Role card B — D task 3, p. 75
Gast

- bestellt ein Frühstück nach eigener Wahl (siehe *Help*-Box auf Seite 75)
- bestellt ein Getränk nach Wahl
- bedankt sich

Unit B

Role card A — D task 4, p. 75
Bastian

- sagt, dass er ein Praktikum im Hotel macht und fragt, was Greg zurzeit in London macht
- fragt, was Greg studieren möchte
- sagt, woher er kommt (Stuttgart)
- sagt, wo seine Heimatstadt liegt
- antwortet, wie das Wetter in Stuttgart ist und fragt, wie das Wetter in London in den nächsten Tagen sein wird
- sagt, dass er sich darüber freut
- verabschiedet sich bis zum Abend

Role cards

Unit B

Role card B — D task 4, p. 75
Greg

- sagt, dass er ein *gap year* in Europa macht, bevor er in Ohio studiert
- sagt, dass er Mathematik studieren möchte und fragt Bastian, woher er kommt
- fragt, wo diese Stadt liegt
- fragt, wie das Wetter dort ist
- antwortet, dass das Wetter sich oft ändert, dass es morgen sonnig werden soll
- verabschiedet sich

Unit 6

Role card A — B 4 task 1, p. 79
Charity worker

Talk about the following things:
- must help poor countries
- rich states and United Nations organizations
- help quickly – time is running out

Role card B — B 4 task 1, p. 79
Biologist

Talk about the following things:
- dangers of overfishing
- no need for exotic seafood
- economic help for poor fishermen

Role card C — B 4 task 1, p. 79
Environmentalist

Talk about the following things:
- polluted rivers
- environmental problems caused by industry
- governments must act

Unit 6

Role card D — B 4 task 1, p. 79
Member of a local environmental group

Talk about the following things:
- clean up your own environment
- local action
- join environmental organizations

Unit 8

Role card A — E task 7, p. 109
Owner of "Stud's"

- You have been quite successful.
- Your company is still growing but not so quickly anymore because of fierce competition.
- You pay employees $3.50 per hour.
- Your employees receive relatively good tips (but not so much from tourists).
- You think your employees are more polite to customers when they work for tips.
- Add other reasonable arguments.

Role card B — E task 7, p. 109
Representative of the employees

- Most of the employees are women.
- They earn $3.50 per hour which is far too little.
- The company is growing and makes a profit of ten million US dollars.
- Tips vary from day to day so employees can never be sure how much they will earn.
- Tourists give no or very small tips.
- Working hours vary so it is difficult to manage a job and a family.
- It is especially difficult for single mothers: some cannot afford proper meals and they need food stamps.
- Add other reasonable arguments.

Grammar files

1 Indefinite article
Unbestimmter Artikel

Form

a	college student university	vor **gesprochenen** Konsonanten
an	interview address hour	vor **gesprochenen** Vokalen

Verwendung

I have bought **a** book for you.	für zählbare Begriffe in der Einzahl
He is **a** teacher.	vor Berufsbezeichnungen

2 Definite article
Bestimmter Artikel

Form

the	course language European	vor **gesprochenen** Konsonanten Aussprache [ðə]
the	engineer office hour	vor **gesprochenen** Vokalen Aussprache [ði:]

Verwendung

the people of London **the** life of Lucy Jordan **the** University of Manchester	bei Substantiven (Personen, Dingen, Abstrakta), wenn sie näher bestimmt sind oder werden
the United States	für Ländernamen im Plural
the Thames, **the** North Sea	für Flüsse und Meere
the Browns	für Eigennamen im Plural
On their tour they visited **the** church.	für die konkrete Bedeutung als Gebäude

Verwendung von Substantiven ohne Artikel
Der Artikel wird abweichend vom Deutschen **nicht** verwendet:

nature, life, time, people	für abstrakte Begriffe und Sammelbezeichnungen, wenn sie nicht näher bestimmt sind oder werden
Trafalgar Square, Buckingham Palace	für Ortsbezeichnungen, bei Eigennamen
Switzerland, Normandy, Lake Windermere	für Länder, Berge und Seen im Singular
church, school, college When does church begin?	für Gebäudebezeichnungen, wenn die normale Nutzung gemeint ist

3 Plural
Mehrzahl

Form

student college	students colleges	Die meisten Nomen bilden den Plural durch Anhängen von -s.
university city	universities cities	Konsonant + y wird zu -ies.
address match	addresses matches	Nach Zischlauten (z. B. s, ss, ch, sh) wird -es angehängt.
man woman child life	**men** **women** **children** **lives**	Einige Nomen haben unregelmäßige Pluralformen.

Verwendung

information, weather, nature, knowledge, work, furniture	Einige Nomen treten nur im Singular auf.
trousers, jeans, glasses, clothes, thanks, customs, savings	Einige Nomen treten nur im Plural auf.
news, the United States, the United Nations, economics, mathematics, electronics **Example:** No news **is** good news.	Einige Nomen treten nur in der Pluralform auf, das Verb steht jedoch im Singular.
family, government, staff, team, band	Sammelnamen – Plural, wenn eher auf die einzelnen Mitglieder hingewiesen wird – Singular, wenn die Gruppe eher in ihrer Gesamtheit gemeint ist

4 Some important prepositions
Zeitliche und Räumliche Präpositionen, Präpositionen der Art und Weise

Zeitliche Präpositionen

on 20th September	**at** six o'clock	**by** day, **by** Wednesday
on Saturday	**at** the age of 16	
on weekdays	**at** night	twelve minutes **to** five
	at noon	
in 1992	**at** midnight	(a) quarter **past** six, half **past** nine
in the morning	**at** the weekend	
in the evening		

Räumliche Präpositionen

go **to** the cinema	**Präpositionen der Art und Weise**
go **to** college	go **by** bus, car, bike
I've been **to** Scotland	go **on** foot
at home	
at school	
at the supermarket	

5 Possessive case
Genitiv

's-Genitiv
Verwendung bei Personen, Tieren, Zeiten, Personenkollektiven

Henry**'s** exam the baker**'s** (shop)	Nomen im Singular + **'s**
his parents**'** computer shop the Greens**'** house	Nomen im Plural + **'**
people**'s** faces children**'s** books	bei Nomen im Plural **ohne** s Anhängung von **'s**
today**'s** newspaper two weeks**'** pay	Bei Zeiten gelten die gleichen Regeln.
Britain's social problems the party's policy	häufig auch bei Staaten, Städten und Institutionen

of-Genitiv
Verwendung bei Sachen

the title **of** the book the price **of** the computers	Der *of*-Genitiv wird im Singular und im Plural verwendet.

6 Comparison of adjectives
Steigerung von Adjektiven

Form

cheap small	cheap**er** small**er**	cheap**est** small**est**	Steigerung der kurzen Adjektive mit -er und -est
nice	nic**er**	nic**est**	stummes -e entfällt
heavy	heav**ier**	heav**iest**	-y wird zu -ier und -iest
big	bi**gg**er	bi**gg**est	Nach kurzen Vokalen wird der Endkonsonant verdoppelt.
good bad little	**better** **worse** **less**	**best** **worst** **least**	Einige Adjektive haben unregelmäßige Steigerungsformen.
careful difficult	**more** careful **more** difficult	**most** careful **most** difficult	Alle dreisilbigen und mehrsilbigen Adjektive und alle zweisilbigen Adjektive, die nicht auf -er, -le, -y, -ow enden, werden mit *more* und *most* gesteigert.
careful difficult	**less** careful **less** difficult	**least** careful **least** difficult	Eine Verminderung der Adjektive ist mit *less* und *least* möglich.

Verwendung

In town centres walking is often **as fast as** going by car.	Gleichheit wird mit *as … as* ausgedrückt.
Travelling by plane is **faster than** travelling by train. Travelling by car is **more expensive than** walking.	Ungleichheit kann mit Hilfe des Komparativs und *than* ausgedrückt werden.
A bicycle is **not so expensive as** (isn't **as expensive as**) a car. A bicycle is **less expensive than** a car.	Eine andere Form Ungleichheit auszudrücken, ist *not so … as* oder umgangssprachlich *not as … as*. Wie im Deutschen kann man auch „weniger als" verwenden.
The Concorde was **the fastest** airliner from Paris to New York.	Der Superlativ wird nur benutzt, wenn mehr als zwei Dinge miteinander verglichen werden.

7 Adjective and adverb
Adjektiv und Adverb

Form

Adjective	Adverb		
cheap	cheap**ly**		Das Adverb wird gebildet aus Adjektiv + -*ly*.
lazy	laz**ily**		-*y* wird zu -*ily*
horrible	horrib**ly**		-*le* wird zu -*ly*
economic	econom**ically**		-*ic* wird zu -*ically*
fast	**fast**		Einige Adverbien bilden unregelmäßige Formen.
good	**well**		

Adjective	Adverb	Adverb	
late	**late** (spät)	**lately** (in letzter Zeit)	Einige Adverbien bilden mehrere Formen.
hard	**hard** (hart)	**hardly** (kaum)	
near	**near** (nah)	**nearly** (beinahe)	

Steigerung von Adverbien

quickly	more quickly	most quickly	Alle abgeleiteten Adverbien auf -*ly* werden mit *more* und *most* gesteigert.
carefully	more carefully	most carefully	
well	better	best	Unregelmäßige Adverbien haben eigene Steigerungsformen.
badly	worse	worst	
fast	faster	fastest	

Verwendung

There are many **new computers** on the market. **They** are still **expensive**.	Adjektive beziehen sich auf Nomen oder Pronomen.
We can't **control** the technology **exactly**. Comics are **really popular** with children. Modern computers work **extremely quickly**. **Fortunately, she e-mailed the information to me in time.**	Adverbien beziehen sich auf Verben, … Adjektive, … Adverbien, … und ganze Sätze.
He **felt nervous** about his new job.	Nach Verben, die einen Zustand beschreiben (z. B. *feel*, *look* (= aussehen), *smell*, *taste*, *sound*, *be*, *become*, *get*, *seem*, *appear*, *keep*) folgt ein Adjektiv.

8 Word order with adverbs and adverbials
Wortstellung bei Adverbien und adverbialen Bestimmungen (a. B.)

Die folgenden Satzstellungen sind üblich.

At nine o'clock he caught the bus **to work**.	Adverbien / a. B. der Zeit stehen am Anfang oder Ende des Satzes. Adverbien / a. B. des Ortes stehen in der Regel am Ende des Satzes.
Mr Woods **always** travels to work by train. He has **never** missed a train in his life.	Adverbien / a. B. der Häufigkeit (z. B. *never, sometimes, often, usually, always*) stehen vor dem Vollverb.
The train arrives **punctually**.	Adverbien / a. B. der Art und Weise stehen in der Regel nach dem Verb (den Verben).
The bus drove **slowly** through **London during the rush hour**.	Treten mehrere Adverbien / a. B. zur gleichen Zeit auf, gilt die Regel: Art und Weise vor Ort und Zeit.

9 Some or any?

Verwendung

I need **some** help with this program. **Some** newspapers in Britain only appear on Sundays.	in Aussagesätzen vor unbestimmten Mengen (etwas) oder Anzahlen (einige)
They didn't make **any** money with the new campaign. Some TV stations do not show **any** adverts.	in verneinten Sätzen vor unbestimmten Mengen oder Anzahlen (kein oder keine)
Have they done **any** research on the new product? Have you got **any** ideas for a new logo?	in Fragesätzen vor unbestimmten Mengen (etwas) oder Anzahlen (welche?)
Would you like me to show you **some** examples?	in Fragesätzen, wenn sie eine Aufforderung, Bitte oder ein Angebot enthalten und wenn die Antwort „ja" erwartet wird.
We never needed **any** electronic devices in the past.	nach Wörtern mit negativer Bedeutung

10 Some / any + -one / -body / -thing / -where

Somebody wants to see you. We haven't been **anywhere** this weekend. Have you got **anything** to say?	Die Regeln zum Gebrauch von *some* und *any* gelten auch für diese Formen.

11 Much – many – a lot of

Form

much a lot of	viel	nicht zählbar
many a lot of	viele	zählbar

Verwendung

He spends **a lot of** time practising his communication skills. **A lot of** (many) people have computers in their homes.	In Aussagesätzen wird in der Regel *a lot of* bevorzugt.
I don't have **a lot of / much** money to spend on computers. There aren't **a lot of / many** experts on the staff.	In verneinten Sätzen kann man beide Formen gebrauchen.
How **much** money do you earn? How **many** adverts did they show? They spend too **much** time in front of the screen.	Nach *how* und *too* muss *much* oder *many* stehen.

12 Little / a little – few / a few

Form

We had **little** help during our training. John had only **a little** time to explain. Last week I spent **less** money than the week before. His latest film made the **least** money.	wenig ein bisschen weniger am wenigsten	unzählbar
Few computers never break down. There are **a few** good adverts on TV. There are **fewer** cars on the roads on Sundays. **The fewest** immigrants are from Norway.	wenige ein paar weniger die wenigsten	zählbar

13 Modal auxiliaries
Modale Hilfsverben

Form

Modale Form	Ersatzform	Bedeutung
must	**have to**	müssen
can	**be able to**	können
can	**be allowed to**	dürfen
mustn't / can't	**not be allowed to**	nicht dürfen
can't	**not be able to**	nicht können
needn't	**not have to**	nicht brauchen/nicht müssen

Verwendung

Cars **must / have to** stop when the lights are red. You **needn't / don't have to** pay in that car park. John **can't / isn't able to** find a parking space.	In der Gegenwart kann entweder die modale Form oder die Ersatzform benutzt werden.
We **had to** turn right at the traffic lights. He **didn't have to** wait as the lights were green. Jane **couldn't / wasn't allowed to** leave her car outside the house, as there was a "No Parking" sign.	Mit Ausnahme von *could* oder *couldn't* können die modalen Hilfsverben keine anderen Zeiten bilden. Für die anderen Zeiten werden die Ersatzformen verwendet.
You **should** go home now. There **may** be some rain today. You **might** even lose your job.	Für einige modale Hilfsverben gibt es keine genau passenden Ersatzformen.

14 Defining relative clauses
Notwendige Relativsätze

Verwendung
Ein Relativsatz ist notwendig, wenn die darin enthaltene Information nötig ist, um zu erkennen, welche Person oder Sache gemeint ist.

The man **who / that** is getting on the bus is on his way home. The boy **who / that** was on the platform was waiting for a friend.	Bei Personen werden die Relativpronomen *who* oder *that* verwendet.
The bus **which / that** is at the lights is going to London. The train **which / that** is leaving right now is heading for Bristol.	Bei Sachen wird *which* oder *that* verwendet.
He greeted the man **(who)** he saw on the platform. He read the paper **(which)** he had bought that morning.	Wenn das Relativpronomen Objekt ist, kann es weggelassen werden.
The woman **whose** name I always forget is coming to see us.	*Whose* (dessen / deren) wird als possessives Relativpronomen gebraucht.

15 Non-defining relative clauses
Nicht notwendige Relativsätze

Verwendung

Ein Relativsatz ist nicht notwendig, wenn die darin enthaltene Information nicht nötig ist, um zu erkennen, welche Person oder Sache gemeint ist.

Henry's wife, **who is 58**, was waiting for him at the station.	Ein Relativsatz wird durch Kommas vom Hauptsatz getrennt.
The train, **which was an Intercity**, left punctually.	*that* darf hier nicht verwendet werden.
Henry, **who I met at the station**, is retiring next week.	In nicht-notwendigen Relativsätzen darf das Relativpronomen nicht entfallen.

The Tenses
Die Zeiten

16 Present simple

Form

I / you / we / they he / she / it	**live** **lives**		in Leeds.	Aussage
I / you / we / they he / she / it	**do not (don't) live** **does not (doesn't) live**		in Birmingham.	Verneinung
Do **Does**	I / you / we / they he / she / it	**(not)**	**live** in Liverpool?	(verneinte) Frage
Why Why	**do** you **does** she	**(not)** **(not)**	**work** on Saturdays? **like** baseball?	

Besonderheiten

Who **How many students**	**likes** **live**	basketball? at home?	Ist das Fragewort Subjekt oder Teil des Subjekts, wird *do / does* nicht verwendet.

Besonderheiten bei der Schreibung der s-Endung

watch, kiss	watch**es**, kiss**es**	*-es* nach Zischlauten
carry, try	carr**ies**, tr**ies**	*-ies*, wenn die Endung *-y* in der Grundform hinter einem Konsonanten steht
go, do	go**es**, do**es**	Ausnahmen beachten!

Verwendung

She **has** a brother.	bei einem Dauerzustand
She **(usually) goes** to college by bus. He **(often) helps** at home.	bei regelmäßigen oder wiederholten Handlungen (oft mit Häufigkeitsadverbien wie *usually, normally, often, sometimes, never, always* – sogenannte *tense markers*)
She **doesn't smoke**.	bei Gewohnheiten
He **has** a flat in Mayfield. I **think** that this **is** a good idea.	bei bestimmten Verben, wenn sie einen Zustand beschreiben, z. B. *be, have, look, think, see, know, like, want*
The train **arrives** at 8 o'clock tomorrow morning.	bei Fahrplänen und Veranstaltungsprogrammen (mit Zukunftsbezug)

17 Present continuous

Form

I	**am**	(not)	**reading** a book.	Aussage und Verneinung
you / we / they	**are**			
he / she / it	**is**			

Am	I	(not)	**reading** a magazine?	Frage und verneinte Frage
Are	you / we / they			Die Kurzform der Verneinung wird
Is	he / she / it			mit *aren't* und *isn't* gebildet.

Besonderheiten bei der Schreibung

come, take	co**ming**, ta**king**	-*e* entfällt
sit, run	si**tting**, ru**nning**	Verdoppelung der Konsonanten am Wortende nach kurzen Vokalen

Verwendung

They **are talking** about their courses.	bei Handlungen, die im Moment des Sprechens stattfinden
She **is studying** for her exam this year. She **is working** at home today.	bei Handlungen, die vorübergehend stattfinden, nicht aber unbedingt im Augenblick
She **is having** a good time. A lot of people **are thinking** about their future.	bei bestimmten Verben (siehe *present simple*), wenn sie eine vorübergehende Handlung und keinen Zustand beschreiben
I **am meeting** him tomorrow.	bei zukünftigen Handlungen (mit Zeitbestimmung)
Some students **are always complaining**.	zur gefühlsbetonten Darstellung von Handlungen in Verbindung mit *always*

18 Past simple

Form

She	work**ed**	in Glasgow	last year.	Aussagen
You	need**ed**	a new car.		Grundform + -ed (Infinitiv)

Besonderheiten

mov**e**	mov**ed**	stummes -e entfällt
tr**y**	tr**ied**	Konsonant + y wird zu ie
sto**p**	sto**pped**	Lautverdopplung
go	**went**	unregelmäßige Verben haben besondere Formen für das *simple past* dabei wird die 2. Form verwendet
meet	**met**	

He	**did not**	need	special software.	Verneinung
We	**(didn't)**	lose	the money.	

Did	you	(not)	**move**	to Glasgow?	(verneinte) Frage
	they		**live**	in Birmingham?	
	it		**take**	more than six months?	
Why did	he	(not)	**stop**	in Liverpool?	

Verwendung

Jane **moved** to Glasgow seven years ago. First she **worked** for a computer company.	bei Handlungen zu einem bestimmten Zeitpunkt oder in einem abgeschlossenen Zeitraum in der Vergangenheit (oft mit einer Zeitbestimmung wie z. B. *yesterday, last year, in 1988, … ago, from … until – tense markers*)

19 Past continuous

Form

I / He / She / It	**was**	(not) (**wasn't**)	**standing**	on the platform.	(verneinte) Aussage
We / You / They	**were**	(not) (**weren't**)			

Verwendung

As/while he **was driving** to the airport, it started to rain. A lot of passengers **were waiting** at the counter when Jason went into the bank.	Für eine Handlung, die schon im Gange war, als eine neue Handlung eintrat, wird die Verlaufsform verwendet.
While **I was reading** a book, my friend **was writing** a letter.	Bei gleichzeitigem Verlauf zweier Handlungen steht die Verlaufsform in beiden Fällen.
What **did** you **do** when Susan **came** in? When she **came** in **I put down** my newspaper and talked to her.	Für Handlungen, die nacheinander stattfanden, wird in beiden Fällen *past simple* benutzt.

20 Present perfect simple

Form

I/You/We/They	have	(not) (haven't)	**had** a car for three years.	(verneinte) Aussage *have/has* + 3. Form
He/She/It	has	(not) (hasn't)	**sold** 20 million CDs. **been** to Scotland.	

Have	I/you/we/they	(not)	**made** a loss? **taken** a photo? **been** here?	(verneinte) Frage
Has	he/she/it			

Verwendung

I **have repaired** the car.	bei Handlungen in der Vergangenheit ohne Zeitangabe – das Ergebnis ist oft wichtiger als die Zeitangabe
They **have sold** 50,000 cars **up till now**.	mit Zeitbestimmungen, die einen Zeitraum beschreiben, der noch andauert, z. B. *today, this week, so far, in the last ten years* – tense markers
He has **already paid** the bill.	mit bestimmten Adverbien wie z. B. *ever, never, always, yet, just, already* – tense markers
How long have you **known** about this particular book? The Browns **have lived** there **for** over three years. We **have lived** here **since** 2006.	bei nicht abgeschlossenen Zuständen mit *how long, since* und *for* – *since* bezieht sich dabei auf einen Zeitpunkt, *for* auf einen Zeitraum. Im Deutschen wird hier das Präsens verwendet, z. B. Wir leben hier seit 2006.

21 Present perfect continuous

Form

| I / you / we / they | **have** | **been standing.** | *Present simple* von *have* + *been* + *-ing*-Form |

Verwendung

| How long have you been waiting?
I've been waiting …
– for half an hour.
– since ten o'clock. | bei Handlungen, die in der Vergangenheit begonnen haben und noch andauern – meist in Verbindung mit *how long*, *since*, *for*
Im Deutschen wird hier das Präsens verwendet – z. B. Ich warte schon seit 10 Uhr. |

22 Past perfect simple

Form

| I / You / He / She /
It / We / They | **had** | **(not)**
(-n't) | **travelled** to Paris. | (verneinte) Aussage |

Verwendung

| After he **had arrived** at the hotel, he went to his room.
When I arrived at the station, the ticket office **had** already **closed**. | für Handlungen oder Zustände, die vor einem Zeitpunkt in der Vergangenheit abgeschlossen waren |

23 Future with 'going to'

Form

I	**am ('m)**	(not)	**going to** watch TV.	(verneinte) Aussage
He / She / It	**is ('s)**			
We / You / They	**are ('re)**			

Am	I		**going to have**	a cup of coffee?	Frage
Is	he / she / it				
Are	we / you / they				

Verwendung

| She **is going to answer** the phone. | bei Absichten und Vorhaben |
| That fax machine **is going to break** down. | bei Vorhersagen, die aufgrund bereits bekannter Fakten oder bisheriger Erfahrungen sicher oder logischerweise in Erfüllung gehen müssen |

24 Will-future

Form

I / You / He / She / It We / They	**will** **will not (won't)**	**use** alternative energy. **waste** water.	Aussage Verneinung
Will	I / you / he / she / it we / they	**use** talking computers?	Frage

Verwendung

Computers **will probably do** most of the work.	bei Vorhersagen mit *hope / suppose / expect* und *probably*
Just a minute, **I'll help** you with your shopping.	bei Entscheidungen, die im Moment des Sprechens getroffen werden
I'll phone you tomorrow, I promise.	bei Versprechen
Will you **make** some coffee, please?	um eine Bitte auszudrücken

25 Question tags
Frageanhängsel

Form

Aussagesatz	Frageanhängsel	
You can drive, Pollution is increasing, Trams will improve our public transport service,	**can't you?** **isn't it?** **won't they?**	Das Hilfsverb wird in dem Frageanhängsel wiederholt. Ist der Aussagesatz positiv, so wird das Frageanhängsel verneint.
Statistics aren't always correct,	**are they?**	Ist der Aussagesatz verneint, so wird das Frageanhängsel bejaht.
We enjoyed the journey, She usually goes to Britain,	**didn't we?** **doesn't she?**	Wenn der Aussagesatz kein Hilfsverb enthält, wird das Frageanhängsel mit *to do* in der Zeit des Aussagesatzes gebildet.

Verwendung
Frageanhängsel werden verwendet:

Air travel is really comfortable, **isn't it?**	beim Wunsch nach Bestätigung
You didn't walk here, **did you?**	bei Überraschung
Oh, it's not another traffic jam, **is it?**	bei Verärgerung
Well, that's a really new idea, **isn't it?**	bei ironischen Aussagen

26 Reported speech
Indirekte Rede

Form
Bei Aussagen ändern sich die Zeitformen, wenn das einleitende Verb in der Vergangenheit steht.

"We are protesting about pollution." → Harry said they **were protesting** about pollution.	*Present tenses* werden zu *past tenses*.
"He doesn't buy cans." → June told me he **didn't buy** cans.	
"Watson's opened four supermarkets in 2008." → Fred pointed out that Watson's **had opened** four supermarkets in 2008.	*Simple past* und *present perfect* werden zu *past perfect*.
"They have started a bus service." → He added that they **had started** a bus service.	
"There will be more 'green' products." → Sue went on to say that there **would be** more 'green' products.	*will* wird zu *would*.

Weitere Änderungen bei Aussagen

"I can save more energy." → Harry told me that **he** could save more energy.	Die Pronomen werden angepasst.
"We are meeting the town planner tomorrow." → Sue added that they were meeting the town planner **the next day**.	Orts- (z. B. *here* wird zu *there*) und Zeitbestimmungen werden angepasst.
"I bought the car three days ago." → He said that he had bought the car **three days before**.	

Fragen

"What are you doing about waste?" → **They asked what we were doing** about waste.	Bei Fragen wird die Wortstellung geändert.
"When did you introduce bicycle routes?" → **We wanted to know when they had introduced** bicycle routes.	

Verwendung
Indirekte Rede wird benutzt, wenn berichtet werden soll, was jemand gesagt oder gefragt hat.

27 Conditionals
Bedingungssätze

Form

Typ 1

If-Satz	Hauptsatz	
If **we fit** a shower,	**we will** save water.	*Present simple* wird für das Verb im If-Satz, Futur mit *will* für das Verb im Hauptsatz verwendet.
If **you go** to Paris,	**you can** see the Eiffel Tower.	
If **you want** to stay alive,	don't drink and drive!	Im Hauptsatz kann in manchen Fällen ein modales Hilfsverb mit Verb oder ein Imperativ stehen.

Typ 2

If-Satz	Hauptsatz	
If the government **developed** solar energy,	there **would be** less pollution.	*Past simple* wird für das Verb im If-Satz, *Conditional I (would)* für das Verb im Hauptsatz verwendet.
If I **were** Environment Minister,	I **could** put my ideas about energy into practice.	*could* oder *might* sind Alternativen zu *would* im Hauptsatz.

Typ 3

If-Satz	Hauptsatz	
If Tom and Kate **had insulated** their roof years ago,	they **would have saved** a lot of money.	*Past perfect* wird für das Verb im If-Satz, *Conditional II (would have)* für das Verb im Hauptsatz verwendet.

Verwendung

Typ 1 wird verwendet, wenn es sich um eine erfüllbare Bedingung in der Gegenwart oder Zukunft handelt: "Was passiert / wird passieren, wenn …?"

Typ 2 wird verwendet, wenn es sich um eine unerfüllbare Bedingung in der Gegenwart handelt: "Was würde passieren, wenn …?"

Typ 3 wird verwendet, wenn über eine nicht mehr erfüllbare Bedingung in der Vergangenheit gesprochen wird: "Was wäre passiert, wenn …?"

28 Passive voice
Passiv

Form

The robots **are equipped** with sensors. This motor **was not made** in Great Britain.	Form von *be* in der jeweiligen Zeit + Partizip Perfekt (3. Form) des Verbs
Now the wheels **can be fitted**. The car **must be tested** first.	Bei der Benutzung von Hilfsverben wird das Hilfsverb + *be* + Partizip Perfekt (3. Form) des Verbs verwendet.

Verwendung

These cars **were made** in Germany. The handbook **is written** in English.	hauptsächlich in der Schriftsprache, wenn der Ausführende unbekannt, unwichtig oder selbstverständlich ist
This information **is checked by** the central computer.	Wenn der Ausführende allerdings genannt werden soll, dann benutzt man die Präposition *by (by-agent)*.
It is said that computers will become even **It is reported** more important in the future. **It is believed** **He is said** to be rich.	bei Verben des Meinens und Berichtens
English **is spoken** here. = Man spricht Englisch. We **will be told** the result later. = Man wird uns später das Ergebnis sagen.	Im Deutschen wird ein Aktivsatz mit ‚man' bevorzugt.

29 Infinitive
Infinitiv

Verwendung ohne *to*

We **must write** a report about our trip to England.	nach den meisten Hilfsverben
Our new teachers **make us work** very hard, but on Friday they **let us go** home early.	nach *make* und *let* + direktem Objekt

Verwendung mit *to*

The teacher **asked me to show** my photos of Newcastle. She **told them to wait** outside for a moment.	nach bestimmten Verben (*ask / tell / advise / expect* etc.)
This is not **easy to understand**. I am **surprised to hear** that.	nach Adjektiven
I do not know **what to do**.	nach Fragewörtern

30 Gerund
Gerundium

Verwendung

Drinking and **driving** is dangerous.	als Subjekt
I **enjoy swimming**.	als Objekt nach Verben ohne Präpositionen, wenn eine allgemeingültige Situation beschrieben wird: z. B. *enjoy / like / dislike / hate / stop / start / avoid / suggest / mind / love / recommend / prefer*
I **look forward to seeing** you again. He is **tired of waiting** here. They saw the **danger of destroying** the environment.	nach Verben / Adjektiven / Substantiven mit Präpositionen
He has helped me a lot **by giving** me that map of Newcastle. The child crossed the road **without looking**.	nach Präpositionen mit adverbialer Bedeutung, z. B. *by / without / instead of*
Normally I enjoy swimming but today I **would prefer to play** tennis. I **remember learning** those rules. = *Ich erinnere mich daran, dass ich die Regeln gelernt habe.* I **must remember to learn** these rules. = *Ich muss daran denken, diese Regeln zu lernen.*	Statt des Gerundiums wird der Infinitiv verwendet, wenn es sich um eine Ausnahmesituation handelt (oft mit *would*) oder wenn die Bedeutung des Satzes die Verwendung des Gerundiums nicht zulässt, z. B. bei *stop / start / remember*.
After talking to the press they started their demonstration.	als Verkürzung von Adverbialsätzen (*after / before*)

31 Participle
Partizip

Form
Es gibt zwei Formen des Partizips.

waiting / going / watching	Partizip Präsens
waited / gone / watched	Partizip Perfekt

Verwendung

The weather forecast for the **coming** week … The weather in New York last week was rather **mixed**.	als Adjektiv
You can find several families **living** in one flat. There are a lot of restaurants there especially **built** for the tourists.	anstelle von Relativsätzen
While talking to his children the minister wrote a note to his secretary. **Feeling tired** the President lay down for a rest.	als Verkürzung von Adverbialsätzen (*while / when / because / as*)

Skills files

1 Lerngewohnheiten

Welcher Lerntyp bin ich?

1. Ich bin ein eher visueller Lerntyp, d.h. ich lerne am besten, indem ich Lerninhalte über das Auge aufnehme, z.B. Bilder anschaue, Texte lese.
D.h. besorgen Sie sich privat häufig englischsprachige Texte, z.B. Comics, Internet, etc. Lesen Sie möglichst viel.

2. Ich bin ein eher auditiver Lerntyp, d.h. ich lerne am besten, indem ich Lerninhalte über das Ohr aufnehme, z.B. Musik höre, Gespräche führe, jemandem zuhöre.
D.h. versuchen Sie die Liedtexte, die Sie hören, zu verstehen und übersetzen Sie diese ins Deutsche. Schauen Sie Nachrichten im Fernsehen auf Englisch an.
Es könnte für Sie beispielsweise hilfreich sein, wenn Sie die Lesetexte in diesem Buch anhand der Tracks unter dem Online-Link anhören, um sich neue Vokabeln besser einprägen zu können.

3. Ich bin ein eher kinästhetischer Lerntyp, d.h. ich lerne am besten, indem ich Lerninhalte über meinen Tastsinn aufnehme, z.B. wenn ich mich bewege, experimentiere, Erfahrungen mache, aktiv werden kann.
D.h. benutzen Sie Selbstlernprogramme (E-Learning) oder versuchen Sie mit englisch- oder amerikanischsprechenden Leuten ins Gespräch zu kommen, z.B. im Irish Pub, in Sportclubs, etc.

Diese drei Lerntypen sind nur die grundlegenden Lerntypen. Studien belegen, dass Menschen besonders schnell und gut lernen, wenn möglichst viele Lernkanäle angesprochen werden, d.h. dass Lernen mit allen Sinnen am effektivsten ist. Nach Möglichkeit sollten neue Lerninhalte demnach durch Lesen, Ansehen, Aktivwerden, Anhören und Sprechen aufgenommen werden. Es könnte für Sie beispielsweise hilfreich sein, wenn Sie die Lesetexte in diesem Buch anhand der CD im Workbook anhören, um sich neue Vokabeln besser einprägen zu können.

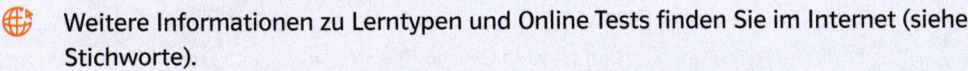
Weitere Informationen zu Lerntypen und Online Tests finden Sie im Internet (siehe Stichworte).

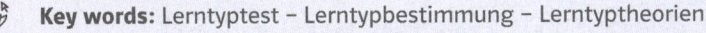
Key words: Lerntyptest – Lerntypbestimmung – Lerntyptheorien

Tipps für alle Lerntypen, um optimal Sprache zu lernen

Lernen Sie regelmäßig!
Lernen Sie regelmäßig Vokabeln und Grammatik, nicht erst kurz vor Ihrer Klausur. Wenn Sie jeden Tag fünf Vokabeln lernen und diese am Wochenende wiederholen, haben Sie schon 25 neue Vokabeln oder englische Redewendungen in einer Woche gelernt.

Nutzen Sie Songtexte, DVDs, Zeitschriften, Internet!
Die englische Sprache begegnet Ihnen mittlerweile überall: in der Werbung, im Fernsehen, im Radio, in Zeitschriften etc. Also halten Sie Ihre Augen und Ohren offen. Sehen Sie sich Ihren Lieblingsfilm doch einmal in der englischen Sprache an.

Analysieren Sie Ihre Fehler!
Machen Sie in jeder Klausur immer wieder dieselben Fehler? Versuchen Sie konkret an Ihren Fehlern zu arbeiten. Nehmen Sie sich die zwei Fehler, die Sie in der letzten Klausur am häufigsten gemacht haben, vor und gehen Sie die Erläuterungen in Ihrer Grammatik noch einmal genau durch. Vielleicht können Sie auch noch ein paar Übungen im *Workbook* dazu machen.

Vermeiden Sie lange und komplizierte Sätze!
Gewöhnen Sie sich schnell an, im Unterricht in der englischen Sprache zu kommunizieren. Wenn Sie Ihre Sätze einfach halten, machen Sie nicht so viele Fehler und fühlen sich sicherer.

2 Interkulturelle Kommunikation

Wenn Sie ins Ausland reisen oder in Ihrem Heimatland auf Menschen aus anderen Ländern treffen, sollten Sie sich eventuell auftretender kultureller Unterschiede bewusst sein. Diese Unterschiede können sich auf unterschiedliche Glaubensvorstellungen, Meinungen, Werte und Normen beziehen.

Deshalb sollten Sie folgende Regeln beachten:
- Respektieren Sie alle Menschen.
- Seien Sie gegenüber dem „Anderssein" aufgeschlossen.
- Interpretieren Sie Verhaltensweisen, die Sie nicht verstehen, nicht als unnormal oder falsch.
- Gehen Sie nicht davon aus, dass es nur einen richtigen Weg gibt zu kommunizieren (Ihren!).
- Informieren Sie sich, wenn möglich, vorher über die kulturellen Hintergründe der anderen Person / des anderen Landes.

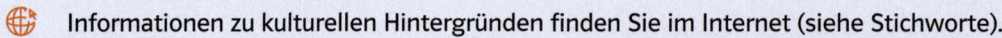 Informationen zu kulturellen Hintergründen finden Sie im Internet (siehe Stichworte).

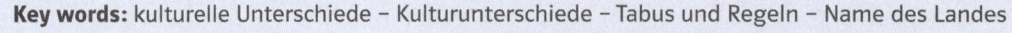 **Key words:** kulturelle Unterschiede – Kulturunterschiede – Tabus und Regeln – Name des Landes

Tipps: Kulturelle Unterschiede

Bekleidung: Wenn Sie ins Ausland reisen, sollten Sie auf Ihre Kleidung achten und sie möglichst den örtlichen Traditionen anpassen. In manchen Ländern gelten kurze Hosen, Miniröcke oder ausgeschnittene Tops als unangemessene Bekleidung in der Öffentlichkeit.

Gestik: Vermeiden Sie ausladende Gestik mit den Händen und Armen. Einige in westlichen Ländern übliche Gesten haben in anderen Ländern keinerlei Bedeutung (z. B. mit den Schultern zucken) oder aber eine gegensätzliche Bedeutung (z. B. bedeutet das Kopfschütteln in Indien „Ja").

Begrüßung: Es gibt verschiedene Begrüßungsarten auf der ganzen Welt (z. B. ist eine Verbeugung die traditionelle Begrüßung in Japan). Um sicher zu gehen, ist es manchmal angebracht, darauf zu warten, wie Ihr Gegenüber die Begrüßung einleitet.

Gesprächsthemen: Seien Sie vorsichtig bei der Wahl der Gesprächsthemen. In den meisten Ländern, so auch in westlichen Industriestaaten, gelten Sexualität, Religion, Politik, Krankheit und Tod als Tabuthemen. Themen, mit denen Sie in den meisten Ländern nicht falsch liegen, sind beispielsweise das Wetter, Sport und Reisen.

Humor: Seien Sie vorsichtig mit Sarkasmus und Humor, da es kulturell bedingt ein unterschiedliches Empfinden darüber gibt, was lustig ist.

Alkohol: In einigen Ländern gilt ein generelles Alkoholverbot und in vielen Ländern ist es verboten, Alkohol in der Öffentlichkeit zu trinken.

Kommunikationsregeln für den Aufenthalt in Amerika

Begrüßung: In der Regel begrüßen Sie sich in den USA, wie in Deutschland, mit einem kurzen Händeschütteln.

Anrede: In der Regel spricht man sich in den USA mit dem Vornamen an. Häufig lassen sich auch Kollegen und Vorgesetzte mit dem Vornamen anreden. Dies ist jedoch kein Zeichen von Freundschaft, Sie sollten trotzdem weiterhin Respekt zeigen.

Höflichkeit: In den USA ist Höflichkeit besonders wichtig und wird sehr ernst genommen. Nach der Begrüßung wird in der Regel gefragt „How are you?" In einem Gespräch sollten Sie auch die Worte *will*, *must* oder *want* vermeiden. Gerne gehört sind dagegen *please*, *might* und *would like to*.

Einladungen: Wenn Sie in den USA eingeladen werden, sollten Sie ein kleines Geschenk mitbringen.

Restaurantbesuch: Im Restaurant warten Sie, bis man Ihnen einen Platz zuweist. Setzten Sie sich nicht einfach an einen freien Tisch.

Warteschlangen: Ob Sie auf den Bus warten, eine öffentliche Toilette aufsuchen möchten, auf dem Postamt sind oder im Supermarkt, es ist immer wichtig, dass Sie sich an das Ende der Reihe stellen und geduldig warten.

Polizeikontrolle: Wenn Sie in den USA von der Polizei angehalten werden sollten, dann legen Sie die Hände auf das Lenkrad und machen so lange nichts, bis Sie zu etwas aufgefordert werden.

Hinweis: Bevor Sie im Ausland arbeiten, sollten Sie sich bei Freunden / Bekannten / Verwandten / Lehrern erkundigen, die bereits in dem Land waren!

Skills Files | Sprachkompetenzen: Rezeption

Exam 3 Hörverstehen

In einigen Klausuren und in der Abschlussprüfung werden Sie gebeten, eine Hörverstehensaufgabe zu bearbeiten. Entweder sollen Sie die Kernaussage des vertonten Textes erfassen (globales Hören) oder Sie sollen bestimmte Details des vertonten Textes herausfinden (selektives Hören). Die Aufgaben zu dem in englischvertonten Text werden auf Deutsch bearbeitet.

Folgende Aufgabentypen kommen beim Hörverstehen in der Prüfung üblicherweise vor:
- Aussagen zum Text auf Deutsch ergänzen: Bei diesem Aufgabentyp werden Sie gebeten, deutsche Sätze auf Deutsch mit Informationen aus dem Hörtext zu ergänzen (siehe z. B. Unit 5 D1, S. 66).
- Fragen zum Text auf Deutsch beantworten: Bei diesem Aufgabentyp werden Sie gebeten, Fragen zum Hörtext auf Deutsch zu beantworten bzw. Aufgaben zum Hörtext zu bearbeiten (siehe z. B. Unit 7 D2, S. 94).

Vor dem Hören

Bevor Sie sich den Text anhören, sollten Sie sich einen Überblick verschaffen, was Sie im Folgenden hören werden. Meist wird der vertonte Text durch eine kurze Situationsbeschreibung eingeleitet.
- Lesen Sie die Einleitung oder die Situationsbeschreibung. Diese gibt in der Regel Informationen über das Thema des vertonten Textes, aber oft auch über die Anzahl/Namen/Rollen der Sprecher und die Situation, d.h. ob es ein Radiointerview ist, eine Werbung, eine Nachrichtensendung, ein Telefongespräch etc.
- Lesen Sie die Aufgabenstellung und eventuell vorgegebene Antwortteile sorgfältig durch, damit Sie wissen, worauf Sie achten sollen. Sollen Sie die Kernaussagen des vertonten Textes erfassen oder sollen Sie auf bestimmte Details achten? Wenn Sie mehrere Fragen oder Aufgaben zu dem Text bearbeiten sollen, denken Sie daran, dass die Abfolge der Aufgaben meistens auch der Reihenfolge entspricht, in der die Informationen im vertonten Text vorkommen. Schreiben Sie Wörter, die Sie eventuell hören werden, auf.
- Wenn ein Raster oder Satzanfänge vorgegeben sind, können Sie diese vorab auf ein Konzeptpapier übertragen. Dies schafft Übersichtlichkeit und erleichtert es Ihnen, dem vertonten Text zu folgen.

Beim Hören

Sie werden den vertonten Text in der Regel insgesamt zweimal hören.
Beim ersten Hören konzentrieren Sie sich auf ein globales Textverständnis und finden heraus, worum es in dem vertonten Text geht.
- Machen Sie sich nur kurze Notizen auf Englisch und verwenden Sie – wenn möglich – Abkürzungen, Anfangsbuchstaben und Symbole. Auf die Rechtschreibung müssen Sie nicht sonderlich achten, weil Sie die Aufgabe ja anschließend auf Deutsch bearbeiten werden. Lassen Sie bei den Abschnitten, die Sie nicht gut verstehen konnten, etwas Platz, um diese Lücken beim zweiten Hören füllen zu können.

- Achten Sie auf bestimmte Signalwörter, die den Text strukturieren und das Verstehen erleichtern:
  Reihenfolgen: first / second, then, next, before, after, later
  Gegensätze: although, however, but, on the other hand
  Gründe / Folgen: because, so, so that
  Vergleiche: more, most, as…as, larger than…
- Konzentrieren Sie sich auf Kernaussagen. Diese werden meist durch häufig wiederholte Schlüsselwörter und durch eine besondere Betonung des Sprechers hervorgehoben.

Zwischen dem ersten und dem zweiten Hören gibt es eine Pause von circa zwei Minuten, die Sie zur Überprüfung und Ergänzung Ihrer ersten Notizen nutzen können. Lesen Sie Ihre Notizen noch einmal in Bezug auf die Aufgabenstellung durch und finden Sie so heraus, auf welche Passagen Sie sich beim zweiten Hören konzentrieren müssen.
Beim zweiten Hören versuchen Sie, eventuelle Lücken zu füllen, und zu kontrollieren, ob Ihre Notizen korrekt sind.

Nach dem Hören

Vervollständigen Sie Ihre Notizen sofort. Wenn Ihnen Details entgangen sind, versuchen Sie, durch die bereits beantworteten Aufgaben die entgangenen Details zu erraten bzw. die Informationen schlau zu kombinieren. Überprüfen Sie zum Schluss, ob Sie die Aufgabe vollständig bearbeitet haben.

Achten Sie auch darauf, dass Sie nur die Informationen aufschreiben, die in der Aufgabenstellung verlangt werden. Wenn Sie beliebig viele zusätzliche Aussagen bzw. Informationen hinzufügen, die sich nicht auf die Aufgabenstellung beziehen, können Ihnen in der Bewertung Punkte abgezogen werden.

4 Hör-Seh-Verstehen

Das Verstehen von Filmen ist im Wesentlichen eine Kombination aus den Kompetenzen Hörverstehen und der Bildbeschreibung. Beim Hörverstehen sollen Sie die Kernaussagen oder bestimmte Details von vertonten Texten benennen. Bei der Bildbeschreibung beschreiben und interpretieren Sie z. B. die Körpersprache von Menschen, die Verwendung von Farben und Licht sowie die Atmosphäre.
▶ Hörverstehen, S. 196   ▶ Fotos und Illustrationen, S. 211

Diese Aspekte werden Sie auch beim Hör-Seh-Verstehen näher betrachten.
In der Regel untersuchen Sie in der Schule keine ganzen Filme, sondern nur kurze Filmausschnitte – so genannte Filmsequenzen – zumeist aus Dokumentarfilmen.

Ein Dokumentarfilm *(documentary)* befasst sich mit tatsächlichen Begebenheiten und Ereignissen. Der Schwerpunkt liegt auf der Sachlichkeit des Films, denn ein Dokumentarfilm soll Informationen zu einem bestimmten Thema bereitstellen.

Deshalb analysieren Sie bei einem Dokumentarfilm zunächst vor allem die Darstellung des Themas, die Vorgehensweise und Intention des Regisseurs und die Wirkung des Filmes auf den Zuschauer.

Grundinformationen

Wenn möglich, sollten die Grundinformationen Folgendes beinhalten:

• Filmgattung,	The documentary (name of film) … was produced by (name of producer) … in (country) … in (year) …
• Filmtitel,	
• Name des Regisseurs oder Produzenten,	
• Erscheinungsort und -zeit,	It is about …
• Thema und Zweck des Films	It shows …

Gesamteindruck

Verschaffen Sie sich einen Gesamteindruck des Filmausschnitts.

• Worum geht es in der Filmsequenz grob *(plot)*?	• This sequence is about … This sequence concentrates on the problem / theme of …
• Gibt es einen Erzähler / Kommentator / Interviewer? Wie wird dieser eingesetzt? *(narrator / commentator and voice-over / interviewer)*	• The narrator wants to inform / influence / manipulate / convince the viewer. The interviewer reacts to the answers with shock / understanding / a lack of understanding / surprise.
• Wo und wann wurde die Filmsequenz gedreht? *(setting)*	• The sequence is set in … The scene / action takes place in …
• Wie ist die Atmosphäre? *(atmosphere)*	• The atmosphere in this sequence is … The music creates a … atmosphere.

Gestaltungselemente

Die Gestaltungselemente eines Films beschäftigen sich mit der Wirkung der filmischen Mittel, z. B. Kameraführung, Lichtgestaltung und Vertonung.

Wie wird die Filmszene gefilmt? Achten Sie auf • Kameraabstand *(distance between the camera and the object)* • Kameraperspektive *(camera position)* • Kamerabewegung *(camera movement)*	• The director uses a long shot / static shot / over-the-shoulder shot in order to show … The scene is shot from … point of view / high-angle / eye-level. The medium shot / close-up / tracking shot / is used to create a … effect. The viewer sees this scene in a … shot. The camera zooms in / out.
Wie werden die gefilmten Szenen vertont? Achten Sie auf: • Dialoge, Monologe, Erzählerkommentare, Interviews • Einsatz von Filmmusik • sonstige Geräusche, z. B. Straßenlärm • Lautstärken	• The film music / sound builds up suspense … The film music / sound provides a shift from one scene to another scene. There is light piano music in the background. The music / sound makes the scene more cheerful / sad / melancholy / aggressive / romantic / authentic / dramatic, etc. The background noise makes the scene more authentic.

5 Leseverstehen

Die Units in diesem Buch enthalten fiktionale und nicht-fiktionale Texte, die Sie im Unterricht lesen werden. Um über diese Texte sprechen zu können, sollten Sie lernen, möglichst schnell zu lesen. Das Gelesene gleichzeitig auch gut zu verstehen, mag Ihnen schwierig vorkommen, z. B. durch unbekanntes Vokabular oder komplizierte Textstrukturen. Deshalb ist es wichtig, systematisch zu lesen, um die Textinhalte zu erfassen.

Tipps: Schwierige Texte leichter verstehen

Überblick gewinnen
Sie überfliegen den gesamten Text recht zügig und ermitteln, was der Inhalt ist. Es ist manchmal hilfreich, die Gesamtaussage des Textes in einem Satz aufzuschreiben, um sich diese besser einprägen zu können.
Beispiel: *The text is about …*

Textaufgaben lesen
Lesen Sie die Fragen, die an den Text gestellt werden. Falls es keine Aufgaben gibt, stellen Sie selber Fragen an den Text!
Beispiel: *Who?, What?, When?, Where?, Why?, How?*

Detailliertes Lesen
Beim zweiten Lesedurchgang lesen Sie den Text Abschnitt für Abschnitt und markieren die wichtigsten Textaussagen oder Schlüsselbegriffe bzw. notieren sich diese auf einem Blatt.

Tipp: Nutzen Sie die Abschnitte als Lesehilfe, d.h. in der Regel wird in jedem neuen Abschnitt ein neuer, weiterführender Aspekt des Themas genannt.
Beispiel: Fragen Sie nach jedem Abschnitt: „Welche Funktion hat dieser Abschnitt?" oder „Welche neuen Aspekte hat dieser Abschnitt aufgeworfen?"

Nachschlagen
Je nach Schwierigkeitsgrad des Textes wird es einzelne Begriffe oder gar ganze Sätze geben, die unverständlich geblieben sind. Klären Sie Unbekanntes mit einem Wörterbuch.
Wenn Sie ganze Sätze nicht verstehen, bitten Sie zunächst einen Mitschüler um Hilfe.
► Mit Texten ohne Wörterbuch umgehen, S. 232
► Mit dem Wörterbuch umgehen, S. 234

Zusammenfassung mit eigenen Worten
Fassen Sie die wichtigsten Aspekte des Textes mit eigenen Worten zusammen. Lösen Sie sich vom Text und finden Sie Ihre eigenen Worte.

6 Einen materialgestützten Aufsatz schreiben

In Klausuren und in der Abschlussprüfung werden Sie aufgefordert, einen Aufsatz über ein bestimmtes Thema zu schreiben. Ihre Aufgabe ist es, eine vorgegebene These zu diskutieren. Dieser Aufsatz dient der argumentativen Auseinandersetzung mit einem Thema, indem verschiedene Aspekte näher beleuchtet werden. Der Aufsatz schließt ab mit einer persönlichen Stellungnahme, die Sie anhand von Argumenten begründen müssen. Ein argumentativer Aufsatz wird im Präsens (Gegenwart) geschrieben.

In der Abschlussprüfung in Baden-Württemberg können Sie zwischen zwei Aufgaben zu unterschiedlichen Themenkomplexen wählen. Jede der beiden Aufgaben besteht aus fünf verschiedenen Materialien in englischer oder deutscher Sprache. Diese bieten Ihnen

Informationen und Anregung, damit Sie sich mit einem bestimmten übergeordneten Thema auseinanderzusetzen können. Von den fünf Materialien sollen Sie mindestens drei der Materialien für Ihren Aufsatz verwenden:

Häufig sind dies:
- Textausschnitt auf Deutsch
- Textausschnitt auf Englisch
- Bildvorlage (Cartoon, Foto, Werbeanzeige)
- Zitate oder provokante These
- Diagramm (Torten-, Säulen-, Liniendiagramm)

Die Materialien stellen verschiedene Aspekte und Perspektiven des Themas dar und sollen Ihnen helfen, sich inhaltlich mit dem Thema auseinanderzusetzen. Aus diesem Grund wird von Ihnen erwartet, dass Sie mindestens drei der fünf Materialien verwenden.

Schritt 1: Klären der Aufgabenstellung

Lesen Sie zunächst die Aufgabenstellung gründlich durch. Schreiben Sie das in der Aufgabenstellung genannte Thema des Aufsatzes auf. Definieren Sie das Thema eindeutig unter Berücksichtigung der Aufgabenstellung.

Schritt 2: Auswertung der Materialien

Es geht darum, die Informationen aus den Materialien für die Diskussion des Themas zu nutzen. Verschaffen Sie sich zuerst einen Überblick über die Materialien, indem Sie diese überfliegen. Konzentrieren Sie sich auf Verständliches und markieren Sie Schlüsselbegriffe bzw. notieren Sie sich diese. Dabei stehen die Hauptaussagen, d. h. insbesondere Fakten sowie Argumente für und gegen die in der Aufgabenstellung genannten Thesen, im Vordergrund. Versuchen Sie auch festzustellen, wie glaubwürdig die Materialien sind. Eine Werbeanzeige ist z. B. keine objektive Quelle, ein Sachbuchartikel ist in der Regel glaubwürdig, ein Zeitungsbericht aus einer Boulevardzeitung ist zweifelhaft.

Schritt 3: Organisation der Informationen

Ergänzen Sie nun die Hauptaussagen der ausgewählten Materialien mit eigenem Hintergrundwissen zu dem Thema. Sie sollten insgesamt etwa fünf Hauptargumente bzw. Hauptthemen haben, die Ihre Position unterstützen bzw. dieser widersprechen. Ordnen Sie die Textaussagen und Ihr eigenes Wissen, indem Sie den Hauptaussagen Teilthemen und Beispiele zuordnen.

Schritt 4: Erstellen der Gliederung

Legen Sie die Reihenfolge der Hauptaussagen und Teilthemen fest.

Schritt 5: Schreiben des Aufsatzes

5.1 Verfassen der Einleitung
Ihre Einleitung soll das Thema / Problem darstellen und das Interesse des Lesers wecken. Sie können z. B.
- eine provokative Aussage machen,

- eine persönliche Erfahrung schildern,
- die aktuelle öffentliche Meinung darstellen,
- aktuelle Statistiken benennen.

Zudem sollen Sie in Ihrer Einleitung:
- die Materialien nennen, die Sie verwenden möchten,
- den Inhalt Ihres Aufsatzes kurz vorstellen,
- einen kurzen Überblick über das Thema / Problem zum gegenwärtigen Zeitpunkt und in der Vergangenheit geben.

Redewendungen

Einleitungssätze

According to the latest statistics …
It is a well-known fact that …

Today there is a lot of discussion about …
Today many people are worried about …

5.2 Verfassen des Hauptteils

Ordnen Sie zunächst Ihre gesammelten Argumente. Eine Möglichkeit ist es, die Argumente vom schwächsten zum stärksten Argument anzuordnen.

Der Hauptteil muss übersichtlich gegliedert sein. Deshalb sollten Sie für jedes neue Argument mit einem neuen Absatz beginnen. Innerhalb eines Absatzes nennen Sie Ihr Argument und in den weiteren Sätzen erläutern Sie dieses anhand von Beispielen, Statistiken und / oder gesammelten Fakten.

Setzen Sie Ihre Sätze in Bezug zueinander, indem Sie passende Bindewörter verwenden. ▶ Bindewörter, S. 237

Verwenden Sie geeignete Adverbien, um Argumente hervorzuheben oder abzuschwächen.

Redewendungen

- **Argumente strukturieren**
  Firstly …, secondly …, finally …
  Moreover …
  In addition …
  Next …
  Then …

- **Begründungen angeben**
  That's why …
  It follows that …
  Because (of) …
  So …
  Therefore …

- **Gegensätze ausdrücken**
  On the one hand … on the other hand …
  However …
  In contrast …

- **Adverbien**
  absolutely – after all – almost – at least – completely – extremely – fortunately – hardly – in fact – mainly – of course – very – particularly – perhaps – really – sadly

5.3 Verfassen des Schlussteils

Im letzten Teil Ihres Aufsatzes ziehen Sie Schlussfolgerungen aus den im Hauptteil aufgeführten Argumenten. Die Schlussfolgerungen sollen das Gesagte kurz zusammenfassen.

Im Anschluss daran geben Sie Ihre eigene Meinung zu dem Thema. Nennen Sie keine neuen Argumente im Schlussteil.

Redewendungen: Schlussfolgerungen

| In conclusion … | All in all … | On the whole … | In my view … |
| As a result … | In short … | In my opinion … | To my mind … |

Schritt 6: Überarbeitung des Aufsatzes

Überprüfen Sie Ihren Aufsatz in zwei Durchgängen:
1. Durchgang: Kontrollieren Sie Ihren Aufsatz auf sachliche Richtigkeit und logischen Aufbau (roter Faden).
2. Durchgang: Prüfen Sie die sprachliche Richtigkeit. Achten Sie hierbei auf Rechtschreibfehler, Grammatik sowie den Satzbau.

7 Eine Inhaltsangabe schreiben

Eine Inhaltsangabe ist ein kurzer Text, in dem Sie die wichtigsten Aspekte eines vorliegenden Textes mit eigenen Worten wiedergeben. Wenn Sie die Inhaltsangabe zu einem Text schreiben, zeigen Sie, dass Sie das Wesentliche des Textes verstanden haben. Eine Inhaltsangabe ist immer eine objektive Darstellung / Version des Originaltextes.

Regeln zum Schreiben einer Inhaltsangabe

- Interpretieren oder kommentieren Sie den Text nicht, sondern schreiben Sie objektiv, worum es in dem Text geht.
- Berücksichtigen Sie wichtige Fakten, Aspekte, Ereignisse.
- Klammern Sie alle unwichtigen Details des Textes aus. Verwenden Sie keine Statistiken, Zahlen oder Zitate.
- Kürzen Sie lange Sätze und vereinfachen Sie den Wortschatz des Textes.
- Schreiben Sie Ihre Inhaltsangabe im Präsens (Gegenwart).
- Fassen Sie sich kurz! Ihre Inhaltsangabe sollte maximal ein Fünftel bis ein Drittel der Länge des Originaltextes haben.

Inhaltsangaben von nicht-fiktionalen Texten

Wenn Sie eine Inhaltsangabe von einem nicht-fiktionalen Text, z. B. Zeitungsartikel, Bericht, Sachtext usw. schreiben sollen, dann folgen Sie den folgenden Schritten:

- Lesen Sie den Originaltext sorgfältig, um das Hauptthema herauszufinden.
- Unterstreichen Sie den Satz, in dem das Hauptthema / die Hauptthese genannt wird.
- Formulieren Sie einen Einleitungssatz für Ihre Inhaltsangabe, der, wenn möglich, Textsorte, Titel des Textes, Autor, Erscheinungsort, Erscheinungsdatum und Hauptthema beinhalten sollte.
  Beispiel: *The newspaper article* "The answer is blowing in the wind" *written by Rick Martin and published in* The Daily USA *on November 12, 2010 is about the first big wind farm project in Nebraska.*

- Lesen Sie nun den Text ein zweites Mal und unterstreichen Sie alle wichtigen Fakten, Ideen, Argumente im Text, die das Hauptthema hervorheben. Hinweis: Keine vollständigen Sätze, sondern nur Stichpunkte.
- Fassen Sie nun die Hauptideen des Textes mit eigenen Worten zusammen. Sie können entweder eine Liste mit Stichpunkten erstellen oder einen Satz zu jedem Abschnitt des Originaltextes schreiben.
- Schreiben Sie einige oder alle Ihrer Sätze um, indem Sie die Intention des Autors hinzufügen. (Siehe Formulierungen zur Autorenintention.)
- Setzen Sie Ihre Sätze in Bezug zueinander, indem Sie passende Bindewörter verwenden.
  ▶ Bindewörter, S. 237

Redewendungen: Formulierungen zur Autorenintention

The author / writer opens with …	He / she emphasizes …
He / she points out that …	He / she explains …
He / she shows that …	He / she concludes with …

Inhaltsangaben von fiktionalen Texten

Wenn Sie eine Inhaltsangabe von einem fiktionalen Text, z. B. Kurzgeschichte, Romanauszug, Gedicht usw. schreiben sollen, dann folgen Sie den nachstehenden Schritten:
- Lesen Sie den Originaltext einmal sorgfältig, um herauszufinden, wer der Hauptcharakter ist und in welcher Situation sich dieser gerade befindet.
- Unterstreichen Sie den / die Hauptcharakter(e) und den Satz, der die Situation am besten beschreibt, in der der Hauptcharakter sich gerade befindet.
- Formulieren Sie einen Einleitungssatz für Ihre Inhaltsangabe, der folgende Punkte beinhalten sollte: Textsorte, Titel des Textes, Autor, Erscheinungsort, Erscheinungsdatum und Hauptcharakter / Situation.
  Beispiel: *The extract from the novel "Cloning Miranda" written by Carol Matas deals with Miranda, a teenage girl, who finds that she has a sister who has been cloned only to save Miranda's life.*
- Lesen Sie nun den Text ein zweites Mal und unterteilen Sie den Text – wenn möglich – in zwei Teile. Der zweite Teil beginnt, wenn sich in der Handlung / Situation etwas ändert oder ein neuer Aspekt hinzukommt. Unterstreichen Sie den Wendepunkt im Text.
- Fassen Sie nun die Handlung des Textes mit eigenen Worten zusammen. Beschreiben Sie hierzu, was passiert und wie die Ereignisse miteinander verbunden sind.
- Setzen Sie Ihre Sätze in Bezug zueinander, indem Sie passende Bindewörter verwenden.
  ▶ Bindewörter, S. 237

Redewendungen: Formulierungen zur Autorenintention

The scene / story / action takes place in …	We get to know … by …
It takes place in the present / past / future.	He / She is confronted with …
	There is a conflict between …
The main character is …	The turning point …
There are two / three / etc. main characters.	At the beginning … / at the end …

8 Ein Protokoll schreiben

Ein Protokoll hält die Inhalte einer Konferenz, Besprechung, Diskussion, eines Referats oder einer Unterrichtsstunde fest. Dadurch ist es den Teilnehmern zu einem späteren Zeitpunkt möglich, die besprochenen Punkte nachzuvollziehen.

Formen des Protokolls

Es gibt verschiedene Formen des Protokollierens, die sich für verschiedene Anlässe eignen. Die beiden geläufigsten Formen – das Verlaufsprotokoll und das Ergebnisprotokoll – finden Sie im Folgenden erklärt:

	Verlaufsprotokoll	Ergebnisprotokoll
Kopfteil	Der Kopfteil sollte möglichst folgende Basisinformationen enthalten: Datum • Uhrzeit (Beginn und Ende) • Ort • Anwesende / Teilnehmer bzw. auch Abwesenheit eingeladener Personen • Leiter der Veranstaltung • Anlass / Thema der Veranstaltung • Tagesordnung	
Hauptteil	• Das Verlaufsprotokoll ist die ausführlichere Form des Protokolls. Es wird Wert gelegt auf den Prozess der Ergebnisfindung. • Geben Sie das Gehörte in zeitlicher Reihenfolge wieder. Dazu gehört auch der Inhalt von Vorschlägen, Diskussionen, Beschlüssen und Abstimmungsergebnissen.	• Das Ergebnisprotokoll ist die Kurzform des Protokolls. Es wird Wert gelegt auf das Festhalten der Ergebnisse der Veranstaltung. • Geben Sie nur die Ergebnisse des Gehörten wieder. Sie müssen deutlich formuliert sein und in der Reihenfolge der Tagesordnungspunkte dokumentiert werden.
Schlussteil	Der Schlussteil Ihres Protokolls sollte Ihre elektronische Signatur oder Kürzel sowie das Datum der Veranstaltung enthalten. Am Ende Ihres Protokolls weisen Sie auf mögliche Anlagen hin, z. B. Arbeitsblätter, die dem Protokoll angehängt werden.	

Protokolle schreiben

- Hören Sie erst genau zu, bevor Sie anfangen zu schreiben.
- Reduzieren Sie das Gehörte auf die Hauptaspekte und schreiben Sie diese stichpunktartig auf.
- Verwenden Sie Abkürzungen, die für Sie zu einem späteren Zeitpunkt aber auch noch verständlich sind. Schreiben Sie Namen und wichtige Begriffe möglichst vollständig auf.
- Schreiben Sie knapp und sachlich. Die eigene Meinung oder Wertungen gehören nicht in ein Protokoll.
- Verfassen Sie das Protokoll im Präsens (Gegenwart) in ganzen Sätzen.
- Gliedern Sie das Protokoll durch sinnvolle Absätze.

Role cards > Grammar Files > **Skills Files** > Vocabulary   **Skills Files**

9 Formelle Briefe und E-Mails schreiben

Formelle Briefe

Wenn Sie einen Brief an einen Geschäftspartner verfassen möchten, müssen Sie sich an bestimmte formale Vorgaben halten. Diese Vorgaben sind nicht einheitlich geregelt, sondern unterscheiden sich in den verschiedenen Kulturkreisen – auch innerhalb des englischsprachigen Raums. Bei englischsprachigen Geschäftsbriefen sollten Sie sich an den britischen Vorgaben orientieren, es sei denn, Sie schreiben an ein Unternehmen in den USA.

Es gibt verschiedene Anlässe für formelle Briefe: Anfragen, Angebote, Beschwerden, Bestellungen, Bewerbungsschreiben, Mahnungen, Mitteilungen, Rechnungen und Reservierungen.

YOUR BOOKS

342 Beaconsfield Road
Liverpool L256EE
England
Tel +44(0)151-1092687
Fax +44(0)151-1092688
www.yourbooks.co....uk
info@yourbooks....com

1 Your ref:
2 Our ref: Ab/Bc

3 15 March 20_

4 Confetti & Co
80 Tottenham Court Road
London WI6 8HR
England

5 Dear Sir or Madam

6 Your advertisement for balloons on the Internet

We refer to your advertisement for your balloons, which we found on the Internet last week.

We are a well established publishing company with subsidiaries all over the world. Our company is planning an introductory day for our new trainees. Therefore we would like to order your balloons for decoration.

Furthermore we saw your special March offer on the Internet and would be pleased if you could send us a confirmation of the validity of your stated prices. Moreover we would be grateful for information about terms of delivery and payment.

We look forward to receiving your answer soon.

7 Yours faithfully

8 *Matt Smith*

9 Matthew Smith
10 Training Manager

---

1 Im Amerikanischen stehen die Bezugszeichen ganz am Ende des Briefs unter den Anlagen.

2 Bezugszeichen des Absenders

3 Das Datum steht normalerweise unterhalb der Bezugszeichen. Es kann aber auch in der ersten Zeile oberhalb der Adressen oder in der ersten Zeile unterhalb der Adressen stehen.
Schreibweisen im Britischen Englisch: Tag, Monat, Jahr; im Amerikanischen Englisch: Monat, Tag, Jahr

4 Die Empfängeradresse steht unter dem Datum.

5 Anrede

6 Betreffzeile

7 Grußformel am Ende des Briefes

8 Unterschrift

9 Vollständiger Name

10 Position

205

Skills Files | Sprachkompetenzen: Produktion

Der folgende Beispielbrief zeigt Ihnen, wie ein Bewerbungsschreiben in Großbritannien in der Regel aufgebaut ist.

1 Lessingstr. 84
44147 Dortmund
Germany

Ms Angela Kelly
Maytree Nursery School
14 Moss Way
Leeds
LS2 9NQ
England

15 February 20_

Dear Ms Kelly

2 **Your advertisement in the Leeds Times of 6 February**

3 With reference to your advertisement in the Leeds Times of 6 February, I would like to apply for the position of a nursery school teacher.

4 After completing my education at Cologne College for Social Care I have been working with *Kindertagesstätte Regenbogenland* in Dortmund since August 20_. I now have great experience in developing the nursery learning environment and developing lesson plans. I feel well qualified for the position advertised.

5 I am particularly interested in this job as I would very much like to gain work experience abroad. As well as speaking fluent English and Spanish, I have working knowledge of French. My mother tongue is of course German.

I can supply references from former employers if you wish.

6 I enclose my curriculum vitae and certified translations of my certificates. Please do not hesitate to contact me if you should require further information.

7 I look forward to hearing from you.

Yours sincerely

Jasmin Kramer

Jasmin Kramer

8 Encs.

---

1 Ihre Adresse ohne Angabe des Namens gehört in die Ecke oben links.

2 Betreffzeile

3 Sagen Sie, worauf Sie sich beziehen (z. B. Anzeige, Telefonat), und nennen Sie den Anlass für den Brief.

4 Stellen Sie sich vor, indem Sie die wichtigsten Qualifikationen und Erfahrungen benennen.

5 Nennen Sie weitere Qualifikationen.

6 Erwähnen Sie die Anlagen Ihres Briefes und weisen Sie darauf hin, dass Sie weitere Zeugnisse usw. senden können.

7 Abschlussworte

8 Encs. = Enclosures (Anlagen)

Formelle E-Mails

Mittlerweile werden verstärkt keine formellen Briefe mehr geschrieben, sondern formelle E-Mails. Sie nehmen zum einen weniger Zeit in Anspruch und sie sind zum anderen schneller beim Empfänger.

Wenn Sie eine formelle E-Mail schreiben, dann müssen Sie den gleichen Kommunikationsregeln folgen wie beim formellen Brief.

Beim Aufbau Ihrer formellen E-Mail gibt es jedoch Unterschiede zum formellen Brief. Das Beispiel zeigt Ihnen, wie eine formelle E-Mail in Großbritannien in der Regel aufgebaut ist:

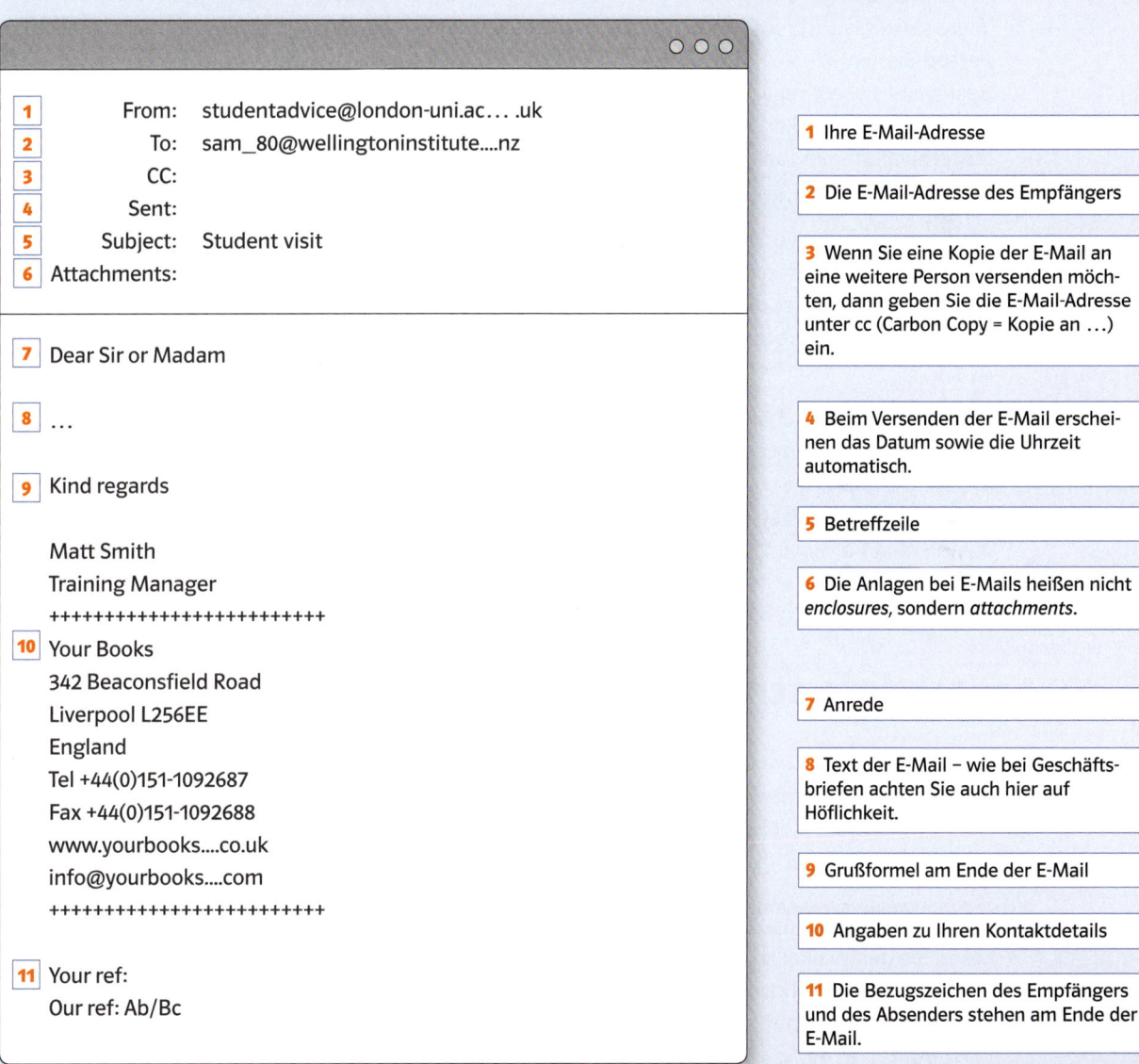

1 From: studentadvice@london-uni.ac….uk
2 To: sam_80@wellingtoninstitute….nz
3 CC:
4 Sent:
5 Subject: Student visit
6 Attachments:

7 Dear Sir or Madam

8 …

9 Kind regards

Matt Smith
Training Manager
+++++++++++++++++++++++++
10 Your Books
342 Beaconsfield Road
Liverpool L256EE
England
Tel +44(0)151-1092687
Fax +44(0)151-1092688
www.yourbooks….co.uk
info@yourbooks….com
+++++++++++++++++++++++++
11 Your ref:
Our ref: Ab/Bc

1 Ihre E-Mail-Adresse

2 Die E-Mail-Adresse des Empfängers

3 Wenn Sie eine Kopie der E-Mail an eine weitere Person versenden möchten, dann geben Sie die E-Mail-Adresse unter cc (Carbon Copy = Kopie an …) ein.

4 Beim Versenden der E-Mail erscheinen das Datum sowie die Uhrzeit automatisch.

5 Betreffzeile

6 Die Anlagen bei E-Mails heißen nicht *enclosures*, sondern *attachments*.

7 Anrede

8 Text der E-Mail – wie bei Geschäftsbriefen achten Sie auch hier auf Höflichkeit.

9 Grußformel am Ende der E-Mail

10 Angaben zu Ihren Kontaktdetails

11 Die Bezugszeichen des Empfängers und des Absenders stehen am Ende der E-Mail.

Skills Files | Sprachkompetenzen: Produktion

Redewendungen

- **Anreden:**
  Dear Sir or Madam
  Dear Sir
  Dear Madam
  Dear Mr Albee
  Dear Ms Howard

- **Schlussformeln:**
  Yours faithfully (Britisch)
  Yours sincerely (Britisch; wenn Sie die Person namentlich kennen)
  Best wishes / Best regards / Kind regards (Britisch und Amerikanisch)
  Sincerely (Amerikanisch)

- **Bezugnahme:**
  We refer to your advertisement …
  Referring to your advertisement …
  We refer to your offer of April 26, 20…
  Your firm has been recommended to us by …

- **Briefanlass und Geschäftsvorstellung:**
  We wish to point out that …
  We should appreciate it if you would …
  We are a medium-sized company importing a wide range of …

- **Informationen / Services erbitten:**
  Would you please send us … ?
  We would be grateful for details of …
  We would like to ask for / to …
  A visit by your representative would be appreciated.

- **Nachrichten übermitteln:**
  We are pleased to inform you that …
  You will be pleased to hear that …
  We are really sorry to inform you that …

- **Abschlussworte:**
  We hope to hear from you soon.
  We look forward to hearing from you soon.
  We look forward to an early reply.
  We hope this information will help you.

- **Struktur:**
  therefore / for this reason
  if / provided that
  however / but
  besides / in addition
  so far / up to now
  still
  as
  so that

10 Leserbriefe schreiben

Der Leserbrief gehört zu den formellen Briefen. In der Regel schreibt man einen Leserbrief an eine Zeitung oder Zeitschrift, wenn man einen Artikel über ein umstrittenes Thema gelesen hat und seine Sichtweise zu diesem Thema äußern möchte. ▶ Formelle Briefe und E-Mails, S. 205

Tipps: Verfassen eines Leserbriefs

- Lesen Sie den Artikel sorgfältig durch und machen Sie sich Notizen zu Aspekten, auf die Sie in Ihrem Leserbrief eingehen möchten.

- Sammeln Sie Ideen für Ihre Argumente und strukturieren Sie diese.

- Fassen Sie sich kurz. Der Stil eines Leserbriefs ist knapp und klar. Wichtig ist, dass Sie sachlich bleiben.

- Schreiben Sie den Leserbrief auf dem Computer und senden Sie ihn per E-Mail.

- Bevor Sie Ihren Leserbrief absenden, lesen Sie ihn nochmals sorgfältig durch und korrigieren Sie alle gefundenen Fehler.

Aufbau des Leserbriefs und Redewendungen

- Anrede:
  To the editor
  Dear editor
  Dear Sir / Dear Madam / Dear Sir or Madam

- In der Einleitung stellen Sie zunächst den Bezug zu dem Zeitungsartikel her. Nennen Sie neben dem Thema auch die Quelle des Artikels, auf den Sie sich beziehen.
  I refer to your report / article on energy consumption in today's / last week's edition of *USA Worldwide*.
  With reference to the article on energy consumption (*USA Worldwide*, 12 June 20…) I would like to point out that …
  I am writing with reference to the article on energy consumption you published in yesterday's issue of *USA Worldwide*.

- Machen Sie Ihre eigene Position zu dem Thema deutlich.
  I agree with your statements on …
  I entirely disagree with …
  I am completely opposed to …

- Im Hauptteil begründen Sie Ihre Position sachlich und zeigen Hintergrundwissen.

- Der Hauptteil besteht aus klar voneinander abgrenzbaren Argumenten, die Sie bestenfalls mit Beispielen veranschaulichen.
  One should not forget that …
  My first / second / final argument …
  Another aspect is that …
  To my mind …

- Im Schlussteil bekräftigen Sie noch einmal Ihre Position zu dem Thema, indem Sie Schlussfolgerungen ziehen und Forderungen aufstellen bzw. Lösungsvorschläge machen.
  I am sure many readers will agree with me when I claim that …
  In conclusion, I would say that …
  All in all, …
  Together, we can …

- Wiederholen Sie Ihre Argumente nicht.

- Der Leserbrief endet ohne Grußformel nur mit Vornamen und Familiennamen.

  ► Bindewörter, S. 237

Beispiel:

To the editor
I am writing about the article "Food pantries falling short" in the Aug. 10 *Press*. The Stanton family represents one in 10 of Michigan households that suffer from hunger. These households are a fraction of the 38 million who go hungry every day in the United States.
These are not statistics; they are humans in the image of God going hungry. The U.S. Conference of Mayors reported that requests for food assistance increased by an average of 12 percent in 24 cities surveyed. More than half of those in need had children, and while many were employed they were unable to put food on their table.
So what can we do? We cannot continue to read articles like this and remain idle. How we treat the hungry in our midst speaks volumes about our hearts, our character and our priorities. This is indeed a moral issue, an issue of justice and one that demands our immediate action.
In addition to donating food to local pantries, we can also call on our legislators to make a difference. A new piece of legislation called the Hunger-Free Communities Act would commit the federal government to cutting hunger in the U.S. in half by 2020, and eliminate it by 2025. This bill needs to be passed as soon as possible. Together, we can end hunger. The question is only when we will choose to solve this problem.
Michael Martin

11 Persönliche Briefe und E-Mails schreiben

Persönliche E-Mails

In den meisten Fällen werden keine persönlichen Briefe mehr geschrieben und mit der Post verschickt, sondern E-Mails. Sie können Ihre E-Mail zwanglos formulieren, so als würden Sie ein Gespräch mit der Person führen. Im Allgemeinen sollten Sie aber denselben Regeln folgen, die für das Schreiben eines Briefes gelten. Bedenken Sie, dass der ausländische Freund einen bestimmten Kommunikationsstil von Ihnen erwarten könnte.

Beispiel:

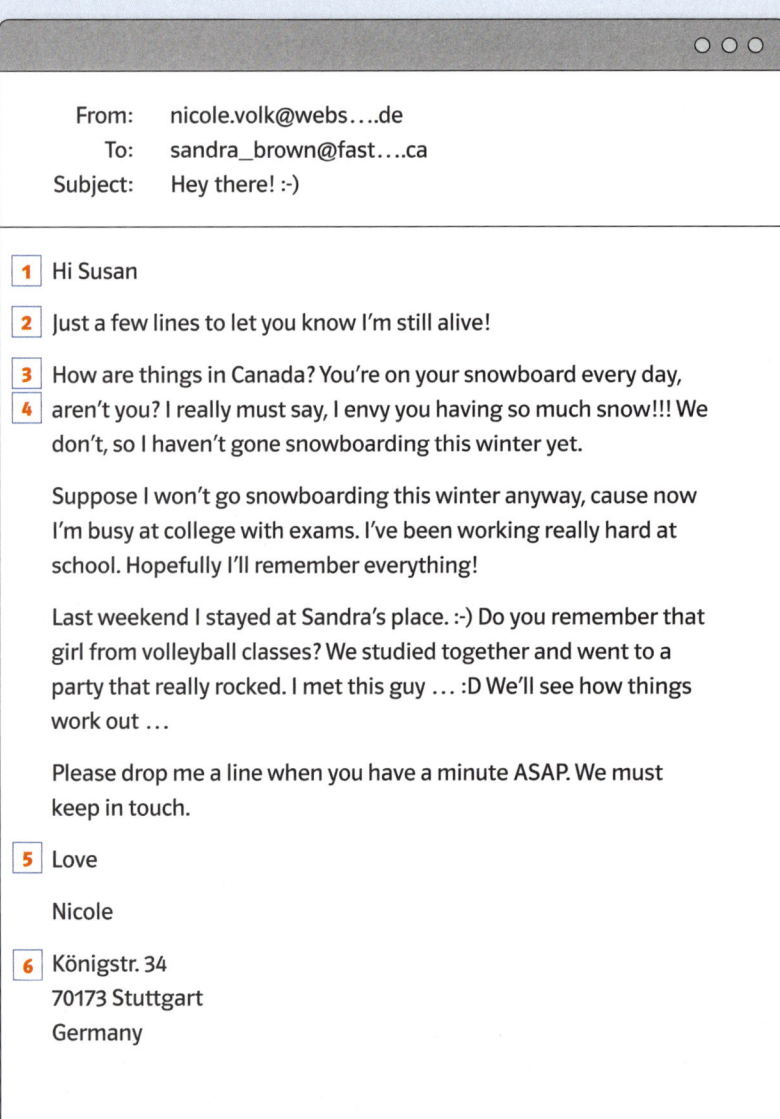

From: nicole.volk@webs….de
To: sandra_brown@fast….ca
Subject: Hey there! :-)

1 Hi Susan

2 Just a few lines to let you know I'm still alive!

3 How are things in Canada? You're on your snowboard every day,
4 aren't you? I really must say, I envy you having so much snow!!! We don't, so I haven't gone snowboarding this winter yet.

Suppose I won't go snowboarding this winter anyway, cause now I'm busy at college with exams. I've been working really hard at school. Hopefully I'll remember everything!

Last weekend I stayed at Sandra's place. :-) Do you remember that girl from volleyball classes? We studied together and went to a party that really rocked. I met this guy … :D We'll see how things work out …

Please drop me a line when you have a minute ASAP. We must keep in touch.

5 Love

Nicole

6 Königstr. 34
70173 Stuttgart
Germany

---

1 Beginnen Sie Ihre E-Mail mit einer Anrede: *Dear + name* (formell) *Hi + name* (informell).

2 Das erste Wort nach der Anrede wird immer groß geschrieben.

3 Gruppieren Sie Ihre Informationen in Sinnabschnitten.

4 Sie können Frageanhängsel verwenden, z. B. *aren't you?, don't you?*

5 Beenden Sie Ihre E-Mail mit einer entsprechenden Schlussfloskel, z. B. *All the best / Best wishes / Bye for now / Love / Lots of love and kisses …*

6 Sie schreiben Ihre Adresse nicht zu Beginn der E-Mail, sondern erst am Ende unterhalb Ihres Namens. Es ist auch üblich die Adresse wegzulassen.

Role cards > Grammar Files > **Skills Files** > Vocabulary

Persönliche E-Mails verfassen

- Wenn Sie eine persönliche E-Mail schreiben, müssen Sie nicht in vollständigen Sätzen schreiben.
  Beispiel: *Suppose I won't go snowboarding this winter anyway, cause I'm busy at college with exams.*

Redemittel

- Freundliche Formulierungen:

Well, …	go back to a topic
Anyway …	summarize the topic
By the way …	change the topic
Of course …	say something is obvious
(Un)luckily …	show good or bad fortune
To be honest …	say what you really mean

- Beispiele für Emoticons / Smileys:

:-)	smiling, happy
:D	large grin
:o	shocked, surprised
:O	shouting

- Beispiele für Abkürzungen:

LOL	laughing out loud
2BCTND	to be continued
AKA	also known as
ASAP	as soon as possible
CM	call me
F2F	face to face
TMI	too much information
THX	thanks
OMG	Oh my God
L8R	later
B4N	Bye for now

Persönliche Briefe

Einen persönlichen Brief schreiben Sie an jemanden, den Sie gut kennen, z. B. an einen Freund oder einen Verwandten. Es gibt ebenfalls keine festen Regeln. Es gibt verschiedene Kommunikationsanlässe: Freundschaftlicher Brief, Liebesbrief, Einladung, Entschuldigung, Glückwunsch / Kondolenz und Danksagung.

12 Fotos und Illustrationen beschreiben / analysieren

Wenn Sie ein Bild analysieren möchten, dann beschreiben Sie das Bild sowohl optisch, d. h. das Aussehen des Bildes, als auch inhaltlich, d. h. den Informationsgehalt. Die Bildanalyse soll so genau sein, dass sich ein blinder Mensch theoretisch das Bild genau vorstellen kann.

Erster Eindruck

- Beschreiben Sie zunächst die Bildart, die Sie sehen, und welche Situation das Bild zeigt.
- Wenn angegeben, nennen Sie die Quellenangabe des Bildes, z. B.: Von wem stammt das Bild? Wer hat es erstellt? Wann ist das Bild entstanden? Welchen Titel trägt das Bild? Wo wurde es veröffentlicht?

Beschreibung des Bildes / des Fotos

- Beschreiben Sie nun detailliert, was Sie auf dem Bild sehen können. Gehen Sie hierbei so vor, dass Sie mit dem wichtigsten Aspekt des Bildes beginnen (im Vordergrund, im Fokus), und nennen Sie erst dann die Details, die im Hintergrund zu sehen sind.
- Achten Sie darauf, dass Sie nur beschreiben und noch nicht interpretieren!
- Was genau zeigt das Bild? Beantworten Sie möglichst die w-Fragen „wer?", „wo?", „was?".
- Beschreiben Sie zudem, wenn möglich, die Körpersprache der Menschen, d.h. Gestik und Mimik, die Beziehung der Menschen zueinander, die Verwendung von Farben, Licht und Symbolen.

Interpretation und Intention

- Versuchen Sie nun, das Bild zu interpretieren, d.h. ziehen Sie Schlussfolgerungen aus dem Beschriebenen hinsichtlich der Intention (Absicht) des Malers / Fotografen.
  - Welche Atmosphäre vermittelt das Bild? Warum wird diese Atmosphäre vermittelt?
  - Welche Botschaft möchte der Maler / Fotograf weitergeben? Und was möchte er / sie damit bewirken?
  - Welche Zielgruppe wird angesprochen?

Wirkung / persönliche Meinung

- Im letzten Teil Ihrer Bildanalyse formulieren Sie Ihren persönlichen Eindruck, den das Bild bei Ihnen hinterlassen hat. Versuchen Sie hierzu immer Beispiele dafür zu geben, welche Elemente des Bildes genau zu Ihrer persönlichen Meinung über das Bild geführt haben.
  - Wie wirkt das Bild auf Sie? Ablehnend oder anziehend?
  - Welche Gefühle weckt das Bild in Ihnen?
  - Bestätigt das Bild die Wirklichkeit oder zeigt es Widersprüche?

Tempus

- Wenn Sie beschreiben, welchen Gegenstand / welche Person Sie in einem Bild sehen, dann verwenden Sie die einfache Form des Präsens. ▶ Present simple, S. 183
  Beispiele:
  There is a young person in the foreground.
  The photo shows …
- Wenn Sie jedoch beschreiben, was die Person in dem Bild gerade tut, dann müssen Sie die Verlaufsform des Präsens verwenden. ▶ Present continuous, S. 184
  Beispiel: *The young person is holding a sign with one hand.*

Redemittel: Bilder und Fotos beschreiben

- **Beschreibung der Bildart und der gezeigten Situation:**
  The picture is a / an illustration / painting / collage / still (from a film) / electronic image …
  The (colour / black-and-white) photograph shows …
  This is a (painting) showing a typical … scene / situation …
  This (collage) illustrates …
  In this (still) you can see (that) …

- **Beschreiben, wo sich etwas im Bild befindet:**
  on the right-hand / left-hand side of the illustration
  At the top / bottom of the photo you can find …
  in the upper right-hand corner
  in the lower left-hand corner
  In the centre of the picture there is …
  In the foreground / background you can see …

- **Interpretation und Intention:**
  The person in the picture looks … (+ adjective)
  The painting gives you the impression that …
  The artist wants to express that …
  Perhaps his / her intention is to show that …
  The illustration is aimed at children …
  Considering the … in the photo you could draw the conclusion that …

- **Beschreibung von Farben und Licht:**
  The colours are bright / dark.
  The photograph is clear / in focus / blurred / not in focus / well-lit.
  The day the photograph was taken on was sunny / cloudy.

- **Beschreibung der Atmosphäre:**
  This creates a / an … atmosphere.
  The main factors that contribute to this atmosphere are …
  The atmosphere is cosy, friendly, funny, happy, lively, peaceful, warm …
  It is chilly, dark, depressing, desperate, sad, scary, serious, terrifying …
  The atmosphere is boring, exotic, hectic, mysterious …
  The … in the photo conveys an atmosphere of great sadness / happiness.

- **Persönliche Meinung:**
  The impression I get from this illustration is that …
  The illustration makes me feel …
  The colours / light the artist has chosen make / makes me feel … (+ adjective)
  In my opinion the painting is supposed to …
  To my mind the photograph would be better if … (+ past simple)
  My first thought when I saw the (photo) was …
  The (collage) is shocking / brilliant / breathtaking / terrifying / impressive / realistic …
  The (painting) reminds me of …

13 Karikaturen beschreiben / analysieren

Eine Karikatur ist eine satirische (spöttische) Darstellung von Menschen oder gesellschaftlichen Situationen. Charakteristisch für Karikaturen ist, dass sie die Realität übertrieben und verformt darstellen mit dem Ziel, einen gesellschaftlichen Zustand, eine Person oder eine Institution zu kritisieren. Meistens besteht eine Karikatur aus einem Bild und einem kurzen Text innerhalb des Bildes, z. B. als Sprechblase, oder unterhalb des Bildes als Bildunterschrift.

Eine Karikatur bedient sich in der Regel zahlreicher Stilmittel, um die Komik einer Situation oder die Eigenheiten einer Person überspitzt darzustellen.

Beispiele:

exaggeration	Übertreibung	Eigenschaften werden überdimensioniert und überzogen dargestellt.
irony	Ironie	Das Gegenteil des Gesagten ist gemeint.
pun	Wortspiel	Beruht auf der Mehrdeutigkeit und Verdrehung von Wörtern
simile	Vergleich	Veranschaulichung einer Aussage, indem sie durch *like* oder *as* mit einem anderen Bereich in Beziehung gesetzt wird
symbol	Symbol	Etwas Konkretes verweist auf etwas Abstraktes.

Wenn Sie eine Karikatur beschreiben und analysieren möchten, beachten Sie „Redemittel: Bilder und Fotos beschreiben" auf Seite 213. ▶ Fotos und Illustrationen, S. 211

Redemittel: Karikaturen beschreiben

- Die Karikatur beschreiben:
  The cartoon consists of an illustration of …
  The illustration shows …
  There is a caption below the cartoon, which says "…".
  In the (first) speech bubble it says "…"
  The text in the speech bubble is spoken by …

- Interpretation der Karikatur:
  The figure is a caricature of …
  The cartoonist exaggerates character traits.
  The person's body language shows that …
  From his / her facial expression you can conclude that …
  … symbolizes / stands for / is a symbol of …

- Die Botschaft der Karikatur:
  The cartoonist's message might be that …
  His point seems to be that …
  Probably his intention is to show that …
  The cartoonist is criticizing the behaviour of …
  He is making fun of …
  He is making a sarcastic comment on …

- Persönliche Meinung:
  I think / I don't think the cartoon is (very) funny because …
  I think / I don't think the cartoon is easy to understand because …
  I agree / I don't agree with the point the cartoonist is making because …

14 Diagramme beschreiben / analysieren

Diagramme sind graphische Darstellungen von numerischen Daten oder Informationen. Sie veranschaulichen Informationen und erleichtern es dem Leser, komplizierte Sachverhalte aufzunehmen.

Je nachdem, was ein Diagramm verdeutlichen soll, werden unterschiedliche Arten von Diagrammen eingesetzt. Im Folgenden finden Sie eine Auswahl der am häufigsten verwendeten Arten von Diagrammen.

Pie chart: Ein Tortendiagramm ist in mehrere Kreissektoren unterteilt, die Teile des Ganzen anzeigen. Es eignet sich besonders, um Anteile darzustellen.

Bar chart: Ein Säulendiagramm oder Balkendiagramm ist ein Diagramm, das die Häufigkeitsverteilung verschiedener Sektoren veranschaulicht. Es eignet sich besonders, um einige wenige Daten miteinander zu vergleichen.

Line graph: Ein Liniendiagramm stellt den funktionellen Zusammenhang von zwei Merkmalen graphisch dar. Es eignet sich besonders gut, um die Entwicklung von Werten graphisch darzustellen.

Diagramme beschreiben

- Nennen Sie zunächst die Art des Diagramms, den Titel, die Quelle, Erscheinungsort und -jahr sowie die Maßeinheiten und Parameter.
- Beschreiben Sie das Diagramm nun detailliert. Machen Sie sich zunächst Notizen. Je nach Art des Diagramms können Sie:
  - den Verlauf der Entwicklung differenziert beschreiben,
  - Einzelwerte vergleichen,
  - Gemeinsamkeiten und Unterschiede benennen,
  - den Kurvenverlauf, die Säulenverteilung, die Sektorverteilung beschreiben,
  - Maximal- und Minimalwerte angeben.
- Achten Sie darauf, dass Ihre Beschreibung nicht zu detailliert ausfällt. Konzentrieren Sie sich nur auf auffällige Entwicklungen oder Zahlen.
- Mit Hilfe Ihrer Notizen formulieren Sie vollständige Sätze, um das Diagramm zu beschreiben.
- Versuchen Sie nun, das Diagramm zu interpretieren, d.h. ziehen Sie Schlussfolgerungen aus dem Beschriebenen und überprüfen Sie gegebenenfalls die Zuverlässigkeit der Quelle.
- Fassen Sie die wichtigsten Ergebnisse des Diagramms in ein bis zwei Sätzen zusammen.

Redemittel: Diagramme beschreiben

- **Bestandsaufnahme der Informationen:**
  The pie chart "US Exports" published in *The Daily USA* in New York in 20… shows in percentage terms what the USA exported in the year 20…

- **Beschreibung:**
  The chart / graph / diagram shows …
  It shows the development from … to …
  The table shows the change of … from … to …
  The chart gives an overview of …
  The time scale runs vertically.
  The weight scale runs horizontally.
  On the y-axis / x-axis you can see …

- **Einen Anstieg beschreiben:**
  There is a noticeable upward trend between … and …
  By 20… figures reached their highest level.
  The number grew / increased.
  The number of … rose slightly / sharply / slowly.

- **Eine Abnahme beschreiben:**
  We notice a downward trend between … and …
  By 20… figures reached their lowest level.
  The number declined / decreased.
  The number fell slightly / slowly / sank sharply.
  The number of … remained unchanged / steady.

- **Unveränderte Werte:**
  Figures remained steady / Figures did not change.

- **Zahlen und Daten:**
  the figures for the last year / the last month, etc.
  the latest figures
  the total number of …
  a significant / an insignificant number of …
  a high percentage of …
  a majority / minority of …
  percentage / amount

- **Mengenbezeichnungen:**
  a total of
  over / under
  nearly / almost / approximately
  exactly
  more / less than
  the same number as
  the same amount of
  from over / under
  one in five
  half / a third / a quarter / two thirds
  100 per cent
  twice / three times as many
  on average

- **Interpretation:**
  The biggest change can be seen in …
  This leads to the assumption that …
  This suggests a relation between … and …

- **Schlussfolgerung:**
  The drastic change may be due to …
  All in all you can say that …
  To sum up … we can say that …

Role cards > Grammar Files > **Skills Files** > Vocabulary

15 Präsentieren

Eine Präsentation oder ein Referat ist eine vorbereitete Vorstellung von Inhalten oder Ergebnissen zu einem bestimmten Thema. Ziel einer Präsentation ist es, die Zuhörer zu informieren.

In der Schule finden häufig Gruppenpräsentationen statt, so dass Sie sich untereinander absprechen sollten, wer welchen Teil übernimmt. ▶ Gruppenarbeit und Projekte, S. 239

Brainstorming

- Verschaffen Sie sich zunächst einen Überblick über das Thema, indem Sie ein Wortnetz zu dem Themenbereich erstellen. ▶ Wortnetze, S. 236
- Sie sollten sich auch Folgendes genau überlegen:
  - Welches Ziel verfolge ich mit der Präsentation?
  - An wen ist die Präsentation adressiert?
  - Welche Hilfsmittel und Medien kann ich verwenden, um erfolgreich zu präsentieren?

Materialsuche

- Sammeln Sie Informationen zu dem Thema. Sie können z. B. in Bibliotheken, Zeitungen, Schulbüchern, Lexika oder dem Internet recherchieren. Oder Sie befragen einen Experten zu dem Thema. ▶ Internetrecherche, S. 241

Konzipierung und Aufbau der Präsentation

- Da Sie möglichst frei sprechen sollten und dies in der Fremdsprache noch etwas schwerer fällt, ist es sinnvoll, wenn Sie sich einen Ablaufplan Ihrer Präsentation erstellen. Sie können z. B. eine Tabelle erstellen, in der die Gliederung, der zeitliche Ablauf und der Einsatz von Medien ersichtlich werden. Den Ablaufplan können Sie sich auf Ihren Rednertisch legen, um während der Präsentation bei Bedarf einen Blick darauf werfen zu können.
- In der Regel können Sie Ihre Präsentation anhand der klassischen Dreiteilung aufbauen: Einstieg – Hauptteil – Schlussteil, wobei Sie den Einstieg und den Schlussteil kurz halten sollten, der Hauptteil kann ausführlicher sein.
- Einstieg: Anrede der Zuhörer und sich vorstellen – Thema vorstellen – Gliederung vorstellen. Dabei ist es sinnvoll, das Interesse der Zuhörer zu wecken. Beginnen Sie z. B. mit einem Zitat, einer Karikatur oder einer provokanten Frage, um die volle Aufmerksamkeit zu erhalten.
- Hauptteil: Gut strukturierte Ausführungen (z. B. chronologische Anordnung der Hauptaspekte) – Beispiele geben – visuelle Hilfsmittel hinzuziehen
- Schlussteil: Zusammenfassung der Hauptaspekte – Dank an die Zuhörer.

Stichwortkarten

- Reduzieren Sie Ihren Vortrag auf die wichtigsten Stichpunkte und schreiben Sie diese auf Karteikarten. Die Stichwortkarten sollten keinesfalls den ganzen Text Ihres Vortrags enthalten. Sie sollten es auch vermeiden, vollständige Sätze aufzuschreiben. Sie können sich auch Stichworte zu Beispielen oder Vokabeln auf den Stichwortkarten notieren.

- Sie sollten die Stichwortkarten so aufteilen, dass Sie während des Vortrags nicht durcheinander geraten. Es ist sinnvoll, für den Einstieg und den Schlussteil jeweils eine Stichwortkarte vorzubereiten. Für den Hauptteil sollten Sie je nach Länge Ihres Vortrags mehrere Karten vorbereiten, z. B. je Hauptaspekt eine Karte.

Visuelle Hilfsmittel

- Die meisten Menschen nehmen nur 30 % über das Ohr auf, aber ca. 70 % über das Auge. Überlegen Sie sich deshalb, welche visuellen Hilfsmittel Ihre Präsentation angemessen unterstützen können.
- Weniger ist mehr! Überfrachten Sie Tafelanschrieb, Plakate, Folien, Handzettel usw. möglichst nicht. Strukturieren Sie diese übersichtlich. ▶ Plakate, S. 244

Vortragsweise

- Wenn Sie nur ablesen, werden sich Ihre Zuhörer schnell langweilen. Sie sollten daher möglichst frei sprechen und nur hin und wieder auf Ihre Stichwortkarten zurückgreifen.
- Sprechen Sie nicht so, wie Sie schreiben, sondern versuchen Sie, natürlich zu sprechen, so dass Ihre Zuhörer Ihnen folgen können. Formulieren Sie möglichst kurze und unkomplizierte Sätze. Verzichten Sie, wenn möglich, auf Fachbegriffe, die Ihren Zuhörern unbekannt sind. Falls Sie doch auf Fachbegriffe zurückgreifen müssen, schreiben Sie diese an die Tafel.
- Nutzen Sie Wiederholungen, um Wichtiges zu betonen.

Stimme und Körpersprache

- Sprechen Sie langsam: So haben Sie länger Zeit, um Ihre Sätze im Englischen zu formulieren.
- Machen Sie Pausen: Die Zuhörer hören das Gesagte vielleicht zum ersten Mal.
- Halten Sie Blickkontakt mit den Zuhörern. Achten Sie auch auf die Reaktionen der Zuhörer.
- Versuchen Sie, Ihre Aussagen durch Gestik und Mimik zu unterstreichen.

Redemittel für die Präsentation

- Einstieg:
  Good morning, my name is …
  Good morning, let me introduce our group. …
  Can everybody hear me alright?
  Can everybody see the board / poster / screen?
  Let me start by saying a few words about …
  The topic of my presentation today is …

- Struktur und Zeitangaben:
  My presentation will last fifteen minutes.
  My presentation is split into four key areas.
  Firstly, … Secondly, … Thirdly, … Finally, …

- Hauptteil:
  Let me give you an example.
  If you look at the screen, you'll see that …
  As you can see on the board / poster …
  That proves my point.
  I'd like to move on to …
  Before we go any further, let's look at …

- Schlussteil:
  Finally …
  I'd like to finish / conclude by saying that …
  To summarize … / To conclude …
  Thank you very much for your attention.
  If you have any questions, please feel free to ask.

16 An einer Diskussion teilnehmen

Diskussionen dienen dem Austausch von Meinungen und Ideen zu einem bestimmten Thema. Sie können uns auch neue Aspekte liefern, wenn wir uns mit unbekannten Themen beschäftigen.
Ob Sie die Diskussion leiten oder an der Diskussion teilnehmen, Sie sollten sich immer gut vorbereiten und sich an die folgenden Regeln halten.

Regeln und Redemittel für die Diskussionsleitung

- Sorgen Sie für einen geordneten Diskussionsablauf und guten Diskussionsstil, d. h. achten Sie besonders auf die Höflichkeit der Diskussionsteilnehmer.

- Halten Sie Ihre eigene Meinung zurück und bleiben Sie immer neutral.

- Geben Sie eine Einführung in das Diskussionsthema und stellen Sie die Diskussionsteilnehmer vor.
  (As you know,) our discussion today is about …
  On my right / left I have … (name of person or group), who is / are in favour of … / against …

- Bestimmen Sie die Reihenfolge der Wortmeldungen.
  Who would like to open the discussion?
  …, would you like to open the discussion?
  The next person to speak is …, followed by … and then …

- Sorgen Sie dafür, dass alle Teilnehmer die gleichen Chancen haben, zu Wort zu kommen.
  Is there anything you would like to say, …?

- Bringen Sie Vielredner dazu, sich kurz zu fassen.
  I'm sorry to interrupt you, but I'm afraid I have to stop you there.
  Sorry, but I must give the others a chance to put forward their arguments now.

- Sorgen Sie dafür, dass immer nur ein Teilnehmer spricht.
  Please wait your turn. You'll have a chance to speak in a minute!
  If you'd just let … finish, please.

- Notieren Sie sich die wichtigsten Ideen / Argumente und fassen Sie die Diskussion am Ende zusammen.
  Time is running out, so I'd like to sum up what we've been discussing.
  We heard from … that …

- Bedanken Sie sich am Ende der Diskussion bei den Teilnehmern für die Teilnahme an der Diskussion.
  Thank you for taking part in the discussion!

Regeln und Redemittel für Diskussionsteilnehmer

- Stellen Sie zunächst sicher, dass Sie das Diskussionsthema richtig verstanden haben.

- Entscheiden Sie, welche Meinung Sie vertreten.

- Wenn Sie ausreichend Zeit haben, kann es sinnvoll sein, sich mit den Gegenargumenten auseinanderzusetzen. Überlegen Sie sich schon vorher, was Sie den Argumenten der anderen Diskussionsteilnehmer entgegensetzen können.

- Sprechen Sie kurz und bleiben Sie beim Thema.

- Bereiten Sie sich gut auf die Diskussion vor, indem Sie sich vor Beginn der Diskussion Argumente zurechtlegen und diese stichpunktartig aufschreiben. Sie sollten Ihre Argumente immer erläutern und begründen können. Es ist auch hilfreich, wenn Sie sich Beispiele überlegen.
  Firstly … secondly … finally …
  First I would like to point out …
  In addition / Moreover / Besides / Furthermore …
  Another significant advantage is …
  On the one hand … on the other hand …
  Consequently / That is why / Therefore …
  However / In contrast to / Nevertheless …
  I think / feel / believe / am of the opinion that …
  To my mind …
  In my opinion …

- Bleiben Sie immer höflich und denken Sie daran, dass es um das Thema geht und nicht um die Personen. Also attackieren Sie nur die Argumente.
  I'm sorry, but I (completely) disagree.
  That's an interesting point, but …
  You've missed the point (entirely).

- Falls Sie etwas nicht richtig verstanden haben und einen Diskussionsteilnehmer unterbrechen möchten, seien Sie höflich.
  Sorry to interrupt, but could you please explain / repeat the point you have just made?

- Gehen Sie auf die Meinungen der anderen Diskussionsteilnehmer ein.
  You are (quite / absolutely) right.
  That's a very good point!
  Absolutely! / Exactly!
  I agree (with you / Laura).
  Andrea made a very valid point when she said that …
  I partly agree with Sven. What he didn't mention was …

Weitere Redemittel für Diskussionsteilnehmer

- Vorschläge machen:
  I suggest that we …
  We would propose that you …
  What do you think about …?
  If I were you, I would …
  Why don't we …

- Auf Vorschläge reagieren:
  That's a good idea! / Fine!
  OK. / Yes, why not?
  OK, if you want, I don't really mind.
  I'm not sure that will work.
  I think it would be a better idea to talk about …
  What about …?

- **Nach einer Meinung fragen:**
  What do you think about …?
  How do you feel about …?
  What is your view on / about …?
  In your opinion what is the best solution?
  What would you say?

- **Mit Zwischenreden umgehen:**
  Can I just finish what I was saying, please?
  Just a second, I haven't quite finished.
  Would you let me / allow me to make my point, please.
  I'll just finish what I wanted to say if you don't mind.
  You could at least let me finish my sentence!

- **Das Thema wechseln:**
  There is something else I'd like to say …
  Have you ever thought of …?
  On the other hand …
  I'd like to bring up another point.

- **Zum eigentlichen Thema zurückkehren:**
  Let's get back to what we were saying / discussing.
  Let's get back to the point.
  As I was saying before, …
  This discussion is getting away from the original topic.
  What we should really be talking about is …

- **Nachfragen bei Verständnisschwierigkeiten:**
  Did I get that right?
  Do you really mean that …?
  Could you explain what you just said / the point you just made again, please?
  Could you give me / us an example, please?

- **Missverständnisse aufklären:**
  I'm sorry, but …
  … that's not what I meant to say (at all)!
  … you've got me (completely) wrong.
  … you've (completely) misunderstood me.
  Sorry, I didn't make myself clear. I'll try and explain again.

17 Eine Debatte führen

Eine Debatte ist eine formale Diskussion über einen Antrag in einer Sitzung *(motion)*, die mit einer Abstimmung über den diskutierten Sachverhalt endet. Ähnlich einer Diskussion ist das Ziel einer Debatte Argumente für oder gegen den Antrag inhaltlich und rhetorisch möglichst überzeugend zu präsentieren.
Eine Debatte folgt klaren Regeln:
- Es gibt einen Vorsitzenden *(chairperson)*, der die Debatte leitet und der darauf achtet, dass die Regeln eingehalten werden. Der Vorsitzende stellt durch eine kurze Einleitung in das Thema den zu diskutierenden Antrag vor. Nach der Diskussion fordert der Vorsitzende die Teilnehmer auf, eine Stimme für oder gegen den Antrag abzugeben.
- Jeder Teilnehmer darf nur einmal für maximal zwei Minuten sprechen.
- Jeder Teilnehmer darf so viele Fragen stellen wie er / sie für notwendig erachtet.
- Wenn ein Teilnehmer sprechen möchte, steht dieser auf, NACHDEM der Redebeitrag eines anderen Teilnehmers zu Ende ist.
- Der Vorsitzende wählt einen der stehenden Teilnehmer aus und erteilt ihr / ihm das Wort. Dabei versucht der Vorsitzende abwechselnd Sprecher aus beiden Lagern auszuwählen.
- Wenn ein Teilnehmer gegen eine der Regeln verstößt, kann dies dem Vorsitzenden mitgeteilt werden. Dies nennt man „*point of order*". Der Vorsitzende wird daraufhin die Anwesenden bitten, die Regeln einzuhalten.

Die Vorbereitung einer Debatte

1. Der Vorsitzende bereitet eine Einleitung in das Thema vor. Die Einleitung sollte einerseits die Anwesenden über das Thema informieren und andererseits den zur Abstimmung stehenden Antrag vorstellen.
2. Die Teilnehmer der Debatte entscheiden sich zunächst, ob sie für eine Annahme des Antrags stimmen möchten oder ob sie den Antrag ablehnen möchten.
3. Die Teilnehmer sammeln Argumente für bzw. gegen den zur Abstimmung stehenden Antrag. Im Anschluss werden die Argumente sortiert. Man beginnt mit dem schwächsten und endet mit dem überzeugendsten Argument.
4. Die Teilnehmer bereiten eine Zusammenfassung ihrer Argumente für ein abschließendes Plädoyer vor. Wichtig ist hierbei, dass die Argumente nicht noch einmal wiederholt werden, sondern zusammenfassend begründet wird, warum der Antrag befürwortet bzw. abgelehnt wird.

Der Ablauf der Debatte

1. Der Vorsitzende stellt das Thema und den Antrag vor.
2. Das erste Argument der befürwortenden Seite *(1st proposition)* wird durch einen Sprecher präsentiert.
3. Das erste Argument der gegnerischen Seite *(1st opposition)* wird durch einen Sprecher präsentiert.
4. Die befürwortende Seite präsentiert ihr zweites Argument *(2nd proposition)*.
5. Die gegnerische Seite präsentiert ihr zweites Argument *(2nd opposition)*.
6. Die beiden Seiten wechseln sich so lange ab, bis alle Argumente präsentiert wurden.
7. Die gegnerische Seite fasst ihre Argumente in einem abschließenden, kurzen Plädoyer zusammen.
8. Die befürwortende Seite fasst ihre Argumente in einem abschließenden, kurzen Plädoyer zusammen.
9. Der Vorsitzende benennt eine Ecke des Klassenraums als „*Aye (Yes) side*" und eine Ecke als „*No side*". Er liest den Antrag noch einmal vor und bittet die Anwesenden um Abstimmung.
10. Die Teilnehmer entscheiden sich anhand der vorgetragenen Argumente für eine Annahme bzw. eine Ablehnung des Antrags und stellen sich in die jeweilige Ecke des Klassenraums.
11. Der Vorsitzende zählt die Stimmen und verkündet das Abstimmungsergebnis.

Redemittel

- **Modes of address and keeping order**
  Mr Chairman / Speaker
  Madam Chairman / Speaker
  Order, order!
  Point of order, Sir / Madam!
  Declined. / Yes please.
  Would you please let … finish his / her statement?
  I have your name on the list. You'll have your turn next.
  Is the Chairman / Speaker aware that …?

- **Opening the debate by the chairperson**
  Ladies and Gentlemen, welcome to this debate.
  Thank you for being here with us today.
  The motion for debate today is …
  What we want to achieve in the future is …
  The subject before us today is …

- **Presenting opening arguments**
  We would like to introduce our stand by giving the following definitions: …
  Let me start with the argument about …
  The first thing we have to consider is that …
  One of the arguments in favour / against this motion is that …

- **Giving further arguments**
  We would like to stress / emphasize that …
  One must take into account that …
  We hear what the opposition are saying but we do not agree. We will show you / prove to you that …
  The proposition have tried to make some good points, however, they forgot to mention that / to think about …
  The opposition unfortunately failed to show …
  We would like to raise another point.
  We should also discuss what this means for …

- **Summing up**
  To summarize what we have just said …
  This motion must fall / stand because …
  After careful consideration, we must conclude that …
  This debate has made it obvious that the motion cannot stand / fall because …
  Now because of … we have to support this motion.

- **Announcing the result**
  The question is (repetition of the motion).
  We have got … Aye (Yes) votes and … No votes. The motion is carried / defeated.

18 Smalltalk machen

Als Smalltalk bezeichnet man eine leichte Unterhaltung ohne Tiefgang. Dabei bietet sich eine gute Möglichkeit, Interesse zu zeigen, freundlich zu kommunizieren und Konflikte zu vermeiden. Bei vielen gesellschaftlichen Ereignissen, z. B. Partys, verbringt man die ganze Zeit mit Smalltalk.

Der Smalltalk hat als gesellschaftlicher Brauch eine hohe Bedeutung, indem er besonders dem unverbindlichen Kennenlernen oder der Auflockerung der Atmosphäre dient. Ein geschäftliches Treffen, ein Telefonat, ein Bewerbungsgespräch etc. können Sie immer mit ein paar Minuten Smalltalk einleiten (und beenden).

Bedenken Sie: „How are you?" ist keine Frage, auf die Sie mit Ihrem persönlichen Befinden antworten sollten. So ist die Frage nicht gemeint, sondern sie stellt in der Regel nur die Einleitung für den Smalltalk dar.

Skills Files | Sprachkompetenzen: Interaktion

Beliebte Themen für Smalltalk

- das Wetter (besonders in Großbritannien)
- Anfahrt zu dem Ort des Gesprächs
- der eigene Wohnort / Wohnort des Gesprächspartners.
- die eigene Familie / die Familie des Gesprächspartners (wenn man die Familie kennt!)
- ein aktueller Film oder eine bekannte Fernsehserie
- Auswahl an Sehenswürdigkeiten, Einkaufsmöglichkeiten, Restaurants etc., die eine bestimmte Stadt bietet
- Sport (z. B. aktuelle internationale Sportveranstaltungen)
- Urlaub
- Schule / Universität / Beruf
- Hobbys und Interessen
- ein Thema aus den aktuellen Nachrichten, das nicht kontrovers ist

Ungeeignete Themen für Smalltalk

- Religiöse Themen
- Politische Themen
- Probleme am Arbeitsplatz
- Beziehungs- oder Familienprobleme

Redemittel

- Ein Gespräch beginnen:
  Hi!
  Hello!
  Do you mind if I join you?
  Nice to see you (again)!
  How are you?
  How are you doing? *(informal)*
  How are things? *(informal)*

- Ein Thema finden:
  Did you see … on TV last night / at the weekend?
  Have you seen the new [James Bond] film yet?
  Did you read about [that terrible train crash] in the newspaper this morning?
  Terrible / Beautiful weather, isn't it?
  How was your journey?
  Have you ever been here before?
  Who do you think is going to win [the football match] this evening?

- Auf den Gesprächspartner eingehen:
  Really?
  I don't believe it!
  Well, I've never heard of anything like that before!
  That's the funniest / most interesting / strangest thing I've heard in ages!
  I couldn't agree more!

- Füllwörter:
  Well, …
  Actually, …
  Let's see, …
  Let me think, …

- Frageanhängsel:
  You know …, don't you?
  He's …, isn't he?
  It hasn't …, has it?

- Das Gespräch beenden:
  It was nice talking to you!
  Excuse me, I've got to go now.
  Hope to see you again soon.
  Hope you get home safely.

  Give my regards to …
  Don't forget to say hello to … for me!
  Have you got my mobile number / my e-mail address so that we can stay in contact?

19 Telefongespräche führen

Im modernen Berufsleben gehören Telefonate in englischer Sprache zum Alltag. Mit etwas Vorbereitung können Ihnen solche Gespräche erheblich leichter fallen.

Vorbereitung auf das Telefongespräch

- Machen Sie sich Stichpunkte in der englischen Sprache oder machen Sie sich eine grobe Skizze über die Punkte, die Sie ansprechen möchten. Das ist besonders wichtig, wenn Sie Geschäftsanrufe tätigen.
- Wenn möglich, finden Sie den Namen und die Durchwahl der Kontaktperson bereits vor dem Telefonat heraus.
- Denken Sie darüber nach, was die Kontaktperson möglicherweise sagen oder fragen wird, und bereiten Sie entsprechende Antworten darauf vor.
- Seien Sie darauf vorbereitet, Wörter zu buchstabieren, insbesondere Namen und Adressen.
- Haben Sie keine Angst, Fehler zu machen.

Während des Telefongesprächs

- Sprechen Sie langsam und deutlich. Stellen Sie Ihre Anfragen eindeutig und sachlich.
- Wenn Sie ein geschäftliches Telefongespräch führen, nennen Sie immer Ihren Vornamen und Ihren Familiennamen und reden Sie die Kontaktperson mit *Mr*, *Mrs* oder *Ms* und ihrem Familiennamen an.
- Wenn Sie ein privates Telefongespräch führen, reicht es, sich mit Ihrem Vornamen zu melden.
- Erwarten Sie nicht, jedes einzelne Wort zu verstehen. Wenn Sie aber meinen, etwas Wichtiges nicht verstanden zu haben, dann fragen Sie nach.

Regeln und Redemittel

- Wenn die Person wiederholen soll, was sie gesagt hat:
  I'm sorry I didn't quite catch what you said. Could you repeat that, please?

- Wenn die Person etwas noch einmal erklären soll:
  I'm sorry, I'm afraid I don't understand what you mean. Could you explain that again, please?
  I'm afraid I couldn't quite follow you. Did you mean …?

- Wenn die Person langsamer sprechen soll:
  Could you speak a little more slowly, please?

- Seien Sie höflich! Denken Sie daran, „bitte" zu sagen, wenn Sie nach Informationen fragen, und „danke", wenn Ihnen geholfen wurde.
  please = bitte
  you're welcome / not at all = bitte schön; gern geschehen

- Nennen Sie Telefonnummern immer als einzelne Zahlen. Wenn die gleiche Zahl zweimal hintereinander vorkommt, können Sie *double* sagen (z. B. *44 = double 4*). Für die Ziffer *0* sagt man sowohl im Britischen als auch im Amerikanischen *Oh*.
  Im Amerikanischen können Sie außerdem auch *zero* sagen.
  07145 12206 = Oh (zero) – seven – one – four – five – one – double two – oh (zero) – six

- Wenn Sie Namen nennen, ist es oftmals hilfreich, wenn Sie diese buchstabieren.
  Would you like me to spell …?
  Would you like me to spell that for you?
  It's spelt …
  I'll just spell that for you. It's …

- Fordern Sie die Kontaktperson höflich dazu auf, Namen etc. zu buchstabieren, um Verwirrung zu vermeiden.
  Could you spell …, please?
  Could you spell that for me, please?
  Would you mind spelling …?
  Would you mind spelling that for me, please?

- Wiederholen Sie die Informationen (Zeiten, Namen, Adressen, Preise etc.), um sicher zu gehen, dass Sie alles richtig verstanden haben.
  Let me just check that I've understood all the information you've given me. …
  Let me just check that I've understood all the information you're asked for correctly.
  I'll just repeat that back to you to make sure I've got everything down correctly. …
  Let me just check that I've spelt your name correctly. …

- Wenn Sie die Kontaktperson nicht richtig hören können, bitten Sie sie, lauter zu sprechen.
  I'm sorry, (it's a very bad line,) I didn't quite catch that! Could you speak up a bit, please?
  Sorry, it's very loud at my end. Would you mind speaking up a bit?

- Wenn Sie denken, dass Sie sich verwählt haben, fragen Sie nach und entschuldigen Sie sich. Legen Sie nicht einfach auf.
  Is that (+ number you want)?
  I'm sorry, I think I've dialled the wrong number.

- Wenn Sie vermuten, dass sich ein Anrufer verwählt hat, erklären Sie ihm dies höflich. Legen Sie nicht einfach auf.
  I'm sorry, but I think you've got the wrong number.
  This is (+ number / name / company name).
  I'm sorry, there's no one here with that name. This is (+ your number / name / company name).

20 Geschäftliche Telefongespräche führen

Wenn Sie ein Telefongespräch mit einem Geschäftspartner führen möchten, können Sie im Wesentlichen den Vorgaben in *Skills File 19*, ▶ Telefongespräche führen, S. 225, folgen. Die Grundlage für ein erfolgreiches Geschäftstelefonat wird in den ersten Minuten gelegt. Sorgen Sie deshalb dafür, dass Sie von Beginn an freundlich sind und deutlich sprechen.

Redemittel

- **Begrüßung:**
  Good morning / Good afternoon …[1]!
  (This is) …[2] speaking.
  Can I help you?
  What can I do for you?

- **Jemand anderen sprechen wollen:**
  Could I speak to …[3], please?
  Can you put me through to …[3], please?
  I'd like to speak to someone in your [sales] department.

- **Einen Gesprächspartner weiterverbinden:**
  Please hold (the line).
  One moment please.
  I'll connect you with …[3]
  I'll connect you with the [sales] department.
  I'll put you through to …[3]

- **Wenn jemand nicht zu sprechen ist:**
  I'm sorry, …[3] isn't here.
  I'm sorry, …[3] isn't available at the moment / today.

- **Nach der richtigen Durchwahl usw. fragen:**
  Can you give me …[3]'s extension number, please?
  I can give you his / her extension number [voice mail number, fax number, e-mail address]. It's …

- **Den Grund für den Anruf nennen:**
  I'd like to receive more information about …
  I'm calling about …

- **Eine Nachricht weitergeben:**
  Could you pass on a message, please?

- **Eine Nachricht entgegennehmen:**
  Would you like to leave a message?
  Can I take a message?
  Would you like me to pass on a message?

- **Eine Nachricht auf einem Anrufbeantworter oder einer Mailbox hinterlassen:**
  Hello, this is …[2] at …[1]. I'm sorry to have missed you.
  I'd be grateful if you could ring me back this morning / afternoon.
  You can get me on my mobile. The number is …
  I'll be in the office all afternoon so you can reach me there.

- **Einen Rückruf vereinbaren:**
  Shall I ask him / her to call you back?
  Could you call back later, please?
  Could you ask him / her to call me back, please? My number is …[4]
  Can I call back later?
  I'll call back later if that's OK.
  When would be the best time to call back?

- **Sich verabschieden:**
  Thanks for your call!
  Thanks for calling!
  Thank you very much for your help!
  Sorry I couldn't be of more help.
  Have a nice day!
  Goodbye!

1 Name Ihrer Firma **2** Ihr Name **3** Name der Person, mit der Sie sprechen wollen **4** Ihre Telefonnummer

Skills Files | Sprachkompetenzen: Mediation

21 Private Telefongespräche führen

Wenn Sie ein privates Telefongespräch in englischer Sprache führen möchten, können Sie im Wesentlichen den Vorgaben in *Skills File 19*, ▶ Telefongespräche führen, S. 225, folgen. Auch die Formulierungen in *Skills File 18*, ▶ Smalltalk machen, S. 223, können hilfreich sein.

Redemittel

- Begrüßung:
  Hello!
  Hello, this is …[1]
  Hello …[2]! It's me …[1]

- Ein Gespräch beginnen:
  How are you?
  How are you doing?
  It's great to hear from you!
  I just thought I'd call and find out how you are.
  I just wanted to ring and let you know that …

- Jemand anderen sprechen wollen:
  Could I speak to …[3], please?
  Is …[3] in, please?
  Do you know when …[3] will be back, please?

- Einen Gesprächspartner weiterreichen:
  Just a second, I'll go and find him/her.
  Hold on a minute, I'll see if he/she is in.

- Eine Nachricht weitergeben:
  Could you give …[3] a message, please?

- Eine Nachricht entgegennehmen:
  I'm afraid he/she can't come to the phone right now. Can I take a message?
  I'm sorry, but he/she isn't in at the moment. Would you like me to take a message?

- Zurückrufen:
  Would it be OK to ring back later?
  What time can I ring back?
  I'll ring back in about half an hour, if that's OK.
  Could you give …[3] my number, please, and ask him/her to ring me back?
  You can try ringing again in about [15 minutes] if you want to.
  He/She should be back at about [11 pm]. Shall I ask him/her to call you back?

- Sich verabschieden:
  Thanks for ringing!
  It was great to hear from you!
  Speak to you again soon, I hope!
  Bye!
  Take care.
  All the best.

[1] Ihr Name [2] Name der Person, die am anderen Ende der Leitung ist [3] Name der Person, die Sie sprechen möchten

Exam

22 Eine Mediation schreiben

Eine Mediation ist die sinngemäße und adressatengerechte Übertragung der wichtigsten Inhaltspunkte eines Textes in eine andere Sprache. In der Abschlussprüfung in Baden-Württemberg werden Sie aufgefordert den Inhalt einer englischen Textvorlage (ca. 600 bis 800 Wörter) gemäß der Aufgabenstellung auf Deutsch wiederzugeben. „Gemäß der Aufgabenstellung" bedeutet bei der Mediation, dass Sie

- dem Text nur die notwendigen Informationen entnehmen, die Sie darstellen sollen,

- die Form des englischen Textes (z. B. Zeitungsartikel) nicht übernehmen, sondern in der Regel eine andere Textsorte erstellen (z. B. Handout),
- aufgefordert werden den Zieltext an einen bestimmten Adressaten zu richten (z. B. Schüler).

Der Sinn einer Mediation besteht nicht darin, den Text zu übersetzen (vgl. Übersetzung, S. 230). Bei einer Mediation geht es darum, die wesentliche Botschaft eines Textes oder bestimmte Äußerungen im Text adressatengerecht ins Deutsche zu verarbeiten.

Bearbeitung einer Mediationsaufgabe

Schritt 1: Sich einen Überblick verschaffen
- Überfliegen Sie den Text, um sich einen allgemeinen Überblick über den Text zu verschaffen (Skimming). ► Antizipieren, Skimming, Scanning, S. 231
- Um welche Textsorte handelt es sich? Worum geht es in dem Text? (Hauptthema) Ist die Quelle vertrauenswürdig? Wird einseitig argumentiert?
- Lesen Sie die Aufgabenstellung sorgfältig durch. Finden Sie heraus, welche Art von Text Sie verfassen und welches Sprachniveau Sie im Hinblick auf die Adressaten (z. B. Schüler, Eltern, Geschäftspartner) verwenden sollen.
- Welchen Verwendungszweck hat der Text, den Sie verfassen sollen? Z. B. Informationen sachlich darstellen; sich mit dem Für und Wider eines Themas auseinandersetzen; Ratschläge erteilen; an Personen appellieren, d. h. sie zum Handeln auffordern; etc.

Schritt 2: Notizen erstellen
- Lesen Sie nun den Text ein zweites Mal. Während Sie lesen, sollten Sie die wichtigsten Begriffe notieren, um die Aufgabe zu bearbeiten (Scanning). ► Antizipieren, Skimming, Scanning, S. 231
- Schreiben Sie sich nur Schlüsselbegriffe auf, keine ganzen Sätze. Achten Sie auf Bindewörter wie *but* / aber; *however* / jedoch; *in contrast* / im Gegensatz usw. Diese Bindewörter leiten oft neue Gesichtspunkte ein.

Schritt 3: Text verfassen
- Wählen Sie ausschließlich die für die Aufgabenstellung relevanten Punkte aus und fassen Sie diese mit Ihren eigenen Worten zusammen. Die Gliederung Ihres Textes muss nicht mit der Gliederung des Originaltextes übereinstimmen. Achten Sie darauf, dass Sie den Text nicht einfach übersetzen. Es wird von Ihnen erwartet, einen logisch aufgebauten Text in vollständigen Sätzen zu verfassen.

Schritt 4: Überprüfen
- Lesen Sie nun Ihren Text noch einmal durch und überprüfen Sie, ob Sie alle relevanten Punkte des Originaltexts auf Deutsch verständlich wiedergegeben haben.
  Überprüfen Sie, ob Sie
  - alle wichtigen Aspekte des Originaltexts genannt haben,
  - keine Beispiele, die im Originaltext genannt werden, übernommen haben,
  - den Text adressatengerecht verfasst haben,
  - die geforderte Textsorte berücksichtigt haben,
  - den Text auf Deutsch verständlich verfasst haben,
  - den Text übersichtlich gestaltet haben.

23 Eine Übersetzung schreiben

Die Übersetzung eines Textes von einer Sprache in eine andere Sprache unterscheidet sich grundlegend von der Mediation. Wenn Sie einen Text übersetzen, dann müssen Sie diesen in eine andere Sprache übertragen. Der Sinn einer Übersetzung besteht darin, den Text so genau wie möglich in der Zielsprache wiederzugeben, ohne die Textsorte oder den Schreibstil zu verändern. Manchmal müssen Sie dazu die Satzstellung ändern oder idiomatische Ausdrücke sinnvoll anpassen.

Bearbeitung einer Übersetzungsaufgabe

Schritt 1: Sich einen Überblick verschaffen
- Überfliegen Sie den Text, um sich einen allgemeinen Überblick über den Text zu verschaffen (Skimming). ► Antizipieren, Skimming, Scanning, S. 231
- Schreiben Sie sich stichpunktartig auf, worum es in dem Text geht. Verwenden Sie hierbei bereits die Zielsprache des zu verfassenden Texts.

Schritt 2: Eine Rohfassung erstellen
- Versuchen Sie sich so nah wie möglich an die Wortwahl des Originaltexts zu halten. Lassen Sie keine Lücken in Ihrer Übersetzung. Wenn Sie die genaue Übersetzung nicht kennen, dann schreiben Sie zunächst das Wort in der Sprache des Originaltexts auf.
- Da es bei einer Übersetzung wichtig ist, dass Sie den Sinn des Textes transportieren, ist die Textsorte des Originaltexts ausschlaggebend dafür, wie nah Sie sich an der Wortwahl des Originaltexts orientieren müssen. Wenn Sie eine Bedienungsanleitung übersetzen, sind Sie möglicherweise enger an die Wortwahl des Originaltexts gebunden als bei einem literarischen Text.
- Für eine Übersetzungsaufgabe erhalten Sie in der Regel eine lange Bearbeitungszeit. Schreiben Sie deshalb Ihre erste Fassung mit einem Bleistift oder am Computer, sodass Sie Wörter ändern und verbessern können.

Schritt 3: Eine zweite Fassung erstellen
- Lesen Sie die erste Fassung sorgfältig durch und versuchen Sie fehlende Wörter oder Satzteile zu übersetzen.
- Versuchen Sie zunächst die Bedeutung der noch fehlenden Wörter aus dem Kontext zu erschließen. ► Umgang mit Texten ohne Wörterbuch, S. 232
- Wenn es Ihnen nicht gelingt, die Wörter aus dem Kontext zu erschließen, dann schlagen Sie diese in einem Wörterbuch nach. ► Umgang mit einem Wörterbuch, S. 234
- Dann vergleichen Sie Ihre zweite Fassung mit dem Originaltext. Stellen Sie sicher, dass Sie keine Satzteile ausgelassen haben.

Schritt 4: Die Übersetzung überprüfen
- Lesen Sie Ihre Übersetzung noch einmal sorgfältig durch und überprüfen Sie, ob sie einwandfrei deutsch bzw. englisch klingt. Falls nicht, überarbeiten Sie diese Passagen noch einmal. Überlegen Sie hier genau, was Sie sagen möchten und wie Sie dies auf Deutsch bzw. Englisch normalerweise ausdrücken würden.

- Lesen Sie sich nun Ihren Text noch einmal durch und überprüfen Sie, ob Ihr Text dem Originaltext entspricht. Überprüfen Sie, ob Sie
  - sinngemäß alles übersetzt haben. Wenn Sie ein Wort nicht übersetzen können und dieses nicht im Wörterbuch finden, paraphrasieren Sie, d. h. umschreiben Sie das Wort.
  - den Schreibstil des Originaltexts übernommen haben.
  - keine falschen Freunde in Ihren Zieltext eingebaut haben (vgl. auch „Falsche Freunde" weiter unten).
  - Redewendungen richtig übersetzt haben.

Falsche Freunde

Falsche Freunde *(false friends)* sind Wörter, die in zwei verschiedenen Sprachen zwar ähnlich aussehen oder ähnlich klingen, aber dennoch unterschiedliche Bedeutungen haben.

Beispiele:

actual ≠ aktuell; = tatsächlich	handy ≠ Handy; = geschickt, handlich
become ≠ bekommen; = werden	rent ≠ Rente; = Miete
brave ≠ brav; = mutig	sensible ≠ sensibel; = vernünftig
gift ≠ Gift; = Geschenk	still ≠ still; = immer noch

24 Antizipieren, Skimming, Scanning

Um die Fragen zu einem Text richtig beantworten zu können, benötigen Sie eine Kombination verschiedener Lesestrategien. Die bekanntesten Lesestrategien sind das Antizipieren, das Skimming und das Scanning.

Antizipieren ist die Leseerwartung, die an einen Text gestellt wird. Es bedeutet, dass Sie vorhersagen, worum es in dem Text gehen könnte, ohne den Text gelesen zu haben. Wenn Sie sich bereits vor dem ersten Lesen Gedanken über den Inhalt des Textes gemacht haben und evtl. sogar Ihr Vorwissen zu dem Thema aktiviert haben, wird es Ihnen leichter fallen, auch schwierige Texte zu verstehen.

Skimming bedeutet, einen Text zu überfliegen, um möglichst schnell einen Gesamteindruck vom Inhalt zu erhalten. Danach sollte es Ihnen möglich sein, in einem Satz den Inhalt wiederzugeben.

Scanning bedeutet, einen Text gezielt auf bestimmte Informationen hin zu filtern.

Antizipieren

Bevor Sie den Text lesen, haben Sie bestimmte Erwartungen, die sich beim späteren Lesen bestätigen lassen oder die Sie verwerfen müssen. Versuchen Sie vorherzusagen, worum es in dem Text gehen könnte.

Beim Antizipieren ist es hilfreich folgende Punkte zu beachten:

- Textsorte (Handelt es sich um einen fiktionalen Text, z. B. Romanauszug, Kurzgeschichte, oder handelt es sich um einen nicht-fiktionalen Text, z. B. Zeitungsartikel, Internetseite, Sachtext, Reisebericht?)
- Erscheinungsdatum und Erscheinungsort des Textes (Geben Erscheinungsdatum und -ort einen Hinweis auf das mögliche Thema des Textes, besonders bei Zeitungsartikeln?)
- Layout und Illustrationen (Bilder, Graphiken)

Skimming

Nach dem Antizipieren überfliegen Sie den Text, um sich einen Gesamtüberblick zu verschaffen. Diese Technik kann beispielsweise besonders hilfreich sein, wenn Sie sich in Ihrer Abschlussprüfung zwischen zwei Texten entscheiden können. Skimming heißt auch, dass Sie ungefähr drei- bis viermal schneller lesen als gewöhnlich.

Beim Skimming ist es hilfreich folgende Punkte zu beachten:
- Lesen Sie die Überschrift(en), um herauszufinden, worum es in dem Text geht.
- Versuchen Sie, sich ganze Abschnitte anzusehen und nicht Wort für Wort zu lesen.
- Lesen Sie nur den ersten und den letzten Satz jedes Abschnittes.

Scanning

Diese Technik des selektiven Lesens kann besonders hilfreich sein, wenn Sie Fragen zum Text beantworten sollen und nur nach relevanten Informationen suchen.

Beim Scanning ist es hilfreich folgende Punkte zu beachten:
- Lesen Sie die Fragen / Aufgaben zum Text sorgfältig durch.
- Lassen Sie Ihre Augen über den Text fliegen und fokussieren Sie dabei Schlüsselbegriffe. Lesen Sie den Text nicht Wort für Wort.
- Markieren Sie Schlüsselbegriffe oder wichtige Details im Text oder notieren Sie diese.
- Versuchen Sie, anhand Ihrer Notizen die Fragen mit Ihren eigenen Worten zu beantworten.

25 Mit Texten ohne Wörterbuch umgehen

Auch wenn Ihnen ein Wörterbuch zur Verfügung steht, lesen Sie den Text mindestens einmal vollständig durch, ohne die unbekannten Wörter nachzuschlagen. Versuchen Sie, die Hauptaussage des Textes zu verstehen.

Texterschließung ohne Wörterbuch

- Überlegen Sie, ob der Kontext, in dem das unbekannte Wort auftaucht, Ihnen hilft, das Wort zu verstehen. So können z. B. angrenzende Worte oder Sätze dabei helfen.
- Manche englische Wörter werden gleichermaßen in der deutschen Sprache verwendet.
  Beispiele: *computer, crash, deadline, international, laptop, loyal, tourist …*
- Manche englische Wörter sind der deutschen Bezeichnung sehr ähnlich.
  Beispiele: *cloning, economy, globalisation, industry, politics, president, technology …*
  Aber achten Sie hier besonders auf „falsche Freunde"!

Beispiele: *brave* = mutig; *sea* = Meer; *sensible* = vernünftig; *to spend money* = Geld ausgeben
- Manche englische Wörter ähneln Wörtern, die Sie aus anderen Fremdsprachen kennen.
  Beispiele: *announce* (French: annoncer), *organic* (Latin: organicus), *solar* (Latin: solaris)
- Bei zusammengesetzten Wörtern kennen Sie vielleicht zumindest einen der beiden Wortteile.
  Beispiele: *high-class, lifestyle, part-time, salesperson, subculture, work experience*
- Bei manchen Wörtern hilft es, sie laut auszusprechen, weil der Klang des Wortes hilft, die Bedeutung zu finden.
  Beispiele: *bang, clap, crisps, hiss, moo, ouch, ping, whisper*
- Versuchen Sie, die Wortfamilie zu ermitteln (siehe unitbegleitendes Vokabular im Schülerbuch ab S. 246 ff.). Ein Teil des Wortes könnte mit einem Ihnen bereits bekannten englischen Wort zusammenhängen. Achten Sie auch auf Vorsilben und Nachsilben.

Vorsilben

- Folgende Vorsilben geben Worten eine negative oder gegensätzliche (≠) Bedeutung:

in-	active ≠ inactive
im-	possible ≠ impossible
il-	literate ≠ illiterate
ir-	relevant ≠ irrelevant
anti-	anti-smoking
counter-	counterrevolution
mis-	to misunderstand
un-	happy ≠ unhappy
de-	to stabilise ≠ to destabilise
dis-	to like ≠ to dislike

- Folgende Vorsilben zeigen einen Anstieg (+) oder eine Abnahme (−) an:

out- (+)	to grow – to outgrow
over- (+)	to heat – to overheat
sub- (−)	standard – substandard
super- (++)	natural – supernatural
under- (−)	to pay – to underpay

- Weitere Vorsilben:

inter-	international
post-	post-war
pre-	pre-school
pro-	pro-abortion
re-	reread
trans-	transatlantic

Nachsilben

- Nachsilben bestimmen den Wortstamm und bilden oft aus Verben und Adjektiven Nomen.

-ation	to nationalize – nationalization	-y	difficult – difficulty
-ence	to differ – difference	-ment	to improve – improvement
-er	to teach – teacher	-ness	happy – happiness
-ing	to begin – beginning	-or	to act – actor

26 Mit dem Wörterbuch arbeiten

Einsprachige Wörterbücher

Das einsprachige Wörterbuch soll bei der Beseitigung von Verständnisproblemen helfen, z. B. wenn Sie einen Text lesen oder einen Text produzieren möchten. Das einsprachige Wörterbuch hilft Ihnen, Wortbedeutungen aus dem Kontext zu entnehmen.

Das Wörterbuch kennenlernen

- Bevor Sie zum ersten Mal mit Ihrem einsprachigen Wörterbuch arbeiten, sollten Sie sich einen Überblick verschaffen, d.h. Sie blättern durch das Wörterbuch und lernen die wichtigsten Hilfen kennen. Nur wenn Sie wissen welche Informationen das Wörterbuch bietet und wo diese stehen, können Sie das Wörterbuch optimal nutzen.
- Achten Sie beispielsweise auf:
  - den Aufbau des Wörterbuchs (Vorspann, Wörterverzeichnis, Nachspann)
  - die Anleitung zur Benutzung
  - das Verzeichnis der Abkürzungen und Symbole
  - verschiedene Listen, z. B. unregelmäßige Verben, Namenslisten
  - Illustrationen und Schaubilder
  - Überblick über die grundlegende Grammatik.
- Nachdem Sie sich einen groben Überblick verschafft haben, schauen Sie sich den Aufbau eines Eintrags genauer an, z. B. das Wort *success*. In einem guten einsprachigen Wörterbuch werden Sie zu dem Eintrag folgende Informationen finden:
  - Schreibung und Worttrennung
  - die verschiedenen Wortarten (Nomen, Verb, Adjektiv, Adverb)
  - Aussprache (anhand von Lautschrift)
  - unregelmäßige Formen
  - die verschiedenen Bedeutungen des Wortes, auch innerhalb einer Wortart
  - Synonyme und Definitionen
  - Beispielsätze zum typischen Gebrauch des Wortes
  - Redewendungen, in denen das Wort verwendet wird.

Mit dem einsprachigen Wörterbuch arbeiten

- Bevor Sie ein Wort nachschlagen, ermitteln Sie die Wortart im Satzzusammenhang, z. B. Nomen, Adjektiv, Verb etc.
- Wenn Sie den Eintrag für das gesuchte Wort gefunden haben, lesen Sie nicht den gesamten Eintrag, sondern beschränken Sie sich auf die Verwendung Ihres Wortes in der gesuchten Wortart.
- Lesen Sie dann alle weiteren Informationen, die Ihnen das Wörterbuch zu dem entsprechenden Stichwort in der gesuchten Wortart gibt, z. B. Beispielsätze oder grammatische Informationen.
- Nehmen Sie sich Zeit zum Lesen des Eintrags und versichern Sie sich, dass Sie die richtige Bedeutung des Wortes gefunden haben. Achten Sie dabei insbesondere auf den Textzusammenhang.

Zweisprachige Wörterbücher

Das zweisprachige Wörterbuch (Englisch-Deutsch, Deutsch-Englisch) soll insbesondere bei der Übertragung von Texten in die andere Sprache helfen, z. B. wenn Sie einen Text übersetzen möchten. Es kann aber auch verwendet werden, um unbekannte Wörter in einem fremdsprachigen Text schnell zu verstehen.

Das Wörterbuch kennenlernen

Bevor Sie zum ersten Mal mit Ihrem zweisprachigen Wörterbuch arbeiten, sollten Sie sich mit dem Wörterbuch vertraut machen. (Siehe Das Wörterbuch kennenlernen auf Seite 234, den ersten Punkt)

- Nachdem Sie sich einen groben Überblick verschafft haben, schauen Sie sich den Aufbau eines Eintrags genauer an, z. B. das Wort *success*. In einem guten zweisprachigen Wörterbuch werden Sie zu dem Eintrag folgende Informationen finden:
  - Schreibung und Worttrennung
  - die verschiedenen Wortarten (Nomen, Verb, Adjektiv, Adverb)
  - Aussprache (anhand von Lautschrift)
  - unregelmäßige Formen
  - die verschiedenen Übersetzungen des Wortes, auch innerhalb einer Wortart
  - Beispielsätze zum typischen Gebrauch des Wortes
  - Redewendungen, in denen das Wort verwendet wird.

Mit dem zweisprachigen Wörterbuch arbeiten

- Bevor Sie ein Wort nachschlagen, ermitteln Sie die Wortart im Satzzusammenhang, z. B. Nomen, Adjektiv, Verb etc.
- Wenn Sie den entsprechenden Eintrag für das Wort gefunden haben, lesen Sie aber nicht den gesamten Eintrag, sondern beschränken Sie sich auf die Verwendung Ihres Wortes in der gesuchten Wortart.
- Lesen Sie zudem alle weiteren Informationen, die Ihnen das Wörterbuch zu dem entsprechenden Stichwort in der gesuchten Wortart gibt, z. B. Beispielsätze.
- Nehmen Sie sich Zeit zum Lesen des Eintrags und versichern Sie sich, dass Sie die richtige Bedeutung des Wortes gefunden haben, ob also die Übersetzung im Textzusammenhang passt.

27 Wortnetze erstellen

Ein Wortnetz eignet sich überall dort, wo Gedanken zu einem bestimmten Thema gesammelt und dargestellt werden sollen, um sich das Thema sinnvoll zu erschließen oder um einen Überblick zu erhalten. Die Grundstruktur eines Wortnetzes ist immer gleich.

Wozu nutzt man Wortnetze?

Brainstorming: Um Ideen zu einem Thema zu sammeln und zusammenzutragen.
Erörterung von Themen: Um Argumente zu strukturieren. Beginnen Sie mit dem Thema der Diskussion und fügen Sie *arguments for* (Thesen) und *arguments against* (Antithesen) hinzu.
Vokabellernen: Um sich neue Wortfelder zu erschließen. Beginnen Sie mit einem Oberthema und fügen Sie alle Wörter hinzu, die sich auf diesen Begriff beziehen.

Erstellen eines Wortnetzes

Sie benötigen ausreichend Platz zum Erstellen des Wortnetzes, z. B. ein ausreichend großes Blatt Papier, Plakat, Tapete, Flipchart. Außerdem brauchen Sie Stifte in verschiedenen Farben.

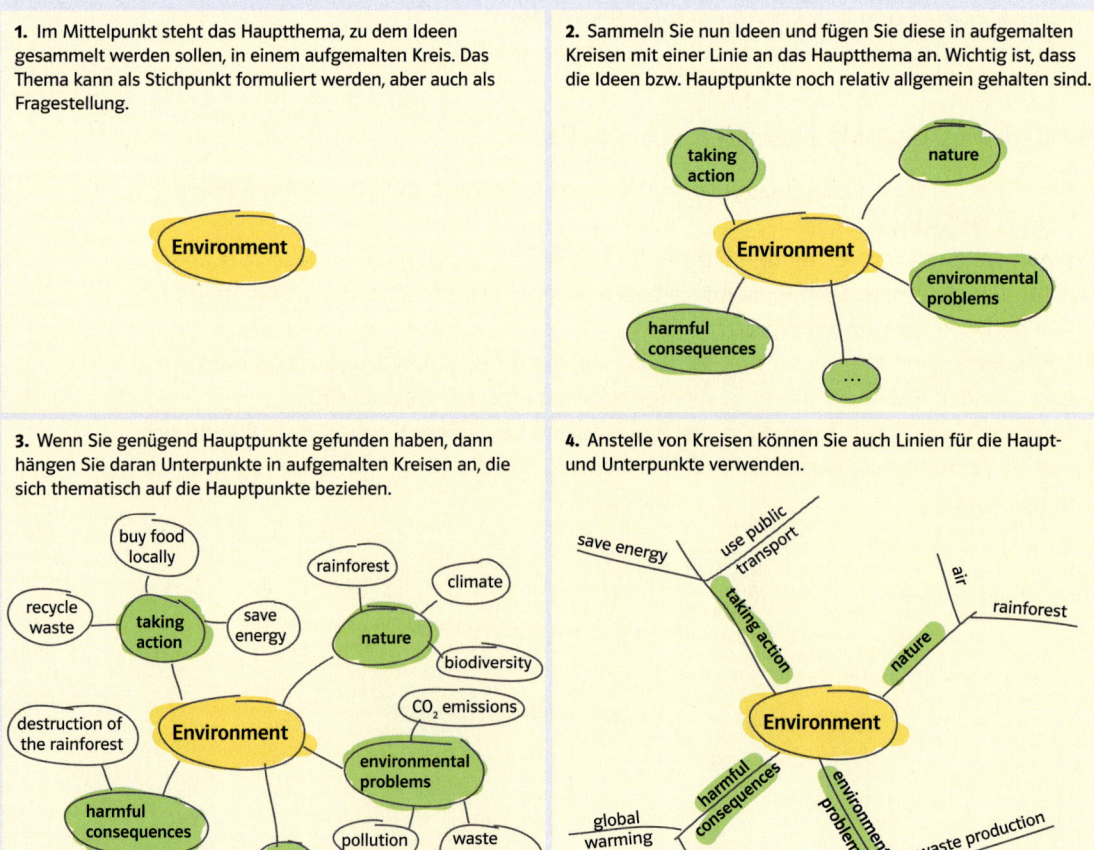

28 Bindewörter verwenden

Bindewörter sind Wörter oder Formulierungen, die Satzglieder, Sätze oder Textabschnitte miteinander verbinden. Diese Bindewörter geben Ihrem Text eine klare Struktur und sie erleichtern es dem Leser, Ihren Ausführungen zu folgen.

Die folgenden Bindewörter sind nur eine kleine Auswahl. Sie sollten eine persönliche Liste mit Bindewörtern führen, die Sie immer wieder erweitern können.

- Eine Reihenfolge anzeigen / Gliederung:
  firstly …, secondly …, finally …
  first of all
  next
  then
  later
  ultimately

  Beispiel: *Next the author describes the activities of the different organizations which help in Zimbabwe.*

- Gedanken / Argumente hinzufügen:
  another
  also
  as well
  in addition / additionally
  too
  moreover
  furthermore
  last but not least

  Beispiel: *Another significant advantage of solar energy is that it doesn't pollute our air.*

- Beispiele geben:
  for example
  for instance

  Beispiel: *The US government is an example of a presidential federal government.*

- Die eigene Einstellung verdeutlichen:
  obviously
  undoubtedly / doubtlessly
  clearly
  generally
  luckily
  fortunately
  unfortunately
  happily / sadly for …

  Beispiel: *Obviously it is wrong to say that tourism always damages our environment.*

- Eine eigene Meinung abgeben:
  in my opinion
  in my view
  to my mind
  Without a doubt

  Beispiel: *To my mind this is not the solution to the economic problems of the people living in this area.*

- Begründungen angeben:
  consequently
  therefore
  as a result
  this is why
  because of
  so

  Beispiel: *This is why more than thirty food companies in Britain have signed a promise to reduce their food transport miles.*

- Vergleiche anstellen:
  compared with
  on the one hand … on the other hand …
  in the same way
  similarly

  Beispiel: *Compared with the situation five years ago children watch TV for longer periods of time.*

- Gegensätze ausdrücken:
  in contrast to
  however
  despite / in spite of

  Beispiel: *Despite all of the arguments mentioned in the text I do not agree with the author's position.*

- Schluss:
  in conclusion
  as a result
  all in all
  in short
  on the whole
  finally
  to sum up

  Beispiel: *To sum up, I am absolutely against the author's demand that pupils in German schools wear uniforms.*

29 Vokabeln systematisch lernen

Wenn Sie eine Sprache lernen, ist es unerlässlich, dass Sie Vokabeln lernen. Je mehr Vokabeln Sie kennen, desto leichter wird es Ihnen fallen, Texte zu verfassen.

Tipps: Neue Vokabeln systematisch sammeln

Alphabetisch (A – Z): Diese Methode ist geeignet, wenn Sie Vokabeln schnell nachschlagen möchten. Allerdings müssen Sie das englische Wort bereits kennen. Wenn Sie einen Text verfassen möchten, ist dies meist nicht der Fall. Deshalb sollten Sie diese Methode mit einer der folgenden kombinieren.

Synonyme oder Antonyme: Sammeln Sie alle Synonyme, d.h. bedeutungsgleichen Wörter, und schreiben Sie diese zusammen auf.
Beispiel: *small, little, tiny*
Oder Sie schreiben Antonyme, d.h. Gegensätze, zusammen auf.
Beispiel: *small ≠ big.*

Wortfamilien: Wenn Sie sich ein Wort notieren, können Sie die anderen Formen (Wortarten) dieses Wortes hinzufügen, d.h. Nomen, Verb, Adjektiv, Adverb. Dadurch erweitern Sie Ihren Wortschatz besonders schnell.
Beispiel: *economy, to economize, economical, economically, economic.*

Wortfelder: Sammeln Sie Vokabeln anhand von thematischen Zusammenhängen.
Beispiel: das Wortfeld *globalisation: industry, travelling, culture, communication, brands, poverty, culture, technology, environment, multiculturalism* usw.

Word webs: Beginnen Sie mit dem Wortfeld, zu dem Sie Vokabeln sammeln möchten, z.B. *globalisation*, und schreiben Sie alles auf, was Ihnen zu diesem Wortfeld einfällt. Strukturieren Sie Ihre Einfälle in einem Word web.
► Wortnetze, S. 236

Kollokationen: Machen Sie sich eine Liste von Wörtern, die oft im Zusammenhang miteinander verwendet werden.
Beispiele: *to draw a conclusion, to make a promise* (Verb + Nomen), *extremely beautiful* (Adverb + Adjektiv), *a handsome man, a tall woman, a powerful computer* (Adjektiv + Nomen) usw.

30 Gruppenarbeit und Projekte durchführen

Gruppenarbeit

Die Arbeit in Gruppen bietet die Chance, sich mit einem Unterrichtsinhalt im Team auseinanderzusetzen. Viele Aufgaben lassen sich besser und schneller in einer Gruppe lösen. Gruppenarbeit dient dem Zweck, gemeinsam zu einer Lösung zu kommen, indem Sie miteinander kommunizieren und Ideen austauschen.

Gruppenzusammensetzung

- Die optimale Gruppengröße beträgt in der Regel 3–5 Personen.
- Gruppen können nach verschiedenen Prinzipien gebildet werden: nach Interesse, nach Sympathie, nach Zufall, nach Stärken und Schwächen. Dabei sollte darauf geachtet werden, dass die Gruppen ungefähr gleich stark gebildet werden und dass sie sich gegenseitig unterstützen.

Vorbereitung der Gruppenarbeit

- Richten Sie sich Ihren Arbeitsplatz so ein, dass Sie gut arbeiten, aber auch gut miteinander kommunizieren können.
- Erstellen Sie sich einen Arbeitsplan. Berücksichtigen Sie hierbei die Zeit, die Ihnen zur Bearbeitung der Aufgabe zur Verfügung steht.
- Verteilen Sie Aufgaben an die einzelnen Gruppenmitglieder. Beachten Sie, dass jeder ungefähr dieselbe Menge an Arbeit hat. Manchmal ist es sinnvoll, schriftlich festzuhalten, wer welche Aufgabe übernimmt.
- Für den Interaktionsprozess in der Gruppe kann es hilfreich sein, dass Sie den einzelnen Gruppenmitgliedern Funktionen zuordnen, z. B. Gruppenleiter, Zeitwächter, Schriftführer, Streitschlichter usw.
- Stellen Sie fest, welche Materialien Sie benötigen, und legen Sie fest, wer welche Materialien besorgt.
  Wenn die Gruppenarbeit über eine Unterrichtseinheit hinausgeht, sollten Sie sich überlegen, ob es eine Möglichkeit gibt, die Materialien aufzubewahren, so dass Sie immer Zugang dazu haben.
- Einigen Sie sich auf eine geeignete Form, um die Ergebnisse zu präsentieren, wenn sie nicht bereits vorgegeben wurde.

Durchführung der Gruppenarbeit

- Gehen Sie immer höflich und respektvoll miteinander um. Lassen Sie alle ausreden und fallen Sie niemandem ins Wort.
- Sie tragen alle die Verantwortung für die Qualität Ihrer Arbeitsergebnisse. Deshalb unterstützen Sie sich gegenseitig und helfen Sie einander bei Problemen.
- Wichtige Arbeitsergebnisse sollten von jedem Gruppenmitglied schriftlich festgehalten werden und nicht nur von einem Schriftführer. So kann es Ihnen nicht passieren, dass Ihnen bei der Präsentation der Arbeitsergebnisse Informationen fehlen.
- Bemühen Sie sich als Arbeitssprache Englisch einzusetzen.

Redemittel

- **Die eigene Meinung ausdrücken:**
  In my opinion / view …
  I think (that) …
  I would like to …
  We should …
  It would be a good idea to …

- **Jemanden unterbrechen:**
  Sorry, may I interrupt you for a second?
  Wait a minute …
  I'm sorry to interrupt but …

- **Das Thema wechseln:**
  Before I forget …
  There is something else I wanted to say …
  By the way …

- **Zum eigentlichen Thema zurückkehren:**
  Let's get back to …
  To get back to what we were talking about …
  As I was saying …

- **Überraschung ausdrücken:**
  Really?
  Are you serious?
  I don't believe it!

- **Zugeständnisse machen:**
  I (partly) agree with you, but …
  Yes, that's true, but …

- **Interesse zeigen:**
  Tell me about your idea.
  Absolutely …
  I'd love to …

- **Rückmeldung geben:**
  That's very kind of you.
  Are you sure?
  I see.
  I like your idea.

- **Jemanden auffordern, etwas zu tun:**
  Could you possibly …?
  Could I ask you to …?
  Do you think you could … please?

- **Vorschläge machen:**
  If I were you I would …
  You could try …
  How about …?

- **Füllwörter:**
  Well, …
  Anyway …
  Actually …
  I mean …
  In fact …

- **Höflichkeitsfloskeln:**
  Please.
  You're welcome.
  Thank you.
  No worries.
  Don't worry.

Projekte

Projekte zeichnen sich dadurch aus, dass Sie mit dem Lehrer gemeinsam ein Thema und die Arbeitsziele festlegen. Bei der Lösung der Aufgabe, der Beschaffung der Materialien / Informationen und der Erstellung eines Produktes arbeiten Sie jedoch selbstständig in Gruppen.

Erfolgreiche Durchführung eines Projektes

- Lesen Sie die Aufgabenstellung sorgfältig und stellen Sie sicher, dass alle Gruppenmitglieder die Aufgabe verstanden haben. Oft ist es bei Projekten der Fall, dass zu Beginn nur das allgemeine Ziel bekannt ist und sich die detaillierten Ziele erst in der Gruppe ergeben, z. B. durch spezifische Betrachtungsweisen des Themas.
  Folgende Fragestellungen zum Verstehen des Arbeitsauftrags können hilfreich sein:
  - Was sollen Sie genau tun und mit welchem Ziel?
  - Gibt es eine zeitliche Begrenzung?
  - Welche Entscheidungen können Sie frei treffen?
  - Sind noch Fragen offen?
- Führen Sie in der Gruppe ein Brainstorming durch:
  - Was wissen Sie bereits über das Thema? Erstellen Sie ein Word web. ▶ Wortnetze, S. 236
  - Welche Aspekte des Themas möchten Sie bearbeiten?
  - Wo finden Sie die Informationen zu dem Thema?
- Planen Sie die Arbeit in Gruppen:
  - Erstellen Sie einen Plan, auf dem festgehalten wird, wer welche Aufgabe übernimmt.
  - Erstellen Sie einen Terminplan, auf dem Sie festhalten, wann bestimmte Aufgaben erledigt sein müssen.
  - Legen Sie fest, wie Sie Ihre Arbeit koordinieren. Wann treffen Sie sich, evtl. auch außerhalb des Unterrichts? Wie tauschen Sie Informationen aus?
- Entscheiden Sie gemeinsam in der Gruppe, wie Sie Ihre Arbeitsergebnisse präsentieren möchten, falls dies nicht in der Aufgabenstellung festgelegt ist.
  Ideen für Präsentationen: Handzettel, Broschüre, Poster, Plakat, Wandzeitung, Video, Hörspiel, Kurzvortrag, PowerPoint-Präsentation …
- Vergessen Sie nicht, alle Quellen zu notieren, die Sie verwendet haben. Sie müssen immer angeben können, wo Sie Informationen, Bilder usw. gefunden haben.

31 Im Internet suchen

Es gibt mittlerweile Millionen von Webseiten im Internet. Das Problem ist jedoch, unter der Vielzahl die gewünschten Informationen zu finden. Sie werden nur sofort fündig, wenn Sie die einschlägige Internet-Adresse bereits kennen oder Sie durch einen Link direkt weitergeleitet werden. Falls beides nicht der Fall ist, müssen Sie auf Suchmaschinen zurückgreifen.

Thema formulieren und eingrenzen

- Bevor Sie sich an den PC setzen, um im Internet nach Informationen zu suchen, sollten Sie sich genau überlegen, welche Informationen Sie benötigen, damit Sie nicht die Orientierung verlieren. Denn das Hauptproblem bei der Recherche im Internet liegt darin, dass man viel Zeit damit verbringt, eine Fülle an unwichtigen und überflüssigen Informationen zu sichten. Um dies zu vermeiden, können Sie z. B. …
  - das Thema präzisieren und evtl. eingrenzen,
  - sinnvolle Stichwörter zum Thema sammeln,
  - themenbezogene Wortfelder erstellen.

Suchanfragen richtig stellen

- Wenn Ihre Suchanfrage zu ungenau ist, werden Sie eine Vielzahl von Informationen erhalten, die zu allgemein sind. Wenn Sie z. B. Informationen zum Thema *TV viewing habits of children* suchen, reicht es nicht aus, das Stichwort *Media* einzugeben. Suchmaschinen bedienen sich teilweise leider unterschiedlicher Suchbegriffe.
  Folgende Eingabearten sind bei den meisten Suchmaschinen möglich:
  - Mehrere Wörter ohne Anführungszeichen
    Beispiel*: TV viewing habits*
    Ergebnis: Alle Texte, in denen <u>entweder</u> *TV* <u>oder</u> *viewing* <u>oder</u> *habits* vorkommen, werden angezeigt.
  - Mehrere Wörter mit Anführungszeichen
    Beispiel: „*TV viewing habits*"
    Ergebnis: Es werden nur Texte angezeigt, in denen die exakte Wortfolge vorkommt.
- Wenn Sie zu wenige Treffer erlangen, überprüfen Sie die Schreibweise, verwenden Sie weniger Begriffe oder versuchen Sie es mit einem anderen Stichwort.
- Wenn Sie zu viele Treffer erlangen, verwenden Sie spezifischere Begriffe oder fügen Sie Stichwörter hinzu.
- Spezielle Begriffe, die aber nicht zu ausgefallen sind, bringen meist gute und eingegrenzte Ergebnisse.

Informationen finden

- Um möglichst schnell und gezielt Informationen zu finden, können Sie Techniken wie Skimming und Scanning verwenden. ► Antizipieren, Skimming, Scanning, S. 231
- Wenn Sie nach einzelnen Wörtern auf einer Seite suchen möchten, können Sie auch Strg+F drücken. Es erscheint dann ein Suchfeld, in das Sie das betreffende Wort eingeben können.

Informationen verarbeiten

- Denken Sie daran, dass jeder Nutzer beliebige Informationen im Internet veröffentlichen kann. Die von Ihnen gefundenen Informationen müssen also nicht immer korrekt sein. Um wertloses Material von wertvollem Material zu unterscheiden, können folgende Fragen hilfreich sein:
  - Wer hat die Webseite veröffentlicht? (z. B. kommerziell vs. nicht kommerziell, Privatperson vs. öffentliche Institution, usw.)
  - Verfolgen die Autoren ein bestimmtes Interesse? (Soll z. B. etwas verkauft werden?)
  - Werden Fakten dargelegt oder Meinungen?
  - Sind die Informationen aktuell? (Wann z. B. wurde die Webseite zum letzten Mal aktualisiert? Von wann sind die Jahreszahlen / Statistiken?)

Favoriten

- Wenn Sie die gesuchten Informationen gefunden haben und später noch einmal auf die Seite zurückgreifen möchten, können Sie die Seite in die Liste der Favoriten aufnehmen. Ihr Browser speichert diese Liste, so dass Sie die Seite jederzeit anzeigen können, ohne erneut suchen zu müssen. Je nach Browser kann diese Liste auch Lesezeichen oder Bookmark heißen. Sie finden die Favoriten in der Menüleiste. Dort klicken Sie auf

„Lesezeichen hinzufügen", während Sie die Seite, die Sie speichern möchten, geöffnet haben. Sie können die Seite auch direkt auf dem Desktop speichern, sodass Sie schnell auf diese Seite zugreifen können.

32 Notizen anfertigen

Informationen, die im Unterricht mündlich präsentiert werden, sind in der Regel die zentralen Lerngegenstände und beinhalten einen großen Teil des prüfungsrelevanten Materials. Mitschriften entstehen im Unterricht durch das Aufschreiben der relevanten Informationen von verschiedenen Quellen, z. B. Unterrichtsgesprächen, Referaten, Hörverständnistexten, Interviews, Filmanalysen usw.

Unabhängig von der Quelle ist bei der Mitschrift besonders wichtig, dass Sie lernen, richtig zuzuhören. In der Regel kann der Mensch nämlich lediglich 30 % des Gehörten behalten. Da die englische Sprache nicht Ihre Muttersprache ist, wird es Ihnen noch schwerer fallen, das gesprochene Englisch zu verstehen und Informationen aufzunehmen. Die folgenden Tipps helfen Ihnen, Ihr Zuhörerverhalten zu verbessern.

Tipps zum richtigen Zuhören

- Wenn Sie nichts oder nur schlecht hören können, verändern Sie Ihre Position. Setzen Sie sich dorthin, wo Sie den Sprecher sehen können und wo Sie nicht von Ablenkungen gestört werden.
- Akzeptieren Sie die Tatsache, dass Sie nicht alles verstehen werden.
- Achten Sie auf die Hauptaussagen des Gesprochenen. Versuchen Sie, Wichtiges von Unwichtigem zu unterscheiden. Konzentrieren Sie sich erst auf Details, wenn Sie die Hauptaussagen verstanden haben.
- Auch wenn Sie für eine Zeit lang dem Gesprochenen nicht folgen können, lassen Sie sich nicht ablenken. Bleiben Sie konzentriert bei der Sache. Oft werden die wichtigen Informationen vom Sprecher im weiteren Verlauf wiederholt.
- Machen Sie sich Notizen, während Sie zuhören. Scheuen Sie sich nicht nachzufragen, wenn Sie etwas nicht verstanden haben.
- Übertragen Sie das Gehörte nicht in Ihre Muttersprache.

Vorbereitung

- Vor Unterrichtsbeginn sollten Sie kurz Ihre Notizen zur vorangegangen Unterrichtsstunde lesen. Dadurch werden Sie sich an den bereits besprochenen Lernstoff erinnern und es wird Ihnen helfen, dem neuen Lernstoff zu folgen.
- Sie sollten immer die Materialien für die Unterrichtsstunde vollständig mitbringen, d. h. Bücher, Hefte, verschiedenfarbige Stifte, Papier, usw.

Notizen erstellen

- Hören Sie erst genau zu, bevor Sie anfangen zu schreiben. Wenn Sie sofort drauflos schreiben, kann es passieren, dass Sie die wichtigste Information verpassen, weil Sie sich gerade auf die Mitschrift konzentrieren.

- Hören Sie auf „Signalsätze", die anzeigen, dass das Folgende besonders wichtig ist, z. B. *Remember that …, The most important point …, In conclusion …*
- Schreiben Sie so schnell und effizient wie möglich, indem Sie nur das Wesentliche schreiben und Kurzsätze bzw. Stichworte aufschreiben. Verwenden Sie Abkürzungen, Symbole und Wortverkürzungen (siehe Tabelle).

Symbole		Abkürzungen		Wortverkürzungen	
&, +	and	p., l.	page, line	med	medicine
=	the same as	i.e.	that is	govt	government
≠	not the same as	e.g.	for example	impt	important
♀	female	cf	compare	yth	youth
♂	male	w/	with	tgt	target
%	percent	w/o	without	cert	certificate

- Informationen, die Sie beim Zuhören nicht verstanden haben, markieren Sie mit einem Fragezeichen (?), so dass Sie später nachfragen oder nachschlagen können.

Überarbeiten der Notizen

- Formulieren Sie Kurzsätze und Stichworte in längere Sätze um.
- Abkürzungen, Symbole und Wortverkürzungen sollten ausgeschrieben werden.
- Beantworten Sie Fragen zu Wörtern oder Informationen, die Sie nicht verstanden haben. Schlagen Sie nach oder fragen Sie Ihre Mitschüler oder Ihren Lehrer.
- Vergleichen Sie Ihre Mitschrift mit der Mitschrift Ihrer Mitschüler. So können Sie Ihre Mitschriften gegenseitig ergänzen.

33 Plakate anfertigen

Ein Plakat ist eine informative, großformatige und übersichtlich gestaltete Form, Arbeitsergebnisse zu präsentieren. In der Regel stehen Plakate nicht für sich alleine, sondern sind als visuelle Unterstützung von Präsentationen gedacht.

Informationen beschaffen und verarbeiten

Bevor Sie mit der Gestaltung des Plakats beginnen, müssen Sie sich mit dem Inhalt beschäftigen. Sammeln Sie Informationen zu Ihrer Aufgabe, lesen Sie Texte, trennen Sie wichtige Informationen von Unwichtigem und fassen Sie schließlich die Inhalte zusammen.

Gliederung der Inhalte

- Auf einem Plakat sollten nie vollständige Sätze stehen, sondern Stichpunkte oder Halbsätze. Deshalb überarbeiten Sie Ihre Zusammenfassungen nun noch einmal, indem Sie Sätze umformulieren und kürzen oder durch Bilder und Symbole ersetzen. Fragen Sie sich an dieser Stelle immer: Welche Botschaft soll das Plakat vermitteln?

- Finden Sie eine passende Überschrift für das Plakat. Die Überschrift sollte nicht zu lang sein, aber für den Leser verständlich. Verwenden Sie also nur Abkürzungen in Überschriften, die allgemein bekannt sind.

Aufbau und Anordnung planen

- Überlegen Sie, ob die Inhalte Ihres Plakats besser im Hochformat oder im Querformat zur Geltung kommen und wie Sie die Überschriften, Textelemente und Bilder anordnen.
- Wenn Sie sich für eine klassische Anordnung der Inhalte entscheiden, dann halten Sie sich an den Aufbau, so wie er im nebenstehenden Schaubild dargestellt ist.
  - Überschrift: über den gesamten Kopf des Plakats,
  - Einleitung: oben links,
  - Schlussfolgerungen: unten links,
  - Sachinformationen und Ergebnisse: füllen den restlichen Platz.

Überschrift
Einleitung

Sachinformationen und Ergebnisse

Schlussfolgerungen

Schrift und Farben

- Ihre Schrift sollte so groß sein, dass sie von allen Positionen des Raumes lesbar ist. Versuchen Sie, gerade zu schreiben. Verwenden Sie möglichst Druckbuchstaben und dicke Stifte.
- Heben Sie Wichtiges durch Farben, Unterstreichungen, Umrahmungen oder Schraffierungen hervor. Verwenden Sie jedoch maximal 3 Farben pro Plakat.

Vocabulary

Basic vocabulary

Abkürzung
AE = Gebrauch im amerikanischen Englisch

A

a couple of   ein paar
a little   etwas, ein bisschen
a lot (of)   viel(e)
a number of   einige
ability   Fähigkeit
abroad   im/ins Ausland
to accept   annehmen, akzeptieren
accident   Unfall
accurate   genau
to achieve   erreichen
active   aktiv
activity   Aktivität
to add   hinzufügen, addieren
additional   zusätzlich
to address; address   adressieren, ansprechen; Adresse
advantage   Vorteil
advert(isement)   Werbeanzeige, Anzeige
to advertise   werben, inserieren
advertiser   Inserent, Werbefachmann
advertising   Werbung
advice   Rat, Ratschlag
to advise   (be)raten
afternoon   Nachmittag
afterwards   danach
again   wieder
against   gegen
age   Alter, Zeitalter
ago   vor
to agree   einverstanden sein, zustimmen
agreement   Übereinstimmung, Übereinkunft, Vereinbarung
to aim (at); aim   (ab)zielen auf; Ziel
air   Luft
airport   Flughafen
alert   Alarm
all   alle(s), ganz

to allow   erlauben
almost   fast, beinahe
alone   allein
along   entlang
already   schon, bereits
also   auch
alternative   Alternative, Wahl; alternativ
although   obwohl
always   immer
among   zwischen, unter
amount   Betrag, Summe, Menge
to analyze   analysieren
angry   wütend
animal   Tier
to announce   bekannt geben, ansagen
announcement   Bekanntgabe, Durchsage
another   noch eine(r, s), ein(e) andere(r, s)
to answer; answer   (be)antworten; Antwort
any   irgendeine(r, s)
any time   jederzeit
anybody   irgendjemand
anyone   irgendjemand
anything   irgendetwas
to appear   (er)scheinen
apple   Apfel
applicant   Bewerber/in
application   Bewerbung
to apply (for)   sich bewerben (um)
area   Gebiet, Bereich
around   um (herum), ungefähr
arrival   Ankunft
to arrive   ankommen
article   Artikel
as   wie, da, als
as well   auch, ebenso gut
to ask (for)   fragen, bitten (um)
at first   anfangs
at home   zu Hause
at last   schließlich, endlich
at least   wenigstens, mindestens, zumindest
at once   sofort
at present   im Augenblick, jetzt
at risk   gefährdet
at the moment   im Moment, jetzt

at work   bei der Arbeit
atmosphere   Atmosphäre
to attend (school)   (Schule) besuchen
attention   Aufmerksamkeit
attitude   Haltung, Einstellung
to attract   anziehen
aunt   Tante
autumn   Herbst
away   weg
awful   furchtbar, schrecklich

B

back   Rücken; zurück
background   Hintergrund, Herkunft
bad   schlecht, schlimm, böse
bag   Tasche, Tüte
baggage   Gepäck
to bake   backen
baker   Bäcker/in
balcony   Balkon
to ban; ban   verbieten, Verbot
bank   Bank (Geldinstitut)
basket   Korb
bathroom   Badezimmer, Toilette
to be able   können
to be afraid (of)   Angst haben (vor)
beach   Strand
beard   Bart
beautiful   schön
because   weil
because of   wegen
to become, (became, become)   werden
bed   Bett
bedroom   Schlafzimmer
before   vor, bevor
to begin, (began, begun)   anfangen, beginnen
beginning   Anfang, Beginn
to behave   sich benehmen, sich verhalten
behaviour   Verhalten, Benehmen
behind   hinter
to believe   glauben
to belong to   gehören zu
best   beste(r, s), am besten
best wishes   alles Gute
better   besser

between zwischen
bicycle Fahrrad
big groß
bike Fahrrad (Kurzform)
bill Rechnung, Gesetzesvorlage, Banknote, Entwurf, Schnabel
bird Vogel
birth Geburt
birthday Geburtstag
bit Stückchen
to bite, (bit, bitten) beißen
black schwarz
blackboard (Wand-)Tafel
to blame (for) verantwortlich machen (für)
block of flats Wohnblock
blog Internet-Tagebuch
blood Blut
blue blau
board Brett, Verpflegung
boat Boot
body Körper
to boil kochen
to book; book buchen; Buch
boot Stiefel
border Grenze
bored gelangweilt
boring langweilig
to borrow sich ausleihen
both beide
bottle Flasche
bottom Boden, unteres Ende
box Schachtel, Kiste, Karton
boy Junge
boyfriend Freund
bread Brot
to break, (broke, broken); break (zer)brechen, kaputt machen; Pause
to break down zusammenbrechen
breakfast Frühstück
bridge Brücke
to bring, (brought, brought) bringen
to broadcast, (broadcast, broadcast) übertragen, senden
brochure Broschüre, Prospekt
brother Bruder
brown braun
to brush; brush bürsten; Bürste
to build, (built, built) bauen
building Gebäude
to burn, (burnt, burnt) brennen
business Geschäft, Betriebswirtschaft
busy beschäftigt, besetzt, belegt
but aber

butcher Metzger/in
to buy, (bought, bought) kaufen
buyer Käufer/in
by durch, mit, bei, neben, bis, um
by the way übrigens

C

cake Kuchen
to calculate (be)rechnen
to call; call (an)rufen, nennen, heißen; Anruf
camera Kamera, Fotoapparat
to camp; camp zelten, lagern; Lager
to campaign; campaign Wahlkampf führen; Kampagne, Wahlkampf
can können; Büchse, Dose
capital Großbuchstabe, Hauptstadt
car Auto
card Karte
to care; care sorgen, gern tun mögen; Sorge
career Beruf, Laufbahn, Karriere
careful vorsichtig, sorgfältig
careless sorglos
cargo Fracht, Ladung
to carry tragen
case Fall, Koffer, Kiste
cash Bargeld
cat Katze
to catch, (caught, caught) fangen
to cause; cause verursachen; Ursache
ceiling Zimmerdecke
centre Zentrum, Mittelpunkt
century Jahrhundert
certain sicher, bestimmt, gewiss
chair Stuhl
chalk Kreide
to change; change wechseln, (sich) (ver)ändern; Änderung, Wechsel(geld)
channel Kanal
chart Schaubild, Tabelle, Karte
cheap billig
to check; check (über)prüfen, kontrollieren; Kontrolle, Rechnung (im Restaurant), *(AE)* Scheck, Prüfung
cheers Tschüs, zum Wohl
cheese Käse
child(ren) Kind(er)
chips Pommes Frites, Kartoffelchips
chocolate Schokolade, Praline
choice Wahl
to choose, (chose, chosen) (aus)wählen
Christmas Weihnachten

church Kirche
cigarette Zigarette
cinema Kino
city Stadt
class (Schul-)Klasse
classmate Klassenkamerad/in
classroom Klassenzimmer
to clean; clean reinigen, putzen; sauber
to clear; clear säubern, räumen; klar
clever klug, schlau, clever
to climb klettern
clock (Wand-)Uhr
to close; close schließen; dicht, nahe
clothes Kleidung
cloud Wolke
coal Kohle
coast Küste
coat Mantel
coffee Kaffee
coin Münze
cold kalt
to collect sammeln, abholen
collection Sammlung
college (Fach-)Hochschule, College
colour Farbe
to comb; comb kämmen; Kamm
to come, (came, come) kommen
comfortable bequem, behaglich
to communicate kommunizieren, übermitteln
communication Kommunikation, Übermittlung
company Gesellschaft, Firma
to compare vergleichen
competition Wettbewerb, Konkurrenz
competitor Konkurrent/in, Wettbewerbsteilnehmer/in
to complete; complete fertigstellen, vervollständigen; vollständig
to connect verbinden
connection Verbindung, Zusammenhang
to contact; contact sich in Verbindung setzen mit; Verbindung, Kontakt
to contain enthalten
container Behälter
to continue fortsetzen, weitermachen, weitergehen
to cook; cook kochen; Koch, Köchin
cooker Herd
to cooperate zusammenarbeiten
cooperation Zusammenarbeit
to copy; copy kopieren, abschreiben; Kopie, Exemplar

Vocabulary | Basic vocabulary

corner Ecke
to correct; correct korrigieren, verbessern; korrekt, richtig
correction Verbesserung, Korrektur
to cost, (cost, cost); cost kosten; Kosten
cotton Baumwolle
to count zählen, ins Gewicht fallen
counter Ladentisch, Schalter
country Land
couple Ehepaar, Paar
course Kurs, Lauf, Gang, Strecke
to cover; cover (be/ab)decken, besetzen; Abdeckung, Umschlag
cow Kuh
to cross überqueren
crossing Kreuzung
crowd (Menschen-)Menge
crowded dicht gedrängt, voll
to cry; cry schreien, weinen; Schrei
cup Tasse
curious neugierig, seltsam
curtain Vorhang
customer Kunde, Kundin
customs Zoll, Zoll-
to cut, (cut, cut); cut schneiden, kürzen; Schnitt
to cycle Fahrrad fahren

D

daily täglich
to damage; damage beschädigen; Schaden
to dance; dance tanzen; Tanz
danger Gefahr
dangerous gefährlich
dark dunkel
darkness Dunkelheit
date Datum, Zeitpunkt, Verabredung
date of birth Geburtsdatum
daughter Tochter
day Tag
dead tot
to deal, (dealt, dealt) (in, with); deal handeln (mit, von); sich befassen mit; Geschäft
dear lieb
death Tod
to decide (sich) entscheiden
decision Entscheidung
deep tief
to deliver liefern, (Rede) halten
delivery Lieferung
department Abteilung

department store Kaufhaus
to depend (on) abhängen (von)
to describe beschreiben
description Beschreibung
to design; design entwerfen, konstruieren; Entwurf, Muster
desk Schreibtisch
to destroy zerstören
destruction Zerstörung
detail Einzelheit, Detail
to develop entwickeln
development Entwicklung
to dial (Telefon) wählen
to dictate diktieren
dictation Diktat
dictionary Wörterbuch
to die sterben
to differ (from) sich unterscheiden (von)
difference Unterschied
different verschieden, unterschiedlich
difficult schwierig, schwer
difficulty Schwierigkeit
dining room Esszimmer
dinner (Mittag-, Abend-)Essen
to direct (to); direct richten, lenken (auf); direkt
direction Richtung
dirty dreckig, schmutzig
disadvantage Nachteil
to disagree (with) anderer Meinung sein, nicht übereinstimmen (mit)
to discuss besprechen, diskutieren
discussion Gespräch, Diskussion
to dislike nicht mögen
distance Entfernung, Strecke, Abstand
doctor Arzt, Ärztin
dog Hund
door Tür
down hinunter, unten
downstairs die Treppe hinunter, unten, im Erdgeschoss
to draw, (drew, drawn) zeichnen, (an)ziehen
drawing Zeichnung
to dream; dream träumen; Traum
to dress; dress (sich) anziehen; Kleid, Kleidung
to drink, (drank, drunk); drink trinken; Getränk
to drive, (drove, driven); drive fahren; Fahrt
driver Fahrer/in
to dry; dry trocknen; trocken

during während
dustbin Mülltonne
duty Pflicht, Zoll

E

each jede(r, s)
each other einander, sich
ear Ohr
early früh
to earn verdienen
earth Erde
east Osten; östlich, Ost-, ostwärts
easy leicht
to eat, (ate, eaten) essen
economy Wirtschaft
edge Kante, Rand, Schneide
to educate erziehen
education Erziehung
to effect; effect durchführen, erzielen, leisten; Wirkung, Effekt
egg Ei
either ... or entweder ... oder
to elect wählen
election Wahl
electric elektrisch
electricity Elektrizität
electronics Elektronik
else sonst
emergency Notfall
to employ beschäftigen, einstellen
employed beschäftigt
employee Angestellte/r, Arbeitnehmer/in
employer Arbeitgeber/in
employment Beschäftigung, Anstellung, Arbeit
empty leer
to end; end (be)enden; Ende, Schluss
energy Energie, Kraft
engine Motor, Triebwerk, Lokomotive
engineer Ingenieur/in, Techniker/in
engineering Technik; technisch
to enjoy genießen, sich freuen an
enjoyable schön, angenehm, unterhaltsam
enough genug
to enquire (about) sich erkundigen (nach), fragen (nach)
enquiry Anfrage, Erkundigung, Untersuchung
to enter eintreten, eingeben
entrance Eintritt, Eingang
envelope Umschlag

environment Umwelt, Umgebung, Umfeld
equal gleich
equipment Ausrüstung, Ausstattung
especial besondere(r, s)
even eben, gleich; sogar, selbst
evening Abend
event Ereignis
ever je, jemals
every jede(r, s)
everybody jeder
everyone jeder
everything alles
everywhere überall
exact genau
exam(ination) Prüfung
example Beispiel
excellent ausgezeichnet, hervorragend
exciting aufregend
to excuse; excuse (sich) entschuldigen; Entschuldigung
exercise Übung, Bewegung
to exist existieren, bestehen
exit Ausgang, Ausfahrt
to expect erwarten
expensive teuer
to experience; experience erleben, erfahren; Erfahrung
to explain erklären
explanation Erklärung
to export; export exportieren, ausführen; Ausfuhr, Export
to express; express ausdrücken, äußern; Schnellzug, als Eilsache
expression Ausdruck
extra besonders
eye Auge

F

to face; face (einer Sache) ins Auge sehen, gegenübertreten; Gesicht
fact Tatsache
factory Fabrik
fair Messe, Markt; gerecht, fair
to fall, (fell, fallen); fall fallen; Fallen, Sturz; (AE) Herbst
false falsch
family Familie
famous berühmt
far weit
fare Fahrpreis, Fahrgeld
farm Bauernhof, Farm
farmer Landwirt

farming Landwirtschaft
fast schnell
fat (adj.); fat dick, fett; Fett
father Vater
favourite Lieblings-
to feed, (fed, fed) füttern, ernähren
to feel, (felt, felt) fühlen
feeling Gefühl
few wenige, paar
field Feld
to fight, (fought, fought); fight kämpfen; Kampf
to fill füllen
final Finale, Endrunde; letzte(r, s), endgültig
to find, (found, found) finden
fine Strafe; fein, schön, gut
to finish; finish beenden, abschließen, aufhören; Ziel, Vollendung
to fire; fire feuern; Feuer
firm Firma; fest, verbindlich
first erste(r, s), zuerst
first of all zuerst, vor allem
to fish; fish fischen; Fisch
to fit (in); fit (zusammen)passen, einbauen; gesund, in Form
to fix befestigen, reparieren, besorgen
flat Wohnung; flach
flight Flug
floor Boden, Stock, Etage
flower Blume
to fly, (flew, flown); fly fliegen; Fliege
to follow folgen
food Essen, Nahrung, Lebensmittel
foot, feet Fuß, Füße
football Fußball
for example zum Beispiel
foreign ausländisch, fremd
forever für immer
to forget, (forgot, forgotten) vergessen
fork Gabel
to form; form formen, gestalten; Form, Formular, Klasse
fortunate glücklich
forward(s) vorwärts
to free; free befreien; frei, kostenlos
freeway (AE) Autobahn
frequent häufig
fresh frisch
fridge Kühlschrank
friend Freund/in
friendly freundlich
front Vorderseite
fruit Obst, Frucht, Früchte

full (of) voll (von, mit)
fun Spaß
furniture Möbel
further weiter
future Zukunft

G

game Spiel
garage Autowerkstatt, Garage
garden Garten
gate Tor
gentleman Herr
to get, (got, got) bekommen, erhalten, werden
to get married heiraten
to get up aufstehen
girl Mädchen
girlfriend Freundin
to give, (gave, given) geben
to give up aufgeben
glad froh
glass Glas
glasses Brille
glove Handschuh
to go, (went, gone) gehen, fahren
to go down untergehen, sinken, fallen
to go on weitergehen, weitermachen
to go shopping einkaufen gehen
to go up hinaufgehen, wachsen, steigen
good gut
goodbye auf Wiedersehen
goods Güter, Waren
to govern regieren
government Regierung
grandfather Großvater
grandmother Großmutter
grandparents Großeltern
grateful dankbar
great groß, großartig
green grün
to greet grüßen
grey grau
grocer Lebensmittelhändler/in
ground Boden
group Gruppe
to grow, (grew, grown) wachsen
grown-up Erwachsene/r
growth Wachstum
to guess; guess (er)raten; Vermutung
guest Gast

H

hair Haar
half Hälfte; halb
hall Flur, Saal
ham Schinken
handbag Handtasche
handkerchief Taschentuch
to hang, (hung, hung) (auf)hängen
to happen geschehen, passieren
happy glücklich, heiter
harbour Hafen
hard hart, schwierig, anstrengend
hardly kaum
hat Hut
to hate; hate hassen; Hass
to have (got), (had, had) haben
to have to müssen
to head; head anführen, fahren nach; Kopf, Leiter
headache Kopfschmerz
headline Überschrift
health Gesundheit
healthy gesund
to hear, (heard, heard) hören
heart Herz
to heat; heat heizen; Hitze
heating Heizung
heavy schwer
height Höhe, Größe
hello hallo
to help; help helfen; Hilfe
helpful hilfreich
here hier
here you are bitte(schön)!
to hesitate zögern
to hide, (hid, hidden) (sich) verstecken
high hoch
high tech Hochtechnologie
hill Hügel
history Geschichte
to hit, (hit, hit); hit schlagen; Schlag, Treffer, Erfolg
to hold, (held, held) halten
hole Loch
holiday Urlaub, Ferien, freier Tag, Feiertag
home Zuhause
homework Hausaufgaben
honest ehrlich
to hope; hope hoffen; Hoffnung
horse Pferd
hospital Krankenhaus
hot heiß, scharf
hour Stunde
house Haus
housewife Hausfrau
housework Hausarbeit
how wie
how are you? wie geht es Dir/Ihnen?
however jedoch
hundred Hundert
hungry hungrig
to hurry; hurry sich beeilen; Eile
to hurt, (hurt, hurt) verletzen
husband Ehemann

I

ice cream Eiskrem
idea Idee, Vorstellung
if wenn, falls, ob
ill krank
illness Krankheit
to imagine sich vorstellen
immediate unmittelbar, unverzüglich
immigrant Einwanderer, Einwanderin
to immigrate einwandern
to import; import einführen, importieren; Einfuhr, Import
importance Wichtigkeit
important wichtig
impossible unmöglich
to improve (sich) verbessern
in fact tatsächlich
in front of vor
in italics kursiv
in my opinion meiner Meinung nach
in time rechtzeitig
inch Zoll (Maßeinheit)
to include einschließen
income Einkommen
to increase; increase zunehmen, steigen, erhöhen; Anstieg
indeed tatsächlich
industry Industrie
to inform informieren
inside in, innerhalb
instead (of) anstatt, stattdessen
to instruct unterrichten, anweisen
instruction Unterricht, Anweisung, (Gebrauchs-)Anleitung
insurance Versicherung
to intend beabsichtigen
interest Interesse, (Plural) Zinsen
interesting interessant
to introduce einführen, vorstellen
introduction Einführung, Vorstellung
to invent erfinden
invention Erfindung
to invest investieren
invitation Einladung
to invite einladen
island Insel
IT Informationstechnik

J

jacket Jacke
jam Marmelade
job Arbeit, Beruf, Job
to join (sich) anschließen, beitreten
journey Reise
juice Saft
to jump; jump springen; Sprung
just genau, soeben, nur

K

to keep, (kept, kept) (be)halten, aufbewahren
key Schlüssel, Haupt-
to kill töten
kilo(gram) Kilo(gramm)
kind Art, Sorte; freundlich
king König
to kiss; kiss küssen; Kuss
kitchen Küche
knee Knie
knife Messer
to knock klopfen
to know, (knew, known) wissen, kennen
knowledge Wissen

L

ladder Leiter
lady Dame
lake See
lamp Lampe
land Land
landlady Vermieterin, Wirtin
landlord Vermieter, Wirt
language Sprache
large weit, groß
to last; last dauern, halten; letzte(r, s)
late spät
later on später
latest neueste(r, s)
to laugh lachen
laughter Gelächter

Role cards > Grammar Files > Skills Files > **Vocabulary**

law Gesetz
to lay, (laid, laid) legen
lazy faul
to lead, (led, led) führen, leiten
leaflet (Hand-)Zettel, Flugblatt
to learn, (learnt, learnt) lernen
learner Lernende/r, Anfänger/in
least wenigste(r, s), geringste(r, s)
to leave, (left, left) (ver)lassen, abfahren
left links; übrig
leg Bein
leisure Freizeit
lemon Zitrone
to lend, (lent, lent) verleihen
length Länge
less weniger
lesson Unterrichtsstunde
to let, (let, let) lassen
letter Brief, Buchstabe
to lie, (lied, lied) lügen
to lie, (lay, lain) liegen
life (lives) Leben
to lift; lift anheben, aufheben; Aufzug, Mitfahrgelegenheit
light Licht, Lampe; hell, leicht
to like; like mögen; wie
to limit; limit beschränken, begrenzen; Grenze, Beschränkung
line Linie, Zeile
lip Lippe
to list; list aufführen, auflisten; Liste
to listen (to) (zu)hören
little klein, wenig
to live; live leben, wohnen; direkt, live
living room Wohnzimmer
to load; load laden; Ladung
local lokal, ortsansässig, örtlich
long lang
to look schauen, (aus)sehen
to look after sich kümmern um
to look for suchen
to look forward to sich freuen auf
to look out aufpassen, hinaussehen
to look up nachschlagen, heraussuchen, aufblicken
lorry Lastwagen
to lose, (lost, lost) verlieren
loss Verlust
lot Menge, Los
lots of viel(e)
loud laut
to love; love lieben; Liebe
lovely hübsch, reizend

low niedrig
luck Glück, Schicksal
lucky glücklich (im Sinne von: Glück haben)
luggage Gepäck
lunch Mittagessen

M

machine Maschine, Gerät, Automat
mad verrückt
madam gnädige Frau
magazine Zeitschrift
mail Post
main Haupt-
mainly hauptsächlich
to make, (made, made) machen, herstellen
man (men) Mann (Männer), Mensch
to manage zu Stande bringen, schaffen, leiten, verwalten
management (Geschäfts-)Leitung, Verwaltung, Durchführung
many viele
map (Land-)Karte
market Markt
marmalade (Orangen-)Marmelade
married verheiratet
to marry heiraten
mass Masse
to match; match passen, zuordnen; Wettkampf, Streichholz
mathematics Mathematik
to matter; matter etwas ausmachen; Angelegenheit
may dürfen
maybe vielleicht
meal Mahlzeit
to mean, (meant, meant) bedeuten, meinen
meaning Bedeutung
(in the) meantime inzwischen, währenddessen
meanwhile inzwischen
meat Fleisch
mechanic Mechaniker/in
media Medien
to meet, (met, met) (sich) treffen, kennenlernen, entsprechen
meeting Treffen
member Mitglied
to mend reparieren
to mention erwähnen
message Mitteilung, Nachricht

method Methode
metre Meter
microwave Mikrowelle
middle Mitte; mittlere(r, s)
midnight Mitternacht
might könnte(n); Gewalt, Macht
mile Meile
milk Milch
to mind; mind etwas ausmachen; Meinung, Gedanken, Verstand
mine Bergwerk
minute Minute
mirror Spiegel
Miss Fräulein
to miss vermissen, verfehlen, verpassen
mistake Fehler
to mix; mix mischen; Mischung
moment Augenblick
money Geld
month Monat
moon Mond
more mehr
morning Morgen
most meiste(r, s), die meisten
mother Mutter
mountain Berg
mouth Mund
to move bewegen, umziehen
movement Bewegung
Mr Herr (Anrede)
Mrs Frau (Anrede für eine verheiratete Frau)
Ms Frau (Anrede)
much viel
mum Mutter, Mama
music Musik
must müssen
must not nicht dürfen

N

to name; name benennen; Name
narrow eng
near nahe
nearby nahe gelegen
nearly fast, beinahe
necessary notwendig
to need; need brauchen, benötigen; Notwendigkeit
neighbour Nachbar/in
neither ... nor weder ... noch
never nie(mals)
new neu

news Nachrichten, Neuigkeit
newspaper Zeitung
next nächste(r, s)
nice nett, schön, hübsch, gut
night Nacht
no kein(e); nein
no longer nicht mehr
no one niemand
nobody niemand
noise Lärm, Geräusch
noisy laut
noon Mittag
north Norden; nördlich, Nord-, nordwärts
nose Nase
not nicht
not either auch nicht
not even nicht einmal
not yet noch nicht
note Notiz
to note notieren, anmerken, bemerken
nothing nichts
to notice; notice bemerken; Aushang, Kenntnis, Beachtung
now jetzt
nowadays heutzutage
nowhere nirgendwo
number Zahl, Nummer, Anzahl
nurse Krankenpfleger/in
nursery school teacher Erzieher/in

O

o'clock Uhr (Zeitangabe)
ocean Meer, Ozean
of course natürlich
off von … weg, aus, weg
to offer; offer anbieten; Angebot
office Büro, Amt
often oft, häufig
oil Öl
old alt
on time pünktlich
once einmal, einst
only nur, erst
to open; open öffnen; offen, geöffnet
opinion Meinung
opposite Gegensatz; andere/r/s
or oder
to order; order bestellen, befehlen; Bestellung, Befehl, Reihenfolge
organization Organisation
to organize organisieren
other andere(r, s)

out of work arbeitslos
outside Außenseite; draußen, außerhalb
to own; own besitzen; eigene(r, s)
owner Eigentümer/in

P

to pack; pack packen; Packung
packet Paket
page Seite
to paint; paint malen; Farbe
pair Paar
paper Papier
parent Elternteil
to park; park parken; Park
part Teil
to pass vorbeigehen, (Prüfung) bestehen, (ein Gesetz) verabschieden, zupassen
passenger Passagier/in, Fahrgast
passport Pass
past Vergangenheit
to pay, (paid, paid); pay bezahlen, zahlen; Lohn, Bezahlung
peace Friede
pen Stift, Füller
pence Plural von Penny
pencil Bleistift
penny Penny (englische Münze)
people Leute, Volk
per cent Prozent
perfect vollkommen, perfekt
perhaps vielleicht
period Periode, Zeitraum, Schulstunde
personal persönlich
petrol Benzin
to phone; phone anrufen, telefonieren; Telefon
photograph Foto
to pick pflücken, wählen
to pick up nehmen, aufheben
picture Bild
piece Stück
pipe Pfeife, Röhre
to place; place stellen, legen; Platz, Ort, Stelle
to plan; plan planen; Plan
plane Flugzeug
to plant; plant pflanzen; Pflanze, Fabrikanlage
plate Teller, Platte, Schild
platform Bahnsteig, Plattform
to play; play spielen; (Schau-)Spiel

player Spieler/in
playground Spielplatz
please bitte
pleasure Vergnügen
pocket Tasche
to point; point zeigen; Punkt
police Polizei
policeman Polizist
policewoman Polizistin
political politisch
politician Politiker/in
politics Politik
to pollute verschmutzen
polluted verschmutzt
pollution Umweltverschmutzung
poor arm, unzureichend, notdürftig
popular beliebt, populär
population Bevölkerung, Population, Bestand
port Hafen
possibility Möglichkeit
possible möglich
post office Post
postcard Postkarte
postman Briefträger, Postbote
pot Topf
potato Kartoffel
pound Pfund
power Kraft, Energie, Strom
power station Kraftwerk
practice Übung
to practise üben
to prefer vorziehen
to prepare vorbereiten, zubereiten
to present; present vorstellen, präsentieren, mit sich bringen; Geschenk, Gegenwart; anwesend, gegenwärtig
to press; press drücken, pressen; Presse
pretty hübsch, ziemlich
price Preis
pride Stolz
prize Preis, Gewinn
probable wahrscheinlich
to produce produzieren, herstellen
producer Hersteller/in, Produzent/in
product Produkt
production Herstellung, Produktion
to profit; profit profitieren; Gewinn
profitable rentabel, einträglich, lohnend
programme Programm, Sendung
to promise; promise versprechen; Versprechen
to pronounce aussprechen

pronunciation Aussprache
to protect schützen
protection Schutz
proud stolz
pub Kneipe
public Öffentlichkeit; öffentlich
to pull ziehen
pupil Schüler/in
purpose Zweck, Absicht
to push; push schieben, stoßen; Stoß
to put, (put, put) setzen, stellen, legen
to put on anziehen, auftragen, aufsetzen
to put up (Hand) heben, bauen, aufstellen

Q

quality Qualität
quantity Menge
quarter Viertel
queen Königin
question Frage
quick schnell
quiet ruhig
quite ganz, ziemlich

R

railway Eisenbahn
to rain; rain regnen; Regen
to raise; raise (hoch)heben, erheben, großziehen, (Thema) anschneiden; Erhöhung, Steigerung
rather ziemlich
to reach erreichen
to read, (read, read) lesen
reader Leser/in
ready fertig, bereit
real wirklich
reality Wirklichkeit
reason Grund
reasonable vernünftig, günstig
to receive erhalten, bekommen
recent jüngst, kürzlich
reception Empfang
receptionist im Empfang arbeitende Person
to record; record aufnehmen; Rekord, Aufnahme, Schallplatte
red rot
regular regelmäßig
relative Verwandte/r; relativ
to relax entspannen, sich erholen

to remain bleiben
to remember sich erinnern an, daran denken
to remind (of) erinnern an
to rent; rent mieten, vermieten; Miete
to repair; repair reparieren; Reparatur
to repeat; repeat wiederholen; Wiederholung
to replace ersetzen
to reply; reply antworten; Antwort
to report; report berichten; Bericht
reputation Ansehen, Ruf
to rescue; rescue retten; Rettung
to rest; rest ruhen; Rest, Ruhe
to result; result resultieren; Ergebnis
to return; return zurückkommen; Rückkehr, Rückgabe
rich reich
to ride, (rode, ridden); ride reiten, fahren; Ritt, Fahrt
right; right richtig, rechts; Recht
to ring, (rang, rung); ring klingeln, anrufen; Ring, Anruf
to rise, (rose, risen); rise (auf)steigen, zunehmen; Aufstieg, Zunahme
river Fluss
road Straße
roof Dach
room Zimmer, Raum, Platz
round rund, herum
rubber (Radier-)Gummi
rubbish Abfall, Müll
to rule; rule herrschen; Regel
to run, (ran, run); run laufen, rennen; Serie, Ablauf

S

sad traurig
safe sicher
safety Sicherheit
sale (Schluss-)Verkauf
salesman/woman Verkäufer/in
salt Salz
same der-/die-/dasselbe, gleiche(r, s)
to save retten, sparen
to say, (said, said) sagen
school Schule
sea Meer
seat Sitz
second Sekunde; zweite(r, s)
secret Geheimnis; geheim
secretary Sekretär/in
to see, (saw, seen) sehen, verstehen

to seem (er)scheinen
to sell, (sold, sold) verkaufen
seller Verkäufer/in
to send, (sent, sent) schicken, senden
to sentence; sentence verurteilen; Satz, Urteil
serious ernst, ernsthaft
to serve (be)dienen, servieren
to service; service (Auto) warten; Dienst, Betrieb
to set, (set, set) setzen, stellen, legen
several mehrere
shall sollen
to share; share teilen; Anteil
sheet Blatt, Bogen
shelf Regal
to shine, (shone, shone) scheinen, leuchten
to ship; ship verschicken; Schiff
shirt Hemd
shoe Schuh
shop Geschäft, Laden
shop assistant Verkäufer/in
short kurz
should sollte(n)
shoulder Schulter
to shout rufen
to show, (showed, shown); show zeigen; Ausstellung, Vorstellung, Show
to shut, (shut, shut) schließen
sick krank
side Seite
sight Sicht, Anblick, Sehenswürdigkeit
to sign; sign unterschreiben; Zeichen
simple einfach
since seit
since then seitdem
to sing, (sang, sung) singen
sir Herr (Anrede)
sister Schwester
to sit, (sat, sat) sitzen
to sit down sich hinsetzen
size Größe
skill Fertigkeit, Fähigkeit, Können
skirt Rock
sky Himmel
to sleep, (slept, slept); sleep schlafen; Schlaf
slim schlank
slow langsam
to slow down verlangsamen
small klein

to smell, (smelt, smelt); smell riechen; Geruch
to smile; smile lächeln; Lächeln
to smoke; smoke rauchen; Rauch
to snow; snow schneien; Schnee
so far bisher, bis jetzt
soap Seife
soccer Fußball
sock Socke
soft weich
solution Lösung
to solve lösen
some einige, etwas
somebody jemand
someone jemand
something etwas
sometimes manchmal
son Sohn
song Lied
soon bald
sorry betrübt, tut mir Leid!, Entschuldigung!
to sound; sound klingen; Geräusch, Klang
south Süden; südlich, Süd-, südwärts
space Raum, Platz, Weltraum
spare time Freizeit
to speak, (spoke, spoken) sprechen
speaker Sprecher/in
special besondere(r, s), spezielle(r, s)
speech Rede
speech bubble Sprechblase
to speed; speed schnell fahren; Geschwindigkeit
to speed up beschleunigen
to spell, (spelt, spelt); spell buchstabieren; Zauber(spruch)
to spend, (spent, spent) ausgeben, verbringen
spoon Löffel
spring Frühling, Quelle, Brunnen
staff Belegschaft, Kollegium
stamp Briefmarke
to stand, (stood, stood) stehen, standhalten
to start; start anfangen, beginnen; Anfang
to state; state erklären, darlegen; Staat, Zustand
station Bahnhof
to stay; stay bleiben; Aufenthalt
still dennoch, noch
stone Stein

to stop; stop beenden, anhalten, aufhören; Halt
to store; store lagern, speichern; *(AE)* Laden, Kaufhaus, Lager
storm Sturm
story Geschichte
strange merkwürdig
street Straße
to strike; strike streiken, schlagen; Streik, Treffer, Schlag
strong stark
to study; study studieren; Studium, Studie
subject Fach, Thema
suburb Vorort
to succeed (in) Erfolg haben (in, bei)
success Erfolg
successful erfolgreich
such solche(r, s)
sudden plötzliche(r, s)
sugar Zucker
to suit; suit passen; Anzug
suitcase Koffer
sum Summe
summer Sommer
sun Sonne
sunshine Sonnenschein
supermarket Supermarkt
supper Abendessen
to suppose annehmen, vermuten
sure sicher
to surprise; surprise überraschen; Überraschung
surprised überrascht
survey Überblick, Umfrage
sweet süß
to swim, (swam, swum) schwimmen
to switch; switch schalten, wechseln; Schalter

T

table Tisch, Tabelle
to take, (took, taken) nehmen
to take part in teilnehmen an
to take place stattfinden
to talk; talk reden, sprechen; Gespräch, Unterhaltung, Vortrag
tall hoch(gewachsen), groß
to taste; taste schmecken, probieren; Geschmack
tasty lecker
tax Steuer
tea Tee

to teach, (taught, taught) lehren, unterrichten
teacher Lehrer/in
team Team, Mannschaft
technical technisch
technology Technik, Technologie
(tele)phone Telefon
television (TV) Fernsehen
to tell, (told, told) erzählen
terrible schrecklich, furchtbar
to test; test testen, überprüfen, untersuchen; Klassenarbeit, Versuch
than als
to thank danken, sich bedanken
that dass; jene(r, s), welche(r, s)
then dann, damals
there dort, da
there is/are es gibt
therefore deshalb
these diese
these days heutzutage
thick dick
thin dünn
thing Ding, Sache
to think, (thought, thought) denken, glauben, meinen
thirsty durstig
this diese(r, s)
those diese, jene
though obwohl, trotzdem
thousand Tausend
through durch
to throw, (threw, thrown) werfen
thus so
ticket Fahr-, Eintrittskarte
tidy ordentlich, aufgeräumt
till bis
time Zeit, Zeitdauer, Uhrzeit
times Mal(e)
tired müde
tobacco Tabak
today heute
toe Zeh
together zusammen
toilet Toilette
tomato Tomate
tomorrow morgen
tongue Zunge
tonight heute Abend
too auch
tool Werkzeug
tooth, teeth Zahn, Zähne
top Spitze, Top, Oberteil
tour (Rund-)Reise, Tour

Role cards > Grammar Files > Skills Files > **Vocabulary**

toward(s) in Richtung
tower Turm
town Stadt
toy Spielzeug
to trade (in); trade handeln (mit); Gewerbe, Handwerk, Handel
traditional traditionell, herkömmlich
traffic Verkehr
traffic light(s) Ampel
to train; train ausbilden, trainieren, eine Ausbildung machen; Zug
training Ausbildung, Training
to translate übersetzen
to translation Übersetzung
to transport; transport transportieren; Transport
to travel reisen, fahren
tree Baum
trip (Kurz-)Reise
trouble Schwierigkeit(en)
trousers Hose
true wahr, richtig
truth Wahrheit
to try; try versuchen; Versuch
to turn (sich) drehen, wenden
to turn left/right links/rechts abbiegen
to turn on/off ein-/ausschalten
to turn over umdrehen, überschlagen
twice zweimal
type Art, Typ
typewriter Schreibmaschine
typical typisch
typist Schreibkraft

U

umbrella Schirm
uncle Onkel
to understand, (understood, understood) verstehen
unemployed arbeitslos
unemployment Arbeitslosigkeit
unfortunate unglücklich
unfortunately leider
unfriendly unfreundlich
unhappy unglücklich
university Universität
until (till) bis
upon auf
upstairs (nach) oben, im Obergeschoss
to use; use gebrauchen; Verwendung
used gebraucht, gewohnt
useful nützlich
useless nutzlos
usual gewöhnlich

V

vacation *(AE)* Ferien
van Lieferwagen
vegetable(s) Gemüse
vehicle Fahrzeug
very sehr
village Dorf
to visit; visit besuchen; Besuch
visitor Besucher/in
vocabulary Wortschatz, Vokabelverzeichnis
voice Stimme
to vote; vote abstimmen, wählen; Abstimmung, Stimme

W

to wait warten
waiter Kellner
waitress Kellnerin
to wake, (woke, woken) (up) wecken, aufwachen
to walk; walk gehen; Spaziergang
wall Wand, Mauer
to want wollen
war Krieg
warehouse Lager
to warm; warm wärmen; warm
to warn warnen
to wash waschen
washing machine Waschmaschine
to waste; waste verschwenden; Abfall, Verschwendung
to watch; watch beobachten, sehen; Uhr
water Wasser
way Weg, Art und Weise
weak schwach
to wear, (wore, worn) (Kleidung) tragen
weather Wetter
week Woche
weekend Wochenende
weight Gewicht
to welcome; welcome willkommen heißen, begrüßen; Willkommen, Empfang
well gut, gesund; na ja ...
well-known bekannt

west Westen, westlich, West-, westwärts
wet nass, feucht
what was
what about ... was ist mit ...
what else was noch
what ... for wofür, wozu
wheel Rad
when wann
where wo
whether ob
which welche(r, s)
while während
white weiß
who wer
whole ganz
whom wem, wen
whose wessen
why warum
wide weit
wife (wives) Ehefrau(en)
will werden; Wille
to win, (won, won) gewinnen
window Fenster
wine Wein
to wish; wish wünschen; Wunsch
within innerhalb
without ohne
woman (women) Frau (Frauen)
wonderful wunderbar
wood Holz, Wald
wool Wolle
word Wort
to work; work arbeiten; Arbeit
worker Arbeiter/in
world Welt
worse schlechter
worst am schlechtesten
worth wert
to write, (wrote, written) schreiben
writer Verfasser/in, Schriftsteller/in
wrong falsch

Y

year Jahr
yellow gelb
yesterday gestern
yet jedoch, schon
you're welcome gern geschehen!
young jung
youth Jugend

Unit vocabulary

Abkürzungen und Zeichen

etw.	= etwas	=	entspricht
pl.	= Plural, Mehrzahl	↔	ist das Gegenteil von
sg.	= Singular, Einzahl	→	verwandt mit
s.o.	= someone	red	Vokabel aus Hörtext oder Video
s.th.	= something		
BE	= britisches Englisch		
AE	= amerikanisches Englisch		

Unit 1 Young people in the world of work

A			
	part-time [ˌpɑːtˈtaɪm]	Teilzeit	↔ full-time
	step [step]	Schritt; Stufe	The steps to this dance are easy.
	post [pəʊst]	Post; Beitrag in einem Blog	
	work placement [ˈwɜːk ˌpleɪsmənt]	Berufspraktikum	= internship (AE)
	insight [ˈɪnsaɪt]	Einblick	a deep understanding of s.th.
	practical [ˈpræktɪkl]	praktisch	↔ impractical
	element [ˈeləmənt]	Element; Aspekt	= aspect
	reception desk [rɪˈsepʃn ˌdesk]	Rezeption	Susan is currently working at the reception desk.
	to check in [ˌtʃek ˈɪn]	einchecken	↔ to check out
	to be on room duty [bi ˌɒn ˈruːm ˌdjuːti]	für den Zimmerservice verantwortlich sein	Susan is on room duty today so she is putting drinks into the mini-bars.
	cleaning staff [ˈkliːnɪŋ ˌstɑːf]	Reinigungspersonal	people in a hotel who clean the rooms
	to tidy up [ˌtaɪdi ˈʌp]	aufräumen	= to clean up
	to get to know [ˌget tə ˈnəʊ]	kennenlernen	to meet s.o. for the first time
	nursery school [ˈnɜːsri ˌskuːl]	Kindergarten; Vorschule	Children go to nursery school up to the age of 5.
	outskirts [ˈaʊtskɜːts]	Stadtrand	= suburbs ↔ downtown (AE) ↔ city centre (BE)
	Munich [ˈmjuːnɪk]	München	Munich is a city in Bavaria.
	challenging [ˈtʃælɪndʒɪŋ]	herausfordernd; anspruchsvoll	→ challenge → to challenge
	outing [ˈaʊtɪŋ]	Ausflug	going somewhere for fun
	working hours (pl.) [ˌwɜːkɪŋ ˈaʊəz]	Arbeitszeit	She works hard. Her working hours are long.
	statement [ˈsteɪtmənt]	Aussage; Statement	The statement is not correct.
	current [ˈkʌrnt]	jetzig; gegenwärtig	The current situation is difficult.
	workplace [ˈwɜːkpleɪs]	Arbeitsplatz	John's workplace is the Lowry Hotel.
	presentation [ˌpreznˈteɪʃn]	Vorstellung; Präsentation	→ to present
	home town [ˈhəʊm ˌtaʊn]	Heimatstadt	the place that you come from
	likes (pl.) [laɪks]	Vorlieben	↔ dislikes
	dislikes (pl.) [ˈdɪslaɪks]	Abneigungen	↔ likes
	personality [ˌpɜːsnˈæləti]	Persönlichkeit	He's kind and friendly. He has a nice personality.
	can't stand s.th. [ˌkɑːnt ˈstænd]	etw. nicht aushalten können	= to dislike a lot
	social networking website [ˌsəʊʃl ˈnetwɜːkɪŋ ˌwebsaɪt]	Internetseite für ein soziales Netzwerk	

B1	**International Diploma** [ˌɪntəˌnæʃnl dɪˈpləʊmə]	internationales Diplom	
	Geography [dʒiˈɒɡrəfi]	Geografie	→ geographical
	Science [saɪəns]	Wissenschaft; Naturwissenschaft	→ scientist → scientific
	Biology [baɪˈɒlədʒi]	Biologie	→ biological → biologist
	Physics [ˈfɪzɪks]	Physik	→ physical → physicist
	Information Technology [ˌɪnfəmeɪʃn tekˈnɒlədʒi]	Informationstechnik	= IT
	project [ˈprɒdʒekt]	Projekt	Ten people worked on the project at a time.
	prompt [prɒmt]	Stichpunkt; Aufforderung	
	to **hand in** [ˌhænd ˈɪn]	abgeben	↔ to hand out
	essay [ˈeseɪ]	Aufsatz	a text written about a specific topic
B3	**lunchtime** [ˈlʌnʃtaɪm]	Mittagszeit	Lunchtime at college is usually between twelve and one o'clock.
	library [ˈlaɪbrəri]	Bibliothek	There are many interesting books in the college library.
	normally [ˈnɔːmli]	normalerweise	= usually
C	**agency** [ˈeɪdʒnsi]	Agentur; Vertretung; Träger	Please contact our agency for more information.
	in order to [ɪn ˈɔːdə tə]	zwecks; um zu	with the plan to do s.th. specific
	disabled [dɪˈseɪbld]	behindert	Disabled people can use this door.
	to **sort out** [ˌsɔːt ˈaʊt]	sortieren; organisieren	= to organize
	chain [tʃeɪn]	Kette	There is a chain of supermarkets across the country.
	checkout [ˈtʃekaʊt]	Kasse	The big supermarkets have fifteen or twenty checkouts.
	apart from [əˈpɑːt frəm]	abgesehen von	except for
	cosmopolitan [ˌkɒzməˈpɒlɪtn]	weltoffen	New York is a cosmopolitan city.
	nationality [ˌnæʃnˈæləti]	Nationalität; Staatsangehörigkeit	→ nation
	multicultural [ˌmʌltɪˈkʌltʃrl]	multikulturell	London and New York are multicultural cities.
	Poland [ˈpəʊlənd]	Polen	Poland is a country and Polish is the language or nationality.
	similar [ˈsɪmɪlə]	ähnlich	↔ different
	to **chill out** [ˌtʃɪl ˈaʊt]	sich entspannen; relaxen	= to relax
	suitable [ˈsuːtəbl]	passend; geeignet	→ to suit
	option [ˈɒpʃn]	Option; Möglichkeit	= possibility
D1	**window shopping** [ˈwɪndəʊ ˌʃɒpɪŋ]	Schaufensterbummel	Window shopping is not expensive because you do not buy anything.
	tiring [ˈtaɪərɪŋ]	ermüdend; anstrengend	→ tired, to tire
	day off [ˌdeɪ ˈɒf]	freier Tag	a holiday for one day
	to **unload** [ʌnˈləʊd]	ausladen	↔ to load
	to **unpack** [ʌnˈpæk]	auspacken	↔ to pack
	sales talk [ˈseɪlz ˌtɔːk]	Verkaufsgespräch	Some shop assistants are very good at sales talk.
	apron [ˈeɪprən]	Schürze	Cooks wear aprons in the kitchen.
	on the right-hand side [ɒn ðə ˌraɪthænd ˈsaɪd]	rechts; auf der rechten Seite	= on the right
	foreground [ˈfɔːɡraʊnd]	Vordergrund	↔ background
	to **scream** [skriːm]	schreien	The movie was so scary that I screamed.
	task [tɑːsk]	Aufgabe	I have to do different tasks every day at work.

Vocabulary | Unit vocabulary

D2	**fashion designer** [ˈfæʃn dɪˌzaɪnə]	Modeschöpfer/in	Karl Lagerfeld is a famous German fashion designer.
	chef [ʃef]	Koch; Köchin	Jamie Oliver is a famous English chef.
	social worker [ˈsəʊʃl ˌwɜːkə]	Sozialarbeiter/in	A social worker helps people in need.
	motor mechanic [ˈməʊtə mɪˌkænɪk]	Kfz-Mechaniker/in	The motor mechanic repaired my car really quickly.
	phrase [freɪz]	Ausdruck	→ phrasal
	to **create** [kriˈeɪt]	schaffen; gestalten	→ creation
	to **install** [ɪnˈstɔːl]	montieren; einbauen	Can you help me to install this new software, please?
	wages (pl.) [ˈweɪdʒɪz]	Lohn; Gehalt	money you get for the work you do
E1	**eco-friendly** [ˌiːkəʊˈfrendli]	umweltfreundlich	= environmentally friendly
	in exchange for s.th. [ɪn ɪksˈtʃeɪndʒ fə]	dafür; im Tausch gegen etw.	in return for s.th. else
	accommodation [əˌkɒməˈdeɪʃn]	Unterkunft	a place where you can stay, e.g. for a holiday
	rural [ˈrʊərl]	ländlich	↔ urban
	long-term [ˌlɒŋˈtɜːm]	Langzeit-	↔ short-term
	to **arrange** [əˈreɪndʒ]	organisieren	= to organize
	to **require** [rɪˈkwaɪə]	verlangen; erfordern; benötigen	= to need
	to **negotiate** [nɪˈgəʊʃieɪt]	verhandeln	The politicians negotiated an agreement.
	host [həʊst]	Gastgeber/in; Moderator/in	↔ guest
	to **dig in** [ˌdɪɡ ˈɪn]	mitmachen	to take an active part
	apprentice [əˈprentɪs]	Auszubildende/r	= trainee
	entire [ɪnˈtaɪə]	ganz	= whole
	all-natural [ˌɔːlˈnætʃrl]	ganz und gar natürlich	↔ artificial
	biodynamic [ˌbaɪədaɪˈnæmɪk]	biodynamisch	using only organic materials for farming
	grape [greɪp]	Traube	fruit used to make wine
	smokehouse [ˈsməʊkhaʊs]	Räucherkammer	building where you can smoke fish, for example
	organic crop [ɔːˌɡænɪk ˈkrɒp]	ökologische Anbauweise	agricultural plants grown in an environmentally friendly way
	irrigation [ˌɪrɪˈɡeɪʃn]	Bewässerung	Because it was so dry the farmer had to install an irrigation system.
	opportunity [ˌɒpəˈtjuːnəti]	Möglichkeit	The job in London is a great opportunity!
	to **milk** [mɪlk]	melken	→ milk
	to **plough** [plaʊ]	pflügen	to work the land
	to **partake** [pɑːˈteɪk]	teilnehmen	to take part in s.th.
	labour [ˈleɪbə]	Arbeit	= work
	to **range** [ˈreɪndʒ]	reichen; sich bewegen	The students range in age from 16 to 19.
	daily chore [ˌdeɪli ˈtʃɔː]	tägliche Aufgabe	task you do every day
	to **contribute** [kənˈtrɪbjuːt]	einen Beitrag leisten; mitarbeiten	→ contribution
	to **rate** [reɪt]	bewerten	to put a value on s.th.
	beneath [bɪˈniːθ]	unter	= under, below
	precaution [prɪˈkɔːʃn]	Vorsichtsmaßnahme	I left my passport in the hotel safe as a precaution.
	stranger [ˈstreɪndʒə]	Unbekannter	→ strange
	unsure [ʌnˈʃɔː]	unsicher	↔ sure
	to **get involved in** [ˌɡet ɪnˈvɒlvd ɪn]	sich engagieren	to take part in s.th.
	destination [ˌdestɪˈneɪʃn]	Ziel	Spain is a popular holiday destination.
	access (sg.) [ˈækses]	Zugang	→ to access

	database [ˈdeɪtəbeɪs]	Datenbank	a collection of pieces of information on a computer
	subscription fee [səbˌskrɪpʃn ˈfiː]	Mitgliedsbeitrag	→ to subscribe
	findings *(pl.)* [ˈfaɪndɪŋz]	Ergebnis	→ to find
	to convince [kənˈvɪns]	überzeugen	We couldn't convince her. She didn't believe us.
E2	**high school** [ˈhaɪ ˌskuːl]	High School *(amerik.)*	school in the USA for people between the ages of 15 and 18
	to grant [grɑːnt]	gewähren; erteilen	to give s.o. s.th. officially
	senior *(AE)* [ˈsiːniə]	Schüler/in im letzten Schuljahr	s.o. in the final year of senior high school
	captain [ˈkæptɪn]	Kapitän/in; Mannschaftsführer/in	leader of a sports team
	lacrosse [ləˈkrɒs]	Lacrosse (Mannschaftssportart)	Lacrosse was first played by North American Indians.
	athletic scholarship [æθˌletɪk ˈskɒləʃɪp]	Stipendium, das einem guten Sportler ermöglicht, einen Studienplatz zu bekommen	I was good at sport so I got an athletic scholarship to go to university.
	Ivy League *(AE)* [ˌaɪvi ˈliːg]	acht Eliteunis in den USA	refers to eight elite universities in the north-east of the US
	SAT *(AE)* [sæt]	Test, der von Studienplatzbewerbern in den USA gefordert wird	SATs are tests taken by people who want to go to university in the US.
	score [skɔː]	Punktestand	Tom's score in the test was 791 points.
	competititve [kəmˈpetɪtɪv]	hart umkämpft; wettbewerbsfähig	→ competition → to compete
	to score [skɔː]	Punkte erzielen	Beth scored badly in the test.
	to make matters worse [ˌmeɪk ˌmætəz ˈwɜːs]	etwas noch schlimmer machen	Ben couldn't get a summer job and to make matters worse he broke his leg on holiday.
	to award [əˈwɔːd]	Preis vergeben; zuerkennen	→ award
	unjust [ʌnˈdʒʌst]	ungerecht	↔ fair
	to deprive of [dɪˈpraɪv ˌəv]	einer Sache berauben	→ deprivation
	definitely [ˈdefɪnətli]	auf jeden Fall	= clearly
	knot [nɒt]	Knoten	a bad feeling
	stomach [ˈstʌmək]	Magen	The patient doesn't feel well. He's had a stomach ache all day.
	admissions director [ədˌmɪʃnz dɪˈrektə]	Zuständige/r für Zulassungen	Jill got an e-mail from the admissions director with an offer of a place at university.
	frustrating [frʌsˈtreɪtɪŋ]	entmutigend; frustrierend	→ frustration → to frustrate
	to misscore [ˌmɪsˈskɔː]	die falsche Punktzahl vergeben	How could they misscore my test and take 100 points off of me?
	fit [fɪt]	die passende Wahl	The job as a teacher is a good fit for Jenny as she likes working with children.
F	**Czech Republic** [ˌtʃek rɪˈpʌblɪk]	Tschechische Republik	The Czech Republic is on the eastern side of Germany.
	laboratory assistant [ləˈbɒrətri əˌsɪstnt]	Laborassistent/in	s.o. who works in a lab
	general [ˈdʒenrl]	allgemein; Haupt-	↔ specific
	detailed [ˈdiːteɪld]	ausführlich	including a lot of information
	medical research [ˌmedɪkl rɪˈsɜːtʃ]	medizinische Forschung	Scientists are doing a lot of medical research into the causes of cancer.
	to mark [mɑːk]	kennzeichnen	→ a mark

Vocabulary | Unit vocabulary

	blood sample [ˈblʌd ˌsɑːmpl]	Blutprobe	The nurse took a blood sample from the patient.
	to **stock** [stɒk]	Lager auffüllen	→ stock
	daily routine [ˌdeɪli ruːˈtiːn]	Tagesablauf	things you do every day
	shopping [ˈʃɒpɪŋ]	Einkäufe	different things that you buy in a shop
	according to [əˈkɔːdɪŋ tə]	gemäß; entsprechend	from what s.o. says or writes
	environmentally friendly [ɪnˌvaɪrnˌmentli ˈfrendli]	umweltfreundlich	Wind energy is environmentally friendly.
	to **vary from** [ˈveəri frəm]	reichen von	to be different in different situations

Unit 2 Getting a job

	to **analyze** [ˈænlaɪz]	analysieren	= to evaluate
	statistics (pl.) [stəˈtɪstɪks]	statistische Angaben; Statistik	The statistics are up to date.
A	**logo** [ˈləʊgəʊ]	Logo; Firmenemblem	= symbol
	paragraph [ˈpærəgrɑːf]	Paragraph; Absatz	The third paragraph of the text describes where he was born.
	origin [ˈɒrɪdʒɪn]	Abstammung; Herkunft	Nobody knows the origin of the song.
	brand [brænd]	Marke	The Levis brand is known all over the world.
	sales (pl.) [seɪlz]	Vertrieb; Verkauf	→ to sell
	wide range [ˌwaɪd ˈreɪndʒ]	großes Angebot; große Auswahl	a big choice or selection
	consumer goods (pl.) [kənˈsjuːmə ˌgʊdz]	Konsumgüter	products that people buy for personal use
	celebrated [ˈseləbreɪtɪd]	gefeiert	→ to celebrate → celebration
	anniversary [ˌænɪˈvɜːsri]	Jubiläum	a day once per year when you celebrate an event
	commercial [kəˈmɜːʃl]	Geschäfts-; geschäftlich; Werbespot	work related to the selling of products or services
	candle maker [ˈkændl ˌmeɪkə]	Kerzenmacher/in	a person or business that produces candles
	soap maker [ˈsəʊp ˌmeɪkə]	Seifenerzeuger/in	a person or company that produces soap
	to **found** [faʊnd]	gründen	= to establish = to set up
	founder [ˈfaʊndə]	Gründer/in	→ to found
	to **launch** [lɔːnʃ]	einführen; auf den Markt bringen	= to introduce
	branded product [ˌbrændɪd ˈprɒdʌkt]	Markenprodukt	product which is better recognized by its trade name, e.g. Tempo tissues
	corporation [ˌkɔːprˈeɪʃn]	großes Unternehmen	a large business
	headquarters (pl.) [ˌhedˈkwɔːtəz]	Zentrale; Stammsitz	The bank has its headquarters in London.
	available [əˈveɪləbl]	erhältlich; verfügbar	This blouse is available in small, medium and large sizes.
	to **acquire s.th.** [əˈkwaɪə]	etw. übernehmen; etw. erwerben	to get or buy s.th.
	net sales (pl.) [ˌnet ˈseɪlz]	Nettoumsatz	↔ gross sales
	billion [ˈbɪliən]	Milliarde	the number 1,000,000,000
	manufacturing [ˌmænjəˈfæktʃrɪŋ]	Fertigung; Produktion; Herstellung; Produktionsbetrieb	→ to manufacture
	unit [ˈjuːnɪt]	Anlage; Einheit	= plant
	to **focus on s.th.** [ˈfəʊkəs ɒn]	sich auf etw. konzentrieren	to concentrate on s.th.
	beauty [ˈbjuːti]	Schönheit	= loveliness = attractiveness
	grooming [ˈgruːmɪŋ]	Pflege	making s.th. attractive
	household care [ˌhaʊshəʊld ˈkeə]	Haushaltspflege	A vacuum and a mop are basic household care products.

	fragrance ['freɪgrəns]	Duft	I wear fragrance spray on special occasions.
	washing powder ['wɒʃɪŋ ˌpaʊdə]	Waschpulver	a powder used for cleaning clothes
	cleaning tool ['kli:nɪŋ ˌtu:l]	Reinigungswerkzeug	A mop is an example of a cleaning tool.
	toilet ['tɔɪlət]	Toilette	= rest room (AE)
	so-called [ˌsəʊ'kɔ:ld]	so gennant	which has a certain name
	term [tɜ:m]	Begriff	a word or expression for s.th.
	soap opera ['səʊp ˌɒprə]	Seifenoper	a regular daytime TV drama which develops over many seasons
	serial ['sɪəriəl]	Serie	a TV show which appears over a long period of time
	to **sponsor** ['spɒnsə]	finanziell unterstützen	→ sponsorship
	relevant ['reləvənt]	wichtig; sachdienlich	= applicable, important
	sector ['sektə]	Branche	Lloyd's is a famous name in the British financial sector.
	to **demand** [dɪ'mɑ:nd]	fordern	The teacher demanded that Sophie sit down.
B1	to **expand** [ɪk'spænd]	vergrößern; erweitern	= to get bigger = to grow
	superstore ['su:pəstɔ:]	großer Supermarkt	a large store that sells a wide variety of products
	independent [ˌɪndɪ'pendənt]	unabhängig	Most teens want to be independent of their parents.
	dealer ['di:lə]	Händler/in	→ to deal
B2	**up to now** [ˌʌp tə 'naʊ]	bis jetzt	so far, until this moment
B3	**born** [bɔ:n]	geboren	I was born in Stuttgart.
	interviewer ['ɪntəvju:ə]	Befrager/in; Interviewer/in	→ interview → interviewee → to interview
	fluency ['flu:ənsi]	Sprachgewandtheit	→ fluent
	work experience (sg.) [ˌwɜ:k ɪk'spɪəriəns]	Berufserfahrung	what you know about a job from working in that area
B4	**bracket** ['brækɪt]	Klammer; Bereich	You put information into brackets when you write a text, if the information is not so important.
	loaf [ləʊf]	Laib	Greg bought a loaf of bread on the way home from work.
C	**application** [ˌæplɪ'keɪʃn]	Bewerbung; Anwendung	→ to apply
	placement ['pleɪsmənt]	Stelle; Praktikum	period of practical experience e.g. in business
	housekeeping ['haʊsˌki:pɪŋ]	Zimmerpflege; Haushaltsführung	tasks like cleaning or vacuuming
	essential [ɪ'senʃl]	notwendig; wesentlich	↔ unnecessary
	with reference to [wɪð 'refrns tə]	mit Bezug auf	with regard to
	open-minded [ˌəʊpn'maɪndɪd]	aufgeschlossen	willing to consider other possibilities or ideas
	facilities (pl.) [fə'sɪlətiz]	Austattung; Einrichtungen	The more stars a hotel has, the more facilties it has for its guests.
	rewarding [rɪ'wɔ:dɪŋ]	lohnend	→ reward → to reward
	certificate [sə'tɪfɪkət]	Zeugnis; Bescheinigung	→ to certify
	further education [ˌfɜ:ðər ˌedʒʊ'keɪʃn]	Aus- und Weiterbildung	After finishing school you can go on to further education such as university.
	to **enable** [ɪ'neɪbl]	ermöglichen	to make possible
	to **enrol** [ɪn'rəʊl]	sich einschreiben	= to sign up for s.th.
	polytechnic university [ˌpɒlɪˌteknɪk ˌju:nɪ'vɜ:səti]	Fachhochschule	higher education institution for technical studies
	Business Studies (pl.) ['bɪznɪs ˌstʌdiz]	Betriebswirtschaftslehre	Marketing and Management are subjects covered in Business Studies.
	Social Studies (pl.) ['səʊʃl ˌstʌdiz]	Gesellschaftslehre	the study of people and societies
	comparable [kəm'pærəbl]	vergleichbar	↔ different ↔ unlike

Vocabulary | Unit vocabulary

active [ˈæktɪv]	aktiv	involved in different activities
leadership [ˈliːdəʃɪp]	Führung; Leitung	→ to lead, leader
working knowledge [ˌwɜːkɪŋ ˈnɒlɪdʒ]	praktische Kenntnisse	When you have a working knowledge of a language you can speak and understand it quite well.
computer skills *(pl.)* [kəmˈpjuːtə ˌskɪlz]	PC-Kenntnisse	ability to use computer software effectively
driver's licence [ˈdraɪvəz ˌlaɪsns]	Führerschein	official document showing that you have passed your driving test, and are allowed to drive
with regard to [wɪð rɪˈɡɑːd tə]	in Bezug auf	considering
qualification [ˌkwɒlɪfɪˈkeɪʃn]	Qualifikation; Abschluss	→ to qualify
D1 **computer technician** [kəmˈpjuːtə tekˌnɪʃn]	Computerfachmann/frau	s.o. who knows a lot about computers and can repair them
bank clerk [ˈbæŋk ˌklɑːk]	Bankkaufmann/frau	person employed by a bank who deals with customers at the counter
electrician [ˌelɪkˈtrɪʃn]	Elektriker/in	→ electricity → electrical
to suit [suːt]	passen; sich eignen	→ suitable
candidate [ˈkændɪdət]	Bewerber/in; Kandidat/in	s.o. being considered for a position in a company
academic year [ˌækədemɪk ˈjɪə]	Schuljahr	= school year
medical [ˈmedɪkl]	medizinisch; gesundheitlich	→ medicine
physiotherapist [ˌfɪziəˈθerəpɪst]	Physiotherapeut/in; Krankengymnast/in	s.o. who helps a patient with massage or special exercises
first hand [ˌfɜːst ˈhænd]	aus erster Hand	= directly
permanent [ˈpɜːmənənt]	fest	↔ temporary
English [ˈɪŋɡlɪʃ]	Engländer/in	= Englishman, Englishwoman, the English
to support [səˈpɔːt]	helfen; unterstützen	= to help
to mind s.th. [maɪnd]	etw. dagegen haben	= to care about s.th.
as long as [əz ˈlɒŋ əz]	solange	= provided that
doctor's surgery [ˌdɒktəz ˈsɜːdʒri]	Arztpraxis	the place where a doctor works
to depend on [dɪˈpend ɒn]	abhängen von	to be based on
as for [ˈæz fə]	bezüglich; was … betrifft	= concerning
to matter [ˈmætə]	von Bedeutung sein; wichtig sein	= to be important
final examination [ˌfaɪnl ɪɡˌzæmɪˈneɪʃn]	Abschlussprüfung	the last major exam of a course
A levels *(pl.)* [ˈeɪˌlevlz]	Abitur	an advanced test in a school subject in the UK, usually at age 18
Chemistry [ˈkemɪstri]	Chemie	→ chemist → chemical
to suffer from [ˈsʌfə]	leiden an	= to experience pain or discomfort
injury [ˈɪndʒri]	Verletzung	→ to injure
to bother [ˈbɒðə]	beunruhigen; stören	to cause worry
physical [ˈfɪzɪkl]	körperlich	A farmer must do a lot of physical work on his farm.
to divorce [dɪˈvɔːs]	sich scheiden lassen	↔ to marry
to fill s.o. in on s.th. [fɪl ˈɪn ɒn]	jmdn. ins Bild setzen	= to explain s.th. to s.o.
laboratory technician [ləˈbɒrətri tekˌnɪʃn]	Labortechniker/in	s.o. who works in a laboratory
to be prepared to do s.th. [bi prɪˈpeəd]	bereit sein, etw. zu tun	↔ to be unwilling to do s.th.
preference [ˈprefrns]	Vorliebe	→ to prefer
bit [bɪt]	etwas; bisschen	↔ a lot

	working week [ˌwɜːkɪŋ ˈwiːk]	Arbeitswoche	the five days that people normally go to work in a week, e.g. Monday to Friday
	shift [ʃɪft]	Schicht; Veränderung	Deborah was very tired after doing a night shift.
D2	**word web** [ˈwɜːd ˌweb]	Wortnetz	a diagram used for brainstorming and linking ideas to a topic
D3	**custom** [ˈkʌstəm]	Brauch; Gewohnheit	It's a custom to wear funny costumes at Halloween.
	uncomfortable [ʌnˈkʌmftəbl]	unwohl	↔ comfortable
	to **take a seat** [ˌteɪk ə ˈsiːt]	sich setzen; Platz nehmen	= to sit down
	self-confidence [ˌselfˈkɒnfɪdns]	Selbstvertrauen	↔ insecurity
	vacancy [ˈveɪknsi]	offene Stelle	→ vacant
	exhausting [ɪɡˈzɔːstɪŋ]	erschöpfend	→ to exhaust
	working conditions (pl.) [ˌwɜːkɪŋ kənˈdɪʃnz]	Arbeitsbedingungen	things which relate to where you work e.g. wages, hours, atmosphere
	precise [prɪˈsaɪs]	präzise	= exact
	around the clock [əˌraʊnd ðə ˈklɒk]	rund um die Uhr	= 24 hours per day
	faux pas [ˌfəʊ ˈpɑː]	Formfehler	s.th. which is not accepted by others
	to **embarrass** [ɪmˈbærəs]	in Verlegenheit bringen	to make s.o. feel unfomfortable
	to **bow** [baʊ]	beugen; sich beugen	to bend the head or body
	calm [kɑːm]	ruhig	= still
	providing [prəˈvaɪdɪŋ]	vorausgesetzt; sofern	if s.th. happens
E1	**time of your life** [ˌtaɪm əv jɔː ˈlaɪf]	einmaliges Erlebnis	a very enjoyable experience
	exotic [ɪɡˈzɒtɪk]	exotisch	unusual, perhaps from a far-away country
	relaxation [ˌriːlækˈseɪʃn]	Erholung	→ to relax
	situated [ˈsɪtʃueɪtɪd]	gelegen	= located
	resort [rɪˈzɔːt]	Ferienort	a place where people spend their holidays
	crystal [ˈkrɪstl]	Kristall	a special type of clear glass
	climate [ˈklaɪmət]	Klima	temperature and weather, related to the Earth's environment
	all year round [ˌɔːl jɪə ˈraʊnd]	ganzjährig	= the whole year
	leisure activity [ˈleʒər ækˌtɪvəti]	Freizeitbeschäftigung	↔ work ↔ duty
	to **comprise** [kəmˈpraɪz]	umfassen	= to consist of
	extensive [ɪkˈstensɪv]	großflächig; umfangreich	→ to extend
	spa centre [ˈspɑː ˌsentə]	Wellnessbereich	wellness facilities in a hotel
	outgoing [ˌaʊtˈɡəʊɪŋ]	aufgeschlossen	↔ shy
	maintenance [ˈmeɪntnəns]	Wartung	→ to maintain
	instructor [ɪnˈstrʌktə]	Lehrer/in	→ to instruct → instruction
	season [ˈsiːzn]	Jahreszeit; Saison	= time of year
	personnel manager [ˌpɜːsnˈel ˌmænɪdʒə]	Personalchef/in	A good personnel manager helps his/her company to find the right people for the right jobs.
	head office [ˌhed ˈɒfɪs]	Firmenzentrale; Hauptgeschäftsstelle; Hauptbüro; Hauptsitz	the most important office of a company
E2	**sharp** [ˈʃɑːp]	stark; scharf	= abrupt
	steady [ˈstedi]	stetig; stabil	= constant
F	**non-food** [ˌnɒnˈfuːd]	Nichtlebensmittel	a product that you cannot eat
	outlet [ˈaʊtlet]	Outlet; Verkaufsstelle; Kanal	a store where you can buy a product
	strength [streŋθ]	Stärke	↔ weakness
	to **summarize** [ˈsʌmraɪz]	zusammenfassen	→ summary

Vocabulary | Unit vocabulary

	Japanese [ˌdʒæpnˈiːz]	japanisch; Japaner/in	→ Japan
	to **shake hands** [ʃeɪk ˈhændz]	sich die Hand geben	a formal greeting where two people join hands
	tip [tɪp]	Rat; Tipp	= hint = advice
	handshake [ˈhænʃeɪk]	Handschlag	Greet your customer with a firm handshake.
	eye-contact [ˈaɪ ˌkɒntækt]	Blickkontakt	when two people look into each other's eyes
	to **pay attention to** [ˌpeɪ əˈtenʃn tə]	beachten	↔ to ignore ↔ to disregard
	UK [juːˈkeɪ]	Vereinigtes Königreich	United Kingdom
	rate [reɪt]	Quote	= amount = quantity

Unit A Cross-cultural communication at work: Preparing for a work placement in London

A		**tunnel** [ˈtʌnl]	Tunnel	The Channel Tunnel links the UK to France.
		flag [flæg]	Flagge	The national flag of the UK is called the Union Jack.
		composition [ˌkɒmpəˈzɪʃn]	Zusammensetzung; Struktur; Aufsatz	The composition of the atmosphere supports life on Earth.
		anthem [ˈænθəm]	Hymne	The national anthem was played during the medal ceremony at the Olympic Games.
		constitution [ˌkɒnstɪˈtjuːʃn]	Verfassung; Grundgesetz	laws and principles according to which a state is governed
B		to **appreciate s.th.** [əˈpriːʃieɪt]	etw. schätzen; etw. wertschätzen	to be thankful for s.th.
		acceptance [əkˈseptəns]	Annahme; Zusage	He wants to study in Leeds. Yesterday he got his letter of acceptance.
		to **be required to do s.th.** [bi rɪˈkwaɪəd tə]	verpflichtet sein, etw. zu tun; erforderlich sein, etw. zu tun	She is required to show her ticket at the gate.
		to **accommodate** [əˈkɒmədeɪt]	Unterkunft bieten	→ accommodation
		B&B [ˌbiːənˈbiː]	Frühstückspension	Bed & Breakfast
		boarding house [ˈbɔːdɪŋ ˌhaʊs]	Pension	a house providing meals and accommodation
		to **confirm** [kənˈfɜːm]	bestätigen	→ confirmation
		to **charge** [tʃɑːdʒ]	berechnen; verlangen	→ charge
		as regards [əz rɪˈɡɑːdz]	was ... betrifft	I have little information as regards her past.
		reference [ˈrefrns]	Empfehlung; Bezug	→ to refer
		stay [steɪ]	Aufenthalt	→ to stay
		polite [pəˈlaɪt]	höflich	↔ impolite
C		to **wonder** [ˈwʌndə]	sich fragen	He wondered if he should go to the party or not.
		including [ɪnˈkluːdɪŋ]	einschließlich; inklusive	The price is € 150 including postage and packaging.
		booking [ˈbʊkɪŋ]	Buchung; Reservierung	reservation
		definite [ˈdefɪnət]	endgültig; eindeutig	↔ indefinite
		on duty [ˌɒn ˈdjuːti]	im Dienst	↔ off duty
		washing machine [ˈwɒʃɪŋ məˌʃiːn]	Waschmaschine	There's a washing machine for dirty T-shirts.
		laundry [ˈlɔːndri]	Wäsche	Look at this pile of dirty laundry!
		informal [ɪnˈfɔːml]	informell; locker; umgangssprachlich	↔ formal
D		**innovation** [ˌɪnəˈveɪʃn]	Innovation; Neuerung	→ innovative
		touristy [ˈtʊərɪsti]	touristisch	→ tourism → tourist
		mod-60s [ˌmɒdˈsɪkstiz]	Subkultur der 60er Jahre	subculture in the UK during the 1960s
		transcendent [trænˈsendənt]	transzendent; überragend	→ transcendence

	mellow [ˈmeləʊ]	locker; heiter	I had a glass of wine and was feeling mellow.
	incapable [ɪnˈkeɪpəbl]	unfähig	↔ capable
	to **figure out** [ˌfɪgərˈaʊt]	kapieren; herausfinden	I can't figure out why she left me.
	cabby [ˈkæbi]	Taxifahrer/in	taxi-driver
	appropriate [əˈprəʊpriət]	geeignet; passend	= suitable
	constant [ˈkɒnstənt]	ständig; andauernd; konstant	= always
	flip side [ˈflɪpsaɪd]	Kehrseite	You should take a look at the flip side of every decision.
	to **shuffle** [ˈʃʌfl]	schlurfen	Walk properly, don't shuffle!
	pavement (BE) [ˈpeɪvmənt]	Bürgersteig	sidewalk (AE)
	rhythm [ˈrɪðm]	Rhythmus	→ rhythmic
	extraordinary [ɪkˈstrɔːdnri]	außergewöhnlich	↔ ordinary
	monument [ˈmɒnjəmənt]	Denkmal	There are many famous monuments in London.
	militaristic [ˌmɪlɪtəˈrɪstɪk]	militaristisch	→ military
	imperial [ɪmˈpɪəriəl]	majestätisch; Reichs-	The imperial palace is extravagant.
	echo [ˈekəʊ]	Echo	You hear a good echo in this cave.
	inappropriate [ˌɪnəˈprəʊpriət]	unangemessen	= inadequate
	anachronistic [əˌnækrəˈnɪstɪk]	anachronistisch; veraltet	→ anachronism
	to **tear down** [ˌteə ˈdaʊn]	einreißen	= to demolish s.th.
	grand [grænd]	prächtig	= magnificent
	benevolence [bɪˈnevləns]	Güte; Mildtätigkeit	kindness and generosity
	kindness [ˈkaɪndnəs]	Freundlichkeit	→ kind
	architecture [ˈɑːkɪtektʃə]	Architektur	→ architect
	empire [ˈempaɪə]	Reich; Imperium	a group of countries under a single ruling power
E	**junction** [ˈdʒʌŋkʃn]	Kreuzung	a place where roads or railway lines meet
	roundabout [ˈraʊndəˌbaʊt]	Kreisverkehr; Karussell	a junction where the traffic goes around a central island
	clockwise [ˈklɒkwaɪz]	im Uhrzeigersinn	↔ anti-clockwise
	headlights (pl.) [ˈhedlaɪts]	Autoscheinwerfer	Turn on your headlights after dusk.
	to **blind** [blaɪnd]	blenden	She was blinded by the sun.
	oncoming [ˈɒnˌkʌmɪŋ]	entgegenkommend; nahend	Be aware of oncoming traffic when you cross the street.
	motorway [ˈməʊtəweɪ]	Autobahn	In some countries you pay to use the motorways.
	carriageway [ˈkærɪdʒweɪ]	Fahrbahn	There is a traffic jam on the southbound carriageway of the motorway.
	built-up area [ˌbɪltʌpˈeəriə]	geschlossene Ortschaft	Mind the speed limit in built-up areas.
	function [ˈfʌŋkʃn]	Funktion	→ to function
	gear [gɪə]	Gang	She has a bicycle with ten gears.
	steering wheel [ˈstɪərɪŋ ˌwiːl]	Lenkrad	Turn the steering wheel to the right.
	Roman [ˈrəʊmən]	römisch; Römer/in	The Roman Empire stretched from the British Isles to Egypt and Iraq.
	sword [sɔːd]	Schwert	In the Middle Ages soldiers fought with swords.
	the British [ðə ˈbrɪtɪʃ]	die Briten	→ Britain
	the French [ðə ˈfrenʃ]	die Franzosen	→ France

Vocabulary | Unit vocabulary

Unit 3 The youth market

	role [rəʊl]	Rolle	→ role-play
	responsible [rɪˈspɒnsəbl]	verantwortungsbewusst; verantwortlich	→ responsibility
A	equipment (sg.) [ɪˈkwɪpmənt]	Geräte; Ausrüstung; Ausstattung	The equipment they have is very old.
	service [ˈsɜːvɪs]	Dienstleistung; Service	→ to service
	item [ˈaɪtəm]	Punkt; Artikel; Stück	They discussed the most important items.
	cosmetics (pl.) [kɒzˈmetɪks]	Kosmetik	products you put on your body, especially the face, to make it more beautiful
	trainers [ˈtreɪnəz]	Turnschuhe	→ to train
	notebook [ˈnəʊtbʊk]	Notebook; Notizbuch	→ to note
	gym [dʒɪm]	Turnhalle; Fitness-Center	I go to the gym twice a week.
	social media [ˌsəʊʃl ˈmiːdiə]	soziale Netzwerk/e	She spends 3 hours every day on social media.
	smart [smɑːt]	ordentlich; gepflegt; schick	↔ untidy, messy
	common [ˈkɒmən]	gemeinsam; verbreitet	↔ uncommon
	chance [tʃɑːns]	Möglichkeit; Gelegenheit; Chance	Is there a chance to talk to her?
	Asia [ˈeɪʒə]	Asien	Asia is the biggest continent in the world.
	aware [əˈweə]	bewusst	→ awareness
	issue [ˈɪʃuː]	Problem; Frage	The city has issues with drugs.
	principle [ˈprɪnsəpl]	Grundsatz; Prinzip	You must be true to your own principles.
	to associate with [əˈsəʊʃieɪt wɪð]	in Verbindung bringen mit	Many people associate flowers with spring.
	figure [ˈfɪɡə]	Zahlen	The accountant presents the latest sales figures.
	to act [ækt]	handeln; fungieren als	→ action
	belief [bɪˈliːf]	Überzeugung; Glaube	→ to believe
	critic [ˈkrɪtɪk]	Kritiker/in	→ to criticize
	attractive [əˈtræktɪv]	attraktiv	↔ unattractive
	to perform [pəˈfɔːm]	funktionieren	The tyres perform well on uneven terrain.
	moreover [mɔːˈrəʊvə]	überdies; außerdem	He knows this car is too expensive. Moreover, he doesn't have any money in his account.
	to discourage [dɪˈskʌrɪdʒ]	entmutigen	↔ to encourage
	label [ˈleɪbl]	Label; Marke	= brand
	confused [kənˈfjuːzd]	verwirrt	I don't understand. I'm confused.
	potential [pəˈtenʃl]	potenziell; eventuell	= possible, likely
	individual [ˌɪndɪˈvɪdʒuəl]	einzelne/r	A team is only as strong as each individual player.
	claim [kleɪm]	Behauptung	→ to claim
	to cheat [tʃiːt]	betrügen	He cheated in the exam.
	humane [hjuːˈmeɪn]	menschenwürdig	→ humanity
	to adapt [əˈdæpt]	anpassen	→ adaptation
	accordingly [əˈkɔːdɪŋli]	folglich; demgemäß	→ in accordance with
	to realize [ˈrɪəlaɪz]	erkennen	→ realization
	value [ˈvæljuː]	Wert	→ valuable
	stress [stres]	Betonung; Stress	→ to stress
	to lay [leɪ]	legen	I laid down the heavy bag for a minute.
	responsibility [rɪˌspɒnsəˈbɪləti]	Verantwortung	→ responsible
B1	above [əˈbʌv]	oben; obenstehend	↔ below
	to exchange [ɪksˈtʃeɪndʒ]	umtauschen; austauschen	When you travel to the UK you must exchange euros for pounds.

	haircut [ˈheəkʌt]	Haarschnitt	I like your new haircut. It's very modern.
B5	twice [twaɪs]	zweimal	Listen. I won't tell you twice.
C1	loan [ləʊn]	Darlehen; Kredit	amount of money given for a period of time
	personal details (pl.) [ˌpɜ:snl ˈdi:teɪlz]	Personendaten	your name, address, birthday etc.
	consequence [ˈkɒnsɪkwəns]	Folge; Konsequenz	the result of s.th.
	mentality [menˈtæləti]	Mentalität; Einstellung	way of thinking
	debt [det]	Schuld; Schulden	→ debtor
	adult [ˈædʌlt]	Erwachsene/r	= grown-up
	at hand [ət ˈhænd]	zur Verfügung; bei der Hand	easy to reach, close-by
	to tend to [tend]	neigen zu; tendieren zu	→ tendency
	understanding [ˌʌndəˈstændɪŋ]	Verständnis	→ understandable → to understand
	to avoid [əˈvɔɪd]	vermeiden	You can avoid the motorway and take the smaller roads.
	institution [ˌɪnstɪˈtju:ʃn]	Institution; Einrichtung	→ institutional
	account [əˈkaʊnt]	Konto	= bank account
	to remark [rɪˈmɑ:k]	anmerken	→ remark
	finances (pl.) [ˈfaɪnænsɪz]	Finanzen	I need help to manage my finances.
	major [ˈmeɪdʒə]	groß; wichtig; Haupt-	↔ minor
	purchase [ˈpɜ:tʃɪs]	Kauf	→ to purchase
	lifestyle [ˈlaɪfstaɪl]	Lebensweise	Their lifestyle is extravagant. They spend a lot of money on luxury goods.
	to struggle [ˈstrʌgl]	abmühen; kämpfen	→ struggle
	to cope with [ˈkəʊp wɪð]	schaffen; zurechtkommen	to be able to deal with s.th. difficult
	school-leaver [ˌsku:l ˈli:və]	Schulabgänger/in	→ school-leaving examination
	advisable [ədˈvaɪzəbl]	ratsam; empfehlenswert	→ advice
	bargain [ˈbɑ:gɪn]	Schnäppchen; guter Kauf	→ to bargain
	charts (pl.) [tʃɑ:ts]	Hitliste	The song has been at the top of the charts for 10 weeks.
	heading [ˈhedɪŋ]	Überschrift	→ to head
	actually [ˈæktʃəli]	eigentlich; tatsächlich	This is actually a very good idea.
	relationship [rɪˈleɪʃnʃɪp]	Beziehung	She has a very good relationship with her parents.
C2	to persuade [pəˈsweɪd]	überzeugen; überreden	→ persuasive
	feedback [ˈfi:dbæk]	Rückmeldungen; Feedback	Positive feedback supports the learning process.
	flexible [ˈfleksɪbl]	flexibel	↔ inflexible
	to react [riˈækt]	reagieren	Nobody reacted to the alarm bell.
	salesperson [ˈseɪlzˌpɜ:sn]	Verkäufer/in	s.o. who sells goods and services
D1	client [ˈklaɪənt]	Kunde; Kundin	People who buy your products are your clients.
	research [rɪˈsɜ:tʃ]	Forschung	→ researcher → to research
	promotion [prəˈməʊʃn]	Förderung; Beförderung; Werbung	→ to promote
	to handle [ˈhændl]	bearbeiten; erledigen; mit etw. umgehen	to deal with
	to hire [haɪə]	beauftragen; anstellen	The hired team did an excellent job.
	interactive [ˌɪntəˈæktɪv]	interaktiv	It's an interactive form. You can fill it in online.
	appointment [əˈpɔɪntmənt]	Termin; Verabredung	arrangement to meet s.o. at a particular time and place

Vocabulary | Unit vocabulary

	creative director [kriˌeɪtɪv dɪˈrektə]	Kreativchef/in	The creative director is responsible for the artistic work.
	account manager [əˈkaʊnt ˌmænɪdʒə]	Kundenbetreuer/in	s.o. in an advertising agency who takes care of clients
	to **specialize** [ˈspeʃlaɪz]	spezialisieren	→ specialist
	to **operate** [ˈɒpreɪt]	tätig sein	The company doesn't operate overseas.
	Chief Marketing Officer [ˌtʃiːf ˈmɑːkɪtɪŋ ˌɒfɪsə]	Marketingchef/in	The Chief Marketing Officer is responsible for the advertising and marketing department of a company.
	to **configure** [kənˈfɪgə]	konfigurieren; gestalten	→ configuration
	to **restrict** [rɪˈstrɪkt]	einschränken; beschränken	→ restriction
	to **control** [kənˈtrəʊl]	kontrollieren	→ control
	obvious [ˈɒbviəs]	offensichtlich	It is obvious that you studied hard. You got an A.
	professional [prəˈfeʃnl]	professionell; berufsmäßig; Profi	↔ unprofessional
	to **do a good job** [ˌduː ə gʊd ˈdʒɒb]	etw. gut machen	The cupboard fits perfectly. You did a good job.
	hands-on [ˌhændzˈɒn]	praktisch; praxisnah	He's a hands-on kind of person. He likes to do things himself.
	demonstration [ˌdemənˈstreɪʃn]	Vorführung	→ to demonstrate
	various [ˈveəriəs]	verschieden; unterschiedlich	→ variety
	unique [juːˈniːk]	einzigartig	This is the last of its kind. It's unique.
	on the spot [ˌɒn ðə ˈspɒt]	sofort; auf der Stelle	= immediately
	to **awaken** [əˈweɪkn]	wecken	→ awake
	up-market [ˌʌpˈmɑːkɪt]	gehoben; hochpreisig	Rich people like to buy up-market products.
	introductory offer [ˌɪntrədʌktri ˈɒfə]	Einführungsangebot	We have just brought a new product onto the market at a lower price as an introductory offer.
	to **be likely** [bi ˈlaɪkli]	wahrscheinlich sein; wahrscheinlich geschehen	It's likely to snow in December.
	to **highlight** [ˈhaɪlaɪt]	hervorheben	Clients should know about this feature. We must highlight it.
	to **get in touch** [ˌget ɪn ˈtʌtʃ]	in Kontakt treten	We'll get in touch as soon as a decision has been made.
	brief [briːf]	Kurzinformation	= briefing
	to **estimate** [ˈestɪmeɪt]	schätzen	Can you estimate how long it will take?
	quotation [kwəˈteɪʃn]	Kostenvoranschlag; Angebot; Zitat	→ to quote
	mobile phone [ˌməʊbaɪl ˈfəʊn]	Handy; Mobiltelefon	= cell phone (AE)
D2	**formula** [ˈfɔːmjələ]	Formel	Use this mathematical formula to get the correct result.
	target [ˈtɑːgɪt]	Ziel	→ to target
	based on [ˈbeɪst ˌɒn]	basierend auf; anhand von	The film is based on a true story.
D3	to **influence** [ˈɪnfluəns]	beeinflussen	→ influential → influence
	to **recognize** [ˈrekəgnaɪz]	erkennen; anerkennen	→ recognizable
	packaging [ˈpækɪdʒɪŋ]	Verpackung	→ to package
	bean [biːn]	Bohne	In Britain you often get baked beans for breakfast.
	tastebud [ˈteɪstbʌd]	Geschmacksknospe	→ tasteful
	mug [mʌg]	umgangssprachlich für Idiot; Trottel	= fool
	to **manipulate** [məˈnɪpjəleɪt]	manipulieren; beeinflussen	→ manipulation
	susceptible [səˈseptəbl]	empfänglich	↔ immune against

	messaging [ˈmesɪdʒɪŋ]	Nachrichtenübermittlung	→ message
	to **affect** [əˈfekt]	beeinflussen; betreffen	= to influence
	stuff [stʌf]	Zeug	= things
	to **transfer** [trænsˈfɜː]	übertragen	→ transferable
	physiology [ˌfɪziˈɒlədʒi]	Physiologie	→ physiological
	to **swallow** [ˈswɒləʊ]	schlucken	A tough truth is hard to swallow.
	to **settle** [ˈsetl]	klarstellen; sich niederlassen	to put s.th. straight
	identical [aɪˈdentɪkl]	identisch	They have the same haircut. To me they look identical.
	flask [flɑːsk]	Thermoskanne; Behälter	You can keep food hot in a flask.
	rascal [ˈræskl]	Bengel; Schelm	= rogue
	to **shake** [ʃeɪk]	schütteln	When you meet s.o., you often shake hands.
	degree [dɪˈgriː]	Grad; Ausmaß; akademischer Grad	The boiling point of water is 100 degrees Celsius.
	salty [ˈsɔːlti]	salzig	I don't like the soup. It's too salty.
	mushy [ˈmʌʃi]	breiig	→ mush
	thread [θred]	Gewinde; Faden	→ to thread s.th.
	definite [ˈdefɪnət]	auf jeden Fall; eindeutig	I'll definitely get back to you tomorrow.
	flavour [ˈfleɪvə]	Geschmack	→ flavoured
	slight [slaɪt]	geringfügig; leicht	= insignificant
	bland [blænd]	fade; farblos	when s.th. does not have a strong taste
	huge [hjuːdʒ]	riesig	↔ tiny
E	**trend** [trend]	Tendenz; Trend	→ trendy
	topic [ˈtɒpɪk]	Thema	= subject
	representative [ˌreprɪˈzentətɪv]	Vertreter/in	→ to represent
	pros and cons [ˌprəʊz ən ˈkɒnz]	Pro und Kontra; Für und Wider	arguments for and against s.th.
	audience [ˈɔːdiəns]	Publikum; Zuhörer	The audience laughed.
	to **download** [ˌdaʊnˈləʊd]	herunterladen	You can download it from the Internet.
	appliance [əˈplaɪəns]	Gerät	a machine you use in the home, especially in the kitchen
	gadget [ˈgædʒɪt]	technisches Gerät	a small mechanical or electronic device
	broadband [ˈbrɔːdbænd]	Breitband	You need a good broadband connection to use the Internet efficiently.
	bureau [ˈbjʊərəʊ]	Büro; Abteilung	= office
	to **double** [ˈdʌbl]	verdoppeln	to make two times as many as before
	user [ˈjuːzə]	Nutzer/in	→ useful
	to **search for s.th.** [ˈsɜːtʃ fə]	nach etw. suchen	→ search
	specific [spəˈsɪfɪk]	bestimmt; spezifisch	= particular
	content [ˈkɒntent]	Inhalt	This website's content has been reviewed by experts.
	via [vaɪə]	über; durch	They reached Germany via Austria.
	to **involve** [ɪnˈvɒlv]	einbeziehen	→ involvement
	feed [fiːd]	Feed; Einspeisung	→ to feed
	to **subscribe** [səbˈskraɪb]	abonnieren	→ subscriber
	provider [prəˈvaɪdə]	Versorger; Anbieter; Provider	→ provision
	to **link** [lɪŋk]	verbinden; koppeln	= to connect
	to **cancel** [ˈkænsl]	absagen; stornieren	→ cancellation
	effective [ɪˈfektɪv]	effektiv; wirksam	↔ ineffective
	to **rely on** [rɪˈlaɪ ɒn]	verlassen auf	→ reliable
	consumption [kənˈsʌmpʃn]	Konsum	→ consumer
	rapid [ˈræpɪd]	schnell; rapide	= quick

Vocabulary | Unit vocabulary

	multi-tasking [ˌmʌltiˈtɑːskɪŋ]	Multitasking	doing more than one thing at the same time
	to **be related to** [bi rɪˈleɪtɪd tə]	betreffen; zu tun haben mit; verwandt sein mit	Climate change is related to human mass consumption.
	survey [ˈsɜːveɪ]	Umfrage	They had a questionnaire for the survey.
	viewer [ˈvjuːə]	Zuschauer/in	Millions of viewers watched Oprah's shows.
	to **switch** [swɪtʃ]	wechseln	We switched providers in order to save money.
	to **admit** [ədˈmɪt]	zugeben	I admit that I made a mistake.
	to **surf** [sɜːf]	surfen	I was surfing the Internet.
	to **point out** [ˌpɔɪntˈaʊt]	hinweisen auf; darlegen	to draw attention to
	significant [sɪɡˈnɪfɪkənt]	bedeutend; deutlich	→ significance
	response [rɪˈspɒns]	Reaktion	→ to respond
	campaign [kæmˈpeɪn]	Kampagne	→ to campaign
	particular [pəˈtɪkjələ]	besonderer/e/es; bestimmt	= special
F	to **treat** [triːt]	behandeln	She treats her employees well.
	ideal [aɪˈdɪəl]	Ideal	→ idealist
	organic [ɔːˈɡænɪk]	biologisch; Bio-	Tom prefers organic food to conventional food.
	cotton [ˈkɒtn]	Baumwolle	The cotton T-shirt is cool when it's hot outside.
	to **spot** [spɒt]	erkennen; wahrnehmen	I spotted her on the train this morning.

Unit 4 Media in our lives

	risk [rɪsk]	Risiko	→ risky
	cartoon [kɑːˈtuːn]	Karikatur	The cartoon is very funny.
A1	**usage** [ˈjuːsɪdʒ]	Gebrauch	→ useful
	percentage [pəˈsentɪdʒ]	Anteil; Prozentsatz	→ percent
	respondent [rɪˈspɒndənt]	befragte Person	→ to respond
	landscape [ˈlænskeɪp]	Landschaft	The calendar displays landscapes from around the world.
	vulnerable [ˈvʌlnrbl]	gefährdet; verletzlich	Marine ecosystems are at risk and so are very vulnerable.
A2	to **refer to s.th.** [rɪˈfɜː tə]	sich beziehen auf etw.	→ reference
	regulator [ˈreɡjəleɪtə]	Regulierungsbehörde; Regulierer	→ to regulate
	habit [ˈhæbɪt]	Gewohnheit	People have good habits and bad habits.
	platform [ˈplætfɔːm]	Plattform	The train to London will stop at platform 7.
	in droves [ɪn ˈdrəʊvz]	in Scharen	in large numbers
	in favour of [ɪn ˈfeɪvərˌəv]	zugunsten	The judge decided in favour of the thief.
	pursuit [pəˈsjuːt]	hier: Beschäftigung; Streben	→ to pursue
	to **publish** [ˈpʌblɪʃ]	publizieren; veröffentlichen	→ publisher
	decline [dɪˈklaɪn]	Rückgang	↔ rise
	precipitous [prɪˈsɪpɪtəs]	sehr steil	very steep
	decade [ˈdekeɪd]	Jahrzehnt	I've known him for decades.
	structural [ˈstrʌktʃrl]	strukturell	→ structure
	era [ˈɪərə]	Ära	This decision marks the start of a new era.
	sense [sens]	Sinn	Your explanation does not make sense.
	radical [ˈrædɪkl]	radikal	He comes up with radical ideas.
	on demand [ɒn dɪˈmɑːnd]	auf Verlangen	The goods are available. We deliver on demand.

	native [ˈneɪtɪv]	Einheimische/r; Inländer/in	He speaks the language. He's a native.
	to **suggest** [səˈdʒest]	hinweisen auf; vorschlagen	→ suggestion
	to **age** [eɪdʒ]	älter werden	She has aged a lot since I last saw her.
	to **identify** [aɪˈdentɪfaɪ]	identifizieren; erkennen	→ identification
B1	**probable** [ˈprɒbəbl]	wahrscheinlich	→ probability
	up-to-date [ˌʌptəˈdeɪt]	aktuell; auf dem neuesten Stand	They follow every trend. They're always up to date.
B2	to **chat** [tʃæt]	plaudern; chatten	Let's chat over coffee.
	browser [ˈbraʊzə]	Browser	→ to browse
	to **click** [klɪk]	klicken	Click here for more information.
	to **switch off** [ˌswɪtʃˈɒf]	ausschalten	Switch off the light please. I want to sleep.
B3	**telecommunications** *(pl.)* [ˌtelɪkəˌmjuːnɪˈkeɪʃnz]	Telekommunikations-	Companies depend on good telecommunications to do business effectively.
	managing director [ˌmænɪdʒɪŋ dɪˈrektə]	Geschäftsführer/in	The managing director is in charge of the business operations of a company.
	to **go ahead** [ˌgəʊ əˈhed]	weiterverfolgen; vorangehen	You can start reading now. Go ahead, please!
	secure [sɪˈkjʊə]	sicher	→ security
	to **expect** [ɪkˈspekt]	erwarten	→ expectation
	computing [kəmˈpjuːtɪŋ]	EDV	Bill has taken a course in computing.
	tablet [ˈtæblət]	Tablet; Schreibtafel	Debbie mainly uses her tablet to play games.
B4	**button** [ˈbʌtn]	Knopf	There was a button missing from his shirt.
	wireless [ˈwaɪələs]	drahtlos	I prefer wireless devices to all those cables.
	to **steal** [stiːl]	stehlen	Some people try to steal money on the Internet.
	recyclable [ˌriːˈsaɪkləbl]	wiederverwertbar	→ recycling
	harmful [ˈhɑːmfəl]	schädlich	↔ harmless
	toxic [ˈtɒksɪk]	giftig	harmful, poisonous
	to **print** [prɪnt]	drucken; ausdrucken	→ printer
C	to **escape** [ɪˈskeɪp]	entgehen; entkommen	to get away
	to **skim** [skɪm]	überfliegen	Don't concentrate on details, just skim the text.
	net piracy [ˌnet ˈpaɪrəsi]	Netzpiraterie	→ net pirate
	prison [ˈprɪzn]	Gefängnis	Criminals go to prison.
	to **beware of** [bɪˈweər əv]	sich in Acht nehmen	Beware of the dog.
	fraud [frɔːd]	Betrug	method by which s.o. tricks people in order to get their money
	bet [bet]	Wette	→ to bet
	to **discover** [dɪˈskʌvə]	entdecken	Columbus discovered America.
	idea [aɪˈdɪə]	Gedanken; Idee	She is full of ideas.
	expert [ˈekspɜːt]	Experte/in	Scientists are experts in their field.
	programming [ˈprəʊgræmɪŋ]	Programmier-	She's a programming expert. She knows how to write code.
	onto [ˈɒntə]	auf	When did smartphones first come onto the market?
	worldwide [ˌwɜːldˈwaɪd]	auf der ganzen Welt; weltweit	The company has offices worldwide.
	crime [kraɪm]	Verbrechen	→ criminal
	criminal [ˈkrɪmɪnl]	kriminell; Kriminelle/r	His criminal energies helped him to escape.
	fantasy [ˈfæntəsi]	Fantasie; Einbildung	Fantasy novels have nothing to do with reality.
	fraudster [ˈfrɔːdstə]	Betrüger/in	→ fraud
	to **target** [ˈtɑːgɪt]	anpeilen; zielen auf	→ target

Vocabulary | Unit vocabulary

	holidaymaker [ˈhɒlədiˌmeɪkə]	Urlauber/in	= vacationer *(AE)*
	deposit [dɪˈpɒzɪt]	Anzahlung; Einzahlung	→ to deposit
	phishing [ˈfɪʃɪŋ]	Phishing	criminal attempt to get passwords, credit card details etc. of Internet users
	attack [əˈtæk]	Angriff	→ attacker
	credit card [ˈkredɪt ˌkɑːd]	Kreditkarte	You don't need cash. You can use your credit card.
	payment [ˈpeɪmənt]	Zahlung	When can we expect payment for the goods we sent you?
	data [ˈdeɪtə]	Daten	We researched it. The new data are up to date.
	auction [ˈɔːkʃn]	Auktion	→ auctioneer
	site [saɪt]	Website	Mark has designed a new homepage for his company's site.
	to **guarantee** [ˌgærnˈtiː]	garantieren	We can't guarantee you a job next month.
	safe [seɪf]	sicher	= secure
	reporter [rɪˈpɔːtə]	Reporter/in	→ to report
	to **investigate** [ɪnˈvestɪgeɪt]	nachgehen; untersuchen	→ investigation
	gang [gæŋ]	Bande; Gruppe	group of people who do (illegal) things together
	to **approach** [əˈprəʊtʃ]	nähern; annähern; ansprechen	Little children shouldn't approach strangers.
	chatroom [ˈtʃætruːm]	Chatroom	online forum where people meet to talk about specific topics
	identity [aɪˈdentəti]	Identität	Someone might try to steal your identity.
	sergeant [ˈsɑːdʒnt]	Sergeant	rank in uniformed organizations, e.g. army, police
	to **register** [ˈredʒɪstə]	registrieren	If you want to receive information from us please register here.
	anonymous [əˈnɒnɪməs]	anonym	→ anonymity
	conversation [ˌkɒnvəˈseɪʃn]	Gespräch; Unterhaltung	= talk
	unpleasant [ʌnˈpleznt]	unangenehm	↔ pleasant
	paedophile [ˈpiːdəfaɪl]	Pädophile/r	Many paedophiles try to contact young children on the Internet.
	victim [ˈvɪktɪm]	Opfer	They counted 23 victims after the attack.
	to **commit** [kəˈmɪt]	begehen	Fraudsters committed several crimes on the Internet.
	undercover [ˌʌndəˈkʌvə]	geheim	Sandra works as an undercover agent.
	investigation [ɪnˌvestɪˈgeɪʃn]	Untersuchung; Ermittlung	→ investigator
D1	to **check out** [ˌtʃek ˈaʊt]	überprüfen; ausprobieren; auschecken	Have you checked out the new restaurant on 5th Street?
	seeker [ˈsiːkə]	Suchende/r	She's an attention seeker.
	to **minimize** [ˈmɪnɪmaɪz]	minimieren	↔ to maximize
	to **reject** [rɪˈdʒekt]	ablehnen	→ rejection
	drug [drʌg]	Droge	It is dangerous to take drugs.
	to **find out** [ˌfaɪnd ˈaʊt]	herausfinden	He found out that she had lied to him.
	negative [ˈnegətɪv]	negativ	↔ positive
	to **be meant to be** [bi ˌment tə ˈbiː]	zu etw. bestimmt sein	He was meant to be a reporter.
	other than [ˈʌðə ðən]	mit Ausnahme von	Other than one brother he has no relatives.
	to **be obsessed with** [bi ˌəbˈsest wɪð]	besessen sein von	→ obsession
	to **refuse** [rɪˈfjuːz]	ablehnen; sich weigern	↔ to accept
	concerned [kənˈsɜːnd]	beunruhigt; betroffen	I'm concerned about climate change.

	addicted to [əˈdɪktɪd tə]	abhängig von	→ addiction
	overuse [ˌəʊvəˈjuːs]	übermäßiger Gebrauch	→ to overuse
	impression [ɪmˈpreʃn]	Eindruck	She has made a good impression.
	screen [ˌskriːn]	Bildschirm	You should limit your child's screen time.
	full-time [ˌfʊlˈtaɪm]	Ganztags-; Vollzeit-	↔ part-time
	plus [plʌs]	plus; sowie	Claire's monthly wage is €4,000 plus overtime.
	overtime [ˈəʊvətaɪm]	Überstunden	He's exhausted from working overtime.
	console [ˈkɒnsəʊl]	Konsole	You need a gaming console to play video games.
	to consume [kənˈsjuːm]	verbrauchen; konsumieren	→ consumer
	substitute [ˈsʌbstɪtjuːt]	Ersatz	→ to substitute
	to collapse [kəˈlæps]	kollabieren; zusammenbrechen	Pat collapsed after running 42 km.
	violence [vaɪəlns]	Gewalt	→ violent
	aspect [ˈæspekt]	Aspekt; Seite	They checked out every aspect of the situation but couldn't find a solution.
D2	**caption** [ˈkæpʃn]	Bildunterschrift	a short description of a photo which is usually given under it
	speech bubble [ˈspiːtʃ ˌbʌbl]	Sprechblase	You can find speech bubbles in a lot of cartoons.
	analysis [əˈnæləsɪs]	Analyse	→ to analyze
	office block [ˈɒfɪs ˌblɒk]	Bürogebäude	Sabrina works as a secretary in that huge office block over there.
D3	**none** [nʌn]	keine/r/s	None of her colleagues came to congratulate her.
	to arise [əˈraɪz]	entstehen	A problem has arisen at work.
	permission [pəˈmɪʃn]	Erlaubnis	→ to permit
	head teacher [ˌhed ˈtiːtʃə]	Schulleiter/in	She works as a head teacher in a school.
	police officer [pəˈliːsˌɒfɪsə]	Polizeibeamte/r	Police officers catch criminals.
	argument [ˈɑːgjəmənt]	Argument; Streit	Your arguments are not very clear.
	device [dɪˈvaɪs]	Gerät	You find electronic devices in every household.
	policy [ˈpɒləsi]	Strategie; Grundsatz; Politik	Phones off! That's our policy at meetings.
E1	**diagram** [ˈdaɪəgræm]	Grafik; Schaubild	The diagram shows the development of smartphones sales in the last five years.
	pace [peɪs]	Geschwindigkeit	The pace of life has increased.
	trillion [ˈtrɪljən]	Billion	the number 1,000,000,000,000
	to make sense of s.th. [ˌmeɪk ˈsens ˌəv]	Sinn hinter etw. sehen; etw. zusammenreimen	I can't make sense of his remark.
	predictable [prɪˈdɪktəbl]	vorhersehbar	→ prediction → to predict
	pattern [ˈpætən]	Muster	a regular and repeated way in which s.th. is done
	creature [ˈkriːtʃə]	Kreatur	→ to create
	funny [ˈfʌni]	eigentümlich; lustig	It's funny that she didn't tell me about the accident.
	in terms of [ɪn ˈtɜːmzˌəv]	hinsichtlich	In terms of sales the book was not successful.
	predictability [prɪˌdɪktəˈbɪləti]	Vorhersehbarkeit	→ to predict → prediction
	gender [ˈdʒendə]	Geschlecht	Your gender – male or female – is given in your passport.
	overwhelming [ˌəʊvəˈwelmɪŋ]	überwältigend	The overwhelming majority voted for Baker.
	male [meɪl]	männlich	↔ female

Vocabulary | Unit vocabulary

	sign-up [ˈsaɪnʌp]	Anmeldung	Get ready for the sign-up for the waiting list. It's at 9 am tomorrow.
	interaction [ˌɪntəˈækʃn]	Interaktion	→ to interact
	theory [ˈθɪəri]	Theorie	→ theoretical
	to **show off** [ˌʃəʊ ˈɒf]	angeben	He likes to show off in front of his friends.
	cop [kɒp]	umgangssprachlich für Polizist	Look out! The cops are coming!
	disaster [dɪˈzɑːstə]	Katastrophe	→ disastrous
	global [ˈgləʊbl]	weltumspannend; global	→ globe
	distinct [dɪˈstɪŋt]	ausgeprägt	different in a way that you can see, feel or hear
	primitive [ˈprɪmɪtɪv]	primitiv	very simple and basic
	human [ˈhjuːmən]	menschlich; Mensch	→ humanity
	mechanism [ˈmekənɪzm]	Mechanismus	→ mechanic
	audio [ˈɔːdiəʊ]	Audio	You can get an audio guide at the front desk.
	bandwidth [ˈbændwɪtθ]	Bandbreite	You need to have a good bandwidth for a satisfactory Internet connection.
	fibre [ˈfaɪbə]	Faser	→ fibre optic cable
	to **absorb** [əbˈzɔːb]	absorbieren; aufsaugen	→ absorption
	eyeglasses [ˈaɪˌglɑːsɪz]	Brille	= glasses
	literal [ˈlɪtrl]	buchstäblich	→ literature
	to **transmit** [trænzˈmɪt]	übertragen	→ transmitter
	to **broadcast** [ˈbrɔːdkɑːst]	senden; ausstrahlen	The radio station broadcasts daily from London.
	scary [ˈskeəri]	unheimlich; furchteinflößend	→ to scare
	prospect [ˈprɒspekt]	Aussicht	The prospects of getting a job in that town are good.
	peak [piːk]	Gipfel; Höchststand; Hoch-	→ to peak
E2	**on the move** [ˌɒn ðə ˈmuːv]	unterwegs	She's never at home. She's always on the move.
	desperate [ˈdesprət]	verzweifelt	→ desperation → to despair
	dull [dʌl]	langweilig	↔ exciting
	spontaneous [spɒnˈteɪniəs]	spontan	→ spontaneity
	surrounded by [səˈraʊndɪd baɪ]	umgeben von	→ surroundings
	armed [ɑːmd]	bewaffnet	↔ unarmed
	rather than [ˈrɑːðə ðən]	lieber als	I would rather play soccer than baseball.
	automatic [ˌɔːtəˈmætɪk]	automatisch	His reaction was automatic.
	spell check [ˈspel tʃek]	Rechtschreibprüfung	Use the spell check on your computer to correct your homework.
	instant [ˈɪnstənt]	sofortig	= prompt
	proper [ˈprɒpə]	richtig; ordentlich; echt	No fast food for me thanks. I need proper food!
	to **confess** [kənˈfes]	gestehen; beichten	→ confession
	nevertheless [ˌnevəðəˈles]	trotzdem; dennoch	= anyhow
	self-confident [ˌselfˈkɒnfɪdnt]	selbstbewusst	→ self-confidence
	optimistic [ˌɒptɪˈmɪstɪk]	optimistisch	→ optimism
	goal-oriented [ˌgəʊlˈɔːriəntɪd]	ergebnisorientiert	Ben is goal-oriented. He wants to get things done.
	talent [ˈtælənt]	Talent	→ talented
	to **concentrate on s.th.** [ˈkɒnsntreɪt ɒn]	sich auf etw. konzentrieren	→ concentration
	single [ˈsɪŋgl]	einzelne/r/s	Not a single word was said.
	period [ˈpɪəriəd]	Zeitraum	→ periodical

	graduate [ˈgrædʒuət]	Absolvent/in	→ to graduate
	to **be willing to do s.th.** [bi ˈwɪlɪŋ tə]	bereit sein, etw. zu tun	I'm more than willing to help you.
	retail [ˈriːteɪl]	Einzelhandel	selling goods in small quantities to consumers
	balance [ˈbæləns]	Balance	→ to balance
	to **decrease** [dɪˈkriːs]	abnehmen	↔ to increase
	continent [ˈkɒntɪnənt]	Kontinent	Asia is the biggest continent, Australia is the smallest.
	truly [ˈtruːli]	wirklich	= really
	citizen [ˈsɪtɪzn]	Bürger/in	Senior citizens often get discounts.
	requirement [rɪˈkwaɪəmənt]	Anforderung	→ to require
F	**chart** [tʃɑːt]	Tabelle; Diagramm	information in the form of a table or diagram
	to **decline** [dɪˈklaɪn]	zurückgehen; fallen	Last year our sales figures declined drastically.
	gradual [ˈgrædʒuəl]	allmählich; stufenweise	= step by step
	drastic [ˈdræstɪk]	drastisch	Zoe has survived some drastic events in her life.
	to **sum up** [ˌsʌm ˈʌp]	zusammenfassen	This sums up the situation perfectly.
	expectation [ˌekspekˈteɪʃn]	Erwartung	→ to expect
	anywhere [ˈeniweə]	überall	You can live anywhere you like.
	to **care about** [ˈkeər əˌbaʊt]	sich interessieren für	I don't care about money.
	challenge [ˈtʃælɪndʒ]	Herausforderung	→ to challenge

Unit 5 Social change

	to **anticipate** [ænˈtɪsɪpeɪt]	erwarten	→ anticipation
	to **scan** [skæn]	flüchtig überfliegen	Scan the text to get a general idea of what it is about.
	benefit [ˈbenɪfɪt]	Vorteil; Wohlfahrtsleistung	→ to benefit
	welfare [ˈwelfeə]	Sozialhilfe; Sozial-; Wohlergehen	Poor families often live on welfare.
A	**breadwinner** [ˈbredˌwɪnə]	Versorger/in; Ernährer/in	Traditionally men were the breadwinners in the family but now women work, too.
	occasional [əˈkeɪʒnl]	gelegentlich	Bert only works occasionally.
	single [ˈsɪŋgl]	alleinerziehend	→ single father → single parent
	to **worry** [ˈwʌri]	sich Sorgen machen	You worry too much. Relax!
	rejection [rɪˈdʒekʃn]	Absage; Ablehnung	→ to reject
	guys *(pl.)* [gaɪz]	umgangssprachlich für Leute; Typen	Come on guys, let's go!
	apart [əˈpɑːt]	getrennt; auseinander	We've been apart for too long. Can't we get together again?
	level [ˈlevl]	Niveau; Gehalt	= height
	migration [maɪˈgreɪʃn]	Migration	→ migrant
	counterpart [ˈkaʊntəpɑːt]	Gegenüber; Gegenpart	The creative director called her counterpart in the other company.
	to **pin** [pɪn]	anstecken; anheften	→ pin
B1	**in return** [ɪn rɪˈtɜːn]	als Gegenleistung; zum Ausgleich	In return for her hard work the company sent her on a holiday to Hawaii.
	to **be in charge of s.th.** [biˌɪn ˈtʃɑːdʒ əv]	für etw. zuständig sein	Jake is in charge of our hardware department.

Vocabulary | Unit vocabulary

	demographic [ˌdeməˈɡræfɪk]	demographisch; bevölkerungsstatistisch	→ demographics
	to **accommodate** [əˈkɒmədeɪt]	aufnehmen; unterbringen; entgegenkommen	→ accommodation
	hardware [ˈhɑːdweə]	Computer-Hardware	Sue is a successful hardware developer.
	concept [ˈkɒnsept]	Konzept; Begriff; Auffassung	You have a different concept of life to me.
B2	**support** [səˈpɔːt]	Unterstützung	→ to support
	in need [ɪn ˈniːd]	bedürftig	= needy
	surplus [ˈsɜːpləs]	überschüssig	more than is needed
	produce [ˈprɒdjuːs]	landwirtschaftliche Erzeugnisse	You get fresh produce at the farmer's market.
	to **move out** [ˌmuːvˈaʊt]	ausziehen	↔ to move in
	to **redecorate** [ˌriːˈdekreɪt]	renovieren	The kitchen badly needs to be redecorated.
	fulfilling [fʊlˈfɪlɪŋ]	erfüllend	Sheila doesn't find her job at the checkout fulfilling.
	skill [skɪl]	Fertigkeit	Cooking is a good skill to have.
B3	**comedian** [kəˈmiːdiən]	Komiker/in	→ comedy
	to **leave out** [ˌliːvˈaʊt]	weglassen	You have left out a word in that sentence.
	Muslim [ˈmʊzlɪm]	muslimisch; Moslem	Most of the people in Arab states are Muslim.
	profession [prəˈfeʃn]	Beruf	→ professional
	comprehensive school [ˌkɒmprɪˈhensɪv ˌskuːl]	Gesamtschule	a type of secondary state school in Britain
	to **give up** [ˌɡɪvˈʌp]	aufgeben	You can succeed. Don't give up!
	to **take up** [ˌteɪkˈʌp]	aufnehmen; anfangen mit	↔ to quit
B4	to **take on** [ˌteɪkˈɒn]	übernehmen; annehmen	Take on this challenge!
C	**carefree** [ˈkeəfriː]	sorglos	↔ worried
	to **indicate** [ˈɪndɪkeɪt]	anzeigen; andeuten	→ indicator
	subheading [ˈsʌbˌhedɪŋ]	Untertitel	The subheading appears under the title of a newspaper article.
	reduction [rɪˈdʌkʃn]	Verringerung	→ to reduce
	academic [ˌækəˈdemɪk]	schulisch; wissenschaftlich	→ academics
	performance [pəˈfɔːməns]	Auftritt; Leistung	→ to perform
	pressure [ˈpreʃə]	Druck	If you have a lot of work to do in a short time, you may feel under pressure.
	to **face** [feɪs]	sich gegenübersehen; konfrontiert sein mit	We are facing a huge climate change problem.
	stressed-out [ˌstrestˈaʊt]	völlig gestresst	Donna is stressed-out. She has been working too hard lately.
	tough [tʌf]	hart; schwierig	→ toughness
	admission [ədˈmɪʃn]	Zulassung; Zugeständnis	→ to admit
	competitive [kəmˈpetɪtɪv]	hart umkämpft	→ competition, to compete
	grade [ɡreɪd]	Note	→ to grade
	to **drop** [drɒp]	sinken; fallen; fallen lassen	= to decline
	out of work [ˌaʊt əv ˈwɜːk]	arbeitslos	= unemployed = jobless
	to **pick up** [ˌpɪkˈʌp]	sich erholen	= to improve
	to **predict** [prɪˈdɪkt]	vorhersagen	→ predictable
	to **juggle** [ˈdʒʌɡl]	unter einen Hut bringen; jonglieren	David must juggle a job, the children and the housework.
	to **catch up with s.o.** [ˌkætʃˈʌp wɪð]	zu jemandem aufschließen	Sheila runs so fast. It's hard to catch up with her.
	banker [ˈbæŋkə]	Bankangestellte/r	→ bank account
	physical therapist [ˌfɪzɪkl ˈθerəpɪst]	Krankengymnast/in	→ physical therapy

	to **determine** [dɪˈtɜːmɪn]	festlegen	→ determination
	timeout [ˌtaɪmˈaʊt]	Auszeit	I'm stressed-out. I need a timeout from work.
	aged [eɪdʒd]	im Alter von	They accept candidates who are aged 18 and over.
	commitment [kəˈmɪtmənt]	Bindung; Engagement	→ to commit
	unpaid [ʌnˈpeɪd]	unbezahlt	The company is only offering unpaid work placements to students.
	voluntary [ˈvɒləntri]	freiwillig	→ volunteer
	to **upgrade** [ʌpˈgreɪd]	aufwerten	Max's job in the company was upgraded and now he's the senior technician.
	CV [ˌsiːˈviː]	Lebenslauf	curriculum vitae
D1	**economics** *(pl.)* [ˌiːkəˈnɒmɪks]	Volkswirtschaftslehre	Sharon is studying economics at university.
	to **prevent** [prɪˈvent]	hindern; verhindern; vermeiden	→ prevention
	circumstances *(pl.)* [ˈsɜːkəmstænsɪz]	Sachverhalt; Umstände	I cannot work under these terrible circumstances.
	numerous [ˈnjuːmrəs]	zahlreich; viel	= many
	treatment [ˈtriːtmənt]	Behandlung	→ to treat
	old age [ˌəʊldˈeɪdʒ]	Alter	George wanted to move into a smaller house in his old age.
	pension [ˈpenʃn]	Rente; Pension	→ pensioner
	scheme [skiːm]	System; Maßnahme	= system
	to **reduce** [rɪˈdjuːs]	reduzieren	→ reduction
	urbanization [ˌɜːbnaɪˈzeɪʃn]	Urbanisation; Verstädterung	→ urban
	to **weaken** [ˈwiːkn]	schwächen	→ weakness
	provision [prəˈvɪʒn]	Versorgung	→ to provide
	senior [ˈsiːniə]	ältere/r/s; Senior	↔ junior
	contract [ˈkɒntrækt]	Vertrag	I have signed a contract for my new job.
	generation [ˌdʒenəˈreɪʃn]	Generation	→ generation gap
	decent [ˈdiːsnt]	angemessen	→ decency
	progress [ˈprəʊgres]	Fortschritt; Fortgang	→ to progress
	effectiveness [ɪˈfektɪvnəs]	Effektivität	→ effective
	to **finance** [ˈfaɪnæns]	finanzieren	→ financial → finances
	benefits *(pl.)* [ˈbenɪfɪts]	Unterstützungszahlungen; Unterstützungsleistungen	→ to benefit
	public [ˈpʌblɪk]	öffentlich	↔ private
D2	**multigenerational** [ˌmʌltɪdʒenəˈreɪʃnl]	Mehrgenerationen-	The town has build a multigenerational house where young and old can live together.
	community [kəˈmjuːnəti]	Gemeinde; Gemeinschaft	→ communal
	to **consist of** [kənˈsɪst əv]	bestehen aus	This study group consists of four students.
	resident [ˈrezɪdnt]	Bewohner/in; Einwohner/in	→ residence
	charity [ˈtʃærɪti]	wohltätige Organisation; gemeinnützige Organisation	→ charitable
	to **provide** [prəˈvaɪd]	zur Verfügung stellen; sorgen für; versorgen	→ provision
	outdoor [aʊtˈdɔː]	Aussen-	↔ indoor
	facility [fəˈsɪləti]	Anlage; Einrichtung	→ to facilitate
	barbecue area [ˈbɑːbɪkjuːˌeəriə]	Grillplatz	→ to barbecue
	car park [ˈkɑːpɑːk]	Parkplatz; Parkhaus	= parking lot *(AE)*
	to **respect** [rɪˈspekt]	respektieren	→ respectable → respect
	diversity [daɪˈvɜːsəti]	Unterschiedlichkeit; Vielfalt	→ diverse
	dependency [dɪˈpendənsi]	Abhängigkeit	→ to depend
	care [keə]	Pflege; Sorgfalt	→ careful

Vocabulary | Unit vocabulary

	lonely [ˈləʊnli]	einsam	Living alone can make you feel lonely.
E1	to **combine** [kəmˈbaɪn]	kombinieren	→ combination
	to **make ends meet** [ˌmeɪk ˌendz ˈmiːt]	über die Runden kommen	I need to find a second job because I can't make ends meet.
	to **earn a living** [ˌɜːn ə ˈlɪvɪŋ]	seinen Lebensunterhalt verdienen	Get an education or you'll never be able to earn a living.
	to **be better off** [bi ˌbetər ˈɒf]	besser dran sein	↔ to be worse off
	to **recover** [rɪˈkʌvə]	genesen	→ recovery
	unsympathetic [ˌʌnsɪmpəˈθetɪk]	mitleidslos	↔ sympathetic
	basically [ˈbeɪsɪkli]	im Grunde; eigentlich	Basically, we need more investment in the business.
	to **give off** [ˌɡɪv ˈɒf]	ausdünsten; verströmen; abgeben	The factory gives off a terrible smell.
	intense [ɪnˈtens]	stark; heftig	→ to intensify
	pitch [pɪtʃ]	Maß	the level of a feeling
	to **tumble** [ˈtʌmbl]	fallen; stürzen	She tumbled down the stairs.
	childminder [ˈtʃaɪldˌmaɪndə]	Babysitter/in	= babysitter
	skincare [ˈskɪnkeə]	Hautpflege	This handcream is an excellent skincare product.
	rank [ræŋk]	Rang; Stand	position in a society
	simultaneous [ˌsɪmlˈteɪniəs]	gleichzeitig	= at the same time
	conventional [kənˈvenʃnl]	herkömmlich; konventionell	→ convention
	damn [dæm]	verdammt	Damn! I've broken my glasses.
	to **buck up** [ˌbʌk ˈʌp]	umgangssprachlich für beeilen	You had better buck up and find a solution!
	flexibility [ˌfleksəˈbɪləti]	Flexibilität	→ flexible
	terrific [təˈrɪfɪk]	grandios; hervorragend	= excellent
	enterprise [ˈentəpraɪz]	Unternehmen; Vorhaben	→ entrepreneur
	amongst [əˈmʌŋst]	inmitten	This enterprise is well established amongst its competitors.
	dinosaur [ˈdaɪnəsɔː]	Dinosaurier	s.o. who is old-fashioned and behind the times
	cocaine [kəˈkeɪn]	Kokain	Cocaine is an illegal drug in our country.
	addict [ˈædɪkt]	Süchtige/r	→ addiction
E2	to **quadruple** [kwɒdˈruːpl]	vervierfachen	to multiply s.th. by four
	economic [ˌiːkəˈnɒmɪk]	wirtschaftlich	→ economical
	factor [ˈfæktə]	Faktor	Social factors such as drug taking can lead to criminal activities.
	primary [ˈpraɪmri]	hauptsächlich	Dana is the primary breadwinner.
	caregiver [ˈkeəˌɡɪvə]	Betreuer/in; Pfleger/in	Women are often the caregivers for elderly parents.
	norm [nɔːm]	Norm	→ normal
	to **represent** [ˌreprɪˈzent]	repräsentieren; vertreten	→ representative
	specifically [spəˈsɪfɪkli]	eigens; speziell	He came here specifically to talk to you.
	role model [ˈrəʊl ˌmɒdl]	Vorbild	It is important for young people to have suitable role models.
	to **navigate** [ˈnævɪɡeɪt]	navigieren	She's trying to navigate this difficult situation.
	assumption [əˈsʌmʃn]	Vermutung; Annahme	→ to assume
	to **promote** [prəˈməʊt]	befördern	→ promotion
	maternity leave [məˈtɜːnəti ˌliːv]	Mutterschaftsurlaub	After she had her baby, Kim was on maternity leave for six months.
	bump [bʌmp]	Erhöhung; Beule	→ bumpy

	no-brainer [nəʊˈbreɪnə]	Kinderspiel; Leichtigkeit	That question is a no-brainer. The answer is clear.
	to **crunch the numbers** [krʌnʃ ðə ˈnʌmbəz]	durchrechnen	to calculate
	childcare [ˈtʃaɪldkeə]	Kinderbetreuung	Tessa's parents pay a lot for childcare every month.
	to **coincide** [ˌkəʊɪnˈsaɪd]	überschneiden	→ coincidence
	regarding [rɪˈgɑːdɪŋ]	bezüglich	Ken has no explanation regarding the bump in the car door.
	workforce [ˈwɜːkfɔːs]	Belegschaft; Gesamtheit der Mitarbeiter	The company has a workforce of 550 employees.
	lean [liːn]	mager	We prefer lean meat for dinner.
	fiscal [ˈfɪskl]	finanziell	The fiscal year ends in March.
	necessity [nəˈsesətiz]	Notwendigkeit	→ necessary
	to **cite** [saɪt]	anführen; zitieren	→ citation
	below [bɪˈləʊ]	unter; unterhalb	The Dead Sea is below sea level.
	poverty [ˈpɒvəti]	Armut	→ poor
	comeback [ˈkʌmbæk]	Comeback; Wiederaufstieg	Don't give up! A comeback is possible.
	to **dominate** [ˈdɒmɪneɪt]	beherrschen	→ domination
	construction [kənˈstrʌkʃn]	Baugewerbe; Bau; Konstruktion	→ to construct
	recession [rɪˈseʃn]	Rezession; Rückgang	The economy saw a major recession in 2009.
	household [ˈhaʊshəʊld]	Haushalt	A fridge is a household appliance.
	strict [strɪkt]	streng	→ strictness
	division [dɪˈvɪʒn]	Teilung; Bereich	→ to divide
F	**roll** [rəʊl]	Brötchen	We had breadrolls for breakfast.
	to **score** [skɔː]	Tor schießen; Punkte erzielen	Beth scored six goals in the match.
	within [wɪˈðɪn]	innerhalb	The store only offers goods within a certain price range.
	manual labour [ˌmænjuəl ˈleɪbə]	körperliche Arbeit	work which is done with your hands
	to **lack** [læk]	mangeln	Naomi lacks patience. She's not very good with kids.

Unit B Cross-cultural communication at work: Living in London

	directions *(pl.)* [dɪˈrekʃnz]	Wegbeschreibung	I'm lost. I need directions to find my way home.
A	**passer-by** [ˌpɑːsəˈbaɪ]	Passant/in	= pedestrian
	turning [ˈtɜːnɪŋ]	Abzweigung	You missed the turning. Take the next one on the right.
	straight on [ˌstreɪt ˈɒn]	geradeaus	= straight ahead
	to **carry on** [ˌkæri ˈɒn]	weitergehen; weitermachen	Carry on with your work! Don't waste time.
B	to **apologize** [əˈpɒlədʒaɪz]	sich entschuldigen	→ apology
	Pleased to meet you. [ˌpliːzd tə ˈmiːt juː]	Schön Sie/dich/euch kennenzulernen.	Good morning, Mr. Turner! Pleased to meet you.
	dialogue [ˈdaɪəlɒg]	Dialog	A constructive dialogue between critics and supporters is necessary.
C	**way of life** [ˌweɪ əv ˈlaɪf]	Lebensart	The way of life in the town is different to that in the country.
	queue [kjuː]	Warteschlange	→ to queue
	pin [pɪn]	Kontaktstift; Stecknadel	Plugs in the UK usually have three pins.
	plug [plʌg]	Stecker	→ to plug in → to plug out

Vocabulary | Unit vocabulary

	to **fry** [fraɪ]	braten	→ frying pan
	bacon [ˈbeɪkn]	Frühstücksspeck	I love bacon and eggs for breakfast.
	sausage [ˈsɒsɪdʒ]	Würstchen	We often grill sausages on the barbecue.
D	to **overhear** [ˌəʊvəˈhɪə]	zufällig mitbekommen	I overheard Maria talking about me.
	trainee [ˌtreɪˈniː]	Auszubildende/r; Trainee; Praktikant/in	→ trainer → to train
	Warsaw [ˈwɔːsɔː]	Warschau	Warsaw is the capital city of Poland.
	the States [ðə ˈsteɪts]	Vereinigte Staaten; USA	You can say the States when you mean the United States of America.
	uni [ˈjuːni]	kurz für: Universität	= university
	logistics [ləˈdʒɪstɪks]	Logistik	Our firm uses a logistics company to send goods to customers.
	Polish [ˈpəʊlɪʃ]	Polnisch	→ Poland
	cereal [ˈsɪəriəl]	Frühstückszerealien	The children eat cereal with milk for breakfast.
	porridge [ˈpɒrɪdʒ]	Hafergrütze	You can make porridge with oats and water or milk.
	muesli [ˈmjuːzli]	Müsli	Muesli has become a popular breakfast dish in Britain.
	scrambled [ˈskræmbld]	Rühr-	Tom made scrambled eggs on toast for breakfast.
	mushroom [ˈmʌʃruːm]	Pilz; Champignon	Mushrooms can be grilled or used in soup.
	tomato [təˈmɑːtəʊ]	Tomate	Dan likes tomato ketchup on his chips.
	drink [drɪŋk]	Getränk	I am so thirsty. I need a drink.
E	to **consider** [kənˈsɪdə]	überlegen; erwägen; betrachten als	→ consideration
	unsettled [ʌnˈsetld]	unbeständig; unruhig	→ to unsettle
	towards [təˈwɔːdz]	in Richtung	I saw Adam. He was coming towards me.
	windy [ˈwɪndi]	windig	It's very windy today.
	northwards [ˈnɔːθwədz]	nach Norden	in a northernly direction
	outbreak [ˈaʊtbreɪk]	Ausbruch	→ to break out
	condition [kənˈdɪʃn]	Zustand; Bedingung; Umstand	You can't go sailing in these weather conditions.
	patchy [ˈpætʃi]	gebietsweise	→ patch
	interlude [ˈɪntəluːd]	kurze Phase; Intermezzo	It rained a lot yesterday. We only had a dry interlude for half an hour.
	ground [graʊnd]	Lagen; Gelände	In Scotland there is a lot of high ground and mountains.
	potential [pəˈtenʃl]	Potenzial; Möglichkeit	The product has great potential.
	flurry [ˈflʌri]	Böe	They predict snow flurries over Berlin.
	who the hell …? [ˌhuː ðə ˈhel]	Wer zum Teufel …?	Who the hell broke my favourite cup?
	script [skrɪpt]	Ansagetext; Drehbuch; Manuskript	Please keep to the script!
	bright [braɪt]	hell; leuchtend	↔ dark
	isle [aɪl]	kleine Insel	a small island
	mainland [ˈmeɪnlənd]	Festland	The weather is too bad to cross from the island to the mainland.
	hazy [ˈheɪzi]	diesig; trüb	→ haze
	brisk [brɪsk]	lebhaft; flott	The wet clothes dried quickly in the brisk wind.
	forecaster [ˈfɔːkɑːstə]	Meteorologe/in; Prognostiker/in	→ to forecast
	bank holiday [ˌbæŋk ˈhɒlədeɪ]	gesetzlicher Feiertag	Bank holidays in Britain usually fall on a Monday.

	forecast [ˈfɔːkɑːst]	Vorhersage	The weather forecast for tomorrow is not good.

Unit 6 Ecology

A	**environmental** [ɪnˌvaɪərnˈmentl]	ökologisch; Umwelt-	→ environment → environmentalist
	genetic [dʒəˈnetɪk]	genetisch	→ gene → geneticist
	to **modify** [ˈmɒdɪfaɪ]	abändern; verändern	→ modification
	extinction [ɪkˈstɪŋkʃn]	Ausrottung	→ to become extinct
	to **tackle** [ˈtækl]	angehen	How do we tackle this problem?
	carbon dioxide, CO₂ [ˌkɑːbn daɪˈɒksaɪd]	Kohlendioxid	How can we reduce carbon dioxide emissions?
	gas [ɡæs]	Gas	Air is a gas.
	atmosphere [ˈætməsfɪə]	Atmosphäre	The atmosphere at the party was great!
	greenhouse [ˈɡriːnhaʊs]	Treibhaus	You can grow tomatoes in a greenhouse in winter.
	to **trap** [træp]	einschließen	If you are trapped, you can't escape.
	in particular [ɪn pəˈtɪkjələ]	insbesondere	I like your hair and the new colour in particular.
	fossil [ˈfɒsl]	fossil	Coal, oil and gas are fossil fuels.
	fuel [ˈfjuːəl]	Kraftstoff; Brennstoff	Planes burn a lot of fuel.
	forest [ˈfɒrɪst]	Wald	The rain forest of the Amazon are in terrible danger.
	in addition [ɪn əˈdɪʃn]	außerdem	Ben plays football and in additon to that he runs twice a week.
	systematic [ˌsɪstəˈmætɪk]	systematisch	The destruction of the forest was systematic.
	centigrade [ˈsentɪɡreɪd]	Grad Celsius	Water boils at 100 degrees centigrade.
	indirect [ˌɪndɪˈrekt]	indirekt	↔ direct
	extreme [ɪkˈstriːm]	extrem	→ extremism
	supply [səˈplaɪ]	Angebot; Versorgung	→ supplier → to supply
	crop [krɒp]	Ernte; Getreide; Feldfrucht	The farmers have had a good crop of apples this year.
	elsewhere [ˌelsˈweə]	anderswo	We can't help you. You have to look elsewhere.
	to **fail** [feɪl]	ausfallen; scheitern	→ failure
	severe [sɪˈvɪə]	ernst; schwer; heftig	Steve's leg hurts a lot. He is in severe pain.
	rainfall [ˈreɪnfɔːl]	Niederschlag; Regen	After two hot weeks the farmers needed rainfall.
	to **take action** [ˌteɪk ˈækʃn]	tätig werden; handeln	If you don't reply, we will have to take action.
	hopefully [ˈhəʊpfəli]	hoffentlich	↔ hope
	dramatic [drəˈmætɪk]	dramatisch; spektakulär	The end of the film was very dramatic.
	rooftop [ˈruːftɒp]	Hausdach	Some people grow grass on their flat rooftops.
	solar panel [ˌsəʊlə ˈpænl]	Sonnenkollektor	We have solar panels on the roof.
	array [əˈreɪ]	Feld; Palette	a large number of things
	to **generate** [ˈdʒenəreɪt]	erzeugen	→ generator
	working day [ˌwɜːkɪŋ ˈdeɪ]	Arbeitstag; Werktag	It's a working day, not a bank holiday. You have to go to work.
	grid [ɡrɪd]	Stromnetz	a system of cables that provides electricity for an area
	to **demonstrate** [ˈdemənstreɪt]	demonstrieren; vorführen	→ demonstration → demonstrator

Vocabulary | Unit vocabulary

	sustainable [sə'steɪnəbl]	nachhaltig; umweltgerecht	→ sustainability
	carbon footprint [ˌkɑːbn 'fʊtprɪnt]	Kohlendioxid-Bilanz	You should reduce your carbon footprint by buying local products.
B1	**developing world** [dɪˌveləpɪŋ 'wɜːld]	Entwicklungsländer	Many countries in Africa belong to the developing world.
	thirst [θɜːst]	Durst	→ thirsty
	gamble ['gæmbl]	Glücksspiel	→ gambler, to gamble
	heartbreaking ['hɑːtˌbreɪkɪŋ]	herzzerreißend	→ heartbreak
	to **benefit from** ['benəfɪt frəm]	Nutzen ziehen aus; profitieren von	→ beneficial
	donation [də'neɪʃn]	Spende	→ to donate
B2	**seafood** ['siːfuːd]	Meeresfrüchte	People on the coast eat a lot of seafood.
	tuna ['tjuːnə]	Thunfisch	You can buy tuna in cans.
	protein ['prəʊtiːn]	Protein; Eiweiß	Seafood is rich in protein.
	catastrophe [kə'tæstrəfi]	Katastrophe	→ catastrophic
	lifetime ['laɪftaɪm]	Leben	This is the chance of a lifetime.
B3	**fund** [fʌnd]	Fonds	an organization which gives money to specific projects
	nearest ['nɪərɪst]	nächstgelegene/r/s	He needs his pills. Where is the nearest pharmacy?
	branch [brɑːnʃ]	Filiale; Zweigstelle	= subsidiary
	membership ['membəʃɪp]	Mitgliedschaft	Your membership starts when you get your members' card from the club.
	leaflet ['liːflət]	Prospekt	= brochure
B4	**drop** [drɒp]	Tropfen	She loves sweets especially chocolate drops.
	to **run out** [ˌrʌn 'aʊt]	sich erschöpfen; zu Ende gehen	The reserves of oil will run out soon.
	overfishing [ˌəʊvə'fɪʃɪŋ]	Überfischung	Several types of fish are dying out because of overfishing.
	fisherman ['fɪʃəmən]	Fischer; Angler	The fishermen go out to sea every night to catch fish.
	to **clean up** [ˌkliːn 'ʌp]	aufräumen; säubern	Please clean up the kitchen when you have finished.
	relating to [rɪ'leɪtɪŋ tə]	bezogen auf; in Bezug auf	Topics relating to politics cause a lot of discussion.
C	**chicken** ['tʃɪkɪn]	Hühnchenfleisch; Huhn	They get fresh eggs from their chickens.
	to **harm** [hɑːm]	schädigen; schaden	= to damage
	conscience ['kɒnʃns]	Gewissen	She cheated and now she has a guilty conscience.
	due to ['djuː tə]	wegen; aufgrund	= because of
	greengrocer ['griːnˌgrəʊsə]	Gemüsehändler/in	The greengrocer sells fresh fruit and vegetables.
	on offer [ˌɒn 'ɒfə]	im Angebot	The supermarket has a wide range of seafood on offer.
	to **process** ['prəʊses]	bearbeiten; verarbeiten	When food is processed you can keep it for longer.
	to **standardize** ['stændədaɪz]	standardisieren	→ standard
	to **package** ['pækɪdʒ]	verpacken	= to wrap
	to **gain** [geɪn]	erwerben; sammeln; erreichen	Teresa is very helpful and has gained a good reputation in her neighbourhood.
	massive ['mæsɪv]	gewaltig; kolossal	= huge
	reaction [ri'ækʃn]	Reaktion	→ to react
	organic [ɔː'gænɪk]	biologisch; Bio-	Tom prefers organic food to conventional food.

	chemical [ˈkemɪkl]	chemisch	→ chemistry → chemist
	fertilizer [ˈfɜːtɪlaɪzə]	Dünger	→ to fertilize
	pesticide [ˈpestɪsaɪd]	Pflanzenschutzmittel	Due to the use of pesticides the fish in this river have died.
	groundwater [ˈɡraʊndˌwɔːtə]	Grundwasser	The quality of our groundwater has improved.
	regulation [ˌreɡjəˈleɪʃn]	Vorschrift; Verordnung	→ to regulate
	to **label** [ˈleɪbl]	etikettieren; beschriften	Please label the packages.
	antibiotic [ˌæntɪbaɪˈɒtɪk]	Antibiotikum	Don't take too many antibiotics!
	contribution [ˌkɒntrɪˈbjuːʃn]	Beitrag	→ to contribute
	conscious [ˈkɒnʃəs]	bewusst	The whole family is very health-conscious.
D1	**society** [səˈsaɪəti]	Gesellschaft	They raise their kids to be responsible members of society.
	trick [trɪk]	Trick; Kniff	→ tricky → to trick
	as though [əz ˈðəʊ]	als ob	She acted as though she hadn't seen him.
	opposition [ˌɒpəˈzɪʃn]	Widerspruch; Widerstand	→ to oppose
	to **reproduce** [ˌriːprəˈdjuːs]	nachproduzieren	→ reproduction
	domestic [dəˈmestɪk]	heimisch; inländisch	↔ foreign
	boomerang [ˈbuːmræŋ]	Bumerang	→ boomerang effect
	to **exceed** [ɪkˈsiːd]	übersteigen; überschreiten	His wishes exceed by far what he can afford.
	soil [sɔɪl]	Erdboden	This is good soil. You can grow anything here.
	erosion [ɪˈrəʊʒn]	Erosion; Abtragung	→ to erode
	lack of [ˈlæk əv]	Mangel an	The children suffer from a serious lack of vitamins.
	instability [ˌɪnstəˈbɪləti]	Instabilität	→ unstable
	planet [ˈplænɪt]	Planet	Venus is the nearest planet to us.
	to **add up** [ˌæd ˈʌp]	aufaddieren	Add up your expenses and you will see how much money you need to earn.
	slogan [ˈsləʊɡən]	Werbespruch	Don't always believe their advertising slogans!
	commentary [ˈkɒməntri]	Kommentar	→ to comment
D2	**hopeless** [ˈhəʊpləs]	hoffnungslos	↔ hopeful
	tonne [tʌn]	metrische Tonne	Jack's truck weighs about 140 tonnes.
	fiction [ˈfɪkʃn]	Fiktion; Annahme	→ fictitious
	canteen [kænˈtiːn]	Kantine	Emma usually has lunch in the canteen at work.
	efficient [ɪˈfɪʃnt]	leistungsfähig; wirksam; tüchtig	↔ inefficient
	enormous [ɪˈnɔːməs]	gewaltig; enorm	= massive = huge
	printer [ˈprɪntə]	Drucker	→ to print
	cartridge [ˈkɑːtrɪdʒ]	Patrone	You can recycle this printer cartridge.
	endless [ˈendləs]	endlos	↔ finite
D3	**sustainability** [səˌsteɪnəˈbɪləti]	Nachhaltigkeit	→ to sustain
	void [vɔɪd]	Lücke	an empty space
	Scandinavian [ˌskændɪˈneɪviən]	skandinavisch	→ Scandinavia
	to **furnish** [ˈfɜːnɪʃ]	einrichten; möblieren	→ furniture
	to **elevate** [ˈeləveɪt]	anheben	→ elevation
	dumbfounded [ˌdʌmˈfaʊndɪd]	sprachlos; verblüfft	= very surprised
	to **usher in** [ˌʌʃər ˈɪn]	einleiten	to cause s.th. to start
	disposable [dɪˈspəʊzəbl]	Wegwerf-	Disposable packaging produces tons of waste.
	guilty [ˈɡɪlti]	schuldig	→ guilt

Vocabulary | Unit vocabulary

furnishings [ˈfɜːnɪʃɪŋz]	Einrichtungsgegenstände	= furniture
traditional [trəˈdɪʃnl]	traditionell	→ tradition
big ticket [ˌbɪg ˈtɪkɪt]	groß; teuer	The salesperson knew immediately that the rich woman was a big ticket customer.
sofa [ˈsəʊfə]	Sofa	= couch
crisp (BE) [krɪsp]	Chip	a salty snack made with potatoes that you buy in packets
regardless [rɪˈgɑːdləs]	ohne Rücksicht	Regardless if the bosses like it or not we have to shut down the system for two hours.
mug [mʌg]	Becher	Not just a small cup; I want a big mug of coffee.
lifespan [ˈlaɪfspæn]	Lebensdauer	The average lifespan of a hamster is two years.
former [ˈfɔːmə]	ehemalige/r/s; frühere/r/s	↔ current
senior executive [ˌsiːniər ɪgˈzekjətɪv]	leitende/r Angestellte/r	a top manager in a company
to **chuck out** [ˌtʃʌk ˈaʊt]	umgangssprachlich für wegwerfen	I don't wear this dress any longer. I'll chuck it out.
chintz [tʃɪnts]	Chintz	brightly coloured material used to cover sofas, for example
to **recycle** [ˌriːˈsaɪkl]	wiederverwerten	→ recycling
sidewalk (AE) [ˈsaɪdwɔːk]	Bürgersteig	pavement (BE)
to **overcome** [ˌəʊvəˈkʌm]	überwinden	He overcame all difficulties.
durable [ˈdjʊərəbl]	haltbar	→ durability
mindset [ˈmaɪndset]	Denkweise	You won't solve this problem unless you change your mindset.
view [vjuː]	Ansicht; Ausblick	→ viewpoint
genuine [ˈdʒenjʊɪn]	echt; ehrlich	= honest
to **dispose** [dɪˈspəʊz]	entsorgen; loswerden	→ disposal
throwaway [ˈθrəʊəweɪ]	Wegwerf-	It's not a throwaway product. It can be repaired.
fashionable [ˈfæʃnəbl]	modisch	→ fashion
E **vertebrate** [ˈvɜːtɪbreɪt]	Wirbel-	Cows and pigs are vertebrate species.
terrestrial [təˈrestriəl]	Erd-; auf dem Festland	Marine and terrestrial ecosystems must be protected.
species (pl.) [ˈspiːʃiːz]	Art; Spezies	There are over 200 species of birds in this country.
freshwater [ˈfreʃwɔːtə]	Süßwasser	↔ saltwater
marine [məˈriːn]	See-	Due to pollution marine wildlife is in danger.
wildlife [ˈwaɪldlaɪf]	Tier- und Pflanzenwelt	Leah is an expert on local wildlife.
to **halve** [hɑːv]	halbieren	A problem shared is a problem halved.
to **decimate** [ˈdesɪmeɪt]	dezimieren; drastisch verringern	→ decimation
unsustainable [ˌʌnsəˈsteɪnəbl]	nicht aufrecht zu erhalten	↔ sustainable
habitat [ˈhæbɪtæt]	Habitat; Lebensraum	Marine habitats are vulnerable.
front page [ˌfrʌnt ˈpeɪdʒ]	Titelseite	This will make front page news.
outdoors (pl.) [ˌaʊtˈdɔːz]	draußen; im Freien	Kids love being outdoors.
inevitable [ɪˈnevɪtəbl]	unvermeidlich	↔ preventable
wellbeing [ˈwelˌbiːɪŋ]	Wohlergehen	He cares a lot about the wellbeing of his family.
driven by [ˈdrɪvn baɪ]	vorangetrieben durch; vorangetrieben von	This catastrophe was driven by human behaviour.
arms (pl.) [ɑːmz]	Waffen; Rüstungsgüter	→ armed → to arm
deforestation [diːˌfɒrɪˈsteɪʃn]	Abholzung	↔ reforestation

steep [sti:p]	steil	The whole group ran up the steep path.
to **calculate** [ˈkælkjəleɪt]	berechnen	You can calculate your carbon footprint online.
in total [ɪn ˈtəʊtl]	insgesamt	= altogether
representative [ˌreprɪˈzentətɪv]	repräsentativ	typical of a group of things
to **reflect** [rɪˈflekt]	widerspiegeln; überlegen	His behaviour reflects a deep anger.
conservation [ˌkɒnsəˈveɪʃn]	Umweltschutz	→ to conserve
resource [rɪˈzɔ:s]	Mittel; Ressourcen	Natural resources are essential for our life on Earth.
ultimately [ˈʌltɪmətli]	letztendlich	→ ultimatum
conflict [ˈkɒnflɪkt]	Streit; Konflikt	They didn't agree and this caused a conflict.
robust [rəˈbʌst]	robust; widerstandsfähig	= strong
indicator [ˈɪndɪkeɪtə]	Indikator; Anzeiger	→ to indicate
to **adopt** [əˈdɒpt]	adoptieren; übernehmen	→ adoption
convention [kənˈvenʃn]	Abkommen	an agreement signed by a number of countries
index [ˈɪndeks]	Index; Kennziffer	This index has risen continuously.
humanity [hju:ˈmænəti]	Menschheit	= humankind
scale [skeɪl]	Maß; Maßstab	In Indonesia forests are burnt on a large scale.
currently [ˈkʌrəntli]	derzeit; zurzeit; momentan	We currently have three placements for EU students.
to **regrow** [ˌri:ˈgrəʊ]	nachwachsen	→ regrowth
to **restock** [ˌri:ˈstɒk]	die Fischbestände sich erholen	to fill up with fish again
to **pump** [pʌmp]	pumpen	→ pump
aquifer [ˈækwɪfə]	wasserführende Schicht	rock which allows groundwater to pass through it
to **replenish** [rɪˈplenɪʃ]	auftanken; auffüllen	↔ to use up
to **emit** [ɪˈmɪt]	ausstoßen; emittieren	→ emission
to **conclude** [kənˈklu:d]	folgern; abschließen	→ conclusion
to **plummet** [ˈplʌmɪt]	stark abfallen; stürzen	= to decrease severely
adviser [ədˈvaɪzə]	Berater/in	→ to advise
whatever [wɒtˈevə]	was auch immer	Take whatever you want from the fridge!
effluent [ˈefluːənt]	Abwasser; Schmutzwasser	= wastewater
to **dump** [dʌmp]	abladen; einleiten	= to unload
India [ˈɪndɪə]	Indien	→ Indian
to **outsource** [ˈaʊtsɔ:s]	outsourcen; ausgliedern	The company outsourced its production to Slovenia.
timber [ˈtɪmbə]	Bauholz	Timber houses don't take long to build.
beef [bi:f]	Rindfleisch	Alice prefers beef to pork.
soya [ˈsɔɪə]	Soja	Sheila adds soya sauce to everything she eats.
chief executive [ˌtʃi:f ɪgˈzekjətɪv]	Firmenchef/in; Vorstandsvorsitzende/r	The chief executive is responsible for the company's policy.
politician [ˌpɒlɪˈtɪʃn]	Politiker/in	→ politics
to **ensure** [ɪnˈʃɔ:]	sicherstellen; gewährleisten	That's dangerous work. You must ensure that the workers are not harmed.
to **value** [ˈvælju:]	schätzen	→ valuable

Vocabulary | Unit vocabulary

Unit 7 The present and future of technology

	technological [ˌteknəˈlɒdʒɪkl]	technologisch	→ technology
A	**biomass** [ˈbaɪəʊˌmæs]	Biomasse	The new biomass power plant will produce enough energy for 300 households.
	renewable [rɪˈnjuːəbl]	erneuerbar	Coal is not a renewable source of energy.
	mountainous [ˈmaʊntɪnəs]	bergig	→ mountain
	agricultural [ˌægrɪˈkʌltʃrl]	landwirtschaftlich	There are large agricultural areas in Ireland.
	region [ˈriːdʒən]	Region; Gebiet	Which region of the country do you come from?
	dozen [ˈdʌzn]	Dutzend	= twelve
	onshore [ˌɒnˈʃɔː]	Festland; auf dem Festland	on land
	offshore [ˌɒfˈʃɔː]	offene See; auf offener See	Offshore wind parks are highly efficient.
	backing [ˈbækɪŋ]	Unterstützung	= support = assistance
	attempt [əˈtempt]	Versuch	→ to attempt
	to **designate** [ˈdezɪgneɪt]	vorsehen; bestimmen	→ designated
	achievable [əˈtʃiːvəbl]	erreichbar	→ achievement
	to **prove** [pruːv]	beweisen; nachweisen	→ proof
	natural gas [ˌnætʃrəl ˈgæs]	Erdgas	A lot of the power stations in Britain run on natural gas.
	North Sea [ˌnɔːθ ˈsiː]	Nordsee	Germany borders the North Sea and the Baltic Sea.
	in the long run [ɪn ðə ˈlɒŋ ˌrʌn]	auf lange Sicht	↔ in the short run
	boost [buːst]	Ankurbelung; Aufschwung	→ to boost
	homegrown [ˌhəʊmˈgrəʊn]	einheimisch; selbst gezogen	We prefer our homegrown vegetables to ones you buy in a supermarket.
	reliance [rɪˈlaɪəns]	Verlass; Vertrauen	→ to rely on
	nuclear power [ˌnjuːkliə ˈpaʊə]	Kernkraft	Nuclear power plants produce electricity
	abundance [əˈbʌndəns]	Fülle; Überfluss	→ abundant
	wave [weɪv]	Welle	In a storm at sea there are big waves.
	substantial [səbˈstænʃl]	erheblich; beträchtlich; wesentlich	→ substance
	excess [ˈekses]	überschüssig	more than is needed
	particularly [pəˈtɪkjələli]	vor allem	This topic is particularly important.
	objection [əbˈdʒekʃn]	Einwand; Widerspruch	→ to object
	conservationist [ˌkɒnsəˈveɪʃnɪst]	Umweltschützer/in	→ to conserve
	outstanding [ˌaʊtˈstændɪŋ]	außerordentlich; besonders	= great
	surroundings *(pl.)* [səˈraʊndɪŋz]	Umgebung	→ to surround
	to **bear** [beə]	tragen; ertragen	= to put up with
	turbine [ˈtɜːbaɪn]	Turbine	A wind farm consists of a large number of turbines.
	object [ˈɒbdʒekt]	Objekt	→ to object
	neighbourhood [ˈneɪbəhʊd]	Nachbarschaft	→ neighbour
	high-voltage [ˌhaɪˈvəʊltɪdʒ]	Hochspannung	↔ low-voltage
	power line [ˈpaʊəˌlaɪn]	Überlandleitung	High-voltage power lines are not popular as they do not look good.
	protest [ˈprəʊtest]	Protest	→ protester → to protest
	party [ˈpɑːti]	Partei	The politician is a member of the Conservative Party.
	low-carbon [ˌləʊˈkɑːbn]	kohlenstoffarm	↔ high-carbon
	to **maintain** [meɪnˈteɪn]	aufrechterhalten; verfechten	→ maintenance

	to **pursue** [pəˈsjuː]	weiterführen; fortfahren	The students pursue their studies with great enthusiasm.
	powerhouse [ˈpaʊəhaʊs]	Kraftwerk	a place where a lot of electricity is produced
	to **encourage** [ɪnˈkʌrɪdʒ]	fördern; ermutigen	→ encouragement
	investment [ɪnˈvestmənt]	Investition	→ to invest → investor
B2	**boiler** [ˈbɔɪlə]	Kessel; Boiler	→ to boil
	steam [stiːm]	Dampf	→ steamy
	generator [ˈdʒenreɪtə]	Generator	→ to generate
	blade [bleɪd]	Turbinenschaufel	The blades of a turbine turn in the wind.
	magnet [ˈmæɡnət]	Magnet	→ magnetic
	finally [ˈfaɪnli]	schließlich; endlich	Tired and hungry we finally arrived at the hotel.
B3	**sweater** [ˈswetə]	Pulli	jumper *(BE)*
	cap [kæp]	Kappe	Please take off your cap.
	earring [ˈɪərɪŋ]	Ohrring	Yvonne loves to wear gold earrings.
B4	**monitor** [ˈmɒnɪtə]	Überwachungsgerät	→ to monitor
	thief [θiːf]	Dieb	A thief stole my money.
	mayor [meə]	Bürgermeister/in	The mayor is the head of the town council.
B5	**hybrid** [ˈhaɪbrɪd]	Hybrid	Some motor companies are testing hybrid cars on the roads.
	hydrogen [ˈhaɪdrədʒən]	Wasserstoff	These are the first hydrogen powered cars on the roads.
C	**tidal** [ˈtaɪdl]	Gezeiten-	Huge tidal waves destroyed the village.
	lagoon [ləˈɡuːn]	Meeresbucht	Look at the blue water in the lagoon.
	estuary [ˈestjʊəri]	Mündungsgebiet	The estuary has a direct connection to the open sea.
	range [reɪndʒ]	Spanne; Intervall	This car is not within my price range.
	bay [beɪ]	Bucht	I love the quiet waters of Dolphin Bay.
	full-scale [ˌfʊlˈskeɪl]	vollständig; umfangreich	They started full-scale operations in May.
	to **take advantage of** [ˌteɪk ədˈvɑːntɪdʒ əv]	sich zunutze machen; ausnutzen	Let's take advantage of the good weather and have a picnic.
	to **split** [splɪt]	teilen; spalten	This piece of cake is too big. Shall we split it?
	atom [ˈætəm]	Atom	→ atomic
	protective [prəˈtektɪv]	schützend	You should wear a protective helmet on your bike.
	breakwater [ˈbreɪkˌwɔːtə]	Wellenbrecher	Breakwaters protect the coast and its harbours.
	square kilometre [ˌskweə kɪˈlɒmɪtə]	Quadratkilometer	Some rich people own 100 square kilometres of land.
	fact [fækt]	Tatsache	I'll tell you some facts about my country.
	emphasis [ˈemfəsɪs]	Betonung; Schwerpunkt	→ to emphasize
	impact [ˈɪmpækt]	Auswirkung; Folge	→ to impact
	phase [feɪz]	Phase	period of time
	to **disturb** [dɪˈstɜːb]	stören	→ disturbance
	in operation [ɪnˌɒpəˈreɪʃn]	in Betrieb	↔ out of operation
	ecological [ˌiːkəˈlɒdʒɪkl]	ökologisch	→ ecology
	plenty [ˈplenti]	Menge; Fülle	→ plentiful
	to **sacrifice** [ˈsækrɪfaɪs]	opfern	→ sacrifice
	unemployment [ˌʌnɪmˈplɔɪmənt]	Arbeitslosigkeit	The government is trying to reduce unemployment by creating new jobs.
	technologist [tekˈnɒlədʒɪst]	Technologe; Technologin	→ technological
	exhaustible [ɪɡˈzɔːstəbl]	erschöpfbar; begrenzt	↔ inexhaustible

	dependent [dɪˈpendənt]	abhängig	↔ independent
	countryside [ˈkʌntrɪsaɪd]	Landschaft; Gegend	Conservationists try to protect the countryside around towns.
	stable [ˈsteɪbl]	stabil	→ stability
	connective [kəˈnektɪv]	Bindewort	→ to connect
	conclusion [kənˈkluːʒn]	Schlussfolgerung	→ to conclude
D1	**surgery** [ˈsɜːdʒri]	Operation	→ surgeon
	medicine [ˈmedsn]	Medizin	→ medical
	examination [ɪɡˌzæmɪˈneɪʃn]	Untersuchung	→ to examine
	disability [ˌdɪsəˈbɪləti]	Behinderung	→ disabled
	artificial [ˌɑːtɪˈfɪʃl]	künstlich	Robots and artificial intelligence belong together.
	insemination [ɪnˌsemɪˈneɪʃn]	Befruchtung	= fertilization
	defibrillator [ˌdiːˈfɪbrɪleɪtə]	Defibrillator	medical machine used to give a shock to s.o.'s heart
	X-ray [ˈeksreɪ]	Röntgenstrahlung; Röntgenbild	The doctor did an X-ray of Peter's arm to see if it was broken.
	ultrasound [ˈʌltrəsaʊnd]	Ultraschall	The doctor used an ultrasound on the patient's body.
	organ transplant [ˈɔːɡən ˌtrænsplɑːnt]	Organtransplantation	Organ transplants can save lives.
	vaccine [ˈvæksiːn]	Impfstoff	→ to vaccinate
	to **outline** [ˈaʊtlaɪn]	umreißen; skizzieren	Please outline the major arguments given in the text.
D2	**disorder** [dɪˈsɔːdə]	Störung	↔ order
	test tube [ˌtestˈtjuːb]	Retorten-	Since the first test tube baby was born in 1978 millions of people have become parents thanks to this method.
	tolerant [ˈtɒlrnt]	tolerant	He is tolerant of people's strange habits.
	up till now [ˌʌp tɪl ˈnaʊ]	bis jetzt	= so far
	desire [dɪˈzaɪə]	Wunsch	= wish
	pre-implantation [ˌpriːɪmplɑːnˈteɪʃn]	Implantation; Einpflanzung	→ to implant
	diagnostics *(pl.)* [ˌdaɪəɡˈnɒstɪks]	Diagnostik	testing s.th. for an illness or disease
	embryo [ˈembriəʊ]	Embryo	→ embryonic
	defect [ˈdiːfekt]	Fehler; Mangel	→ defective
	trisomy [ˈtrɪsəmi]	Trisomie	Trisomy is a genetic disorder.
	Down's syndrome [ˈdaʊnz ˌsɪndrəʊm]	Downsyndrom	Down's syndrome is another word for trisomy.
	to **give birth** [ˌɡɪv ˈbɜːθ]	gebären; zur Welt bringen	Susan already had two children when she gave birth to twins.
	would-be [ˈwʊdbi]	angehend	Would-be authors can present their work on the Internet.
	procedure [prəˈsiːdʒə]	Verfahren; Ablauf	→ to proceed
	intelligence [ɪnˈtelɪdʒns]	Intelligenz	→ intelligent
	illegal [ɪˈliːɡl]	illegal	= unlawful
	sceptical [ˈskeptɪkl]	skeptisch; kritisch	→ sceptic
	alarm bell [əˈlɑːm ˌbel]	Alarmglocke	The alarm bell rings when there is a fire.
	experiment [ɪkˈsperɪmənt]	Experiment	→ to experiment
	ethical [ˈeθɪkl]	ethisch; moralisch	→ ethics
	tweet [twiːt]	kurzer Textbeitrag über ein Mikroblog-Dienst; Tweet	
D3	**scientific** [ˌsaɪənˈtɪfɪk]	wissenschaftlich	→ science

Role cards > Grammar Files > Skills Files > **Vocabulary**

	to **select** [sɪˈlekt]	selektieren; auswählen	→ selection
	female [ˈfiːmeɪl]	weiblich	↔ male
	to **roll** [rəʊl]	ausrollen; rollen	The ball rolled slowly to a stop.
	pink [pɪŋk]	rosa; pink	Emma loves her pink overalls.
	fingernail [ˈfɪŋɡəneɪl]	Fingernagel	Mary likes to paint her fingernails black.
	conception [kənˈsepʃn]	Empfängnis	→ to conceive
	to **separate** [ˈsepreɪt]	trennen; abtrennen	→ separation
	sperm [spɜːm]	Spermium; Sperma	Sperm can be stored in a sperm bank for future use.
	to **screen** [skriːn]	überprüfen; durchsehen	Pat's job is to screen patients to find out if they have any illnesses.
	to **undergo** [ˌʌndəˈɡəʊ]	unterziehen	They must undergo a strict screening process.
	indication [ˌɪndɪˈkeɪʃn]	Indikation; Befund	→ to indicate
	to **approve** [əˈpruːv]	anerkennen; genehmigen	→ approval
	prevention [prɪˈvenʃn]	Verhinderung; Vermeidung	→ to prevent
	disease [dɪˈziːz]	Krankheit	Although it is serious the patient can handle the disease.
	represented [ˌreprɪˈzentɪd]	vertreten; vorhanden	→ representation
	selection [sɪˈlekʃn]	Auswahl	→ to select
	devastating [ˈdevəsteɪtɪŋ]	verheerend	→ devastation
	muscular [ˈmʌskjələ]	muskulär	→ muscle
	dystrophy [ˈdɪstrəfi]	Dystrophie	disease where the muscles get weaker until the person can no longer walk
	suffering [ˈsʌfrɪŋ]	Leiden	→ to suffer
	bottom line [ˌbɒtəm ˈlaɪn]	Entscheidende	That's my bottom line. I won't change my mind.
	sheet [ʃiːt]	Blatt	I'll write a list. Have you got a sheet of paper?
	institute [ˈɪnstɪtjuːt]	Institut	→ institutional
	to **take into consideration** [ˌteɪk ˌɪntə kənˌsɪdrˈeɪʃn]	in Betracht ziehen; berücksichtigen	= to consider
D4	**designer** [dɪˈzaɪnə]	Designer/in	→ to design
	to **hold on** [ˌhəʊld ˈɒn]	warten; festhalten	Hold on, what did he just say?
	to **contradict** [ˌkɒntrəˈdɪkt]	widersprechen	→ contradiction
	partly [ˈpɑːtli]	teilweise	= in parts
	critical [ˈkrɪtɪkl]	kritisch; entscheidend	He is very critical of our modern society.
	compromise [ˈkɒmprəmaɪz]	Kompromiss	→ to compromise
	to **argue** [ˈɑːɡjuː]	argumentieren; Argumente darlegen	→ argument
E	**hunger** [ˈhʌŋɡə]	Hunger	→ hungry
	to **feed** [fiːd]	füttern	At the zoo they must feed the animals.
	to **swell** [swel]	schwellen; anschwellen	After the accident his knee swelled up like a balloon.
	leader [ˈliːdə]	Leiter/in; Führer/in	→ leadership → to lead
	to **starve** [stɑːv]	hungern	→ starvation
	straightforward [ˌstreɪtˈfɔːwəd]	einfach; unkompliziert	= simple = basic
	maize (BE) [meɪz]	Mais	corn (AE)
	Spain [speɪn]	Spanien	→ Spanish
	red tape [ˌred ˈteɪp]	Bürokratie; Papierkrieg	The conservationists had to work through a lot of red tape before they were able to buy the piece of land.
	to **block** [blɒk]	blockieren	→ blockade

Vocabulary | Unit vocabulary

despite [dɪˈspaɪt]	trotz	= in spite of
nutritional [ˌnjuːˈtrɪʃnl]	Ernährungs-	Being a vegetarian has many nutritional benefits.
reward [rɪˈwɔːd]	Vorzug; Belohnung	→ rewarding → to reward
to **breed** [briːd]	züchten	→ breeder
variety [vəˈraɪəti]	Vielfalt; Auswahl	→ to vary
unacceptable [ˌʌnækˈseptəbl]	inakzeptabel; unzumutbar	↔ acceptable
to **stress** [stres]	betonen	Let me stress that we must come to a conclusion!
European [ˌjʊərəˈpiːən]	europäisch; Europäer/in	→ Europe
fit for purpose [ˌfɪt fə ˈpɜːpəs]	zweckdienlich	= appropriate
to **urge** [ɜːdʒ]	drängen	→ urgent
to **outweigh** [aʊtˈweɪ]	aufwiegen; wettmachen	The benefits far outweigh the disadvantages.
to **perceive** [pəˈsiːv]	wahrnehmen	→ perception
to **debate** [dɪˈbeɪt]	diskutieren; erörtern	They debated all night and couldn't reach an agreement.
to **mature** [məˈtjʊə]	sich entwickeln; reifen	→ maturity
campaigner [kæmˈpeɪnə]	Aktivist/in	→ to campaign
ignorance [ˈɪgnrns]	Ignoranz; Ahnungslosigkeit	→ to ignore
bureaucratic [ˌbjʊərəˈkrætɪk]	bürokratisch	→ bureaucracy
inertia [ɪˈnɜːʃə]	Trägheit	→ inert
swath [swɒθ]	große Menge	a lot of s.th.
promising [ˈprɒmɪsɪŋ]	vielversprechend	→ to promise → promise
to **boost** [buːst]	ankurbeln; fördern	→ boost
yield [jiːld]	Ertrag	→ to yield
great deal [ˌgreɪt ˈdiːl]	ziemlich viel	= a lot
productivity [ˌprɒdʌkˈtɪvəti]	Produktivität	→ to produce
inroad [ˈɪnrəʊd]	Eingriff	Medical bills have made deep inroads into the patient's savings.
unfed [ʌnˈfed]	ungefüttert; ohne Nahrung	→ to feed
wilderness [ˈwɪldənəs]	Wildnis	→ wild
cultivation [ˌkʌltɪˈveɪʃn]	Landbau	→ to cultivate
perspective [pəˈspektɪv]	Perspektive	Look at the problem from Pete's perspective.
case [keɪs]	Fall; Angelegenheit	The case is closed. No more discussions, please!
strain [streɪn]	Belastung; Anstrengung	→ to strain
shortage [ˈʃɔːtɪdʒ]	Knappheit; Mangel	↔ abundance
starvation [stɑːˈveɪʃn]	Hungern; Verhungern	→ to starve
worsening [ˈwɜːsnɪŋ]	Verschärfung; Verschlechterung	→ to worsen → worse
to **deploy** [dɪˈplɔɪ]	einsetzen	= to use = to introduce
to **smooth** [smuːð]	ebnen	→ smoothie
path [pɑːθ]	Pfad; Weg	I've walked down that path before.
deployment [dɪˈplɔɪmənt]	Verwendung; Einsatz	→ to deploy
bacteria *(pl.)* [bækˈtɪəriə]	Bakterien	→ bacterial
stomach [ˈstʌmək]	Magen	The patient doesn't feel well. He's had a stomachache all day.
resistant [rɪˈzɪstnt]	resistent; widerstandsfähig	→ resistance
foodstuff [ˈfuːdstʌf]	Nahrungsmittel	Bread and milk are two examples of foodstuffs.
to **compete** [kəmˈpiːt]	an einem Wettkampf teilnehmen; konkurrieren	→ competition

	patent ['peɪtnt]	Patent	New products can be protected by patents.
	ecosystem ['iːkəʊˌsɪstəm]	Ökosystem	→ ecological
	make-up ['meɪkʌp]	Zusammensetzung; Aufbau	Please explain the make-up of your company.
	overnight [ˌəʊvə'naɪt]	über Nacht	↔ during the day
	immoral [ɪ'mɒrl]	unmoralisch	↔ ethical
	religious [rɪ'lɪdʒəs]	religiös	→ religion
	kosher ['kəʊʃə]	koscher	quality of and way of preparing food according to Jewish religious laws
	bee [biː]	Biene	Bees make honey.
	butterfly ['bʌtəflaɪ]	Schmetterling	Butterflies are colourful insects.
	allergic to [ə'lɜːdʒɪk tə]	allergisch auf	→ allergy
	substance ['sʌbstns]	Substanz	→ substantial
F	**sheep** [ʃiːp]	Schaf; Schafe	The plural form of 'sheep' is also 'sheep'.
	advance [ɑd'vɑːns]	Fortschritt; Vorstoß	→ to advance

Unit 8 The service industry

A1	**agriculture** ['ægrɪkʌltʃə]	Landwirtschaft	→ agricultural
A2	**tourism** ['tʊərɪzm]	Tourismus	Tourism is big business in Spain.
	ferry ['feri]	Fähre	→ ferry harbour
	Continent ['kɒntɪnənt]	europäisches Festland	For many Britons the Continent seems far away.
	boom [buːm]	wirtschaftlicher Aufschwung	↔ downturn
	tour guide ['tʊə ˌgaɪd]	Reiseführer/in	= travel guide
	training on the job [ˌtreɪnɪŋ ɒn ðə 'dʒɒb]	Ausbildung am Arbeitsplatz	The company gives training on the job to new employees.
	temporary ['temprəri]	vorübergehend; befristet	We are staying in temporary accommodation.
	to deal with ['diːl wɪð]	umgehen mit	Receptionists have to deal with all kinds of complaints in their job.
	people skills *(pl.)* ['piːpl ˌskɪlz]	soziale Kompetenz	= interpersonal skills
	communicative [kə'mjuːnɪkətɪv]	kommunikativ	→ to communicate
	operator ['ɒpreɪtə]	Betreiber; Veranstalter	→ to operate
	passion [ˌpæʃn]	Leidenschaft	→ passionate
	to work one's way up [ˌwɜːk wʌnz weɪ 'ʌp]	sich hocharbeiten	Nora worked her way up from cashier to manager.
	to boom [buːm]	boomen; florieren	The economy has boomed for five years.
	dedicated ['dedɪkeɪtɪd]	engagiert	This service would not exist if were not for the dedicated volunteers.
	orientation [ˌɔːrien'teɪʃn]	Orientierung	→ to orientate oneself
	Far East [ˌfɑːr 'iːst]	Fernost	Indonesia is the best place to travel to in the Far East.
	Central America [ˌsentrl ə'merɪkə]	Mittelamerika	Costa Rica is a country in Central America.
B1	**square** [skweə]	Platz	Let's meet in the square in front of the church.
	opera ['ɒprə]	Oper	→ opera singer
	temple ['templ]	Tempel	Millions of tourists visit Thailand's temples every year.
	France [frɑːns]	Frankreich	→ French
	Russia ['rʌʃə]	Russland	→ Russian
	Statue of Liberty [ˌstætʃuː əv 'lɪbəti]	Freiheitsstatue	The Statue of Liberty has greeted millions of immigrants to the US.

Vocabulary | Unit vocabulary

	Eiffel Tower [ˌaɪfl ˈtaʊə]	Eiffelturm	a popular sight in Paris
	Moscow [ˈmɒskəʊ]	Moskau	the capital city of Russia
B2	**for hire** [fə ˈhaɪə]	zu mieten; zu vermieten	There were no cars for hire at the airport so we took a taxi.
	litter [ˈlɪtə]	Abfall	→ to litter
	towel [taʊəl]	Handtuch	Can you give me a towel, please? My hands are wet.
B3	**imagination** [ɪˌmædʒɪˈneɪʃn]	Phantasie; Vorstellungskraft	→ to imagine
	Majorca [məˈjɔːkə]	Mallorca	a Spanish island that is popular with tourists
	lottery [ˈlɒtri]	Lotto; Lotterie	Grandad won one million euros in the lottery.
B4	**honeymoon** [ˈhʌnimuːn]	Hochzeitsreise	a trip taken by a newly married couple
	Ireland [ˈaɪələnd]	Irland	→ Irish
	otherwise [ˈʌðəwaɪz]	sonst	Hurry up, otherwise we'll be late.
	trendy [ˈtrendi]	modisch; schick	= fashionable = up-to-date
	jealous [ˈdʒeləs]	eifersüchtig	→ jealousy
	never mind [ˌnevə ˈmaɪnd]	schon gut	= all right
C	**World War II** [ˌwɜːldwɔː ˈtuː]	Zweiter Weltkrieg	= Second World War
	to **explode in size** [ɪkˌspləʊd ɪn ˈsaɪz]	explosionsartig wachsen	→ explosion
	remote [rɪˈməʊt]	abgelegen; unnahbar	The doctor had trouble reaching the sick man who lived in a very remote area.
	attraction [əˈtrækʃn]	Attraktion	→ to attract
	revenue [ˈrevnjuː]	Einnahmen; Umsatz	Government revenues rose by 2% last year because of the higher rate of tax.
	to **amount to** [əˈmaʊnt tə]	sich belaufen auf	Ben's debts amount to 10,000 euros.
	drinking water [ˈdrɪŋkɪŋ ˌwɔːtə]	Trinkwasser	water that is clean enough to drink
	coastal [ˈkəʊstl]	Küsten-	→ coast
	litre [ˈliːtə]	Liter	You should drink two litres of water every day.
	shower [ʃaʊə]	Dusche	Did you have a bath or a shower this morning?
	golf course [ˈgɒlf ˌkɔːs]	Golfplatz	→ golfer
	intensive [ɪnˈtensɪv]	intensiv	↔ extensive
	reserve [rɪˈzɜːv]	Rücklage; Reserve	s.th. you store to use later
	to **contaminate** [kənˈtæmɪneɪt]	verunreinigen	→ contamination
	well [wel]	Brunnen	Don't drink that water! The well is contaminated.
	farmland [ˈfɑːmlænd]	Ackerland	area where crops are grown
	transatlantic [ˌtrænzətˈlæntɪk]	transatlantisch	Transatlantic relations have improved between Europe and the US.
	return flight [rɪˌtɜːn ˈflaɪt]	Hin- und Rückflug	We booked a return flight to London.
	to **hop onto** [ˌhɒp ˈɒntə]	einsteigen in; aufspringen	The schoolchildren hopped onto the bus.
	long-distance [ˌlɒŋˈdɪstns]	Langstrecke	Kurt is a long-distance runner. He runs one or two marathons every year.
	Caribbean [ˌkærɪˈbiːən]	Karibik	Jamaica is a Caribbean island.
	global warming [ˌgləʊbl ˈwɔːmɪŋ]	Erderwärmung	Global warming is already having a negative influence on our environment.
	ironically [aɪˈrɒnɪkli]	ironischerweise	→ irony
	ghetto [ˈgetəʊ]	Ghetto	part of a city in which a group of people lives in isolation
	respect [rɪˈspekt]	Respekt	→ respectful
	thoughtfully [ˈθɔːtfəli]	mit Bedacht; rücksichtsvoll	→ to think → thought

	far-away [ˌfɑːrəˈweɪ]	weit entfernt	↔ close by ↔ nearby
	to **rephrase** [riˈfreɪz]	umformulieren	That wasn't polite! Please rephrase your request.
D1	**self-employed** [ˌselfɪmˈplɔɪd]	selbstständig	↔ employed
	salary [ˈsælri]	Lohn; Gehalt	John asked his employer for an increase in salary.
	excellent [ˈekslnt]	exzellent; hervorragend	= outstanding
	recognized [ˈrekəɡnaɪzd]	anerkannt	→ recognition
	sporty [ˈspɔːti]	sportlich	→ sportsman → sportswoman
	licence [ˈlaɪsns]	Lizenz	→ licence holder
	weekly [ˈwiːkli]	wöchentlich	once a week
	session [ˈseʃn]	Einheit; Sitzung	The trainer charges customers 10 pounds per session.
	process [ˈprəʊses]	Prozess; Vorgang; Verfahren	→ to process
	to **coach** [kəʊtʃ]	trainieren	→ coach
	athletic [æθˈletɪk]	Sport-	→ athlete
	rehabilitation [ˌriːhəˌbɪlɪˈteɪʃn]	Rehabilitation	→ to rehabilitate
	heart attack [ˈhɑːt əˌtæk]	Herzinfarkt	The old man died of a heart attack.
D2	to **recommend** [ˌrekəˈmend]	empfehlen	→ recommendation
	schedule [ˈʃedjuːl]	Zeitplan; Terminplan	→ to schedule
	emotion [ɪˈməʊʃn]	Gefühl	→ emotional
D3	**in the open air** [ɪn ðiˌəʊpn ˈeə]	draußen; im Freien	= outdoors
	middle-aged [ˌmɪdlˈeɪdʒd]	mittleren Alters	being between youth and old age
	elderly [ˈeldəli]	älter	These seats are reserved for elderly people.
	workout [ˈwɜːkaʊt]	Training	The sportsman follows a daily workout routine.
	crash diet [ˌkræʃ ˈdaɪət]	Gewaltkur	↔ balanced diet
	to **fizzle out** [ˌfɪzl ˈaʊt]	im Sande verlaufen	The trainee started out highly motivated but his enthusiasm fizzled out.
	down the line [ˌdaʊn ðə ˈlaɪn]	irgendwann; später	= later
	sedentary [ˈsedntri]	sitzend	Most of my friends have sedentary jobs in offices.
	motivated [ˈməʊtɪveɪtɪd]	motiviert	→ motivation
	'cos [kəz]	weil	short for: because
	to **reveal** [rɪˈviːl]	enthüllen; aufzeigen	= to show
	survey [ˈsɜːveɪ]	befragen	asked about a specific topic
	resolution [ˌrezəˈluːʃn]	Vorsatz	= decision
	heath [hiːθ]	Heideland	area of land where not much can grow
	sufficient [səˈfɪʃnt]	genug; genügend; ausreichend	My grades are sufficient to get into college.
	to **seize up** [ˌsiːz ˈʌp]	einrosten	Get up and move or you'll seize up!
	fad [fæd]	Modeerscheinung; Laune	Don't worry, it's just a fad. It'll pass.
	approach [əˈprəʊtʃ]	Herangehensweise; Ansatz	→ to approach
E	**tip** [tɪp]	Trinkgeld	→ to tip
	harsh [hɑːʃ]	hart; rau	= severe
	inequality [ˌɪnɪˈkwɒləti]	Ungleichheit; Unterschied	→ unequal
	shocking [ˈʃɒkɪŋ]	entsetzlich; schrecklich; schockierend	→ to shock
	mood [muːd]	Stimmung	→ moody
	colleague [ˈkɒliːɡ]	Kollege; Kollegin	The colleagues at work get along very well.
	superior [suːˈpɪəriə]	Vorgesetzte/r	↔ subordinate
	establishment [ɪˈstæblɪʃmənt]	Unternehmen; Betrieb	→ to establish

Vocabulary | Unit vocabulary

	throughout [θruːˈaʊt]	im ganzen; durchwegs	Sales went up throughout the year.
	grocery [ˈɡrəʊsri]	Lebensmittel-	We buy food in the grocery store around the corner.
	hardship [ˈhɑːdʃɪp]	Not; Entbehrung	A lot of people suffered hardship during the war.
	panel [ˈpænl]	Forum; Ausschuss	→ panel discussion
	obstacle [ˈɒbstəkl]	Hindernis	The company's main obstacle to success is the tough competition in the market.
	inattentive [ˌɪnəˈtentɪv]	unaufmerksam	↔ attentive
	federal [ˈfedrl]	Bundes-	FBI is short for Federal Bureau of Investigation.
	legislation [ˌledʒɪˈsleɪʃn]	Gesetze; Gesetzgebung	→ legal
	to eliminate [ɪˈlɪmɪneɪt]	beseitigen; ausschließen	→ elimination
	sub-wage [ˌsʌbˈweɪdʒɪz]	Niedriglohn	pay that is below the legal minimum wage
	pay stub [ˈpeɪ ˌstʌb]	Gehaltszettel	You can take the pay stub off of your pay check and keep it as a record.
	paycheck [ˈpeɪtʃek]	Gehaltszettel; Gehaltsabrechnung	pay cheque (BE)
	to claim s.th. as income [kleɪm əzˈɪnkʌm]	als Einkommen angeben; versteuern	Jane had to claim the money she got from a Saturday job as income.
	insecurity [ˌɪnsɪˈkjʊərəti]	Unsicherheit	→ insecure
	to interview [ˈɪntəvjuː]	ein Vorstellungsgespräch haben	to do an interview
	food stamp [ˈfuːd ˌstæmp]	Lebensmittelmarke	A lot of poor people rely on food stamps.
	authority [ɔːˈθɒrəti]	Autorität; Behörde	→ authoritarian
	setting [ˈsetɪŋ]	Rahmen	The garden is a nice setting for the party.
	brunch [brʌnʃ]	Brunch	Come over for brunch on Sunday at about 11 a.m.
	server (AE) [ˈsɜːvə]	Bedienung; Kellner/in	→ to serve
	to reverse [rɪˈvɜːs]	umkehren	to be the opposite of s.th.
	fierce [fɪəs]	stark; heftig	= strong = intense
F	**output** [ˈaʊtpʊt]	Leistung; Ausstoß	The factory's output increased by 5 per cent.
	overweight [ˌəʊvəˈweɪt]	übergewichtig	These days many people eat too much and are overweight.

Unit C Cross-cultural communication at work: Working in London

A	**to cover for s.o.** [ˈkʌvə fə]	für jemanden einspringen	You can take a break. I'll cover for you.
	fax machine [ˈfæks məʃiːn]	Faxgerät	In the digital age fax machines are a thing of the past.
	straight ahead [ˌstreɪt əˈhed]	geradeaus	Walk straight ahead and the station is about 400 metres away.
	corridor [ˈkɒrɪdɔː]	Gang	= hallway
	to pop in [ˌpɒpˈɪn]	vorbeischauen	We'll pop in to see you while we're in the area.
	executive suite [ɪɡˌzekjətɪv ˈswiːt]	Luxussuite; hier: Chefetage	place where managers work and meet business partners
	pan [pæn]	Pfanne	You use a pan to fry eggs.
	millennium [mɪˈleniəm]	Millenium; Jahrtausend	→ millennial
C	**reservation** [ˌrezəˈveɪʃn]	Reservierung	= booking
	twin room [ˈtwɪn ˌruːm]	Zweibettzimmer	a hotel room with two separate beds
	family name [ˈfæmli ˌneɪm]	Familienname	Jenny's family name is Evans.
	double room [ˈdʌbl ˌruːm]	Doppelzimmer	A double room has only one bed while a twin room has two.

Role cards > Grammar Files > Skills Files > **Vocabulary**

	given name [ˈgɪvn ˌneɪm]	Vorname	= first name
	absolutely [ˌæbsəˈluːtli]	absolut	You're absolutely right!
	valid [ˈvælɪd]	gültig	→ validity
D	**misunderstanding** [ˌmɪsʌndəˈstændɪŋ]	Missverständnis	The manager appeared unfriendly because she didn't shake his hand. What a terrible misunderstanding!
	thumb [θʌm]	Daumen	Your test result is excellent. Two thumbs up!
	forefinger [ˈfɔːfɪŋɡə]	Zeigefinger	finger next to your thumb
	circle [sɜːkl]	Kreis	A circle is perfectly round.
	appreciation [əˌpriːʃiˈeɪʃn]	Wertschätzung; Würdigung	Show your appreciation with a bouquet of flowers.
	Saudi Arabia [ˌsaʊdiəˈreɪbiə]	Saudi-Arabien	→ Saudi Arabian
	Arab [ˈærəb]	arabisch; Araber/in	= Arabian
	Spanish [ˈspænɪʃ]	Spanisch	→ Spaniard → Spain
	Mexico [ˈmeksɪkəʊ]	Mexiko	→ Mexican

Unit 9   Living and working in a globalized world

	globalized [ˈgləʊblaɪzd]	globalisiert	→ global → globalization
A	**migrant** [ˈmaɪgrnt]	Wander-; herumziehend	→ migration
	expat [ˌekˈspæt]	im Ausland lebende Person; Auswanderer/in	short for: expatriate
	to **emigrate** [ˈemɪgreɪt]	auswandern	↔ to immigrate
	Brits [brɪts]	die Briten	= the British
	for short [fə ˈʃɔːt]	abgekürzt	His name is Benjamin but we call him Ben for short.
	to **make a living** [ˌmeɪk ə ˈlɪvɪŋ]	Lebensunterhalt bestreiten; Auskommen haben	I can't make a living from working three days in a café.
	building worker [ˈbɪldɪŋ ˌwɜːkə]	Bauarbeiter/in	= construction worker
	to **migrate** [maɪˈgreɪt]	einwandern; abwandern; auswandern	→ migrant → migration
	majority [məˈdʒɒrəti]	Mehrheit	↔ minority
	Canada [ˈkænədə]	Kanada	Canada's official languages are English and French.
	racism [ˈreɪsɪzm]	Rassismus	→ racist
	Canadian [kəˈneɪdiən]	kanadisch; Kanadier/in	Being born in Canada makes you a Canadian.
	accent [ˈæksnt]	Akzent	He speaks with an Australian accent.
	Paki [ˈpæki]	Pakistaner/in	negative word to describe s.o. from Pakistan
	monkey [ˈmʌŋki]	Affe	Children like to watch the monkeys playing at the zoo.
	race [reɪs]	Rasse; Rennen	Asians and Africans are different races.
	unsafe [ʌnˈseɪf]	unsicher	↔ safe
	prejudice [ˈpredʒədɪs]	Vorurteil	We have to fight racial prejudices.
B	**tutor** [ˈtjuːtə]	Tutor/in	→ tutorial
	to **advise** [ədˈvaɪz]	beraten	→ adviser
	likes and dislikes (pl.) [ˌlaɪks ən ˈdɪslaɪks]	Vorlieben und Abneigungen	A mother knows her son's likes and dislikes.
	cricket [ˈkrɪkɪt]	Kricket	Cricket is a popular game in Britain and India.
	novel [ˈnɒvl]	Roman	→ novelist
	guideline [ˈgaɪdlaɪn]	Richtlinie	At the border control you must follow the guidelines.

Vocabulary | Unit vocabulary

C	sewing [ˈsəʊɪŋ]	Näh-	→ to sew
	garment [ˈgɑːmənt]	Kleidungsstück; Kleidung	Winter garments include gloves and woollen hats.
	exploitation [ˌeksplɔɪˈteɪʃn]	Ausbeutung	→ to exploit
	legal [ˈliːgl]	rechtlich; gesetzlich; juristisch	↔ illegal
	to detail [ˈdiːteɪl]	einzeln aufführen; genau berichten	Please detail your points for the meeting.
	inadequate [ɪˈnædɪkwət]	unzureichend; unzulänglich	↔ adequate
	bullying [ˈbʊliɪŋ]	Mobbing	→ bully → to bully
	retailer [ˈriːteɪlə]	Einzelhändler/in	a company that sells directly to consumers
	day in day out [deɪ ɪn deɪ ˈaʊt]	Tag für Tag	= every day
	to observe [əbˈzɜːv]	beachten; beobachten	= to follow = to respect
	to quit [kwɪt]	kündigen; aufhören	= to resign
	shed [ʃed]	Schuppen	There is a wooden shed at the bottom of the garden.
	South-east Asia [ˌsaʊθiːst ˈeɪʒə]	Südostasien	→ South-east Asian
	Eastern Europe [ˌiːstn ˈjʊərəp]	Osteuropa	→ Eastern European
	to force [fɔːs]	zwingen	Refugees are often forced to leave their home country.
	backyard [bækˈjɑːd]	Hinterhof	Debbie grows flowers in her backyard.
	to violate [ˈvaɪəleɪt]	verstoßen gegen	→ violation → violator
	sought after [ˈsɔːt ɑːftə]	gesucht	wanted by many people but not easy to get
	invisible [ɪnˈvɪzəbl]	unsichtbar	↔ visible
	Romanian [rʊˈmeɪniən]	rumänisch; Rumäne/in	→ Romania
	Hungarian [hʌŋˈgeəriən]	ungarisch; Ungar/in	→ Hungary
	undocumented [ʌnˈdɒkjəmentɪd]	nicht registriert; undokumentiert	= not registered
	Nigerian [naɪˈdʒɪəriən]	Nigerianer/in	→ Nigeria
	Belgium [ˈbeldʒəm]	Belgien	→ Belgian
	unskilled [ʌnˈskɪld]	ungelernt	↔ skilled
	to be supposed to do s.th. [bi səˈpəʊst tə]	tun sollen	= to be expected to do s.th.
	addressee [ˌædresˈiː]	Adressat; Empfänger/in	→ to address
	to refer to [rɪˈfɜː tə]	sich beziehen auf	→ reference
	Bangladesh [ˌbæŋgləˈdeʃ]	Bangladesch	→ Bangladeshi
	Vietnam [ˌvjetˈnæm]	Vietnam	→ Vietnamese
D1	ready-made [ˌrediˈmeɪd]	gebrauchsfertig; von der Stange	= off the shelf
	rush [rʌʃ]	große Eile	→ to rush
	to set up [ˌset ˈʌp]	errichten; einrichten	The company has set up a new branch in Dover.
	unsuitable [ʌnˈsuːtəbl]	ungeeignet	↔ suitable
	to bar [bɑː]	vergittern; versperren	The cat can't climb out of the window. It is barred.
	fire exit [ˈfaɪər eksɪt]	Notausgang	= emergency exit
	workshop [ˈwɜːkʃɒp]	Werkstatt	Sharon repairs electrical goods in a workshop.
	underground [ˌʌndəˈgraʊnd]	unterirdisch	= below ground
	ventilation [ˌventɪˈleɪʃn]	Belüftung	→ to vent → ventilator
	to pay attention [ˌpeɪ əˈtenʃn]	aufmerksam sein	Please pay attention!
	governmental [ˌgʌvnˈmentl]	Regierungs-	→ to govern
	insufficient [ˌɪnsəˈfɪʃnt]	unzureichend	↔ sufficient
	Bangladeshi [ˌbæŋgləˈdeʃi]	bangladeschisch; Bangladescher/in	→ Bangladesh

	shopper [ˈʃɒpə]	Käufer/in	→ to go shopping → to shop
	definitely [ˈdefɪnətli]	auf jeden Fall	= obviously
	to **sort through** [ˌsɔːt ˈθruː]	durchsehen	Sort through your clothes and take out the things you do not need.
	neon sign [ˌniːɒn ˈsaɪn]	Lichtreklame	The neon sign at the hotel was flashing on and off.
D2	**Third World** [ˌθɜːd ˈwɜːld]	Dritte Welt	= developing world
D3	**emerging** [ɪˈmɜːdʒɪŋ]	aufstrebend	= up-and-coming
	frontier [ˈfrʌntɪə]	Grenze; Grenzland	= boundary
	high-tech [ˌhaɪˈtek]	Hightech; Hochtechnologie	The high-tech sector offers attractive jobs to young professionals.
	ancient [ˈeɪnʃnt]	alt; uralt	very old
	amidst [əˈmɪdst]	inmitten	= surrounded by
	chaos [ˈkeɪɒs]	Chaos	→ chaotic
	bold [bəʊld]	kühn; keck	= courageous
	mecca [ˈmekə]	Mekka	Thailand is a tourist mecca.
	showcase [ˈʃəʊkeɪs]	Vorzeigeprojekt; Schaukasten	→ to showcase
	to **lure** [ljʊə]	ködern; anlocken	The TV lured me away from my homework.
	investor [ɪnˈvestə]	Investor/in; Kapitalanleger/in	→ to invest
	on a par [ɒn ə ˈpɑː]	auf einer Stufe; gleichwertig	= comparable
	court [kɔːt]	Feld; Gericht	The employees can use the company tennis court.
	pitching range [ˈpɪtʃɪŋ ˌreɪndʒ]	Übungsbereich beim Golf	an area for practising golf
	Prime Minister [ˌpraɪm ˈmɪnɪstə]	Premierminister	The Prime Ministers of the European countries met in Brussels.
	spa [spɑː]	Heilbad; Heilquelle	Our spa offers excellent swimming and sauna facilities.
	Indian [ˈɪndɪən]	Inder/in	→ India
	to **trade in** [ˌtreɪd ˈɪn]	eintauschen	= to exchange
	overseas [ˌəʊvəˈsiːz]	in Übersee; im Ausland	Lara left her home country to live overseas ten years ago.
	elite [ɪˈliːt]	Elite	= best = first-class
	to **graduate** [ˈɡrædjueɪt]	akademischen Grad erlangen; absolvieren	= to finish one's education = to get a degree
	cubicle [ˈkjuːbɪkl]	an drei Seiten von halbhohen Wänden umgebene Arbeitsnische	Each office worker has a cubicle to work in.
	buck *(AE)* [bʌk]	Dollar	= an American dollar
	adjustment [əˈdʒʌstmənt]	Anpassung	→ to adjust
	thrill [θrɪl]	Nervenkitzel	→ thrilling
	adventure [ədˈventʃə]	Abenteuer	We went on an adventure holiday in South America.
	allure [əˈljʊə]	Reiz; Faszination	= attraction = charm
	to **recruit** [rɪˈkruːt]	anwerben; einstellen	= to engage = to employ
	giant [ˈdʒaɪənt]	Riese; Gigant	→ gigantic
	interviewee [ˌɪntəvjuˈiː]	Befragte/r	→ interviewer
D4	to **cooperate** [kəʊˈɒpreɪt]	kooperieren; zusammenarbeiten	→ cooperation
	satellite [ˈsætlaɪt]	Satellit	You can receive a lot of TV stations via satellite.
	free movement [ˌfriː ˈmuːvmənt]	Freizügigkeit	The EU guarantees free movement within its borders.
	so far [ˌsəʊ ˈfɑː]	bisher; bis jetzt	= up to now
E	**style** [staɪl]	Stil	→ stylish

Vocabulary | Unit vocabulary

unethical [ʌnˈeθɪkl]	skrupellos; unethisch	morally wrong
resurgence [rɪˈsɜːdʒns]	Wiederaufleben	= revival
abuse [əˈbjuːs]	Missbrauch	→ to abuse → abuser
clothing [ˈkləʊðɪŋ]	Kleidung	= garment
co-founder [ˌkəʊˈfaʊndə]	Mitbegründer/in	→ to found
scarf [skɑːf]	Schal	→ scarves *(pl.)*
to **entail** [ɪnˈteɪl]	bedeuten; zur Folge haben	= to result in
superior to [suːˈpɪəriə tə]	besser als	↔ inferior to
distant [ˈdɪstnt]	entfernt; weit entfernt	↔ close by
tentative [ˈtentətɪv]	vorläufig	= not final = provisional
fundamental [ˌfʌndəˈmentl]	grundsätzlich	= basic
concern [kənˈsɜːn]	Frage; Belang; Bedenken	→ concerned
endeavour [ɪnˈdevə]	Anstrengung; Bemühung	= effort
extent [ɪkˈstent]	Umfang; Ausmaß	= degree
turn-around time [ˈtɜːnəraʊnd ˈtaɪm]	Umschlagszeit; Abfertigungszeit	Airports have longer turn-around times due to stricter security.
zero [ˈzɪərəʊ]	Null	We expect temperatures below zero tonight.
security [sɪˈkjʊərəti]	Sicherheit	→ secure
collapse [kəˈlæps]	Zusammenbruch	→ to collapse
spirit [ˈspɪrɪt]	Geist	→ spirited
cuff [kʌf]	Hemdmanschette	part of a shirt nearest to your hand
to **fray** [freɪ]	ausfransen	Look at the bottoms of your jeans, they are all frayed.
sleeve [sliːv]	Ärmel	→ sleeveless
gardening [ˈgɑːdnɪŋ]	das Gärtnern	→ gardener
rag [ræg]	Lumpen; Lappen	Ken used an old rag to clean his bike.
ounce [aʊns]	Unze (Gewichtseinheit)	1 ounce is 28.35 grams.
to **extract** [ɪkˈstrækt]	gewinnen; extrahieren	The company extracts methane gas from waste.
effort [ˈefət]	Anstrengung; Bemühung	→ effortless
tailor [ˈteɪlə]	Schneider/in	→ tailor-made
miller [ˈmɪlə]	Müller/in	→ to mill
fabric [ˈfæbrɪk]	Stoff	The clothing company sells many beautiful fabrics.
monochrome [ˈmɒnəkrəʊm]	einfarbig; monochrom	having only one colour
proof [pruːf]	Beweis; Nachweis	→ to prove
turnover [ˈtɜːnˌəʊvə]	Umsatz; Fluktuation	= sales volume
to **minimise** [ˈmɪnɪmaɪz]	minimieren	↔ to maximise
to **certify** [ˈsɜːtɪfaɪ]	zertifizieren; bescheinigen	→ certificate
supplier [səˈplaɪə]	Lieferant/in; Zulieferer/in	→ to supply
cutter [ˈkʌtə]	Zuschneider/in; Cutter/in	→ to cut
finisher [ˈfɪnɪʃə]	Finisher; Person, die die letzten Arbeitsschritte durchführt	→ to finish
weaving [ˈwiːvɪŋ]	das Weben	→ to weave
quarter [ˈkwɔːtə]	Viertel	3.15 p.m. is a quarter past three in the afternoon.
menswear [ˈmenzweə]	Männerbekleidung	You can find suits and ties in the menswear section.
to **preach** [priːtʃ]	predigen	→ preacher
fantastic [fænˈtæstɪk]	großartig; fantastisch	= great
accessories *(pl.)* [əkˈsesriz]	Accessoires; Zubehör	In the accessories section of a shop you can find bags and belts.

	to **deserve** [dɪˈzɜːv]	verdienen	If you work hard you deserve to succeed.
	criterion [kraɪˈtɪəriən]	Kriterium	→ criteria *(pl.)*
	to **exploit** [ɪkˈsplɔɪt]	ausbeuten; ausnutzen	→ exploitation
	American [əˈmerɪkən]	amerikanisch; Amerikaner/in	→ America
	fault [fɔːlt]	Fehler	→ faulty
	comment [ˈkɒment]	Kommentar	→ to comment
	point of view [ˌpɔɪnt_əv ˈvjuː]	Standpunkt; Ansicht	= opinion = view
F	to **oppress** [əˈpres]	unterdrücken	→ oppression
	to **take charge** [ˌteɪk ˈtʃɑːdʒ]	selbst in die Hand nehmen	Take charge of your life and follow your dreams.
	to **flee** [fliː]	fliehen	= to get away = to escape
	risky [ˈrɪski]	riskant	= dangerous = unsafe
	studies *(pl.)* [ˈstʌdiz]	Studium	→ student
	champagne [ʃæmˈpeɪn]	Champagner	The hotel offers champagne and caviar for breakfast.
	wealthy [ˈwelθi]	reich	→ wealth
	developed country [dɪˌveləpt ˈkʌntriz]	Industrieland	European countries are so-called developed countries.
	fraction [ˈfrækʃn]	Bruchteil	→ to fracture
	exchange [ɪksˈtʃeɪndʒ]	Austausch	The two countries agreed on an exchange of prisoners.
	industrialized [ɪnˈdʌstriəlaɪzd]	industrialisiert	Some industrialized countries struggle with high rates of unemployment.
	to **replace** [rɪˈpleɪs]	ersetzen	→ replacement
	landfill site [ˈlænfɪl ˌsaɪt]	Mülldeponie	= dump
	council [ˈkaʊnsl]	Rat; Gemeinderat	The city council introduced higher parking fees in the city centre.
	textiles *(pl.)* [ˈtekstaɪlz]	Textilien	anything made of fabric
	straight [streɪt]	geradewegs; direkt	→ straightforward
	to **total** [ˈtəʊtl]	sich summieren; sich belaufen auf	Our town has debts totalling over three million pounds.
	equivalent [ɪˈkwɪvlənt]	Pendant; Äquivalent	→ to equate to
	handful [ˈhænfʊl]	Handvoll	The little boy picked up a handful of sand.
	to **dub** [dʌb]	bezeichnen als; synchronisieren	We dubbed the horse "Flash" because it was so fast.
	to **discard** [dɪˈskɑːd]	abladen	= to dump = to dispose of
	high street [ˈhaɪ ˌstriːt]	Einkaufsstraße; Haupteinkaufsstraße	Many big stores are located on the high street in our town.
	hospice [ˈhɒspɪs]	Hospiz; Sterbeklinik	Working as a hospice nurse can be rewarding but also challenging.
	to **mend** [mend]	flicken; reparieren	I took my mobile to a shop that mends broken phones.
	artisan [ˌɑːtɪˈzæn]	Kunsthandwerker/in	a skilled worker who usually makes s.th. by hand
	transformation [ˌtrænsfəˈmeɪʃn]	Umwandlung	→ to transform
	reuse [ˌriːˈjuːs]	Wiederverwendung	→ to reuse
	mattress [ˈmætrəs]	Matratze	The mattress on the bed was very hard.
	stuffing [ˈstʌfɪŋ]	Füllmaterial	→ to stuff
	insulation [ˌɪnsjəˈleɪʃn]	Wärmedämmung; Isolierung	→ to insulate

Unit 10 International organizations and politics

	to **research** [rɪˈsɜːtʃ]	recherchieren; forschen	= to look into
	civil rights [ˌsɪvl ˈraɪts]	Bürgerrechte	→ civil rights activist
	political [pəˈlɪtɪkl]	politisch	→ politician → politics
	participation [pɑːˌtɪsɪˈpeɪʃn]	Teilnahme	→ to participate
A	**need** [niːd]	Bedürfnis	→ needy
	basic [ˈbeɪsɪk]	grundlegend; Grund-	Most young English people have a basic knowledge of French.
	human being [ˌhjuːmən ˈbiːɪŋ]	Mensch; menschliches Wesen	→ humankind
	shelter [ˈʃeltə]	Behausung; Obdach	→ to shelter
	nutritious [njuːˈtrɪʃəs]	nahrhaft	→ nutrition
	universal [ˌjuːnɪˈvɜːsl]	allgemein; allgemeingültig; weltweit	→ universe
	declaration [ˌdekləˈreɪʃn]	Erklärung; Deklaration	→ to declare
	to **define** [dɪˈfaɪn]	definieren	→ definition
	to **inherit** [ɪnˈherɪt]	erben	to receive s.th. from s.o. when that person dies
	to **loan** [ləʊn]	leihen; verleihen	→ loan → to lend
	to **deny** [dɪˈnaɪ]	verweigern; leugnen	→ denial
	dignity [ˈdɪgnəti]	Würde	→ dignified
	entitled [ɪnˈtaɪtld]	berechtigt	The employer is entitled to ask for references.
	document [ˈdɒkjəmənt]	Dokument	→ to document
	to **divide** [dɪˈvaɪd]	teilen	The teacher divided the class into two groups.
	classic [ˈklæsɪk]	klassisch	This accident is a classic example of the dangers of drinking and driving.
	freedom of speech [ˌfriːdəm əv ˈspiːtʃ]	Redefreiheit	In the USA they enjoy freedom of speech.
	equality [ɪˈkwɒləti]	Gleichheit	→ equal
	solidarity [ˌsɒlɪˈdærəti]	Solidarität; Zusammenhalt	when members of a group agree with one another
	to **apply to** [əˈplaɪ tə]	anwenden auf; gelten für; betreffen	This law applies to everyone living in this country.
	collective [kəˈlektɪv]	gemeinsam; gemeinschaftlich	→ collection
	self-determination [ˌselfdɪˌtɜːmɪˈneɪʃn]	Selbstbestimmung	→ self-determined
	existence [ɪgˈzɪstns]	Vorhandensein; Existenz	→ to exist
	to **discriminate against** [dɪˈskrɪmɪneɪt əˌgenst]	diskriminieren	→ discrimination
	to **torture** [ˈtɔːtʃə]	foltern	→ torturer
	standing [ˈstændɪŋ]	Bedeutung; Ansehen	= prestige
	binding [ˈbaɪndɪŋ]	verbindlich; rechtsverbindlich	= obligatory
	violation [ˌvaɪəˈleɪʃn]	Verletzung; Verstoß	→ to violate
	to **monitor** [ˈmɒnɪtə]	überwachen; kontrollieren	= to supervise = to check
	headquarters *(pl.)* [ˌhedˈkwɔːtəz]	Zentrale; Stammsitz	The bank has its headquarters in London.
	humanitarian [hjuːˌmænɪˈteəriən]	humanitär	→ human
	aid [eɪd]	Hilfe; Unterstützung	→ first aid
B1	to **integrate** [ˈɪntɪgreɪt]	integrieren; sich integrieren	→ integration
	curriculum [kəˈrɪkjələm]	Lehrplan	→ curriculum vitae

	to **put into practice** [ˌpʊt ˌɪntə ˈpræktɪs]	in die Tat umsetzen; realisieren	Now that you have learned how to write a letter of application you should put it into practice.
	democratic [ˌdeməˈkrætɪk]	demokratisch	→ democracy
	openness [ˈəʊpnnəs]	Offenheit; Freimütigkeit	Sarah's openness helps me to understand her better.
	tolerance [ˈtɒlrns]	Toleranz	→ to tolerate
B3	**series** [ˈsɪəriːz]	Serie; Reihe	Jake loves watching soap series on TV.
	listener [ˈlɪsnə]	Zuhörer/in	→ to listen
	to **succeed in** [səkˈsiːd ɪn]	gelingen; erfolgreich sein	→ successful
C	**surveillance** [sɜːˈveɪləns]	Überwachung	= observation
	to **conflict with** [kənˈflɪkt wɪð]	im Widerspruch stehen zu	→ conflict
	privacy [ˈpraɪvəsi]	Privatsphäre	I need some privacy! Please close the door.
	threat [θret]	Bedrohung; Drohung	→ to threaten
	to **enshrine** [ɪnˈʃraɪn]	bewahren	→ shrine
	parliamentary [ˌpɑːləˈmentri]	parlamentarisch	→ parliament
	assembly [əˈsembli]	Versammlung	→ to assemble
	to **encompass** [ɪnˈkʌmpəs]	umfassen	= to comprise
	suspicion [səˈspɪʃn]	Verdacht; Argwohn	→ suspicious
	wrongdoing [ˈrɒŋduːɪŋ]	Fehlverhalten	= misconduct
	deliberately [dɪˈlɪbrətli]	vorsätzlich; absichtlich	= on purpose
	systematical [ˌsɪstəˈmætɪkl]	systematisch	→ system
	cyber-terrorist [ˈsaɪbəˌterərɪst]	Cyber-	→ cyberbullying
	encryption [ɪnˈkrɪpʃn]	Verschlüsselung	→ to encrypt
	to **acknowledge** [əkˈnɒlɪdʒ]	bestätigen; anerkennen	→ acknowledgement
	targeted [ˈtɑːgɪtɪd]	gezielt	→ to target
	suspected [səˈspektɪd]	verdächtigt	→ suspect → to suspect
	organised [ˈɔːgnaɪzd]	organisiert	→ organisation
	review [rɪˈvjuː]	Bericht; Besprechung	→ to review
	to **carry out** [ˌkæri ˈaʊt]	ausführen	The renovation is carried out by skilled craftsmen.
	evidence [ˈevɪdns]	Beweis; Nachweis	→ evident
	controversial [ˌkɒntrəˈvɜːʃl]	umstritten	→ controversy
	emotional [ɪˈməʊʃnl]	emotional; gefühlsbetont	→ emotion
D1	**rebel** [ˈrebl]	Rebell	→ rebellious → to rebel
	baron [ˈbærn]	Baron	→ baroness
	to **arrest** [əˈrest]	verhaften	The police arrested the criminal.
	to **imprison** [ɪmˈprɪzn]	inhaftieren; einsperren	→ imprisonment
	except [ɪkˈsept]	außer	I have done all of the exercises except for the last one.
	judgement [ˈdʒʌdʒmənt]	Urteil	→ judge → to judge
	equal [ˈiːkwəl]	Gleichgestellte/r	→ equality
	to **delay** [dɪˈleɪ]	verzögern; verschieben	→ delay
	justice [ˈdʒʌstɪs]	Gerechtigkeit	↔ injustice
	democracy [dɪˈmɒkrəsi]	Demokratie	→ democratic
	to **examine** [ɪgˈzæmɪn]	untersuchen	→ examination
	United Kingdom [juːˌnaɪtɪd ˈkɪŋdəm]	Vereinigtes Königreich	Great Britain and Northern Ireland
	publication [ˌpʌblɪˈkeɪʃn]	Veröffentlichung	→ to publish
	Middle Ages [ˌmɪdl ˈeɪdʒɪz]	Mittelalter	→ medieval
	to **shape** [ʃeɪp]	formen; prägen	→ shape

Vocabulary | Unit vocabulary

	freedom of expression [ˌfriːdəm əv ɪkˈspreʃn]	Recht auf freie Meinungsäußerung	= freedom of speech
	trial [traɪəl]	Verhandlung; Prozess	The trial of the accused murderer went on for months.
	to **assign** [əˈsaɪn]	zuordnen	→ assignment
	constitutional law [ˌkɒnstɪtjuːʃnl ˈlɔː]	Staatsrecht	→ constitution
	to **specify** [ˈspesɪfaɪ]	genau bezeichnen	→ specification
	to **date back to** [ˌdeɪt ˈbæk tə]	zurückreichen	This tool dates back to the Middle Ages.
	to **take for granted** [ˌteɪk fə ˈɡrɑːntɪd]	als selbstverständlich betrachten	Don't take peace for granted. A war can easily break out.
	property [ˈprɒpəti]	Eigentum	After you buy a house it is your property.
	motto [ˈmɒtəʊ]	Motto; Leitspruch	a principle that guides a person
	brotherhood [ˈbrʌðəhʊd]	Brüderlichkeit	→ brotherly
	to **lower** [ˈləʊə]	senken	Lowering taxes is a good way to get votes.
D2	**chancellor** [ˈtʃɑːnslə]	Kanzler/in	head of the German government
	president [ˈprezɪdnt]	Präsident/in	→ to preside
	to **appoint** [əˈpɔɪnt]	ernennen; bestellen	→ appointment
	cabinet [ˈkæbɪnət]	Kabinett; Schränkchen	→ cabinet minister
	constituency [kənˈstɪtjuənsi]	Wahlbezirk	→ to constitute
	to **propose** [prəˈpəʊz]	vorschlagen	→ proposal
D3	to **engage** [ɪnˈɡeɪdʒ]	sich engagieren	→ engagement
	conduct [ˈkɒndʌkt]	Verhalten; Benehmen	→ to conduct
	theatrical [θiˈætrɪkl]	theatralisch	→ theatre
	out of touch [ˌaʊt əv ˈtʌtʃ]	lebensfremd	My sister has no idea of fashion. She is out of touch with modern trends.
	slightly [ˈslaɪtli]	geringfügig; etwas	= a little
	memory [ˈmemri]	Erinnerung	→ memorable
	housing [ˈhaʊzɪŋ]	Wohnbau; Wohnungen	→ welfare housing
	to **intend** [ɪnˈtend]	beabsichtigen	→ intention
	chronic [ˈkrɒnɪk]	chronisch	Coleen suffers from chronic bronchitis.
	extortionate [ɪkˈstɔːʃnət]	ungeheuer; unverschämt; Wucher-	= excessive = exorbitant
	to **congratulate** [kənˈɡrætʃʊleɪt]	gratulieren	→ congratulations
	honourable [ˈɒnrəbl]	ehrenwert	→ honour → to honour
	resounding [rɪˈzaʊndɪŋ]	rauschend; durchschlagend	= sweeping
	victory [ˈvɪktri]	Sieg	→ victorious
	bench [benʃ]	Bank; Sitzbank	→ backbencher
	disagreement [ˌdɪsəˈɡriːmənt]	Meinungsverschiedenheit; Unstimmigkeit	→ to disagree
	delighted [dɪˈlaɪtɪd]	entzückt; begeistert	→ delight → to delight
	council house [ˌkaʊnsl ˈhaʊs]	Sozialwohnung	= social housing
	previous [ˈpriːviəs]	früher; vorhergehend	Glenn worked as a mechanic in his previous job.
	innovative [ˈɪnəveɪtɪv]	innovativ; erfinderisch	→ innovation
	aspiration [ˌæspɪˈreɪʃn]	Streben; Sehnsucht	→ to aspire
	to **criticize** [ˈkrɪtɪsaɪz]	kritisieren	→ criticism → to criticize
D4	**debate** [dɪˈbeɪt]	Debatte	→ to debate
	convincing [kənˈvɪnsɪŋ]	überzeugend	→ conviction → to convince
	proposer [prəˈpəʊzə]	Antragsteller/in	→ to propose
	opponent [əˈpəʊnənt]	Gegner/in	→ to oppose
	motion [ˈməʊʃn]	Antrag	The motion went through. There were no opponents.

Role cards > Grammar Files > Skills Files > **Vocabulary**

E	**refugee** [ˌrefjʊˈdʒiː]	Flüchtling	a person who flees to a foreign country
	fortress [ˈfɔːtrəs]	Festung	→ to fortify
	criticism [ˈkrɪtɪsɪzm]	Kritik	→ critic
	to **accuse s.o. of s.th.** [əˈkjuːz ˌsʌmbədi əv ˌsʌmθɪŋ]	jdn. wegen etw. beschuldigen	→ accusation
	to **fuel** [ˈfjuːəl]	anheizen	→ fuel
	crisis [ˈkraɪsɪs]	Krise	→ crisis management
	drowning [ˈdraʊnɪŋ]	das Ertrinken	→ to drown
	Mediterranean [ˌmedɪtrˈeɪniən]	Mittelmeer	Italy has many miles of Mediterranean shore.
	coalition [ˌkəʊəˈlɪʃn]	Koalition	→ to form a coalition
	to **resource** [rɪˈzɔːs]	personell ausstatten	→ resource
	search [sɜːtʃ]	Suche	→ to search
	rescue [ˈreskjuː]	Rettung	→ to rescue
	mission [ˈmɪʃn]	Mission	→ missionary
	to **re-establish** [ˌriːɪˈstæblɪʃ]	wieder einführen; wiederherstellen	Some groups want to re-establish the Deutsche Mark.
	to **condemn** [kənˈdem]	verurteilen	→ condemnation
	failure [ˈfeɪljə]	Versagen; Scheitern	→ to fail
	asylum [əˈsaɪləm]	Asyl	→ asylum seeker
	zone [zəʊn]	Zone; Gebiet	Only a few correspondents report from war zones.
	Syria [ˈsɪriə]	Syrien	→ Syrian
	to **declare** [dɪˈkleə]	erklären; verkünden	→ declaration
	immigration [ˌɪmɪˈgreɪʃn]	Einwanderung	→ immigrant
	solution [səˈluːʃn]	Lösung	→ to solve
	to **drown** [draʊn]	ertrinken	Don't swim too far. You might drown.
	refuge [ˈrefjuːdʒ]	Schutz; Zuflucht	= shelter
	smuggler [ˈsmʌglə]	Schmuggler	→ to smuggle
	blame [bleɪm]	Schuld; Verschulden	→ to blame
	to **capsize** [kæpˈsaɪz]	kentern	The boat capsized and sank.
	fishing [ˈfɪʃɪŋ]	das Fischen	→ to fish
	appalling [əˈpɔːlɪŋ]	entsetzlich; mies	= horrid
	human trafficker [ˌhjuːmən ˈtræfɪkə]	Schlepper	→ human trafficking
	survivor [səˈvaɪvə]	Überlebende/r	→ to survive
	to **claim** [kleɪm]	behaupten; beanspruchen	→ claimant
	on board [ˌɒn ˈbɔːd]	an Bord	↔ off board
	vessel [ˈvesl]	Schiff	Only oceangoing vessels should make this trip.
	Italian [ɪˈtæliən]	italienisch; Italiener/in	→ Italy
	investigator [ɪnˈvestɪgeɪtə]	Ermittler/in	→ to investigate
	locked inside [ˌlɒkt ɪnˈsaɪd]	eingeschlossen; eingesperrt	My keys are locked inside the car.
	hull [hʌl]	Schiffsrumpf; Schiffskörper	The tanker was fully laden so its hull was low in the water.
	distress [dɪˈstres]	Notlage; Bedrängnis	= emergency
	to **emerge** [ɪˈmɜːdʒ]	bekannt werden; sich abzeichnen	= to become apparent
	military [ˈmɪlɪtri]	militärisch; Militär	Soldiers must get used to many military routines.
	premier [ˈpremɪə]	Premierminister/in	= prime minister
	to **sink** [sɪŋk]	versenken; versinken	The boat was hit by a monster wave and sank.
	Libyan [ˈlɪbiən]	libysch; Libyer/in	→ Libya

Vocabulary | Unit vocabulary

foreign secretary [ˌfɒrən ˈsekrətri]	Außenminister/in	→ foreign ministry
home secretary [ˌhəʊm ˈsekrətri]	Innenminister/in	→ interior ministry
measure [ˈmeʒə]	Maßnahme	= step
patrol [pəˈtrəʊl]	Patrouille; Streife	→ patrol boat
to **capture** [ˈkæptʃə]	fangen; einfangen; abfangen	to gain control of
Sicilian [sɪˈsɪliən]	sizilianisch; Sizilianer/in	→ Sicily
condemnation [ˌkɒndemˈneɪʃn]	Verurteilung	→ to condemn
tide [taɪd]	Strom; Ebbe und Flut	upward and downward movement of the level of the ocean
shore [ʃɔː]	Ufer; Küste	→ shoreline
Greece [griːs]	Griechenland	→ Greek
death toll [ˈdeθ ˌtəʊl]	Zahl der Todesopfer	The death toll after the earthquake was enormous.
to **fund** [fʌnd]	finanzieren	= to finance
comprehensive [ˌkɒmprɪˈhensɪv]	umfassend	The comprehensive report included all of the details of the accident.
callous [ˈkæləs]	gefühllos; kaltschnäuzig	feeling no emotion
bloc [blɒk]	Block	a group of countries
courageous [kəˈreɪdʒəs]	mutig	→ courage
vast [vɑːst]	riesig; enorm	= huge
cemetery [ˈsemətri]	Friedhof	Paris has many famous cemeteries.
to **pander to** [ˈpændə tə]	begünstigen	= to promote
xenophobic [ˌzenəˈfəʊbɪk]	fremdenfeindlich	→ xenophobia
populist [ˈpɒpjəlɪst]	populistisch; Volks-; Populist/in	Some politicians argue with populist theories.
to **poison** [ˈpɔɪzn]	vergiften	→ poisonous
signatory [ˈsɪgnətri]	Unterzeichner/in	→ to sign
gloomy [ˈgluːmi]	düster; bedrückend	→ gloom
backdrop [ˈbækdrɒp]	Hintergrund; Kulisse	The setting sun makes a nice backdrop for a photo.
tragedy [ˈtrædʒədi]	Tragödie	→ tragic
to **access** [ˈækses]	erreichen	= to enter
to **take into account** [teɪk ˌɪntʊ əˈkaʊnt]	berücksichtigen	= to consider
F to **attempt** [əˈtemt]	versuchen; sich bemühen	→ attempt
classification [ˌklæsɪfɪˈkeɪʃn]	Klassifizierung; Einstufung	→ to classify
untouchable [ʌnˈtʌtʃəbl]	unantastbar	which should not be affected or changed
dignified [ˈdɪgnɪfaɪd]	würdevoll; würdig	→ dignity
discrimination [dɪˌskrɪmɪˈneɪʃn]	Diskriminierung; Benachteiligung	→ to discriminate
interior [ɪnˈtɪəriə]	innen; intern	→ interior designer
mount [maʊnt]	Halterung; Gestell	→ to mount
implementation [ˌɪmplɪmenˈteɪʃn]	Einführung	→ to implement
irresponsible [ˌɪrɪˈspɒnsəbl]	verantwortungslos	↔ responsible
chamber [ˈtʃeɪmbə]	Kammer	→ Commons Chamber → Lords Chamber
MP [ˌemˈpiː]	Abgeordnete/r	short for: Member of Parliament
Secretary of State for Defence [ˌsekrətri əv ˌsteɪt fə dɪˈfens]	Verteidigungsminister/in	ministry of defence
editor [ˈedɪtə]	Herausgeber/in; Redakteur/in	→ to edit

Unit 11 Young people – leisure and health

A

	inactive [ɪˈnæktɪv]	träge; inaktiv	↔ active
	loafer [ˈləʊfə]	Faulenzer/in; Gammler/in	→ to loaf
	to **progress** [prəˈgres]	fortschreiten	→ progress
	touch [tʌtʃ]	Berührung	→ to touch
	comfort [ˈkʌmfət]	Behaglichkeit; Trost	→ comfortable
	recently [ˈriːsntli]	kürzlich	→ recent
	monitoring [ˈmɒnɪtrɪŋ]	Überwachung; Kontrolle	→ to monitor
	to **bring about** [ˌbrɪŋ əˈbaʊt]	bewirken	= to create = to produce = to generate
	tracking [ˈtrækɪŋ]	Verfolgung	→ to track
	neck [nek]	Hals	→ necklace
	to **relieve** [rɪˈliːv]	entlasten	→ relief
	tension [ˈtenʃn]	Spannung	→ tense
	to **get carried away** [get ˌkærɪd əˈweɪ]	von etwas mitgerissen werden	Sorry, I that I shouted at you. I got carried away.
	addictive [əˈdɪktɪv]	süchtig machend	→ addict → addiction

B

	to **skip** [skɪp]	auslassen; überspringen	It's a boring meeting, let's skip it!
	anxiety [æŋˈzaɪəti]	Besorgnis; Angst	→ anxious
	to **soar** [sɔː]	sprunghaft steigen; in die Höhe schnellen	to rise a lot to increase a lot
	self-esteem [ˌselfɪˈstiːm]	Selbstwertgefühl	Josh's self-esteem is soaring. He won the match.
	annual [ˈænjuəl]	jährlich; Jahres-	Christmas is an annual holiday.
	startling [ˈstɑːtlɪŋ]	alarmierend; überraschend	→ to startle
	anxious [ˈæŋkʃəs]	besorgt; bang	= worried
	to **slim down** [ˌslɪm ˈdaʊn]	abnehmen	= to lose weight
	worrying [ˈwʌriɪŋ]	beunruhigend; besorgniserregend	= alarming
	proportion [prəˈpɔːʃn]	Anteil; Proportion	number or percentage of s.th.
	correlation [ˌkɒrəˈleɪʃn]	Zusammenhang; Beziehung	→ to correlate
	youngster [ˈjʌŋstə]	Jugendliche/r	a young person
	to **agonise** [ˈægənaɪz]	sich den Kopf zerbrechen; sich quälen	→ agony
	high-calorie [ˌhaɪˈkælri]	kalorienreich	→ calories
	anyway [ˈeniweɪ]	ohnehin; sowieso	Ask Tom to get some milk. He's going shopping anyway.
	alarmed [əˈlɑːmd]	beunruhigt; aufgeschreckt	Don't be alarmed! It's just a quick test.
	to **come under fire** [ˌkʌm ˌʌndə ˈfaɪə]	unter Beschuss geraten	The politician came under fire for corruption.
	shape [ʃeɪp]	Figur; Form; Gestalt	→ to shape
	skinny [ˈskɪni]	mager; dünn	= thin
	mannequin [ˈmænɪkɪn]	Schaufensterpuppe	I love the dress on the mannequin in the shop window.
	ridiculous [rɪˈdɪkjələs]	lächerlich	= absurd = laughable
	insecure [ˌɪnsɪˈkjʊə]	unsicher	↔ secure
	downturn [ˈdaʊntɜːn]	Abschwung	↔ boom
	consistent [kənˈsɪstnt]	einheitlich	→ consistency
	to **occur** [əˈkɜː]	vorkommen	→ occurrence
	to **evaluate** [ɪˈvæljueɪt]	bewerten; beurteilen	→ evaluation
	alongside [əˌlɒŋˈsaɪd]	neben; daneben	Sheila often walks her dog alongside the train tracks.

Vocabulary | Unit vocabulary

	to **rehearse** [rɪˈhɜːs]	proben; einüben	→ rehearsal
	representation [ˌreprɪzenˈteɪʃn]	Darstellung; Vertretung	→ to represent
	celebration [ˌseləˈbreɪʃn]	Feier	→ to celebrate
	worry [ˈwʌri]	Sorge	→ to worry
	plausible [ˈplɔːzɪbl]	plausibel; einleuchtend; glaubhaft	→ plausibility
	to **be aware of s.th.** [bɪ əˈweər əv ˈsʌmθɪŋ]	sich etw. bewusst sein	→ awareness
	exposure [ɪkˈspəʊʒə]	Aussetzen; Kontakt	→ to expose
	undesirable [ˌʌndɪˈzaɪrəbl]	unerwünscht	↔ desirable
C	**binge drinking** [ˌbɪndʒ ˈdrɪŋkɪŋ]	Besäufnis; Komasaufen	drinking large quantities of alcohol in a short time
	brain [ˈbreɪn]	menschliches Gehirn	Too much alcohol can cause damage to the human brain.
	to **trigger** [ˈtrɪgə]	auslösen	→ trigger
	irreparable [ɪˈrepəbl]	nicht mehr zu reparieren; irreparabel	→ to repair
	long-lasting [ˌlɒŋˈlɑːstɪŋ]	langlebig; haltbar	Too much sugar can have a long-lasting and negative effect on your health.
	adolescence [ˌædəˈlesns]	Jugend	→ adolescent
	abnormality [ˌæbnɔːˈmæləti]	Unregelmäßigkeit; Auffälligkeit	→ abnormal
	enduring [ɪnˈdjʊərɪŋ]	bleibend; dauerhaft	→ to endure
	maturity [məˈtjʊərəti]	Reife	→ mature
	to **refine** [rɪˈfaɪn]	verfeinern	The petrol in your car comes from refined oil.
	cognitive [ˈkɒgnətɪv]	kognitiv; Wahrnehmungs-	A child's cognitive development is as important as its physical development.
	hippocampus [ˌhɪpəˈkæmpəs]	Hippocampus	a major component of the human brain
	cell [sel]	Zelle	→ cellular
	immature [ˌɪməˈtjʊə]	unreif	↔ mature
	to **associate with** [əˈsəʊʃieɪt wɪð]	verbinden mit	People often associate drug-taking with young criminals.
	immaturity [ˌɪməˈtjʊərəti]	Unreife	↔ maturity
	to **disrupt** [dɪsˈrʌpt]	stören; unterbrechen	→ disruption
	maturation [ˌmætjrˈeɪʃn]	Reife	→ to mature
	eager [ˈiːgə]	eifrig; begierig	→ eagerness
	to **explore** [ɪkˈsplɔː]	erforschen	→ explorer → exploration
	ongoing [ˌɒnˈgəʊɪŋ]	in Gang befindlich; laufend	= current
	immeasurable [ɪˈmeʒrəbl]	unermesslich	→ to measure → measurement
	outlook [ˈaʊtlʊk]	Perspektive; Aussicht	= perspective
	vigilance [ˈvɪdʒɪləns]	Wachsamkeit	→ vigilant
	addiction [əˈdɪkʃn]	Sucht; Abhängigkeit	→ addict → addicted
	rational [ˈræʃnl]	vernünftig; rational	↔ irrational
	to **bond** [bɒnd]	eine Verbindung eingehen	→ bond
	traumatised [ˈtrɔːmətaɪzd]	traumatisiert	→ trauma
	step-parent [ˈstepˌpeərnt]	Stiefelternteil	→ stepmother → stepfather

Unit 12 Modern media and advertising

A	**widespread** [ˈwaɪdspred]	weit verbreitet	= common
	to **rocket** [ˈrɒkɪt]	in die Höhe schießen	→ to skyrocket
	to **keep in touch** [ˌkiːp ɪn ˈtʌtʃ]	in Verbindung bleiben	Bye for now. We must keep in touch!

	sex [seks]	Geschlecht	She mustn't talk to a member of the other sex.
	to **mention** ['menʃn]	erwähnen	Did Dan mention the new plans?
	upcoming [ˈʌpˌkʌmɪŋ]	bevorstehend	= imminent
	boredom [ˈbɔːdəm]	Langeweile	→ boring
	awareness [əˈweənəs]	Bewusstsein	→ aware
	to **be spied on** [bi ˈspaɪd ɒn]	ausspioniert werden	→ to spy
B	**profile** [ˈprəʊfaɪl]	Profil	Tim looks better in his profile picture than he does in reality.
	torment [ˈtɔːment]	Pein; Qual	→ tormentor
	sociology [ˌsəʊsiˈɒlədʒi]	Soziologie	→ sociological
	trusting [ˈtrʌstɪŋ]	vertrauensvoll	↔ distrustful
	to **recall** [rɪˈkɔːl]	sich erinnern	→ recollection
	to **scar** [skɑː]	Wunden hinterlassen	→ scar
	appearance [əˈpɪərns]	Aussehen	→ to appear
	abuser [əˈbjuːzə]	Missbraucher/in	→ to abuse
	to **escalate** [ˈeskəleɪt]	eskalieren	→ escalation
	aggressive [əˈgresɪv]	aggressiv	↔ meek
	stalkerish [ˈstɔːkərɪʃ]	wie Stalking	→ to stalk
	to **crash** [kræʃ]	verunglücken; abstürzen	→ crash test dummy
	frustrating [frʌsˈtreɪtɪŋ]	entmutigend; frustrierend	→ frustration → to frustrate
	to **engage with** [ɪnˈgeɪdʒ wɪð]	sich einlassen mit; sich abgeben mit	→ engagement
	bully [ˈbʊli]	Bully; Mobber/in	→ to bully
	reverberation [rɪˌvɜːbrˈeɪʃn]	Auswirkung	→ to reverberate
	concentration [ˌkɒnsnˈtreɪʃn]	Konzentration	→ to concentrate
	to **harass** [ˈhærəs]	belästigen; drangsalieren	→ harassment
	impunity [ɪmˈpjuːnəti]	Straffreiheit	= without being punished
	terms and conditions [ˌtɜːmz ən kənˈdɪʃnz]	Geschäftsbedingungen	You can access the bank's terms and conditions via this link.
	to **release** [rɪˈliːs]	freigeben; veröffentlichen	→ release
	salacious [səˈleɪʃəs]	anzüglich	= insinuating
	closed off [ˌkləʊzd ˈɒf]	verschlossen	= withdrawn
	guarded [ˈgɑːdɪd]	vorsichtig	= reserved
	criminology [ˌkrɪmɪˈnɒlədʒi]	Kriminologie	→ criminal
	to **type** [taɪp]	tippen	Where did you learn to type so fast?
	to **stick with s.o.** [ˈstɪk wɪð ˌsʌmwʌn]	an jemandem haften bleiben; jemanden weiterhin beschäftigen	The bike accident I had at the age of five still sticks with me.
C	to **ban** [bæn]	verbieten	→ ban
	complex [ˈkɒmpleks]	komplex; kompliziert	→ complexity
	discretionary [dɪˈskreʃnri]	verfügbar	= disposable
	point of sale [ˌpɔɪnt əv ˈseɪl]	Verkaufsort	
	concert [ˈkɒnsət]	Konzert	→ concert hall
	sexualization [ˌsekʃuəlaɪˈzeɪʃn]	Sexualisierung	
	strategy [ˈstrætədʒi]	Strategie	→ strategic
	core [kɔː]	Zentrum; Herzstück	→ hard-core
	regulatory [ˈregjələtri]	regulierend	→ regulation
	complementary [ˌkɒmplɪˈmentri]	ergänzend; komplementär	→ to complement
	stakeholder [ˈsteɪkˌhəʊldə]	Interessengruppe	= interest group
	to **wink** [wɪŋk]	zwinkern	→ wink

Vocabulary | Unit vocabulary

	to **pester** [ˈpestə]	plagen; bedrängen	→ pest
	civilised [ˈsɪvlaɪzd]	zivilisiert	→ civil
	to **require s.o. to do s.th.** [rɪˌkwaɪə ˌsʌmwʌn tə ˈduː ˌsʌmθɪŋ]	etw. von jemandem verlangen	All guests are required to take off their shoes.
	to **impact** [ɪmˈpækt]	beeinflussen	= effect
	billboard [ˈbɪlbɔːd]	Plakatwand	type of advertising found in public places
	banner ad [ˌbænərˈæd]	Werbebanner	→ advertisement

Unit 13 Young people and society

A	to **grow up** [ˌɡrəʊˈʌp]	aufwachsen	He grew up in the USA.
	gun [ɡʌn]	Schusswaffe	→ gun law
	prostitution [ˌprɒstɪˈtjuːʃn]	Prostitution	→ prostitute
	gang warfare [ˌɡæŋ ˈwɔːfeə]	Bandenkrieg	The only way to stop gang warfare is to create jobs for young people.
	crack [kræk]	Crack	→ crack addict
	phone box [ˈfəʊn ˌbɒks]	Telefonzelle	Nowadays it is difficult to find a phone box in towns.
	heroin [ˈherəʊɪn]	Heroin	Heroin is an addictive drug.
	to **inject** [ɪnˈdʒekt]	spritzen; einspritzen	→ injection
	subway (BE) [ˈsʌbweɪ]	Unterführung für Fußgänger	a tunnel under a road
	to **stab** [stæb]	stechen; (er)stechen	He was attacked by a gang and stabbed.
	generally [ˈdʒenrli]	im Allgemeinen; eigentlich	People in the office are generally very friendly.
	homeless [ˈhəʊmləs]	obdachlos	→ homelessness
	to **beg** [beɡ]	betteln	→ beggar
	stereotype [ˈsteriətaɪp]	Stereotyp; Klischee	→ to stereotype
	hostel [ˈhɒstl]	Herberge	→ youth hostel
	dining [ˈdaɪnɪŋ]	Ess-	→ dining table
	privileged [ˈprɪvlɪdʒd]	begünstigt; privilegiert	→ privilege
	fairly [ˈfeəli]	einigermaßen	= reasonably
	rosy [ˈrəʊzi]	rosig	= bright
	to **close down** [ˌkləʊz ˈdaʊn]	schließen; stilllegen	= to shut down
	to **push off** [ˌpʊʃˈɒf]	hinunterstoßen; abstoßen	The attacker tried to push the man off the cliff.
	ladder [ˈlædə]	Leiter	We need a ladder to reach the apples on the tree.
B	to **campaign for s.th.** [kæmˈpeɪn fə ˌsʌmθɪŋ]	für etwas kämpfen	→ campaigner
	Down's syndrome [ˈdaʊnz ˌsɪndrəʊm]	Downsyndrom	Down's syndrome is another word for trisomy 21.
	coach [kəʊtʃ]	Reisebus	The coach from York to London is cheaper than the train.
	fellow student [ˌfeləʊ ˈstjuːdnt]	Mitstudent/in; Kommilitone/Kommilitonin	s.o. you study with at college
	borough [ˈbʌrə]	Stadtbezirk	Queens is one of the five boroughs of New York.
	mainstream [ˈmeɪnstriːm]	herkömmlich; Regel-	Ben listens to mainstream pop music.
	residential catering college [ˌrezɪdenʃl ˈkeɪtrɪŋ ˌkɒlɪdʒ]	College mit Unterkunft und Verpflegung	Students can live in the residential catering college.
	waitress [ˈweɪtrəs]	Kellnerin	→ waiter

	fortunate [ˈfɔːtʃnət]	glücklich	→ fortune
	postcode (BE) [ˈpəʊstkəʊd]	Postleitzahl	= zip code (AE)
	post-16 [ˌpəʊstsɪkˈstiːn]	nach dem 16. Lebensjahr	when s.o. is older than 16
	specialist [ˈspeʃlɪst]	fachlich	→ to specialize
	to offer [ˈɒfə]	anbieten	→ offer
	battle [ˈbætl]	Kampf; Schlacht	→ battlefield
	to secure [sɪˈkjʊə]	sichern	→ security
	funding [ˈfʌndɪŋ]	finanzielle Unterstützung	→ to fund
	to serve [sɜːv]	dienen; bedienen	server (AE)
	local [ˈləʊkl]	hiesig	→ location
	hygiene [ˈhaɪdʒiːn]	Hygiene; Sauberkeit	→ hygenic
	spot on [ˌspɒtˈɒn]	treffend	= to the point
	to prevent from doing s.th. [prɪˈvent frəm]	von etwas abhalten	→ prevention
	reliant on [rɪˈlaɪənt ɒn]	abhängig sein von	→ reliance
	to embed [ɪmˈbed]	einbetten	The idea became embedded in his mind.
	ethos [ˈiːθɒs]	Ethos	= principles
	semi-independent [ˌsemiɪndɪˈpendnt]	relativ unabhängig	Students like to earn money in the holidays so they can be semi-independent of their parents.
	to write off [ˌraɪtˈɒf]	abschreiben	This car is totally damaged. You can write it off.
	to deprive of [dɪˈpraɪv əv]	einer Sache berauben	→ deprivation
	intervention [ˌɪntəˈvenʃn]	Eingriff; Intervention	→ to intervene
	vital [ˈvaɪtl]	entscheidend; wesentlich	→ vitality
	to empower [ɪmˈpaʊə]	befähigen	The new law empowers the police to search anyone on the street at night.
	beyond [bɪˈɒnd]	jenseits; außerhalb	How you can eat raw meat is beyond my imagination.
	arrangement [əˈreɪndʒmənt]	Gestaltung; Regelung	→ to arrange
	communally [kəˈmjuːnli]	in Gemeinschaft; gemeinsam	community
	autism [ˈɔːtɪzm]	Autismus	→ autistic
	delightful [dɪˈlaɪtfəl]	entzückend; reizend	= lovely
	cycling [ˈsaɪklɪŋ]	Radfahren	→ cyclist
	earnestness [ˈɜːnɪstnəs]	Ernsthaftigkeit	→ earnest
	achievement [əˈtʃiːvmənt]	Leistung; Erfolg	→ to achieve
C	**powder keg** [ˈpaʊdə ˌkeg]	Pulverfass	a dangerous situation
	to spark [spɑːk]	auslösen; entzünden	→ spark
	violent [ˈvaɪələnt]	gewalttätig	→ violence
	confrontation [ˌkɒnfrənˈteɪʃn]	Konfrontation	→ to confront
	to shatter [ˈʃætə]	zerschlagen	= to destroy
	racial [ˈreɪʃl]	Rassen-; rassisch	→ race
	harmony [ˈhɑːməni]	Harmonie	→ harmonious
	notion [ˈnəʊʃn]	Vorstellung; Auffassung	= idea
	to take hold [teɪk ˈhəʊld]	sich durchsetzen	This trend will never take hold.
	elite [ɪˈliːt]	Elite	= best = first-class
	cheerful [ˈtʃɪəfəl]	fröhlich; heiter	= happy
	passage [ˈpæsɪdʒ]	Verabschiedung	→ to pass
	cathartic [kəˈθɑːtɪk]	reinigend	= liberating
	roar [rɔː]	Gebrüll	→ to roar

Vocabulary | Unit vocabulary

to **blame for** [ˈbleɪm fə]	für etwas verantwortlich machen	Mike was innocent but he was still blamed for the accident.
to **murder** [ˈmɜːdə]	ermorden	→ murderer
to **ruin** [ˈruːɪn]	ruinieren	→ ruin
unarmed [ʌnˈɑːmd]	unbewaffnet	↔ armed
to **shoot** [ʃuːt]	schießen; erschießen	J.F. Kennedy was shot in Dallas.
disputed [dɪˈspjuːtɪd]	umstritten	→ dispute
circumstance [ˈsɜːkəmstæns]	Umstand	The circumstances of his death are not clear.
complaint [kəmˈpleɪnt]	Beschwerde	→ to complain
borne out [ˌbɔːn ˈaʊt]	bekräftigt; bestätigt	→ to bear out
official [əˈfɪʃl]	offiziell	↔ unofficial
attorney general [əˌtɜːni ˈdʒenrl]	Generalstaatsanwalt	The attorney general is appointed as the chief legal officer by the government.
penalty [ˈpenlti]	Strafe	The penalty will not stop people from stealing.
to **issue** [ˈɪʃuː]	verhängen; ausstellen; ausgeben	The judge issued an order to search the building.
minor [ˈmaɪnə]	gering; geringfügig	↔ major
offence [əˈfens]	Vergehen	→ offender → to offend
to **uncover** [ʌnˈkʌvə]	aufdecken	↔ to cover
resentment [rɪˈzentmənt]	Ärger; Verbitterung	→ to resent
bureaucrat [ˈbjʊərəkræt]	Bürokrat	→ bureaucratic
to **impose** [ɪmˈpəʊz]	verhängen; auferlegen	The police impose a heavy fine for drunken driving.
regime [reɪˈʒiːm]	Ordnung; System	system of order in a country
to **resemble** [rɪˈzembl]	gleich sein	→ resemblance
to **police** [pəˈliːs]	überwachen	→ policeman → policewoman
to **erupt** [ɪˈrʌpt]	ausbrechen	→ eruption
relentlessly [rɪˈlentləsli]	unerbittlich	not willing to change an opinion or decision
to **defend** [dɪˈfend]	verteidigen	→ defence
councillor [ˈkaʊnslə]	Stadtrat/rätin	→ city council
to **persist** [pəˈsɪst]	bestehen bleiben	→ persistent
savage [ˈsævɪdʒ]	grausam	= brutal = uncivilized = rude
segregated [ˈsegrɪgeɪtɪd]	nach Rassen getrennt	→ segregation
real estate agent [ˌrɪəlɪsteɪt ˈeɪdʒnt]	Immobilienmakler/in	The real estate agent showed us some houses that were for sale.
anatomy [əˈnætəmi]	Analyse	= analysis
white-collar [ˌwaɪtˈkɒlə]	im Büro tätig	The white-collar workers work in the offices of the firm.
blue-collar [ˌbluːˈkɒlə]	gewerblich tätig	The blue-collar workers work on the production line of the firm.
median [ˈmiːdiən]	Mittelwert	average

Unit 14 Technology, energy and environment

A	**beekeeper** [ˈbiːkiːpə]	Imker/in	Beekeepers keep bees to produce honey
	Thames [temz]	Themse	The Thames is a river that runs through London.
	power plant [ˈpaʊə ˌplɑːnt]	Kraftwerk	= generating plant
	flooding [ˈflʌdɪŋ]	Überschwemmung	→ to flood

	twice over [ˌtwaɪs ˈəʊvə]	zweimalig; zweimal hintereinander	I had to explain it twice over before he finally agreed.
	unpredictable [ˌʌnprɪˈdɪktəbl]	unvorhersehbar; unberechenbar	↔ predictable
	steppe [step]	Steppe	You can find steppe land in Siberia.
	desert [ˈdezət]	Wüste	There's no water in the desert.
	lot [lɒt]	Grundstück; Parzelle	The architects divided the land for the new houses into lots.
	creation [kriˈeɪʃn]	Schöpfung; Schaffung	→ creator
	Christian [ˈkrɪstʃən]	Christ/in	→ to christen
B	to **join forces** [ˌdʒɔɪn ˈfɔːsɪz]	sich zusammenschließen; sich zusammentun	Students and teachers have joined forces to raise money for the new heating system.
	initiative [ɪˈnɪʃətɪv]	Initiative	→ to initiate
	to **state** [steɪt]	erklären; festlegen	→ statement
	to **put out of business** [ˌpʊt aʊt əv ˈbɪznɪs]	aus dem Markt drängen	The local food store was put out of business by the big supermarket.
	storage [ˈstɔːrɪdʒ]	Speicherung	→ to store
	transmission [trænzˈmɪʃn]	Weiterleitung; Übertragung	→ to transmit
	to **undercut** [ˌʌndəˈkʌt]	unterbieten	to cost less than s.th. else
	feasible [ˈfiːzəbl]	machbar; möglich	= manageable
	to **loom** [luːm]	sich abzeichnen	A future of hunger and thirst looms over many people in Africa.
	advocate [ˈædvəkət]	Befürworter/in	↔ opponent
	to **decarbonise** [ˌdiːˈkɑːbənaɪz]	entkarbonisieren	→ carbon
	to **commit oneself** [kəˈmɪt wʌnˌself]	sich festlegen; verpflichten	April committed herself to helping her parents financially.
	launch [lɔːnʃ]	Markteinführung; Start	→ to launch
	urgent [ˈɜːdʒnt]	dringend; eilig	→ urgency
	pathway [ˈpɑːθweɪ]	Pfad	= path
	gross domestic product [ˌɡrəʊs dəˌmestɪk ˈprɒdʌkt]	Bruttoinlandsprodukt	short form: GDP
	consortium [kənˈsɔːtiəm]	Vereinigung; Zusammenschluss	A large consortium took over the mall.
	to **reap** [riːp]	ernten	= to harvest
	emeritus professor [ɪˌmerɪtəs prəˈfesə]	Professor im Ruhestand	a professor who has retired
	to **crack** [kræk]	knacken; aufknacken	= to solve
	to **head** [hed]	leiten	= to direct
	breakthrough [ˈbreɪkθruː]	Durchbruch	Apollo 11 was a breakthrough in space travel.
	to **postpone** [pəʊsˈpəʊn]	verschieben	= to delay
	atmospheric [ˌætməsˈferɪk]	atmosphärisch	→ atmosphere
	to **abate** [əˈbeɪt]	abflauen; nachlassen	= to subside
	drought [draʊt]	Dürre	= aridity
	flood [flʌd]	Überschwemmung	The flood destroyed the buildings.
	livelihood [ˈlaɪvlihʊd]	Lebensunterhalt	Pete earns his livelihood by selling electronic equipment.
C	**census** [ˈsensəs]	Befragung; Volkszählung	In the last census they found out that the population had increased dramatically.
	creator [kriˈeɪtə]	Schöpfer/in; Erschaffer/in	→ to create
	obsolete [ˈɒbsliːt]	veraltet; außer Gebrauch	We don't use typewriters anymore. They're obsolete.
	merely [ˈmɪəli]	bloß; lediglich	= only = just
	to **ease** [iːz]	erleichtern; lindern	→ at ease
	balanced [ˈbælənst]	ausgewogen	→ to balance

Vocabulary | Unit vocabulary

dominant ['dɒmɪnənt]	beherrschend; dominierend	→ to dominate
to **contract** [kən'trækt]	unter Vertrag nehmen	→ contract
to **offset** [ˌɒf'set]	kompensieren; ausgleichen	= to compensate
repetitive [rɪ'petətɪv]	sich wiederholend	→ to repeat
laborious [lə'bɔːriəs]	mühsam; anstrengend	→ labour
to **substitute** ['sʌbstɪtjuːt]	ersetzen	→ substitution
muscle ['mʌsl]	Muskel	Doing sport helps to build muscles.
to **shrink** [ʃrɪŋk]	schrumpfen	→ shrinkage
profound [prə'faʊnd]	tiefgreifend	The overuse of electronic devices has a profound effect on children.
historic [hɪ'stɒrɪk]	historisch	→ history
raw [rɔː]	roh; rau; grob	Raw sugar has not been refined.
nursing auxiliary [ˌnɜːsɪŋ ɔːg'zɪliəri]	nicht geprüfter Krankenpfleger; nicht geprüfte Krankenpflegerin	Nursing is not an easy job.
essentials (pl.) [ɪ'senʃlz]	lebenswichtige Güter	→ essential
oxygen ['ɒksɪdʒən]	Sauerstoff	We need oxygen to breathe.
ordinary ['ɔːdnri]	gewöhnlich	↔ extraordinary
to **invent** [ɪn'vent]	erfinden	→ inventor
revolutionary [ˌrevə'luːʃnri]	revolutionär	→ revolution

Unit 15 Globalization and migration

A	**originally** [ə'rɪdʒnli]	ursprünglich	→ origin
	Jamaica [dʒə'meɪkə]	Jamaika	→ Jamaican
	West Indies [ˌwest 'ɪndiːz]	Westindische Inseln	→ West Indian
	cab [kæb]	Taxi	= taxi
	hostility [hɒs'tɪləti]	Anfeindung; Feindschaft	→ hostile
	to **abuse** [ə'bjuːz]	missbrauchen	→ abuser
	minority [maɪ'nɒrəti]	Minderheit	↔ majority
	cost of living [ˌkɒst əv 'lɪvɪŋ]	Lebenshaltungskosten	The cost of living in London has risen dramatically over the last few years.
	paradise ['pærədaɪs]	Paradies	Adam and Eve lived in paradise.
	standard of living [ˌstændəd əv 'lɪvɪŋ]	Lebensstandard	The Royals enjoy a high standard of living.
	rarely ['reəli]	selten; kaum	↔ frequently
	the Scots [ðə 'skɒts]	die Schotten	→ Scottish
	bagpipes (pl.) ['bægpaɪps]	Dudelsack	The bagpipes is a traditional Scottish musical instrument.
	whisky (BE) ['wɪski]	Whisky	whiskey (AE)
	engaged [ɪn'geɪdʒd]	verlobt	→ engagement
	Scottish ['skɒtɪʃ]	schottisch	→ Scotland → Scot
	relations (pl.) [rɪ'leɪʃnz]	Verwandtschaft	= relatives
B	**healthcare** ['helθˌkeə]	Gesundheitsfürsorge; Gesundheitsversorgung	→ healthcare system
	to **stretch** [stretʃ]	ausdehnen; strecken	Before you go jogging you should stretch your legs.
	catalyst ['kætlɪst]	Katalysator; Beschleuniger	s.th. that causes a big change
	empowerment [ɪm'paʊəmənt]	Ermächtigung; Bevollmächtigung	→ to empower
	joint [dʒɔɪnt]	gemeinsam	→ joint venture

presence ['prezns]	Präsenz	→ present
Cambodia [kæm'bəʊdiə]	Kambodscha	→ Cambodian
Lesotho [lə'suːtuː]	Lesotho	a kingdom in southern Africa
Nicaragua [ˌnɪkr'æɡuə]	Nicaragua	→ Nicaraguan
Haiti ['heɪti]	Haiti	→ Haitian
Jordan ['dʒɔːdn]	Jordanien	→ Jordanian
Indonesia [ˌɪndə'niːʒə]	Indonesien	→ Indonesian
sustained [sə'steɪnd]	anhaltend; nachhaltig	→ sustainability
Vietnamese [ˌvjetnə'miːz]	vietnamesisch	→ Vietnam
industrial [ɪn'dʌstriəl]	industriell; Industrie-	→ industrialized
to **lag behind** [læɡ bɪ'haɪnd]	hinterherhinken; zurückbleiben	The old man lagged behind the rest of the runners.
sewer ['səʊə]	Näher/in	→ to sew
occupation [ˌɒkjə'peɪʃn]	Beruf; Beschäftigung	→ to occupy
supervisor ['suːpəvaɪzə]	Abteilungsleiter/in; Leiter/in	→ to supervise
to **exclude** [ɪk'skluːd]	ausschließen	→ exclusion
dynamics [daɪ'næmɪks]	Dynamik; Kräftespiel	→ dynamic
to **retain** [rɪ'teɪn]	behalten; beibehalten	→ retainer
to **pave** [peɪv]	pflastern	→ pavement
per capita [pə 'kæpɪtə]	pro Kopf	→ per capita expenditure
gender gap ['dʒendə ˌɡæp]	Geschlechterkluft (z.B. auf dem Arbeitsmarkt)	a difference e.g. in pay or working hours, between men and women
remittance [rɪ'mɪtns]	Überweisung	→ to remit
head on [ˌhed'ɒn]	frontal; von vorn	The cars crashed head on.
business sense ['bɪznɪs ˌsens]	Geschäftssinn	You should have some basic business sense to run a small firm.
absenteeism [ˌæbsn'tiːɪzm]	Fernbleiben; Krankfeiern	→ absentee
dispute [dɪ'spjuːts]	Streitigkeit; Auseinandersetzung	→ to dispute
trade union [ˌtreɪd 'juːnjən]	Gewerkschaft	Trade unions fight for workers' rights.
to **bargain** ['bɑːɡɪn]	handeln; verhandeln	→ bargain
on behalf of [ɒn bɪ'hɑːf əv]	im Auftrag von; im Namen von	Jessie spoke on behalf of her boss at the meeting as he was ill.
barrier ['bæriə]	Barriere; Hindernis	→ to barricade
to **remove** [rɪ'muːv]	entfernen; räumen	→ removal
doubt [daʊt]	Zweifel	→ doubtful
to **grasp** [ɡrɑːsp]	greifen; ergreifen; festhalten	→ grasp
C **co-op** ['kəʊɒp]	Kooperative	→ to cooperate
to **combat** ['kɒmbæt]	bekämpfen	= to fight
Gaelic ['ɡeɪlɪk]	gälisch	Gaelic is a language spoken by some Irish and Scottish people.
Punjabi [pʌn'dʒɑːbiː]	Pandschabi	→ Punjab
Pakistani [ˌpækɪ'stɑːni]	pakistanisch	→ Pakistan
Indian ['ɪndiən]	indisch	→ India
to **stitch** [stɪtʃ]	nähen; steppen	→ stitch
pillar ['pɪlə]	Säule	The tall pillars were used to support the building.
surgical ['sɜːdʒɪkl]	chirurgisch	→ surgeon
fire escape ['faɪər ɪˌskeɪp]	Notausgang; Feuerleiter	emergency exit used in case of fire
fire extinguisher ['faɪər ɪkˌstɪŋɡwɪʃə]	Feuerlöscher	You use a fire extinguisher to put out a fire.
basement ['beɪsmənt]	Untergeschoss	= cellar

Vocabulary | Unit vocabulary

governing body [ˌgʌvnɪŋ ˈbɒdi]	Aufsichtsrat; Dachverband	The governing body of the company voted to expand its business in China.
premium [ˈpriːmiəm]	Prämie	The company pays a 3% premium on long-term investments.
certification [ˌsɜːtɪfɪˈkeɪʃn]	Zertifizierung; Beurkundung	→ to certify
to **verify** [ˈverɪfaɪ]	nachweisen; nachprüfen	→ verification

Alphabetical word list

Die Seitenzahl bezieht sich auf das erste Vorkommen der Vokabel im Buch.

Abkürzungen und Zeichen
AE = amerikanisches Englisch
BE = britisches Englisch
* = unregelmäßiges Verb
(pl.) = Plural, Mehrzahl
(sg.) = Singular, Einzahl

A

to abate abflauen, nachlassen 160
abnormality Unregelmäßigkeit, Auffälligkeit 144
above oben, obenstehend 38
absenteeism Fernbleiben, Krankfeiern 166
to absorb absorbieren, aufsaugen 56
abundance Fülle, Überfluss 89
abuse Missbrauch 124
to abuse missbrauchen 164
abuser Missbraucher/in 148
academic schulisch, wissenschaftlich 65
academic year Schuljahr 26
accent Akzent 117
acceptance Annahme, Zusage 33
access *(sg.)* Zugang 16
to access erreichen 137
accessories *(pl.)* Accessoires, Zubehör 125
to accommodate Unterkunft bieten 33, aufnehmen, unterbringen, entgegenkommen 62
accommodation Unterkunft 16
accordingly folglich, demgemäß 37
according to gemäß, entsprechend 19
account Konto 40
account manager Kundenbetreuer/in 42
accredited akkreditiert, anerkannt 17
to accuse s.o. of s.th. jdn. wegen etw. beschuldigen 136
achievable erreichbar 89
achievement Leistung, Erfolg 154
to acknowledge bestätigen, anerkennen 132
to acquire s.th. übernehmen, erwerben 21
to act handeln, fungieren als 37
active aktiv 25

actually eigentlich, tatsächlich 41
to adapt anpassen 37
addict Süchtige/r 68
addicted to abhängig von 54
addiction Sucht, Abhängigkeit 145
addictive süchtig machend 140
addressee Adressat, Empfänger/in 121
to add up aufaddieren 82
adjustment Anpassung 123
admission Zulassung, Zugeständnis 65
admissions director Zuständige/r für Zulassungen 17
to admit zugeben 45
adolescence Jugend 144
to adopt adoptieren, übernehmen 85
adult Erwachsene/r 40
advance Fortschritt, Vorstoß 99
adventure Abenteuer 123
advisable ratsam, empfehlenswert 40
to advise beraten 118
adviser Berater/in 85
advocate Befürworter/in 159
to affect beeinflussen, betreffen 43
affluent wohlhabend 17
to afford sich leisten 17
affordable erschwinglich, günstig 17
to age älter werden 49
aged im Alter von 65
agency Agentur, Vertretung, Träger 12
aggressive aggressiv 148
to agonise sich den Kopf zerbrechen, sich quälen 141
agricultural landwirtschaftlich 88
agriculture Landwirtschaft 100
aid Hilfe, Unterstützung 129
alarm bell Alarmglocke 94
alarmed beunruhigt, aufgeschreckt 141
A levels *(pl.)* Abitur 26
allergic to allergisch auf 97
all-natural ganz und gar natürlich 16
allure Reiz, Faszination 123
all year round ganzjährig 28
alongside neben, daneben 142
American amerikanisch, Amerikaner/in 125
AmeriCorps amerikanische Organisation, die Jugendliche auf dem Weg zur Berufsfindung unterstützt 17
amidst inmitten 123
amongst inmitten 68
to amount to sich belaufen auf 104

anachronistic anachronistisch, veraltet 35
analysis Analyse 55
to analyze analysieren 20
anatomy Analyse 157
ancient alt, uralt 123
anniversary Jubiläum 21
annual jährlich, Jahres- 141
anonymous anonym 53
anthem Hymne 32
antibiotic Antibiotikum 80
to anticipate erwarten 60
anxiety Besorgnis, Angst 141
anxious besorgt, bang 141
anyway ohnehin, sowieso 141
anywhere überall 58
apart getrennt, auseinander 61
apart from abgesehen von 12
to apologize sich entschuldigen 73
appalling entsetzlich, mies 136
appearance Aussehen 147
appliance Gerät 45
application Bewerbung, Anwendung 24
to apply to anwenden auf, gelten für, betreffen 129
to appoint ernennen, bestellen 134
appointment Termin, Verabredung 42
to appreciate s.th. etw. schätzen, wertschätzen 33
appreciation Wertschätzung, Würdigung 115
apprentice Auszubildende/r 16
to approach nähern, annähern, ansprechen 53
approach Herangehensweise, Ansatz 107
appropriate geeignet, passend 35
to approve anerkennen, genehmigen 95
apron Schürze 14
aquifer wasserführende Schicht 85
Arab arabisch, Araber/in 115
architecture Architektur 35
to argue argumentieren, Argumente darlegen 95
argument Argument, Streit 55
***to arise** entstehen 55
armed bewaffnet 57
arms Waffen, Rüstungsgüter 85
around the clock rund um die Uhr 27
to arrange organisieren 16
arrangement Gestaltung, Regelung 154
array Feld, Palette 77

Vocabulary | Alphabetical word list

to arrest verhaften 134
artificial künstlich 94
artisan Kunsthandwerker/in 127
as for bezüglich, was … betrifft 26
Asia Asien 37
as long as solange 26
aspect Aspekt, Seite 54
as regards was … betrifft 33
assembly Versammlung 132
to assign zuordnen 134
to associate with in Verbindung bringen mit 37, verbinden mit 144
assumption Vermutung, Annahme 69
as though als ob 82
asylum Asyl 136
at hand zur Verfügung, bei der Hand 40
athletic Sport- 106
atmosphere Atmosphäre 76
atmospheric atmosphärisch 160
atom Atom 92
attack Angriff 53
attempt Versuch 89
to attempt versuchen, sich bemühen 138
attorney general Generalstaatsanwalt 156
attraction Attraktion 104
attractive attraktiv 37
auction Auktion 53
audience Publikum, Zuhörer 44
audio Audio 56
Australia Australien 17
authority Autorität, Behörde 109
autism Autismus 154
automatic automatisch 57
available erhältlich, verfügbar 21
to avoid vermeiden 40
to awaken wecken 42
to award Preis vergeben; zuerkennen 17
aware bewusst 37
awareness Bewusstsein 146

B

B&B Frühstückspension 33
backdrop Hintergrund, Kulisse 137
backing Unterstützung 89
backpacking Rucksacktourismus 17
backyard Hinterhof 120
bacon Frühstücksspeck 74
bacteria *(pl.)* Bakterien 97
bagpipes Dudelsack 164
balance Balance 57
balanced ausgewogen 162
to ban verbieten 149

bandwidth Bandbreite 56
Bangladesh Bangladesch 121
Bangladeshi bangladeschisch, Bangladescher/in 122
bank clerk Bankkaufmann/frau 26
banker Bankangestellte/r 65
bank holiday gesetzlicher Feiertag 75
banner ad Werbebanner 151
to bar vergittern, versperren 122
barbecue area Grillplatz 67
bargain Schnäppchen, guter Kauf 41
to bargain handeln, verhandeln 166
baron Baron 134
barrier Barriere, Hindernis 166
based on basierend auf, anhand von 43
basement Untergeschoss 167
basic grundlegend, Grund- 128
basically im Grunde, eigentlich 68
battle Kampf, Schlacht 153
bay Bucht 92
bean Bohne 43
°to bear tragen, ertragen 89
beauty Schönheit 21
°to be aware of s.th. sich etw. bewusst sein 142
°to be better off besser dran sein 68
bee Biene 97
beef Rindfleisch 85
beekeeper Imker/in 158
to beg betteln 152
°to be in charge of s.th. für etw. zuständig sein 62
Belgium Belgien 120
belief Überzeugung, Glaube 37
°to be likely wahrscheinlich sein, wahrscheinlich geschehen 42
below unter, unterhalb 69
°to be meant to be zu etw. bestimmt sein 54
bench Bank, Sitzbank 135
beneath unter 16
benefit Vorteil, Wohlfahrtsleistung 60
to benefit from Nutzen ziehen aus, profitieren von 78
benefits *(pl.)* Unterstützungszahlungen, Unterstützungsleistungen 66
benevolence Güte, Mildtätigkeit 35
°to be obsessed with besessen sein von 54
°to be on room duty für den Zimmerservice verantwortlich sein 8
°to be prepared to do s.th. bereit sein, etw. zu tun 26

°to be related to betreffen, zu tun haben mit, verwandt sein mit 45
°to be required to do s.th. verpflichtet sein, etw. zu tun, erforderlich sein, etw. zu tun 33
°to be spied on ausspioniert werden 146
°to be supposed to do s.th. tun sollen 121
bet Wette 53
°to beware of sich in Acht nehmen 52
°to be willing to do s.th. bereit sein, etw. zu tun 57
beyond jenseits, außerhalb 154
big ticket groß, teuer 83
billboard Plakatwand 151
billion Milliarde 21
binding verbindlich, rechtsverbindlich 129
binge drinking Besäufnis, Komasaufen 144
biodynamic biodynamisch 16
Biology Biologie 10
biomass Biomasse 88
bit etwas, ein bisschen, bisschen 26
blade Turbinenschaufel 90
blame Schuld, Verschulden 136
to blame for für etwas verantwortlich machen 156
bland fade, farblos 43
to blind blenden 35
bloc Block 137
to block blockieren 96
blood sample Blutprobe 18
blue-collar gewerblich tätig 157
boarding house Pension 33
boiler Kessel, Boiler 90
bold kühn, keck 123
booking Buchung, Reservierung 34
boom wirtschaftlicher Aufschwung 101
to boom boomen, florieren 101
boomerang Bumerang 82
boost Ankurbelung, Aufschwung 89
to boost ankurbeln, fördern 96
boredom Langeweile 146
born geboren 23
borne out bekräftigt, bestätigt 156
borough Stadtbezirk 153
to bother beunruhigen, stören 26
bottom line Entscheidende 95
to bow beugen, sich beugen 27
bracket Klammer, Bereich 23
brain menschliches Gehirn 144
branch Filiale, Zweigstelle 79
brand Marke 20

branded product Markenprodukt 21
breadwinner Versorger/in, Ernährer/in 60
breakthrough Durchbruch 160
breakwater Wellenbrecher 92
°**to breed** züchten 96
brief Kurzinformation 42
bright hell, leuchtend 75
°**to bring about** bewirken 140
brisk lebhaft, flott 75
Brits die Briten 117
broadband Breitband 45
to broadcast senden, ausstrahlen 56
brotherhood Brüderlichkeit 134
browser Browser 50
brunch Brunch 109
buck Dollar
to buck up beeilen 68
building worker Bauarbeiter/in 117
built-up area geschlossene Ortschaft 35
bully Bully, Mobber/in 148
bullying Mobbing 120
bump Erhöhung, Beule 69
bureau Büro, Abteilung 45
bureaucrat Bürokrat 156
bureaucratic bürokratisch 96
business sense Geschäftssinn 166
Business studies Betriebswirtschaftslehre 25
butterfly Schmetterling 97
button Knopf 51

C

cab Taxi 164
cabby Taxifahrer/in 35
cabinet Kabinett, Schränkchen 134
to calculate berechnen 85
callous gefühllos, kaltschnäuzig 137
calm ruhig 27
Cambodia Kambodscha 165
campaign Kampagne 45
campaigner Aktivist/in 96
to campaign for s.th. für etwas kämpfen 153
Canada Kanada 117
Canadian kanadisch, Kanadier/in 117
to cancel absagen, stornieren 45
candidate Bewerber/in, Kandidat/in 26
candle maker Kerzenmacher/in 21
canteen Kantine 83
can't stand s.th. etw. nicht aushalten können 9
cap Kappe 91

to capsize kentern 136
captain Kapitän/in; Mannschaftsführer/in 17
caption Bildunterschrift 55
to capture fangen, einfangen, abfangen 137
carbon dioxide Kohlendioxid 76
carbon footprint Kohlendioxid-Bilanz 77
care Pflege, Sorgfalt 67
to care about sich interessieren für 59
carefree sorglos 64
caregiver Betreuer/in, Pfleger/in 69
Caribbean Karibik 104
car park Parkplatz, Parkhaus 67
carriageway Fahrbahn 35
to carry on weitergehen, weitermachen 73
to carry out ausführen 132
cartoon Karikatur 48
cartridge Patrone 83
case Fall, Angelegenheit 96
catalyst Katalysator, Beschleuniger 165
catastrophe Katastrophe 79
°**to catch up with s.o.** zu jemandem aufschließen 65
cathartic reinigend 156
celebrated gefeiert 21
celebration Feier 142
cell Zelle 144
cemetery Friedhof 137
census Befragung, Volkszählung 162
centigrade Grad Celsius 77
Central America Mittelamerika 101
cereal Frühstückszerealien 75
certificate Zeugnis, Bescheinigung 24
certification Zertifizierung, Beurkundung 168
to certify zertifizieren, bescheinigen 125
chain Kette 12
challenge Herausforderung 59
challenging herausfordernd, anspruchsvoll 9
chamber Kammer 139
champagne Champagner 126
chance Möglichkeit, Gelegenheit, Chance 37
chancellor Kanzler/in 134
chaos Chaos 123
to charge berechnen, verlangen 33
charity wohltätige Organisation, gemeinnützige Organisation 66
chart Tabelle, Diagramm 58
charts *(pl.)* Hitliste 41
to chat plaudern, chatten 50

chatroom Chatroom 53
to cheat betrügen 37
to check in einchecken 8
checkout Kasse 12
to check out überprüfen, ausprobieren, auschecken 54
cheerful fröhlich, heiter 156
chef Koch, Köchin 15
chemical chemisch 80
Chemistry Chemie 26
chicken Hühnchenfleisch, Huhn 80
chief executive Firmenchef/in, Vorstandsvorsitzende/r 85
Chief Marketing Officer Marketingchef/in 42
childcare Kinderbetreuung 69
childminder Babysitter/in 68
to chill out sich entspannen, relaxen 12
chintz Chintz 83
Christian Christ/in 159
chronic chronisch 135
to chuck out wegschmeißen 83
circle Kreis 115
circumstance Umstand 156
circumstances *(pl.)* Sachverhalt, Umstände 66
to cite anführen, zitieren 69
citizen Bürger/in 57
civilised zivilisiert 151
civil rights Bürgerrechte 128
claim Behauptung 37
to claim behaupten, beanspruchen 136
to claim s.th. as income als Einkommen angeben, versteuern 108
classic klassisch 129
classification Klassifizierung, Einstufung 138
cleaning staff Reinigungspersonal 8
cleaning tool Reinigungswerkzeug 21
to clean up aufräumen, säubern 79
to click klicken 50
client Kunde, Kundin 42
climate Klima 28
clockwise im Uhrzeigersinn 35
closed off verschlossen 148
to close down schließen, stilllegen 153
clothing Kleidung 124
to coach trainieren 106
coach Reisebus 153
coalition Koalition 136
coastal Küsten- 104
cocaine Kokain 68
co-founder Mitbegründer/in 124
cognitive kognitiv, Wahrnehmungs- 144

Vocabulary | Alphabetical word list

to coincide überschneiden 69
to collapse kollabieren, zusammenbrechen 54
collapse Zusammenbruch 124
colleague Kollege, Kollegin 108
collective gemeinsam, gemeinschaftlich 129
to combat bekämpfen 167
to combine kombinieren 68
comeback Comeback, Wiederaufstieg 69
comedian Komiker/in 63
°**to come under fire** unter Beschuss geraten 142
comfort Behaglichkeit, Trost 140
comment Kommentar 125
commentary Kommentar 82
commercial Geschäfts-, geschäftlich, Werbespot 21
to commit begehen 53
commitment Bindung, Engagement 65
to commit oneself sich festlegen, verpflichten 159
common gemeinsam, verbreitet 36
communally in Gemeinschaft, gemeinsam 154
communicative kommunikativ 101
community Gemeinde, Gemeinschaft 66
comparable vergleichbar 25
to compete an einem Wettkampf teilnehmen, konkurrieren 97
competitive hart umkämpft 17
complaint Beschwerde 156
complementary ergänzend, komplementär 150
complex komplex, kompliziert 150
composition Zusammensetzung, Struktur, Aufsatz 32
comprehensive umfassend 137
comprehensive school Gesamtschule 63
to comprise umfassen 28
compromise Kompromiss 95
computer skills PC-Kenntnisse 25
computer technician Computerfachmann/frau 26
computing EDV 51
to concentrate on s.th. sich auf etw. konzentrieren 57
concentration Konzentration 148
concept Konzept, Begriff, Auffassung 62
conception Empfängnis 95
concern Frage, Belang, Bedenken 124
concerned beunruhigt, betroffen 54
concert Konzert 150
to conclude folgern, abschließen 85

conclusion Schlussfolgerung 93
to condemn verurteilen 136
condemnation Verurteilung 137
condition Zustand, Bedingung, Umstand 75
conduct Verhalten, Benehmen 135
to confess gestehen, beichten 57
to configure konfigurieren, gestalten 42
to confirm bestätigen 33
conflict Streit, Konflikt 85
to conflict with im Widerspruch stehen zu 132
confrontation Konfrontation 156
confused verwirrt 37
to congratulate gratulieren 135
connective Bindewort 93
conscience Gewissen 80
conscious bewusst 81
consequence Folge, Konsequenz 40
conservation Umweltschutz 85
conservationist Umweltschützer/in 89
to consider überlegen, erwägen, betrachten als 75
consistent einheitlich 142
to consist of bestehen aus 66
console Konsole 54
consortium Vereinigung, Zusammenschluss 160
constant ständig, andauernd, konstant 35
constituency Wahlbezirk 134
constitution Verfassung, Grundgesetz 32
constitutional law Staatsrecht 134
construction Baugewerbe, Bau, Konstruktion 69
to consume verbrauchen, konsumieren 54
consumer goods *(pl.)* Konsumgüter 21
consumption Konsum 45
to contaminate verunreinigen 104
content Inhalt 45
continent Kontinent 57
Continent europäisches Festland 101
contract Vertrag 66
to contract unter Vertrag nehmen 162
to contradict widersprechen 95
to contribute einen Beitrag leisten, mitarbeiten 16
contribution Beitrag 80
to control kontrollieren 42
controversial umstritten 133
convention Abkommen 85
conventional herkömmlich, konventionell 68

conversation Gespräch, Unterhaltung 53
to convince überzeugen 17
convincing überzeugend 135
co-op Kooperative 167
to cooperate kooperieren, zusammenarbeiten 123
cop umgangssprachlich für Polizist 56
to cope with schaffen, zurechtkommen 40
core Zentrum, Herzstück 150
corporation großes Unternehmen 21
correlation Zusammenhang, Beziehung 141
corridor Gang 113
'cos weil 111
cosmetics Kosmetik 36
cosmopolitan weltoffen 12
cost of living Lebenshaltungskosten 164
cotton Baumwolle 46
council Rat, Gemeinderat 127
council house Sozialwohnung 135
councillor Stadtrat/rätin 156
counterpart Gegenüber, Gegenpart 61
countryside Landschaft, Gegend 93
courageous mutig 137
court Feld, Gericht 123
to cover for s.o. für jemanden einspringen 112
crack Crack 152
to crack knacken, aufknacken 160
to crash verunglücken, abstürzen 148
crash diet Gewaltkur 107
to create schaffen, gestalten 15
creation Schöpfung, Schaffung 159
creative director Kreativchef/in 42
creator Schöpfer/in, Erschaffer/in 162
creature Kreatur 56
credit card Kreditkarte 53
cricket Kricket 119
crime Verbrechen 53
criminal kriminell, Kriminelle/r 53
criminology Kriminologie 148
crisis Krise 136
crisp Chip 83
criterion Kriterium 125
critic Kritiker/in 37
critical kritisch, entscheidend 95
criticism Kritik 136
to criticize kritisieren 135
crop Ernte, Getreide, Feldfrucht 77
to crunch the numbers durchrechnen 69
crystal Kristall 28
cubicle an drei Seiten von halbhohen Wänden umgebene Arbeitsnische 123

cuff Hemdmanschette 125
cultivation Landbau 96
culture Kultur 17
current jetzig, gegenwärtig 9
currently derzeit, zurzeit, momentan 85
curriculum Lehrplan 130
custom Brauch, Gewohnheit 27
cutter Zuschneider/in, Cutter/in 125
CV Lebenslauf 65
cyber-terrorist Cyber- 132
cycling Radfahren 154
Czech Republic Tschechische Republik 18

D

daily chore tägliche Aufgabe 16
daily routine Tagesablauf 18
damn verdammt 68
data Daten 53
database Datenbank 16
to date back to zurückreichen 134
day in day out Tag für Tag 120
day off freier Tag 14
dealer Händler/in 22
*to deal with umgehen mit 101
death toll Zahl der Todesopfer 137
to debate diskutieren, erörtern 96
debate Debatte 135
debt Schuld, Schulden 40
decade Jahrzehnt 49
to decarbonise entkarbonisieren 159
decent angemessen 66
to decimate dezimieren, drastisch verringern 85
declaration Erklärung, Deklaration 128
to declare erklären, verkünden 136
decline Rückgang 49
to decline zurückgehen, fallen 58
to decrease abnehmen 57
dedicated engagiert 101
defect Fehler, Mangel 94
to defend verteidigen 156
to defer verschieben 17
defibrillator Defibrillator 94
to define definieren 129
definite endgültig, eindeutig 34, auf jeden Fall 17
definitely auf jeden Fall 122
deforestation Abholzung 85
degree Grad, Ausmaß, akademischer Grad 43
to delay verzögern, verschieben 134
deliberately vorsätzlich, absichtlich 132
delighted entzückt, begeistert 135

delightful entzückend, reizend 154
to demand fordern 21
democracy Demokratie 134
democratic demokratisch 130
demographic demographisch, bevölkerungsstatistisch 62
to demonstrate demonstrieren, vorführen 77
demonstration Vorführung 42
to deny verweigern, leugnen 129
dependency Abhängigkeit 67
dependent abhängig 93
to depend on abhängen von 26
to deploy einsetzen 96
deployment Verwendung, Einsatz 96
deposit Anzahlung, Einzahlung 53
to deprive of einer Sache berauben 17
desert Wüste 159
to deserve verdienen 125
to designate vorsehen, bestimmen 89
designer Designer/in 95
desire Wunsch 94
desperate verzweifelt 57
despite trotz 96
destination Ziel 16
to detail einzeln aufführen, genau berichten 120
detailed ausführlich 18
to determine festlegen 65
devastating verheerend 95
developed country Industrieland 126
developing world Entwicklungsländer 78
device Gerät 55
diagnostics *(pl.)* Diagnostik 94
diagram Grafik, Schaubild 56
dialogue Dialog 73
*to dig in mitmachen 16
dignified würdevoll, würdig 138
dignity Würde 129
dining Ess- 152
dinosaur Dinosaurier 68
directions *(pl.)* Wegbeschreibung 72
disability Behinderung 94
disabled behindert 12
disagreement Meinungsverschiedenheit, Unstimmigkeit 135
disaster Katastrophe 56
to discard abladen 127
to discourage entmutigen 37
to discover entdecken 53
discretionary verfügbar 150
to discriminate against diskriminieren 129

discrimination Diskriminierung, Benachteiligung 138
disease Krankheit 95
dislikes *(pl.)* Abneigungen 9
disorder Störung 94
disposable Wegwerf- 83
to dispose entsorgen, loswerden 83
dispute Streitigkeit, Auseinandersetzung 166
disputed umstritten 156
to disrupt stören, unterbrechen 144
distant entfernt, weit entfernt 124
distinct ausgeprägt 56
distress Notlage, Bedrängnis 137
to disturb stören 92
diversity Unterschiedlichkeit, Vielfalt 67
to divide teilen 129
division Teilung, Bereich 69
to divorce sich scheiden lassen 26
*to do a good job etw. gut machen 42
doctor's surgery Arztpraxis 26
document Dokument 129
domestic heimisch, inländisch 82
dominant beherrschend, dominierend 162
to dominate beherrschen 69
donation Spende 78
to double verdoppeln 45
doubt Zweifel 166
to download herunterladen 45
down the line irgendwann, später 107
downturn Abschwung 142
Down's syndrome Downsyndrom 94
dozen Dutzend 89
dramatic dramatisch, spektakulär 77
drastic drastisch 58
drink Getränk 75
drinking water Trinkwasser 104
driven by vorangetrieben durch, vorangetrieben von 85
driver's licence Führerschein 25
to drop sinken, fallen, fallen lassen 65
drop Tropfen 79
drought Dürre 160
to drown ertrinken 136
drowning das Ertrinken 136
drug Droge 54
to dub bezeichnen als, synchronisieren 127
due to wegen, aufgrund 80
dull langweilig 57
dumbfounded sprachlos, verblüfft 83
to dump abladen, einleiten 85
durable haltbar 83

Vocabulary | Alphabetical word list

dynamics Dynamik, Kräftespiel 166
dystrophy Dystrophie 95

E

eager eifrig, begierig 144
to earn a living seinen Lebensunterhalt verdienen 68
earnestness Ernsthaftigkeit 154
earring Ohrring 91
to ease erleichtern, lindern 162
Eastern Europe Osteuropa 120
echo Echo 35
eco-friendly umweltfreundlich 16
ecological ökologisch 92
economic wirtschaftlich 69
economics *(pl.)* Volkswirtschaftslehre 66
ecosystem Ökosystem 97
editor Herausgeber/in, Redakteur/in 139
effective effektiv, wirksam 45
effectiveness Effektivität 66
efficient leistungsfähig, wirksam, tüchtig 83
effluent Abwasser, Schmutzwasser 85
effort Anstrengung, Bemühung 125
Eiffel Tower Eiffelturm 102
elderly älter 107
electrician Elektriker/in 26
element Element, Aspekt 8
to elevate anheben 83
to eliminate beseitigen, ausschließen 108
elite Elite 123
elsewhere anderswo 77
to embarrass in Verlegenheit bringen 27
to embed einbetten 154
embryo Embryo 94
to emerge bekannt werden, sich abzeichnen 137
emerging aufstrebend 123
emeritus professor Professor im Ruhestand 160
to emigrate auswandern 116
to emit ausstoßen, emittieren 85
emotion Gefühl 106
emotional emotional, gefühlsbetont 133
emphasis Betonung, Schwerpunkt 92
empire Reich, Imperium 35
to empower befähigen 154
empowerment Ermächtigung, Bevollmächtigung 165
to enable ermöglichen 25
to encompass umfassen 132
to encourage fördern, ermutigen 89

encryption Verschlüsselung 132
endeavour Anstrengung, Bemühung 124
endless endlos 83
enduring bleibend, dauerhaft 144
to engage sich engagieren 135
engaged verlobt 164
to engage with sich einlassen mit, sich abgeben mit 148
English Engländer/in 26
enormous gewaltig, enorm 83
enriching bereichernd 17
to enrol sich einschreiben 25
enrolment Anmeldung 17
to enshrine bewahren 132
to ensure sicherstellen, gewährleisten 85
to entail bedeuten, zur Folge haben 124
enterprise Unternehmen, Vorhaben 68
entertainment Unterhaltung 17
entire ganz 16
entitled berechtigt 129
environmental ökologisch, Umwelt- 76
environmentally friendly umweltfreundlich 19
equal Gleichgestellte/r 134
equality Gleichheit 129
equipment Geräte, Ausrüstung, Ausstattung 36
equivalent Pendant, Äquivalent 127
era Ära 49
erosion Erosion, Abtragung 82
to erupt ausbrechen 156
to escalate eskalieren 148
to escape entgehen, entkommen 52
essay Aufsatz 10
essential notwendig, wesentlich 24
essentials lebenswichtige Güter 162
establishment Unternehmen, Betrieb 108
to estimate schätzen 42
estuary Mündungsgebiet 92
ethical ethisch, moralisch 94
ethos Ethos 154
European europäisch, Europäer/in 96
to evaluate bewerten, beurteilen 142
evidence Beweis, Nachweis 132
examination Untersuchung 94
to examine untersuchen 134
to exceed übersteigen, überschreiten 82
excellent exzellent, hervorragend 106
except außer 134
excess überschüssig 89
to exchange umtauschen, austauschen 38

exchange Austausch 126
to exclude ausschließen 166
executive suite Luxussuite, Chefetage 113
exhaustible erschöpfbar, begrenzt 93
exhausting erschöpfend 27
existence Vorhandensein, Existenz 129
exotic exotisch 28
to expand vergrößern, erweitern 22
expat *(short for)* **expatriate** im Ausland lebende Person, Auswanderer/in 116
to expect erwarten 51
expectation Erwartung 58
experiment Experiment 94
expert Experte/in 53
to explode in size explosionsartig wachsen 104
to exploit ausbeuten, ausnutzen 125
exploitation Ausbeutung 120
exploration Entdeckung 17
to explore erforschen 144
exposure Aussetzen, Kontakt 142
extensive großflächig, umfangreich 28
extent Umfang, Ausmaß 124
extinction Ausrottung 76
extortionate ungeheuer, unverschämt, Wucher- 135
to extract gewinnen, extrahieren 125
extraordinary außergewöhnlich 35
extreme extrem 77
eye-contact Blickkontakt 31
eyeglasses Brille 56

F

fabric Stoff 125
to face sich gegenübersehen, konfrontiert sein mit 65
facilities *(pl.)* Austattung, Einrichtungen 24
facility Anlage, Einrichtung 66
fact Tatsache 92
factor Faktor 69
fad Modeerscheinung, Laune 107
to fail ausfallen, scheitern 77
failure Versagen, Scheitern 136
fairly einigermaßen 153
fantastic großartig, fantastisch 125
fantasy Fantasie, Einbildung 53
far-away weit entfernt 105
Far East Fernost 101
farmland Ackerland 104
fashionable modisch 83
fashion designer Modeschöpfer/in 15

fault Fehler 125
faux pas Formfehler 27
fax machine Faxgerät 113
feasible machbar, möglich 159
federal Bundes- 108
fee Gebühr 17
feed Feed, Einspeisung 45
*****to feed** füttern 96
feedback Rückmeldungen, Feedback 41
fellow student Mitstudent/in, Kommilitone/Kommilitonin 153
female weiblich 95
ferry Fähre 101
fertilizer Dünger 80
fibre Faser 56
fiction Fiktion, Annahme 83
fierce stark, heftig 109
figure Zahlen 37
to figure out kapieren, herausfinden 35
to fill s.o. in on s.th. jmdn. ins Bild setzen 26
final examination Abschlussprüfung 26
finally schließlich, endlich 90
to finance finanzieren 66
finances *(pl.)* Finanzen 40
financial finanziell 17
findings *(pl.)* Ergebnis 17
*****to find out** herausfinden 54
fingernail Fingernagel 95
finisher Finisher, Person, die die letzten Arbeitsschritte durchführt 125
fire escape Notausgang, Feuerleiter 167
fire exit Notausgang 122
fire extinguisher Feuerlöscher 167
first hand aus erster Hand 26
fiscal finanziell 69
fisherman Fischer, Angler 79
fishing das Fischen 136
fit die passende Wahl 17
fit for purpose zweckdienlich 96
fix Lösung 17
to fizzle out im Sande verlaufen 107
flag Flagge 32
flask Thermoskanne, Behälter 43
flavour Geschmack 43
*****to flee** fliehen 126
flexibility Flexibilität 68
flexible flexibel 41
flip side Kehrseite 35
flood Überschwemmung 160
flooding Überschwemmung 158
fluency Sprachgewandtheit 23
flurry Böe 75

to focus on s.th. sich auf etw. konzentrieren 21
food stamp Lebensmittelmarke 109
foodstuff Nahrungsmittel 97
to foot the bill die Rechnung bezahlen 17
to force zwingen 120
forecast Vorhersage 75
forecaster Meteorologe/in, Prognostiker/in 75
forefinger Zeigefinger 115
foreground Vordergrund 14
foreign secretary Außenminister/in 137
forest Wald 76
for hire zu mieten, zu vermieten 102
former ehemalige/r/s, frühere/r/s 83
formula Formel 43
for short abgekürzt 117
fortress Festung 136
fortunate glücklich 153
fossil fossil 76
to found gründen 21
founder Gründer/in 21
fraction Bruchteil 126
fragrance Duft 21
France Frankreich 102
fraud Betrug 52
fraudster Betrüger/in 53
to fray ausfransen 125
freedom of expression Recht auf freie Meinungsäußerung 134
freedom of speech Redefreiheit 129
free movement Freizügigkeit 123
freshwater Süßwasser 84
frontier Grenze, Grenzland 123
front page Titelseite 85
frustrating entmutigend, frustrierend 17
to fry braten 74
fuel Kraftstoff, Brennstoff 76
to fuel anheizen 136
fulfilling erfüllend 62
full-scale vollständig, umfangreich 92
full-time Ganztags-, Vollzeit- 54
function Funktion 35
fund Fonds 79
to fund finanzieren 137
fundamental grundsätzlich 124
funding finanzielle Unterstützung 153
funny eigentümlich, lustig 56
to furnish einrichten, möblieren 83
furnishings Einrichtungsgegenstände 83
further education Aus- und Weiterbildung 25

G

gadget technisches Gerät 45
Gaelic gälisch 167
to gain erwerben, sammeln, erreichen 80
gamble Glücksspiel 78
gang Bande, Gruppe 53
gang warfare Bandenkrieg 152
gap year Pause zwischen Schule und Universität bzw. Arbeitsbeginn 17
gardening das Gärtnern 125
garment Kleidungsstück, Kleidung 120
gas Gas 76
gear Gang 35
gender Geschlecht 56
gender gap Geschlechterkluft z.B. auf dem Arbeitsmarkt 56
general allgemein, Haupt- 18
generally im Allgemeinen, eigentlich 152
to generate erzeugen 77
generation Generation 66
generator Generator 90
genetic genetisch 76
genuine echt, ehrlich 83
Geography Geografie 10
*****to get carried away** von etwas mitgerissen werden 140
*****to get in touch** in Kontakt treten 42
*****to get involved in** sich engagieren 16
*****to get to know** kennenlernen 8
ghetto Ghetto 104
giant Riese, Gigant 123
*****to give birth** gebären, zur Welt bringen 94
*****to give off** ausdünsten, verströmen, abgeben 68
*****to give up** aufgeben 63
global weltumspannend, global 56
globalized globalisiert 116
global warming Erderwärmung 104
gloomy düster, bedrückend 137
*****to go ahead** weiterverfolgen, vorangehen 51
goal-oriented ergebnisorientiert 57
golf course Golfplatz 104
governing body Aufsichtsrat, Dachverband 167
governmental Regierungs- 122
grade Note 65
gradual allmählich, stufenweise 58
graduate Absolvent/in 57
to graduate akademischen Grad erlangen, absolvieren 123

Vocabulary | Alphabetical word list

grand prächtig 35
to grant gewähren, erteilen 17
grape Traube 16
to grasp greifen, ergreifen, festhalten 166
great deal ziemlich viel 96
Greece Griechenland 137
greengrocer Gemüsehändler/in 80
greenhouse Treibhaus 76
grid Stromnetz 77
grocery Lebensmittel- 108
grooming Pflege 21
gross domestic product Bruttoinlandsprodukt 160
ground Lagen, Gelände 75
groundwater Grundwasser 80
°to grow up aufwachsen 152
to guarantee garantieren 53
guarded vorsichtig 148
guideline Richtlinie 119
guilty schuldig 83
gun Schusswaffe 152
guys (pl.) Leute, Typen 61
gym Turnhalle, Fitness-Center 36

H

habit Gewohnheit 49
habitat Habitat, Lebensraum 85
haircut Haarschnitt 38
Haiti Haiti 165
to halve halbieren 85
handful Handvoll 127
to hand in abgeben 10
to handle bearbeiten, erledigen, mit etw. umgehen 42
handshake Handschlag 31
hands-on praktisch, praxisnah 42
to harass belästigen, drangsalieren 148
hardship Not, Entbehrung 108
hardware Computer-Hardware 62
to harm schädigen, schaden 80
harmful schädlich 51
harmony Harmonie 156
harsh hart, rau 108
hazy diesig, trüb 75
to head leiten 160
heading Überschrift 41
headlights (pl.) Autoscheinwerfer 35
head office Firmenzentrale, Hauptgeschäftsstelle, Hauptsitz 28
head on frontal, von vorn 166
headquarters (pl.) Zentrale, Stammsitz 21

head teacher Schulleiter/in 55
healthcare Gesundheitsfürsorge, Gesundheitsversorgung 165
heart attack Herzinfarkt 106
heartbreaking herzzerreißend 78
heath Heideland 107
heroin Heroin 152
high-calorie kalorienreich 141
to highlight hervorheben 42
high school High School (amerik.) 17
high street Einkaufsstraße, Haupteinkaufsstraße 127
high-tech Hightech, Hochtechnologie 123
high-voltage Hochspannung 89
hippocampus Hippocampus 144
to hire beauftragen, anstellen 42
historic historisch 162
°to hold on warten, festhalten 95
holidaymaker Urlauber/in 53
homegrown einheimisch, selbst gezogen 89
homeless obdachlos 152
home secretary Innenminister/in 137
home town Heimatstadt 9
honeymoon Hochzeitsreise 103
honourable ehrenwert 135
hopefully hoffentlich 77
hopeless hoffnungslos 83
to hop onto einsteigen in, aufspringen 104
hospice Hospiz, Sterbeklinik 127
host Gastgeber/in, Moderator/in 16
hostel Herberge 152
hostility Anfeindung, Feindschaft 164
household Haushalt 69
household care Haushaltspflege 21
housekeeping Zimmerpflege, Haushaltsführung 24
housing Wohnbau, Wohnungen 135
huge riesig 43
hull Schiffsrumpf, Schiffskörper 137
human menschlich, Mensch 56
human being Mensch, menschliches Wesen 128
humane menschenwürdig 37
humanitarian humanitär 129
humanity Menschheit 85
human trafficker Schlepper 136
Hungarian ungarisch, Ungar/in 120
hunger Hunger 96
hybrid Hybrid 91
hydrogen Wasserstoff 91
hygiene Hygiene, Sauberkeit 154

I

idea Gedanken, Idee 53
ideal Ideal 46
identical identisch 43
to identify identifizieren, erkennen 49
identity Identität 53
ignorance Ignoranz, Ahnungslosigkeit 96
illegal illegal 94
imagination Phantasie, Vorstellungskraft 103
immature unreif 144
immaturity Unreife 144
immeasurable unermesslich 145
immigration Einwanderung 136
immoral unmoralisch 97
impact Auswirkung, Folge 92
to impact beeinflussen 151
imperial majestätisch, Reichs- 35
implantation Implantation, Einpflanzung 94
implementation Einführung 138
to impose verhängen, auferlegen 156
impression Eindruck 54
to imprison inhaftieren, einsperren 134
impunity Straffreiheit 148
inactive träge, inaktiv 140
in addition außerdem 76
inadequate unzureichend, unzulänglich 120
inappropriate unangemessen 35
inattentive unaufmerksam 108
incapable unfähig 35
including einschließlich, inklusive 34
independent unabhängig 22
index Index, Kennziffer 85
India Indien 85
Indian Inder/in 123, indisch 167
to indicate anzeigen, andeuten 64
indication Indikation, Befund 95
indicator Indikator, Anzeiger 85
indirect indirekt 77
individual einzelne/r 37
Indonesia Indonesien 165
in droves in Scharen 49
industrial industriell, Industrie- 165
industrialized industrialisiert 127
inequality Ungleichheit, Unterschied 108
inertia Trägheit 96
inevitable unvermeidlich 85
in exchange for s.th. dafür, im Tausch gegen etw. 16
in favour of zugunsten 49
to influence beeinflussen 43

Role cards > Grammar Files > Skills Files > **Vocabulary**   Vocabulary

informal informell, locker, umgangssprachlich 34
Information Technology Informationstechnik 10
to inherit erben 129
initiative Initiative 159
to inject spritzen, einspritzen 152
injury Verletzung 26
in need bedürftig 62
innovation Innovation, Neuerung 35
innovative innovativ, erfinderisch 135
in operation in Betrieb 92
in order to zwecks, um zu 12
in particular insbesondere 76
in return als Gegenleistung, zum Ausgleich 62
inroad Eingriff 96
insecure unsicher 142
insecurity Unsicherheit 108
insemination Befruchtung 94
insight Einblick 8
instability Instabilität 82
to install montieren, einbauen 15
instant sofortig 57
institute Institut 95
institution Institution, Einrichtung 40
instructor Lehrer/in 28
insufficient unzureichend 122
insulation Wmedmung, Isolierung 127
to integrate integrieren, sich integrieren 130
intelligence Intelligenz 94
to intend beabsichtigen 135
intense stark, heftig 68
intensive intensiv 104
interaction Interaktion 56
interactive interaktiv 42
interior innen, intern 138
interlude kurze Phase, Intermezzo 75
in terms of hinsichtlich 56
International Diploma internationales Diplom 10
intervention Eingriff, Intervention 154
to interview ein Vorstellungsgespräch haben 108
interviewee Befragte/r 123
interviewer Befrager/in, Interviewer/in 23
in the long run auf lange Sicht 89
in the open air draußen, im Freien 107
in total insgesamt 85
introductory offer Einführungsangebot 42
to invent erfinden 163

to investigate nachgehen, untersuchen 53
investigation Untersuchung, Ermittlung 53
investigator Ermittler/in 137
investment Investition 89
investor Investor/in, Kapitalanleger/in 123
invisible unsichtbar 120
to involve einbeziehen 45
Ireland Irland 103
ironically ironischerweise 104
irreparable nicht mehr zu reparieren, irreparabel 144
irresponsible verantwortungslos 138
irrigation system Bewässerung 16
isle kleine Insel 75
issue Problem, Frage 37
to issue verhängen, ausstellen, ausgeben 156
Italian italienisch, Italiener/in 137
item Punkt, Artikel, Stück 36
Ivy League (AE) acht Eliteunis in den USA 17

J

Jamaica Jamaika 164
Japanese japanisch, Japaner/in 31
jealous eifersüchtig 103
to join forces sich zusammenschließen, sich zusammentun 159
joint gemeinsam 165
Jordan Jordanien 165
judgement Urteil 134
to juggle unter einen Hut bringen, jonglieren 65
junction Kreuzung 35
justice Gerechtigkeit 134

K

°**to keep in touch** in Verbindung bleiben 146
kindness Freundlichkeit 35
kosher koscher 97
knot Knoten 17

L

label Label, Marke 37
to label etikettieren, beschriften 80
laboratory assistant Laborassistent/in 18

laboratory technician Labortechniker/in 26
laborious mühsam, anstrengend 162
labour Arbeit 16
to lack mangeln 71
lack of Mangel an 82
lacrosse Lacrosse (Mannschaftssportart) 17
ladder Leiter 153
to lag behind hinterherhinken, zurückbleiben 165
lagoon Meeresbucht 92
landfill site Mülldeponie 127
landscape Landschaft 48
to launch einführen, auf den Markt bringen 21
launch Markteinführung, Start 159
laundry Wäsche 34
°**to lay** legen 37
leader Leiter/in, Führer/in 96
leadership Führung, Leitung 25
leaflet Prospekt 79
lean mager 69
°**to leave out** weglassen 63
legal rechtlich, gesetzlich, juristisch 120
legislation Gesetze, Gesetzgebung 108
leisure activity Freizeitbeschäftigung 28
Lesotho Lesotho 165
level Niveau, Gehalt 61
library Bibliothek 11
Libyan libysch, Libyer/in 137
licence Lizenz 106
lifespan Lebensdauer 83
lifestyle Lebensweise 40
lifetime Leben 79
likes (pl.) Vorlieben 9
likes and dislikes (pl.) Vorlieben und Abneigungen 119
to link verbinden, koppeln 45
listener Zuhörer/in 131
literal buchstäblich 56
litre Liter 104
litter Abfall 102
livelihood Lebensunterhalt 160
loaf Laib 23
loafer Faulenzer/in, Gammler/in 140
loan Darlehen, Kredit 40
to loan leihen, verleihen 129
local hiesig 153
locked inside eingeschlossen, eingesperrt 137
logistics Logistik 74
logo Logo, Firmenemblem 20
lonely einsam 67

323

Vocabulary | Alphabetical word list

long-distance Langstrecke 104
long-lasting langlebig, haltbar 144
long-term Langzeit- 16
to loom sich abzeichnen 159
lot Grundstück, Parzelle 159
lottery Lotto, Lotterie 103
low-carbon kohlenstoffarm 89
to lower senken 134
lunchtime Mittagszeit 11
to lure ködern, anlocken 123

M

magnet Magnet 90
mainland Festland 75
mainstream herkömmlich, Regel- 153
to maintain aufrechterhalten, verfechten 89
maintenance Wartung 28
maize (BE) Mais 96
major groß, wichtig, Haupt- 40
Majorca Mallorca 103
majority Mehrheit 117
*****to make a living** Lebensunterhalt bestreiten, Auskommen haben 117
*****to make ends meet** über die Runden kommen 68
to make matters worse etwas noch schlimmer machen 17
*****to make sense of s.th.** Sinn hinter etw. sehen, etw. zusammenreimen 56
make-up Zusammensetzung, Aufbau 97
male männlich 56
managing director Geschäftsführer/in 51
to manipulate manipulieren, beeinflussen 43
mannequin Schaufensterpuppe 142
manual labour körperliche Arbeit 71
manufacturing Fertigung, Produktion, Herstellung, Produktionsbetrieb 21
marine See- 84
to mark kennzeichnen 18
massive gewaltig, kolossal 80
maternity leave Mutterschaftsurlaub 69
to matter von Bedeutung sein, wichtig sein 26
mattress Matratze 127
maturation Reife 144
to mature sich entwickeln, reifen 96
maturity Reife 144
mayor Bürgermeister/in 91
meaningful sinnvoll 17
measure Maßnahme 137
mecca Mekka 123

mechanism Mechanismus 56
median Mittelwert 157
medical medizinisch, gesundheitlich 26
medical research medizinische Forschung 18
medicine Medizin 94
Mediterranean Mittelmeer 136
mellow locker, heiter 35
membership Mitgliedschaft 79
memory Erinnerung 135
to mend flicken, reparieren 127
menswear Männerbekleidung 125
mentality Mentalität, Einstellung 40
to mention erwähnen 146
merely bloß, lediglich 162
messaging Nachrichtenübermittlung 43
Mexico Mexiko 115
middle-aged mittleren Alters 107
Middle Ages Mittelalter 134
migrant Wander-, herumziehend 116
to migrate einwandern, abwandern, auswandern 117
migration Migration 61
militaristic militaristisch 35
military militärisch, Militär 137
to milk melken 16
millennium Millenium, Jahrtausend 113
miller Müller/in 125
to mind s.th. etw. dagegen haben 26
mindset Denkweise 83
to minimise minimieren 125
to minimize minimieren 54
minor gering, geringfügig 156
minority Minderheit 164
to misscore die falsche Punktzahl vergeben 17
mission Mission 136
misunderstanding Missverständnis 115
mobile phone Handy, Mobiltelefon 42
to modify abändern, verändern 76
mod-60s Subkultur der 60er Jahre 35
monitor Überwachungsgerät 91
to monitor überwachen, kontrollieren 129
monitoring Überwachung, Kontrolle 140
monkey Affe 117
monochrome einfarbig, monochrom 125
monument Denkmal 35
mood Stimmung 108
moreover überdies, außerdem 37
Moscow Moskau 102
motion Antrag 135
motivated motiviert 107
motor mechanic Kfz-Mechaniker/in 15

motorway Autobahn 35
motto Motto, Leitspruch 134
mount Halterung, Gestell 138
mountainous bergig 88
to move out ausziehen 62
MP Abgeordnete/r 139
muesli Müsli 75
mug Idiot, Trottel 43, Becher 83
multicultural multikulturell 12
multigenerational Mehrgenerationen- 66
multi-tasking Multitasking 45
Munich München 9
to murder ermorden 156
muscle Muskel 162
muscular muskulär 95
mushroom Pilz, Champignon 75
mushy breiig 43
Muslim muslimisch, Moslem 63

N

nationality Nationalität, Staatsangehörigkeit 12
native Einheimische/r, Inländer/in 49
natural gas Erdgas 89
to navigate navigieren 69
nearest nächstgelegene/r/s 79
necessity Notwendigkeit 69
neck Hals 140
need Bedürfnis 128
negative negativ 54
to negotiate verhandeln 16
neighbourhood Nachbarschaft 89
neon sign Lichtreklame 122
net piracy Netzpiraterie 52
net sales (pl.) Nettoumsatz 21
never mind schon gut 103
nevertheless trotzdem, dennoch 57
Nicaragua Nicaragua 165
Nigerian Nigerianer/in 120
no-brainer Kinderspiel, Leichtigkeit 69
none keine/r/s 55
non-food Nichtlebensmittel 30
norm Norm 69
normally normalerweise 11
North Sea Nordsee 89
northwards nach Norden 75
notebook Notebook, Notizbuch 36
notion Vorstellung, Auffassung 156
novel Roman 119
nuclear power Kernkraft 89
numerous zahlreich, viel 66

Vocabulary

nursery school Kindergarten, Vorschule 9
nursing auxiliary nicht geprüfter Krankenpfleger, nicht geprüfte Krankenpflegerin 162
nutritional Ernährungs- 96
nutritious nahrhaft 128

O

object Objekt 89
objection Einwand, Widerspruch 89
to observe beachten, beobachten 120
obsolete veraltet, außer Gebrauch 162
obstacle Hindernis 108
obvious offensichtlich 42
occasional gelegentlich 60
occupation Beruf, Beschäftigung 166
to occur vorkommen 142
offence Vergehen 156
to offer anbieten 153
office block Bürogebäude 55
official offiziell 156
*****to offset** kompensieren, ausgleichen 162
offshore offene See, auf offener See 89
old age Alter 66
on a par auf einer Stufe, gleichwertig 123
on behalf of im Auftrag von, im Namen von 166
on board an Bord 136
oncoming entgegenkommend, nahend 35
on demand auf Verlangen 49
on duty im Dienst 34
ongoing in Gang befindlich, laufend 144
on offer im Angebot 80
onshore Festland, auf dem Festland 89
on the move unterwegs 56
on the right-hand side rechts, auf der rechten Seite 14
on the spot sofort, auf der Stelle 42
onto auf 53
open-minded aufgeschlossen 24
openness Offenheit, Freimütigkeit 130
opera Oper 102
to operate tätig sein 42
operator Betreiber, Veranstalter 101
opponent Gegner/in 135
opportunity Möglichkeit 16
opposition Widerspruch, Widerstand 82
to oppress unterdrücken 126
optimistic optimistisch 57

option Option, Möglichkeit 13
ordinary gewöhnlich 163
organic biologisch, Bio- 80
organic crop ökologische Anbauweise 16
organised organisiert 132
organ transplant Organtransplantation 94
orientation Orientierung 101
origin Abstammung, Herkunft 20
originally ursprünglich 164
other than mit Ausnahme von 54
otherwise sonst 103
ounce Unze (Gewichtseinheit) 125
outbreak Ausbruch 75
outdoor Aussen- 66
outdoors draußen, im Freien 85
outgoing aufgeschlossen 28
outing Ausflug 9
outlet Outlet, Verkaufsstelle, Kanal 30
to outline umreißen, skizzieren 94
outlook Perspektive, Aussicht 145
out of touch lebensfremd 135
out of work arbeitslos 65
output Leistung, Ausstoß 110
outskirts Stadtrand 9
to outsource outsourcen, ausgliedern 85
outstanding außerordentlich, besonders 89
to outweigh aufwiegen, wettmachen 96
*****to overcome** überwinden 83
overfishing Überfischung 79
*****to overhear** zufällig mitbekommen 74
overnight über Nacht 97
overseas in Übersee, im Ausland 123
overtime Überstunden 54
overuse übermäßiger Gebrauch 54
overweight übergewichtig 111
overwhelming überwältigend 56
oxygen Sauerstoff 163

P

pace Geschwindigkeit 56
to package verpacken 80
packaging Verpackung 43
paedophile Pädophile/r 53
Paki Pakistaner/in 117
Pakistani pakistanisch 167
pan Pfanne 113
to pander to begünstigen 137
panel Forum, Ausschuss 108
paradise Paradies 164
paragraph Paragraph, Absatz 20
parliamentary parlamentarisch 132

*****to partake** teilnehmen 16
to participate teilnehmen 17
participation Teilnahme 128
particular besonderer/e/es, bestimmt 45
particularly vor allem 89
partly teilweise 95
part-time Teilzeit 8
party Partei 89
passage Verabschiedung 156
passer-by Passant/in 72
passion Leidenschaft 101
patchy gebietsweise 75
patent Patent 97
path Pfad, Weg 96
pathway Pfad 160
patrol Patrouille, Streife 137
pattern Muster 56
to pave pflastern 166
pavement Bürgersteig 35
to pay attention aufmerksam sein 122
*****to pay attention to** beachten 31
paycheck Gehaltszettel, Gehaltsabrechnung 108
payment Zahlung 53
pay stub Gehaltszettel 108
peak Gipfel, Höchststand, Hoch- 56
penalty Strafe 156
pension Rente, Pension 66
people skills soziale Kompetenz 101
per capita pro Kopf 166
to perceive wahrnehmen 96
percentage Anteil, Prozentsatz 48
to perform funktionieren 37
performance Auftritt, Leistung 65
period Zeitraum 57
permanent fest 26
permission Erlaubnis 55
to persist bestehen bleiben 156
personal details *(pl.)* Personendaten 40
personality Persönlichkeit 9
personnel manager Personalchef/in 28
perspective Perspektive 96
to persuade überzeugen, überreden 41
to pester plagen, bedrängen 151
pesticide Pflanzenschutzmittel 80
phase Phase 92
phishing Phishing 53
phone box Telefonzelle 152
phrase Ausdruck 15
physical körperlich 26
physical therapist Krankengymnast/in 65
Physics Physik 10
physiology Physiologie 43

Vocabulary | Alphabetical word list

physiotherapist Physiotherapeut/in, Krankengymnast/in 26
to pick up sich erholen 65
pillar Säule 167
to pin anstecken, anheften 61
pin Kontaktstift, Stecknadel 74
pink rosa, pink 95
pitch Maß 68
pitching range Übungsbereich beim Golf 123
placement Stelle 24
planet Planet 82
platform Plattform 49
plausible plausibel, einleuchtend, glaubhaft 142
Pleased to meet you. Schön Sie/dich/euch kennenzulernen. 73
plenty Menge, Fülle 92
to plough pflügen 16
plug Stecker 74
to plummet stark abfallen, stürzen 85
plus plus, sowie 54
point of sale Verkaufsort 150
point of view Standpunkt, Ansicht 125
to point out hinweisen auf, darlegen 45
to poison vergiften 137
Poland Polen 12
to police überwachen 156
police officer Polizeibeamte/r 55
policy Strategie, Grundsatz, Politik 55
Polish Polnisch 74
polite höflich 34
political politisch 128
politician Politiker/in 85
polytechnic university Fachhochschule 25
to pop in vorbeischauen 113
populist populistisch, Volks-, Populist/in 137
porridge Hafergrütze 75
post Post, Beitrag in einem Blog 8
post-16 nach dem 16. Lebensjahr 153
postcode (BE) Postleitzahl 153
to postpone verschieben 160
potential potenziell, eventuell 37
potential Potenzial, Möglichkeit 75
poverty Armut 69
powder keg Pulverfass 156
powerhouse Kraftwerk 89
power line Überlandleitung 89
power plant Kraftwerk 158
practical praktisch 8
to preach predigen 125
precaution Vorsichtsmaßnahme 16

precipitous sehr steil 49
precise präzise 27
to predict vorhersagen 65
predictability Vorhersehbarkeit 56
predictable vorhersehbar 56
preference Vorliebe 26
prejudice Vorurteil 117
premier Premierminister/in 137
premium Prämie 167
presence Präsenz 165
presentation Vorstellung, Präsentation 9
president Präsident/in 134
pressure Druck 65
to prevent hindern, verhindern, vermeiden 66
to prevent from doing s.th. von etwas abhalten 154
prevention Verhinderung, Vermeidung 95
previous früher, vorhergehend 135
primary hauptsächlich 69
Prime Minister Premierminister 123
primitive primitiv 56
principle Grundsatz, Prinzip 37
to print drucken, ausdrucken 51
printer Drucker 83
prison Gefängnis 52
privacy Privatsphäre 132
privileged begünstigt, privilegiert 153
probable wahrscheinlich 50
procedure Verfahren, Ablauf 94
to process bearbeiten, verarbeiten 80
process Prozess, Vorgang, Verfahren 106
produce landwirtschaftliche Erzeugnisse 62
productivity Produktivität 96
profession Beruf 63
professional professionell, berufsmäßig, Profi 42
profile Profil 147
profound tiefgreifend 162
programming Programmier- 53
progress Fortschritt, Fortgang 66
to progress fortschreiten 140
project Projekt 10
promising vielversprechend 96
to promote befördern 69
promotion Förderung, Beförderung, Werbung 42
prompt Stichpunkt, Aufforderung 10
proof Beweis, Nachweis 125
proper richtig, ordentlich, echt 57
property Eigentum 134
proportion Anteil, Proportion 141

to propose vorschlagen 134
proposer Antragsteller/in 135
pros and cons Pro und Kontra, Für und Wider 44
prospect Aussicht 56
prostitution Prostitution 152
protective schützend 92
protein Protein, Eiweiß 79
protest Protest 89
to prove beweisen, nachweisen 89
to provide zur Verfügung stellen, sorgen für, versorgen 66
provider Versorger, Anbieter, Provider 45
providing vorausgesetzt, sofern 27
provision Versorgung 66
public öffentlich 66
publication Veröffentlichung 134
to publish publizieren, veröffentlichen 49
to pump pumpen 85
Punjabi Pandschabi 167
purchase Kauf 40
to pursue weiterführen, fortfahren 89
pursuit Beschäftigung, Streben 49
to push off hinunterstoßen, abstoßen 153
***to put into practice** in die Tat umsetzen, realisieren 130
***to put out of business** aus dem Markt drängen 159

Q

to quadruple vervierfachen 69
qualification Qualifikation, Abschluss 25
quarter Viertel 125
queue Warteschlange 74
to quit kündigen, aufhören 120
quotation Kostenvoranschlag, Angebot, Zitat 42

R

race Rasse, Rennen 117
racial Rassen-, rassisch 156
racism Rassismus 117
radical radikal 49
rag Lumpen, Lappen 125
rainfall Niederschlag, Regen 77
to range reichen, sich bewegen 16
range Spanne, Intervall 92
rank Rang, Stand 68
rapid schnell, rapide 45
rarely selten, kaum 164

Role cards > Grammar Files > Skills Files > **Vocabulary**

rascal Bengel, Schelm 43
to rate bewerten 16
rate Quote 31
rather than lieber als 57
rational vernünftig, rational 145
raw roh, rau, grob 162
to react reagieren 41
reaction Reaktion 80
ready-made gebrauchsfertig, von der Stange 122
real estate agent Immobilienmakler/in 157
to realize erkennen 37
to reap ernten 160
rebel Rebell 134
to recall sich erinnern 147
recently kürzlich 140
reception desk Rezeption 8
recession Rezession, Rückgang 69
to recognize erkennen, anerkennen 43
recognized anerkannt 106
to recommend empfehlen 106
to recover genesen 68
to recruit anwerben, einstellen 123
recyclable wiederverwertbar 51
to recycle wiederverwerten 83
to redecorate renovieren 62
red tape Bürokratie, Papierkrieg 96
to reduce reduzieren 66
reduction Verringerung 64
to re-establish wieder einführen, wiederherstellen 136
reference Empfehlung, Bezug 13
to refer to sich beziehen auf 49
to refine verfeinern 144
to reflect widerspiegeln, überlegen 85
refuge Schutz, Zuflucht 136
refugee Flüchtling 136
to refuse ablehnen, sich weigern 54
regarding bezüglich 69
regardless ohne Rücksicht 83
regime Ordnung, System 156
region Region, Gebiet 88
to register registrieren 53
°to regrow nachwachsen 85
regulations Vorschrift, Verordnung 80
regulator Regulierungsbehörde, Regulierer 49
regulatory regulierend 150
rehabilitation Rehabilitation 106
to rehearse proben, einüben 142
to reject ablehnen 54
rejection Absage, Ablehnung 61
relating to bezogen auf, in Bezug auf 79

relations Verwandtschaft 165
relationship Beziehung 41
relaxation Erholung 28
to release freigeben, veröffentlichen 148
relentlessly unerbittlich 156
relevant wichtig, sachdienlich 21
reliance Verlass, Vertrauen 89
reliant on abhängig sein von 154
to relieve entlasten 140
religious religiös 97
to rely on verlassen auf 45
to remark anmerken 40
remittance Überweisung 166
remote abgelegen, unnahbar 104
to remove entfernen, räumen 166
renewable erneuerbar 88
repetitive sich wiederholend 162
to rephrase umformulieren 105
to replace ersetzen 127
to replenish auftanken, auffüllen 85
reporter Reporter/in 53
to represent repräsentieren, vertreten 69
representation Darstellung, Vertretung 142
representative Vertreter/in 44
representative repräsentativ 85
represented vertreten, vorhanden 95
to reproduce nachproduzieren 82
to require verlangen, erfordern, benötigen 16
requirement Anforderung 57
to require s.o. to do s.th. etw. von jemandem verlangen 151
rescue Rettung 136
research Forschung 42
to research recherchieren, forschen 128
to resemble gleich sein 156
resentment Ärger, Verbitterung 156
reserve Rücklage, Reserve 104
resident Bewohner/in, Einwohner/in 66
residential catering college College mit Unterkunft und Verpflegung 153
resistant resistent, widerstandsfähig 97
resolution Vorsatz 107
resort Ferienort 28
resounding rauschend, durchschlagend 135
resource Mittel, Ressourcen 85
to resource personell ausstatten 136
to respect respektieren 67
respect Respekt 104
respondent befragte Person 48
response Reaktion 45

responsibility Verantwortung 37
responsible verantwortungsbewusst, verantwortlich 36
to restock die Fischbestände sich erholen 85
to restrict einschränken, beschränken 42
resurgence Wiederaufleben 124
retail Einzelhandel 57
retailer Einzelhändler/in 120
to retain behalten, beibehalten 166
return flight Hin- und Rückflug 104
reuse Wiederverwendung 127
to reveal enthüllen, aufzeigen 107
revenue Einnahmen, Umsatz 104
reverberation Auswirkung 148
to reverse umkehren 109
review Bericht, Besprechung 132
revolutionary revolutionär 163
reward Vorzug, Belohnung 96
rewarding lohnend 24
rhythm Rhythmus 35
ridiculous lächerlich 142
risk Risiko 48
risky riskant 126
roar Gebrüll 156
robust robust, widerstandsfähig 85
to rocket in die Höhe schießen 146
role model Vorbild 69
roll Brötchen 70
to roll ausrollen, rollen 95
Roman römisch, Römer/in 35
Romanian rumänisch, Rumäne/in 120
rooftop Hausdach 77
rosy rosig 153
roundabout Kreisverkehr, Karussell 35
to ruin ruinieren 156
°to run out sich erschöpfen, zu Ende gehen 79
rural ländlich 16
rush große Eile 122
Russia Russland 102

S

to sacrifice opfern 92
safe sicher 53
salacious anzüglich 148
salary Lohn, Gehalt 106
sales *(pl.)* Vertrieb, Verkauf 20
salesperson Verkäufer/in 41
sales talk Verkaufsgespräch 14
salty salzig 43
SAT *(AE)* Test, der von Studienplatzbewerbern

327

Vocabulary | Alphabetical word list

in den USA gefordert wird 17
satellite Satellit 123
Saudi Arabia Saudi-Arabien 115
sausage Würstchen 74
savage grausam 156
scale Maß, Maßstab 85
to scan flüchtig überfliegen 60
Scandinavian skandinavisch 83
to scar Wunden hinterlassen 147
scarf Schal 124
scary unheimlich, furchteinflößend 56
sceptical skeptisch, kritisch 94
schedule Zeitplan, Terminplan 106
scheme System, Maßnahme 66
scholarship Stipendium in Form eines Geldbetrages, der einmal ausbezahlt wird 17
school-leaver Schulabgänger/in 40
Science Wissenschaft, Naturwissenschaft 10
scientific wissenschaftlich 95
score Punktestand 17
to score Tor schießen, Punkte erzielen 70
Scottish schottisch 164
scrambled Rühr- 75
to scream schreien 14
screen Bildschirm 54
to screen überprüfen, durchsehen 95
script Ansagetext, Drehbuch, Manuskript 75
seafood Meeresfrüchte 79
search Suche 136
to search for s.th. nach etw. suchen 45
season Jahreszeit, Saison 28
Secretary of State for Defence Verteidigungsminister/in 139
sector Branche 21
secure sicher 51
to secure sichern 153
security Sicherheit 124
sedentary sitzend 107
seeker Suchende/r 54
segregated nach Rassen getrennt 157
to seize up einrosten 107
to select selektieren, auswählen 95
selection Auswahl 95
self-confidence Selbstvertrauen 27
self-confident selbstbewusst 57
self-determination Selbstbestimmung 129
self-employed selbstständig 106
self-esteem Selbstwertgefühl 141
semi-independent relativ unabhängig 154

senior (AE) Schüler/in im letzten Schuljahr 17; ältere/r/s, Senior 66
senior executive leitende/r Angestellte/r 83
sense Sinn 49
separate zusätzlich, separat 17
to separate trennen, abtrennen 95
sergeant Sergeant 53
serial Serie(n) 21
series Serie, Reihe 131
to serve dienen, bedienen 153
server (AE) Bedienung, Kellner/in 109
service Dienstleistung, Service 36
session Einheit, Sitzung 106
***to set s.o. back** jmdm. kosten 17
setting Rahmen 109
to settle klarstellen, sich niederlassen 43
***to set up** errichten, einrichten 122
severe ernst, schwer, heftig 77
sewer Näher/in 166
sewing Näh- 120
sex Geschlecht 146
sexualization Sexualisierung 150
***to shake** schütteln 43
***to shake hands** sich die Hand geben 31
to shape formen, prägen 134
shape Figur, Form, Gestalt 142
sharp stark, scharf 29
to shatter zerschlagen 156
shed Schuppen 120
sheep Schaf, Schafe 98
sheet Blatt 95
shelter Behausung, Obdach 128
shift Schicht, Veränderung 26
shocking entsetzlich, schrecklich, schockierend 108
***to shoot** schießen, erschießen 156
shopper Käufer/in 122
shopping Einkäufe 19
shore Ufer, Küste 137
shortage Knappheit, Mangel 96
showcase Vorzeigeprojekt, Schaukasten 123
shower Dusche 104
to show off angeben 56
to shrink schrumpfen 162
to shuffle schlurfen 35
Sicilian sizilianisch, Sizilianer/in 137
sidewalk Bürgersteig 83
signatory Unterzeichner/in 137
significant bedeutend, deutlich 45
sign-up Anmeldung 56
similar ähnlich 12
simultaneous gleichzeitig 68

single einzelne/r/s 57, alleinerziehend 60
***to sink** versenken, versinken 137
site Website 53
situated gelegen 28
skill Fertigkeit 62
to skim überfliegen 52
skincare Hautpflege 68
skinny mager, dünn 142
to skip auslassen, überspringen 141
sleeve Ärmel 125
slight geringfügig, leicht 43
slightly geringfügig, etwas 135
to slim down abnehmen 141
slogan Werbespruch 82
smart ordentlich, gepflegt, schick 36
smokehouse Räucherkammer 16
to smooth ebnen 96
smuggler Schmuggler 136
soap maker Seifenerzeuger/in 21
soap opera Seifenoper 21
to soar sprunghaft steigen, in die Höhe schnellen 141
so-called so gennant 21
social media soziale Netzwerk/e 36
social networking website Internetseite für ein soziales Netzwerk 9
Social Studies (pl.) Gesellschaftslehre 25
social worker Sozialarbeiter/in 15
society Gesellschaft 82
sociology Soziologie 147
sofa Sofa 83
so far bisher, bis jetzt 123
soil Erdboden 82
solar panel Sonnenkollektor 77
solidarity Solidarität, Zusammenhalt 129
solution Lösung 136
to sort out sortieren, organisieren 12
to sort through durchsehen 122
sought after gesucht 120
South Africa Südafrika 17
South-east Asia Südostasien 120
soya Soja 85
spa Heilbad, Heilquelle 123
spa centre Wellnessbereich 28
Spain Spanien 96
Spanish Spanisch 115
to spark auslösen, entzünden 156
specialist fachlich 153
to specialize spezialisieren 42
species (pl.) Art, Spezies 84
specific bestimmt, spezifisch 45
specifically eigens, speziell 69
to specify genau bezeichnen 134

speech bubble Sprechblase 55
spell check Rechtschreibprüfung 57
sperm Spermium, Sperma 95
spirit Geist 125
°to split teilen, spalten 92
to sponsor finanziell unterstützen 21
spontaneous spontan 57
sporty sportlich 106
to spot erkennen, wahrnehmen 47
spot on treffend 154
square Platz 102
square kilometre Quadratkilometer 92
to stab stechen, (er)stechen 152
stable stabil 93
stakeholder Interessengruppe 150
stalkerish wie Stalking 148
to standardize standardisieren 80
standard of living Lebensstandard 164
standing Bedeutung, Ansehen 129
startling alarmierend, überraschend 141
starvation Hungern, Verhungern 96
to starve hungern 96
to state erklären, festlegen 159
statement Aussage, Statement 9
statistics *(pl.)* statistische Angaben, Statistik 20
Statue of Liberty Freiheitsstatue 102
stay Aufenthalt 33
steady stetig, stabil 29
°to steal stehlen 51
steam Dampf 90
steep steil 85
steering wheel Lenkrad 35
step Schritt, Stufe 8
step-parent Stiefelternteil 145
steppe Steppe 159
stereotype Stereotyp, Klischee 152
°to stick with s.o. an jemandem haften bleiben, jemanden weiterhin beschäftigen 148
stipend Stipendium in Form eines Geldbetrages, der in regelmäßigen Abständen ausbezahlt wird 17
to stitch nähen, steppen 167
to stock Lager auffüllen 18
stomach Magen 17
storage Speicherung 159
straight geradewegs, direkt 127
straight ahead geradeaus 113
straightforward einfach, unkompliziert 96
straight on geradeaus 73
strain Belastung, Anstrengung 96
stranger Unbekannter 16

strategy Strategie 150
strength Stärke 30
stress Betonung, Stress 37
to stress betonen 96
stressed-out völlig gestresst 65
to stretch ausdehnen, strecken 165
strict streng 69
structural strukturell 49
to struggle abmühen, kämpfen 40
studies *(pl.)* Studium 126
stuff Zeug 43
stuffing Füllmaterial 127
style Stil 124
subheading Untertitel 64
to subscribe abonnieren 45
subscription fee Mitgliedsbeitrag 16
substance Substanz 97
substantial erheblich, beträchtlich, wesentlich 89
substitute Ersatz 54
to substitute ersetzen 162
sub-wage Niedriglohn 108
subway Unterführung für Fußgänger 152
to succeed in gelingen, erfolgreich sein 131
to suffer from leiden an 26
suffering Leiden 95
sufficient genug, genügend, ausreichend 107
to suggest hinweisen auf, vorschlagen 49
to suit passen, sich eignen 26
suitable passend, geeignet 13
to summarize zusammenfassen 30
to sum up zusammenfassen 58
superior Vorgesetzte/r 108
superior to besser als 124
superstore großer Supermarkt 22
supervisor Abteilungsleiter/in, Leiter/in 166
supplier Lieferant/in, Zulieferer/in 125
supply Angebot, Versorgung 77
to support helfen, unterstützen 26
support Unterstützung 62
to surf surfen 45
surgery Operation 94
surgical chirurgisch 167
surplus überschüssig 62
surrounded by umgeben von 57
surroundings *(pl.)* Umgebung 89
surveillance Überwachung 132
survey Umfrage 45
surveyed befragen 107
survivor Überlebende/r 136

susceptible empfänglich 43
suspected verdächtigt 132
suspicion Verdacht, Argwohn 132
sustainability Nachhaltigkeit 83
sustainable nachhaltig, umweltgerecht 77
sustained anhaltend, nachhaltig 165
to swallow schlucken 43
swath große Menge 96
sweater Pulli 91
°to swell schwellen, anschwellen 96
to switch wechseln 45
to switch off ausschalten 50
sword Schwert 35
Syria Syrien 136
systematic systematisch 76
systematical systematisch 132

T

tablet Tablet, Schreibtafel 51
to tackle angehen 76
tailor Schneider/in 125
°to take action tätig werden, handeln 77
°to take advantage of sich zunutze machen, ausnutzen 92
°to take a seat sich setzen, Platz nehmen 27
°to take charge selbst in die Hand nehmen 126
°to take for granted als selbstverständlich betrachten 134
°to take hold sich durchsetzen 156
°to take into account berücksichtigen 137
°to take into consideration in Betracht ziehen, berücksichtigen 95
°to take on übernehmen, annehmen 63
°to take up aufnehmen, anfangen mit 63
talent Talent 57
target Ziel 43
to target anpeilen, zielen auf 53
targeted gezielt 132
task Aufgabe 14
tastebud Geschmacksknospe 43
°to tear down einreißen 35
technological technologisch 88
technologist Technologe, Technologin 93
telecommunications *(pl.)* Telekommunikations- 51
temple Tempel 102
temporary vorübergehend, befristet 101
to tend to neigen zu, tendieren zu 40
tension Spannung 140

tentative vorläufig 124
term Begriff 21
terms and conditions Geschäftsbedingungen 148
terrestrial Erd-, auf dem Festland 84
terrific grandios, hervorragend 68
test tube Retorten- 94
textiles *(pl.)* Textilien 127
Thames Themse 158
theatrical theatralisch 135
the British die Briten 35
the French die Franzosen 35
theory Theorie 56
the Scots die Schotten 164
the States Vereinigte Staaten, USA 74
thief Dieb 91
Third World Dritte Welt 122
thirst Durst 78
thoughtfully mit Bedacht, rücksichtsvoll 104
thread Gewinde, Faden 43
threat Bedrohung, Drohung 132
thrill Nervenkitzel 123
throughout im ganzen, durchwegs 108
throwaway Wegwerf- 83
thumb Daumen 115
tidal Gezeiten- 92
tide Strom, Ebbe und Flut 137
to tidy up aufräumen 8
timber Bauholz 85
time of your life einmaliges Erlebnis 28
timeout Auszeit 65
tip Rat, Tipp 31, Trinkgeld 108
tiring ermüdend, anstrengend 14
toilet Toilette 21
tolerance Toleranz 130
tolerant tolerant 94
tomato Tomate 75
tonne metrische Tonne 83
topic Thema 44
torment Pein, Qual 147
to torture foltern 129
to total sich summieren, sich belaufen auf 127
touch Berührung 140
tough hart, schwierig 65
tour guide Reiseführer/in 101
tourism Tourismus 101
touristy touristisch 35
towards in Richtung 75
towel Handtuch 102
toxic giftig 51
tracking Verfolgung 140
to trade in eintauschen 123

trade union Gewerkschaft 166
traditional traditionell 83
tragedy Tragödie 137
trainee Auszubildende/r, Trainee, Praktikant/in 74
trainers Turnschuhe 36
training on the job Ausbildung am Arbeitsplatz 101
transatlantic transatlantisch 104
transcendent transzendent, überragend 35
to transfer übertragen 43
transformation Umwandlung 127
transmission Weiterleitung, Übertragung 159
to transmit übertragen 56
to trap einschließen 76
to treat behandeln 46
treatment Behandlung 66
trend Tendenz, Trend 44
trendy modisch, schick 103
trial Verhandlung, Prozess 134
trick Trick, Kniff 82
to trigger auslösen 144
trillion Billion 56
trisomy Trisomie 94
truly wirklich 57
trusting vertrauensvoll 147
to tumble fallen, stürzen 68
tuna Thunfisch 79
tunnel Tunnel 32
turbine Turbine 89
turn-around time Umschlagszeit, Abfertigungszeit 124
turning Abzweigung 72
turnover Umsatz, Fluktuation 125
tutor Tutor/in 118
tweet kurzer Textbeitrag über ein Mikroblog-Dienst, Tweet 94
twice zweimal 39
twice over zweimalig, zweimal hintereinander 158
to type tippen 148

U

UK Vereinigtes Königreich 31
ultimately letztendlich 85
ultrasound Ultraschall 94
unacceptable inakzeptabel, unzumutbar 96
unarmed unbewaffnet 156
uncomfortable unwohl 27
to uncover aufdecken 156

undercover geheim 53
°to undercut unterbieten 159
°to undergo unterziehen 95
underground unterirdisch 122
understanding Verständnis 40
undesirable unerwünscht 142
undocumented nicht registriert, undokumentiert 120
unemployment Arbeitslosigkeit 92
unethical skrupellos, unethisch 124
unfed ungefüttert, ohne Nahrung 96
uni kurz für: Universität 74
unique einzigartig 42
unit Anlage, Einheit 21
United Kingdom Vereinigtes Königreich 134
universal allgemein, allgemeingültig, weltweit 128
unjust ungerecht 17
to unload ausladen 14
to unpack auspacken 14
unpaid unbezahlt 65
unpleasant unangenehm 53
unpredictable unvorhersehbar, unberechenbar 158
unsafe unsicher 117
unsettled unbeständig, unruhig 75
unskilled ungelernt 120
unsuitable ungeeignet 122
unsure unsicher 16
unsustainable nicht aufrecht zu erhalten 85
unsympathetic mitleidslos 68
untouchable unantastbar 138
upcoming bevorstehend 146
to upgrade aufwerten 65
up-market gehoben, hochpreisig 42
up till now bis jetzt 94
up-to-date aktuell, auf dem neuesten Stand 50
up to now bis jetzt 22
urbanization Urbanisation, Verstädterung 66
to urge drängen 96
urgent dringend, eilig 160
usage Gebrauch 48
user Nutzer/in 45
to usher in einleiten 83

V

vacancy offene Stelle 27
vaccine Impfstoff 94
value Wert 37

to value schätzen 85
variety Vielfalt, Auswahl 96
various verschieden, unterschiedlich 42
to vary from reichen von 19
vast riesig, enorm 137
ventilation Belüftung 122
to verify nachweisen, nachprüfen 168
vertebrate Wirbel- 84
vessel Schiff 137
via über, durch 45
victim Opfer 53
victory Sieg 135
Vietnam Vietnam 121
Vietnamese vietnamesisch 165
view Ansicht, Ausblick 83
viewer Zuschauer/in 45
vigilance Wachsamkeit 145
to violate verstoßen gegen 120
violation Verletzung, Verstoß 129
violence Gewalt 54
violent gewalttätig 156
visa Visum 17
vital entscheidend, wesentlich 154
void Lücke 83
voluntary freiwillig 65
to volunteer sich freiwillig melden 17
vulnerable gefährdet, verletzlich 48

W

wages *(pl.)* Lohn, Gehalt 15
waitress Kellnerin 153
Warsaw Warschau 74
washing machine Waschmaschine 34
washing powder Waschpulver 21
wave Welle 89
way of life Lebensart 74

to weaken schwächen 66
wealthy reich 126
weaving das Weben 125
weekly wöchentlich 106
welfare Sozialhilfe, Sozial-, Wohlergehen 60
well Brunnen 104
wellbeing Wohlergehen 85
West Indies Westindische Inseln 164
whatever was auch immer 85
whisky Whisky 164
white-collar im Büro tätig 157
who the hell wer zum Teufel 75
wide range großes Angebot, große Auswahl 21
widespread weit verbreitet 146
wilderness Wildnis 96
wildlife Tier- und Pflanzenwelt 85
window shopping Schaufensterbummel 14
windy windig 75
to wink zwinkern 151
wireless drahtlos 51
within innerhalb 70
with reference to mit Bezug auf 24
with regard to in Bezug auf 25
to wonder sich fragen 34
word web Wortnetz 27
work experience *(sg.)* Berufserfahrung 23
workforce Belegschaft, Gesamtheit der Mitarbeiter 69
working conditions *(pl.)* Arbeitsbedingungen 27
working day Arbeitstag, Werktag 77
working holiday Arbeitsurlaub 17
working hours *(pl.)* Arbeitszeit 9

working knowledge praktische Kenntnisse 25
working week Arbeitswoche 26
to work one's way up sich hocharbeiten 101
workout Training 107
workplace Arbeitsplatz 9
work placement Berufspraktikum 8
workshop Werkstatt 122
World War II Zweiter Weltkrieg 104
worldwide auf der ganzen Welt, weltweit 53
to worry sich Sorgen machen 61
worry Sorge 142
worrying beunruhigend, besorgniserregend 141
worsening Verschärfung, Verschlechterung 96
would-be angehend 94
***to write off** abschreiben 154
wrongdoing Fehlverhalten 132

X

xenophobic fremdenfeindlich 137
X-ray Röntgenstrahlung, Röntgenbild 94

Y

yield Ertrag 96
youngster Jugendliche/r 141

Z

zero Null 124
zone Zone, Gebiet 136

Operatoren

In der folgenden Tabelle sind die wichtigsten Arbeitsanweisungen (= Operatoren), die im Schülerbuch und in Prüfungen vorkommen können aufgelistet. Die römischen Zahlen beziehen sich dabei auf den jeweiligen Anforderungsbereich: I = comprehension, II = analysis, III = comment.

Operatoren	Definitionen	Beispiele
analyse, examine II	*analysieren, untersuchen:* Beschreiben und erläutern Sie detailliert bestimmte Aspekte des Textes.	Analyse the diagram. Examine the author's use of language.
comment III	*kommentieren, eine Stellungnahme abgeben:* Drücken Sie deutlich Ihre Meinung zu einem bestimmten Thema aus und begründen Sie diese durch Belege und Beispiele.	Comment on the suggestion made in the text that a 'lack of women in the armed forces demonstrates a weakness in the role of women in society'.
compare II–III	*vergleichen:* Zeigen Sie Ähnlichkeiten und Unterschiede auf.	Compare X's and Y's views on education.
contrast II	*kontrastieren:* Stellen Sie die Unterschiede zwischen zwei oder mehreren Dingen dar.	Contrast the author's idea of human aggression with the theories of aggression you have read about.
describe I–II	*beschreiben:* Geben Sie eine detaillierte Darstellung von etwas.	Describe the photo. (I) Describe the way the writer creates an atmosphere of suspense. (II)
discuss III	*diskutieren:* Untersuchen Sie ein Thema argumentativ, indem Sie Argumente dafür und dagegen präsentieren.	Discuss the advantages and disadvantages of globalization.
explain II	*erklären:* Beschreiben und definieren Sie etwas im Detail.	Explain the link between the slogan and the commentary.
illustrate II	*veranschaulichen:* Erklären Sie einen Sachverhalt anhand von Beispielen.	Illustrate the author's use of language.
outline I	*umreißen:* Präsentieren Sie die Hauptpunkte eines Themas, indem Sie Details auslassen.	Outline the author's views on love, marriage and divorce.
point out, state I	*darlegen:* Stellen Sie einen Sachverhalt deutlich dar.	State briefly the main developments in the family described in the text.
summarize, write a summary I	*zusammenfassen:* Geben Sie eine kurze Darstellung der Hauptaspekte des Textes.	Summarize the information given in the text about the dangers of cloning.

Phrases for speaking

Nachfragen bei Verständnisschwierigkeiten

Did I get that right?
Do you really mean that …?
Could you explain the point you just made again, please?
Could you give me / us an example, please?

Die eigene Meinung ausdrücken

In my opinion / view …
I think (that) …
I would like to …
It would be a good idea to …

Nach einer Meinung fragen

What do you think about …?
What is your view on / about …?
What would you say?

Vorschläge machen

I suggest that we …
What do you think about …?

Auf Vorschläge reagieren

That's a good idea! / Fine!
OK. / Yes, why not?
What about (+ gerund) … instead?

Missverständnisse aufklären

I'm sorry, but that's not what I meant to say (at all)!
Sorry, I didn't make myself clear. I'll try and explain again.

Jemanden unterbrechen

Sorry, may I interrupt you for a second?
Wait a minute …

Jemanden auffordern, etwas zu tun

Could you possibly …?
Could I ask you to …?

Höflichkeitsfloskeln

You're welcome.
Thank you.
Don't worry.

Phrases for writing

Argumentieren und begründen

That's why …
It follows that …
Because (of) …
Moreover …
However …

Schlussfolgerungen ziehen

In conclusion …
As a result …
All in all …
To my mind …

Formulierungen zur Autorenintention

The author / writer opens with …
He / she points out that …
He / she shows that …
He / she explains …
He / she concludes with …

Bilder beschreiben und analysieren

The photo / illustration shows …
   at the top / bottom
   in the upper right-hand corner
   in the lower left-hand corner
   in the foreground / background
The person in the centre of the picture looks …
   (+ adjective)
Perhaps the photographer's intention is to show that …
Considering the … in the photo you could draw the conclusion that …

Cartoons beschreiben und analysieren

The cartoon consists of an illustration of …
There is a caption below the cartoon which says "…"
In the (first) speech bubble it says "…"
The cartoonist's message might be that …
The cartoonist is criticizing the behaviour of …

Connectives

Eine Reihenfolge anzeigen / Gliederung

firstly ..., secondly ..., finally ...
first of all ... next ... then/later

Gedanken/Argumente hinzufügen

another
in addition / additionally
moreover

furthermore
last but not least

Beispiele geben

for example

for instance

Die eigene Einstellung verdeutlichen

obviously / clearly

generally

Eine eigene Meinung abgeben

in my opinion
to my mind

without a doubt

Begründungen angeben

consequently
therefore
as a result

this is why
because of

Vergleiche anstellen

compared with
on the one hand ... on the other hand ...
in the same way

Gegensätze ausdrücken

in contrast to
however

despite / in spite of

Schluss

in conclusion
as a result
on the whole

to sum up
in the end

Phrases to describe statistics

Allgemeine Beschreibung

The chart / graph / diagram ... published in ... shows the development from ... to ...
It shows the share of ... / the number of ...

Arten von Diagrammen

pie chart / bar graph / line graph

Einen Anstieg beschreiben

There is a noticeable upward trend between ... and ...
By 20 ... figures reached their highest level.
The number of ... increased / rose slightly / sharply / slowly.

Eine Abnahme beschreiben

We notice a downward trend between ... and ...
By 20 ... figures reached their lowest level.
The number declined / decreased slightly / slowly.
The number fell / sank sharply.

Unveränderte Werte

Figures remained steady / did not change.

Zahlen und Daten

the figures for the last year / the last month, etc.
the total number of ...
a significant / an insignificant number of ...
a high percentage of ...
a majority / minority of ...

Mengenbezeichnungen

a total of
over / under
nearly / almost /
  approximately
more / less than
the same number as /
  the same amount of

one in five
eight out of ten
half / a third / a quarter /
  two thirds
twice / three times as many
on average

Interpretation

The change in ... leads to the assumption that ...
This suggests a relation between ... and ...

Schlussfolgerung

The drastic change may be due to ...
All in all ... we can say that ...

Bildquellennachweis

Umschlag Corbis (xPACIFICA), Berlin; **Umschlag** Avenue Images GmbH (Westend61), Hamburg; **8.1** Thinkstock (istock/kadmy), München; **8.2** Thinkstock (istock/anyaivanova), München; **8.3** Thinkstock (istock/omgimages), München; **10.1** Fotolia.com (63014931), New York; **10.2** shutterstock.com (Antonio Guillem), New York, NY; **10.3** iStockphoto (Solovyova), Calgary, Alberta; **10.4** Fotolia.com (Robert Kneschke), New York; **12** Fotolia.com (contrastwerkstatt), New York; **14** iStockphoto (sturti), Calgary, Alberta; **15.1** iStockphoto (sturti), Calgary, Alberta; **15.2** shutterstock.com (dotshock), New York, NY; **15.3** Fotolia.com (Diego Cervo), New York; **15.4** iStockphoto (GlobalStock), Calgary, Alberta; **15.5** iStockphoto (Christopher Futcher), Calgary, Alberta; **15.6** shutterstock.com (wavebreakmedia), New York, NY; **16** iStockphoto (VladTeodor), Calgary, Alberta; **17** shutterstock.com (Mike Broglio), New York, NY; **19.1** iStockphoto (Squaredpixels), Calgary, Alberta; **19.2** iStockphoto (Louis-Paul St-Onge), Calgary, Alberta; **20.1** iStockphoto (luchezar), Calgary, Alberta; **20.2** iStockphoto (olaser), Calgary, Alberta; **20.3** iStockphoto (ollo), Calgary, Alberta; **20.4** iStockphoto (wellesenterprises), Calgary, Alberta; **21** iStockphoto (Sharrocks), Calgary, Alberta; **26.1** Fotolia.com (Pkchai), New York; **26.2** Fotolia.com (Alexander Raths), New York; **26.3** iStockphoto (PhotoAttractive), Calgary, Alberta; **26.4** Fotolia.com (javiindy), New York; **27** Klett-Archiv, Stuttgart; **28** iStockphoto (nicalfc), Calgary, Alberta; **32.1** iStockphoto (fazon1), Calgary, Alberta; **32.2** Mauritius Images (The Photolibrary Wales/Alamy), Mittenwald; **32.3** shutterstock.com (Lukassek), New York, NY; **33** shutterstock.com (Peter Bernik), New York, NY; **34** iStockphoto (Tassii), Calgary, Alberta; **35** shutterstock.com (balounm), New York, NY; **36.1** Thinkstock (lzf), München; **36.2** iStockphoto (Leonardo Patrizi), Calgary, Alberta; **36.3** shutterstock.com (videnko), New York, NY; **36.4** iStockphoto (Izabela Habur), Calgary, Alberta; **40** Thinkstock (Brand X Pictures), München; **42** Fotolia.com (dizain), New York; **42.1** iStockphoto (Oktay Ortakcioglu), Calgary, Alberta; **42.2** iStockphoto (sturti), Calgary, Alberta; **42.3** iStockphoto (monkeybusinessimages), Calgary, Alberta; **42.4** iStockphoto (andresr), Calgary, Alberta; **43.1** iStockphoto (Rawpixel Ltd), Calgary, Alberta; **43.2** Video(s) supplied by BBC Worldwide Learning, London; **46** Fotolia.com (Syda Productions), New York; **47.1** shutterstock.com (Dirima), New York, NY; **47.2** shutterstock.com (Jacob Lund), New York, NY; **47.3** shutterstock.com (Ann Haritonenko), New York, NY; **48** Thinkstock (scanrail), München; **49** iStockphoto (sturti), Calgary, Alberta; **50** iStockphoto (Cathy Yeulet), Calgary, Alberta; **51** iStockphoto (monkeybusinessimages), Calgary, Alberta; **52.1** Fotolia.com (ra2 studio), New York; **52.2** Fotolia.com (dragonstock), New York; **54.1** iStockphoto (sturti), Calgary, Alberta; **54.2** Thinkstock (iStockphoto), München; **52.3** shutterstock.com (Inna Sokolovska), New York, NY; **54.3** iStockphoto (leezsnow), Calgary, Alberta; **55.1; 55.2** www. CartoonStock.com, Bath; **55.3** iStockphoto (Neustockimages), Calgary, Alberta; **57** Fotolia.com (bokan), New York; **60.1** iStockphoto (mikeinlondon), Calgary, Alberta; **60.2** Thinkstock (Jupiterimages), München; **60.3** iStockphoto (FredFroese), Calgary, Alberta; **61.1** shutterstock.com (tommaso79), New York, NY; **61.2** shutterstock.com (Goran Bogicevic), New York, NY; **61.3** shutterstock.com (Syda Productions), New York, NY; **61.4** shutterstock.com (Diego Cervo), New York, NY; **61.5** Mauritius Images (Janine Wiedel Photolibrary/Alamy), Mittenwald; **61.6** shutterstock.com (ibreakstock), New York, NY; **61.7** shutterstock.com (Cylonphoto), New York, NY; **62** iStockphoto (IS_ImageSource), Calgary, Alberta; **65** iStockphoto (Tassii), Calgary, Alberta; **65** Mauritius Images (Gary Roebuck/Alamy), Mittenwald; **66** shutterstock.com (RonTech3000), New York, NY; **67.1** iStockphoto (Volodymyr Kyrylyuk), Calgary, Alberta; **67.2** Fotolia.com (goodluz), New York; **68** shutterstock.com (michaeljung), New York, NY; **68** iStockphoto (monkeybusinessimages), Calgary, Alberta; **72.1** iStockphoto (justhavealook), Calgary, Alberta; **72.2** iStockphoto (Leadinglights), Calgary, Alberta; **72.3** shutterstock.com, New York, NY; **72.4** shutterstock.com (Peter Bernik), New York, NY; **73** iStockphoto (annebaek), Calgary, Alberta; **74.1** shutterstock.com (Claudio Divizia), New York, NY; **74.2** iStockphoto (simoningate), Calgary, Alberta; **74.3; 74.4** shutterstock.com (Monkey Business Images), New York, NY; **74.5** iStockphoto (claudiodivizia), Calgary, Alberta; **74.6** iStockphoto (tirc83), Calgary, Alberta; **75** shutterstock.com (Tupungato), New York, NY; **76.1** shutterstock.com (Mykola Mazuryk), New York, NY; **76.2** shutterstock.com (PR Image Factory), New York, NY; **76.3** dreamstime.com (Luca Barausse), Brentwood, TN; **76.4** Fotolia.com (kanvag), Calgary, Alberta; **77** iStockphoto (zstockphotos), Calgary, Alberta; **78** iStockphoto (Bartosz Hadyniak), Calgary, Alberta; **79** iStockphoto (paulprescott72), Calgary, Alberta; **82** Thinkstock (Hemera), München; **83** shutterstock.com (FotograFFF), New York, NY; **84.1** WWF Deutschland, Berlin; **84.2** shutterstock.com (Robert Adrian Hillman), New York, NY; **84.3** shutterstock.com (Vertes Edmond Mihai), New York, NY; **84.4** shutterstock.com (yyang), New York, NY; **87.1** iStockphoto (MsLightBox), Calgary, Alberta; **87.2** Fotolia.com (mur162), New York; **87.3** laif (Pierre GLEIZES/REA), Köln; **88.1** Fotolia.com (Paul Stock), New York; **88.2** shutterstock.com (Elena Elisseeva), New York, NY; **88.3** Fotolia.com (Wolfgang Reiss), New York; **88.4** Fotolia.com (Gerhard Seybert), New York; **91.1** iStockphoto (windujedi), Calgary, Alberta; **91.2** iStockphoto (Praiwun), Calgary, Alberta; **92.1; 92.2** Tidal Lagoon Power Ltd, Cheltenham Gloucester; **94.1** iStockphoto (skynesher), Calgary, Alberta; **94.2** iStockphoto (filrom), Calgary, Alberta; **94.3** shutterstock.com (Tashatuvango), New York, NY; **94.4** shutterstock.com (surassawadee), New York, NY; **94.5** iStockphoto (koya79), Calgary, Alberta; **94.6** shutterstock.com (sfam_photo), New York, NY; **95** Video(s) supplied by BBC Worldwide Learning, London; **99** shutterstock.com (vitstudio), New York, NY; **100.1** Picture-Alliance (Russian Look), Frankfurt; **100.2** iStockphoto (AlexRaths), Calgary, Alberta; **100.3** iStockphoto (MachineHeadz), Calgary, Alberta; **100.4** iStockphoto (emholk), Calgary, Alberta; **102.1** iStockphoto (R-J Seymour), Calgary, Alberta; **102.2** shutterstock.com (Halfpoint), New York, NY; **103** Thinkstock (Wavebreakmedia Ltd), München; **106.1** shutterstock.com (Monkey Business Images), New York, NY; **106.2** Fotolia.com (Christian Jung), New York; **106.3** Fotolia.com (pressmaster), New York; **106.4; 106.7** iStockphoto (PeopleImages), Calgary, Alberta; **106.5** shutterstock.com (gpointstudio), New York, NY; **106.6** Thinkstock (m-gucci), München; **107** Fotolia.com (Martinan), New York; **108** Fotolia.com (Africa Studio), New York; **112** iStockphoto (Steve Debenport), Calgary, Alberta; **114** BBC Information and archives, London; **116.1** Thinkstock (Ron Chapple Stock), München; **116.2** Reuters (Rogan Ward), Frankfurt; **117** Fotolia.com (IjinanDesign), New York; **119.1** iStockphoto (m-imagephotography), Calgary, Alberta; **119.2** iStockphoto (ScottOSmith), Calgary, Alberta; **120** shutterstock.com (topten22photo), New York, NY; **122.1** Imago (Xinhua), Berlin; **122.2** www.CartoonStock.com (Schley, Karsten), Bath; **123** Video(s) supplied by BBC Worldwide Learning, London; **124** iStockphoto (Abdolhamid Ebrahimi), Calgary, Alberta; **126** iStockphoto (Ababsolutum), Calgary, Alberta; **128.1** iStockphoto (onepony), Calgary, Alberta; **128.2** Fotolia.com (LuckyImages), New York; **128.3** shutterstock.com (Baloncici), New York, NY; **128.4** shutterstock.com (TACstock), New York, NY; **130** shutterstock.com (Free Wind 2014), New York, NY; **131** shutterstock.com (wavebreakmedia), New

York, NY; **132.2** www.CartoonStock.com (Royston Robertson), Bath; **135** Parliament Recording Unit, London; **136.1** www.CartoonStock.com (Schley, Karsten), Bath; **136.2** ddp images GmbH (Infophoto), Hamburg; **139** shutterstock.com (Dutourdumonde Photography), New York, NY; **140.1** Fotolia.com (Martinan), New York; **140.2** iStockphoto (Leonardo Patrizi), Calgary, Alberta; **140.3** iStockphoto (pixdeluxe), Calgary, Alberta; **140.4** iStockphoto (Predrag Vuckovic), Calgary, Alberta; **142** iStockphoto (MachineHeadz), Calgary, Alberta; **144** shutterstock.com (Anilinn), New York, NY; **146.1** Fotolia.com (Nicola De Mitri), New York; **146.2** iStockphoto (sturti), Calgary, Alberta; **150** www.CartoonStock.com (McCracken, Theresa), Bath; **152.1** iStockphoto (Aldo Murillo), Calgary, Alberta; **152.2** shutterstock.com (Photographee.eu), New York, NY; **152.3** dreamstime.com (Steve Mann), Brentwood, TN; **154** iStockphoto (skynesher), Calgary, Alberta; **155** shutterstock.com (R. Gino Santa Maria), New York, NY; **157.1** www.CartoonStock.com (Greenberg, Steve), Bath; **158.1** iStockphoto (AMR_Photos), Calgary, Alberta; **158.2** Fotolia.com (Gina Sanders), New York; **158.3** iStockphoto (andreveen), Calgary, Alberta; **160** iStockphoto (Jorisvo), Calgary, Alberta; **162** www.CartoonStock.com (Eales, Stan), Bath; **164.1** Fotolia.com (Andrey_Arkusha), New York; **164.2** iStockphoto (Chris Schmidt), Calgary, Alberta; **164.3** shutterstock.com (Robert Kneschke), New York, NY; **166** iStockphoto (Liuser), Calgary, Alberta; **167** iStockphoto (EdStock), Calgary, Alberta; **168** iStockphoto (mrPliskin), Calgary, Alberta; **168** Fotolia.com (AnKudi), New York; **169** www.CartoonStock.com (McMillan, Stephanie), Bath.

Textquellennachweis

16 by Will Coldwell, © The Guardian.com, November 26, 2013; **31** Grafik „Employment rate (aged 16 to 64) from January to March 1971 to March to May 2015 Source: Labour Force Survey - Office for National; **48** Source: Pew Research Center. „In Changing News Landscape, Even Television is Vulnerable." September 27, 2012. www.journalism.org; **49** by John Plunkett, © The Guardian.com, December 15, 2014; **69** by Kate Dailey, © BBC News Magazine, June 5, 2014; **84** Infographic Living Planet Index © WWF; **85** by Damian Carrington, © The Guardian.com, September 30, 2014; **96** ©The Guardian.com, March 16, 2014; **108** by Jana Kasperkevic, © The Guardian.com, January 19, 2014; **124** by David Evans © The Guardian.com,November 14, 2014; **124** by Louise Gray © The Telegraph, May 31 2012; **108** Grafik „More Continue to be concerned with coutry's Protection over civil Lieberties. Survey conducted Jan. 7-11, 2015 by Pew Research Center;**132** by Luke Harding © The Guardian.com, January 26, 2015;**133** by Nicolas Richter © Süddeutsche Zeitung 1.Juni, 2015; **133** (c) Mikko Hypponen. Source: www.huffingtonpost.com/tedtalks, February 4, 2014; **136** by Cahal Milmo and Michael Day © The Independent, April 20, 2015; **141** by Daniel Boffey © The Guardian.com, August 2, 2015; **143** by Sabine Menkens © Die Welt, 23. April, 2015; **144** by Lizzie Parry © The Daily Mail, April 27, 2015; **145** by Russell Brand, Guardian News & Media Ltd. March 9,2013; **145** by Johann Hari, © The Guardian.com, January 2, 2015; **145** Source: Health and Social Care Information Centre, U.K.; **147** by Charlotte Philby © The Independent, August 10, 2014; **149** familie.de/Vision Net AG, Leonrodstraße 52, 80636 München; **150** by Bo Viktor Nylund, UNICEF, published in The Guardian; **151** by Steuart Henderson Britt, Herald Tribune October 30, 1956, in: Oxford Dictionary of American quotations; **151** by Jonathan Kent, Telegraph Media Group Limited, April 11, 2013; **154** by Andy Merriman © The Guardian.com, August 19, 2014;**155** by Sebastian Moll, Zeit Online 30. Juli 2015; **156** by Jon Swaine © The Guardian.com, August 20, 2014; **156** From Jonathan Kozol, Savage Inequalities: Children in American's Schools New York, NY: Crown Publishers; **156** From Jay-Z, Best Life Magazine 3/20/2009; **157** From blackdemographics.com; **160** by Steve Connor © The Independent, June 2, 2015; **161** by Dierkes Meinolf, Spiegel.de,16. Februar 1987; **162** by Katie Allen © Guardian News & Media Ltd. August 18,2015; **163** © Progressio.org.uk, February 5, 2014; **163** © Tim O'Reilly, futurist and software pioneer. Source: http://readwrite.com/2004/11/17/tim_oreilly_int_1, November 17, 2004; **157** by Douglas Adams from The salmon of doubt: Hitchhiking the galaxy one last time; **166** by Dan Rees © The Guardian.com, March 7, 2014; **167** by Owen Duffy © The Guardian.com, July 27, 2015; **168** by Axel Hansen, Die Zeit, 18. August 2014; **168** From Fairtrade.org.uk; **169.1** by Kagera Co-Operative Union Field officer, Olivia Mwombeki, Tanzania; **169**.2 by Franklin D. Roosvelt; **169.3** by Jerry Greenfield, The New York Times, November 16, 2010.

Sollte es in einem Einzelfall nicht gelungen sein, den korrekten Rechteinhaber ausfindig zu machen, so werden berechtigte Ansprüche selbstverständlich im Rahmen der üblichen Regelungen abgegolten.